INTRODUCTION TO
BASIC
PROGRAMMING

Final Thurs 10:00 - 11:50

SHELLY & CASHMAN BOOKS

Introduction to BASIC Programming

Introduction to Computers and Data Processing

Introduction to Computer Programming Structured COBOL

Advanced Structured COBOL Program Design and File Processing

Business Systems Analysis and Design

Computer Programming RPG II

Introduction to Computer Programming ANSI COBOL

ANSI COBOL Workbook

Advanced ANSI COBOL Disk/Tape Programming Efficiencies

Introduction to Computer Programming RPG

Introduction to Flowcharting and Computer Programming Logic

Introduction to Computer Programming IBM System/360 Assembler Language

IBM System/360 Assembler Language Workbook

IBM System/360 Assembler Language Disk/Tape Advanced Concepts

DOS Utilities Sort/Merge Multiprogramming

OS Job Control Language

DOS Job Control for Assembler Language Programmers

DOS Job Control for COBOL Programmers

Introduction to Computer Programming System/360 PL/I

INTRODUCTION TO
BASIC
PROGRAMMING

Gary B. Shelly
Educational Consultant
Brea, California

&

Thomas J. Cashman, CDP, B.A., M.A.
Long Beach City College
Long Beach, California

ANAHEIM PUBLISHING COMPANY
2632 Saturn St., Brea, CA 92621
(714) 993-3700

ISBN 0-88236-118-X

Printed in the United States of America

10987654

Table of Contents

CHAPTER THREE
ARITHMETIC OPERATIONS

CHAPTER FOUR
COMPARING

CHAPTER FIVE
MORE ON COMPARING

CHAPTER SIX
LOOPING — INTERACTIVE PROGRAMMING

Objectives

CHAPTER SEVEN
ARRAYS

CHAPTER EIGHT
MENUS, ARRAYS, SUBROUTINES, AND SORTING

CHAPTER NINE
STRING PROCESSING

CHAPTER TEN
FILES, REPORT GENERATION, AND FUNCTIONS

PREFACE

BASIC was developed in 1965 by Dr. John Kemeny and Dr. Thomas Kurtz at Dartmouth College for use in an academic environment. Its use has expanded considerably since then, particularly since its adoption in the late 1970's as the primary language on microcomputers. Today, it is probably the most widely used language in the world, with many minicomputers and over 1 million microcomputers using it as the main programming language.

When BASIC was developed in 1965, only a few of the characteristics of a good programming language as we know them today had been recognized. Further, little significant research had been published on how to design and write a good program. During that era, a program which produced the correct output was considered a good program. Little or no consideration was given to the need for reviewing a program at some future date.

In the years since BASIC was created, considerable maturity has occurred in the computing industry, particularly with respect to the programming process. The techniques of structured programming, with a heavy emphasis on developing logic using well-defined control structures and writing code which is easy to read, understand, and modify, have become widely accepted in the industry.

Unfortunately, this acceptance has not always been applied in the development of programs written in the BASIC language. Most periodicals serving those who use the BASIC language illustrate programs which are so poorly written that only the original programmer can decipher the processing taking place. Many BASIC textbooks illustrate trivial examples that violate the most fundamental rules of modern program design and coding. These books urge students to get on the computer and try different methods without instruction in the use of good program design and coding. Indeed, statements have even been made in textbooks that modern programming techniques cannot be taught when using the BASIC language. Such statements reflect a complete lack of understanding about the concepts of modern program design. Good program design is not dependent upon the programming language used. The programming language is merely the vehicle to implement the program design. Good program design using the control structures of structured programming can be implemented clearly and easily in any programming language.

The widespread use of BASIC as the first programming language taught to students and the use of poorly designed and written programs in the first programming course has led to considerable difficulty in later programming courses. For example, students who have been allowed or even encouraged to write programs in any format using any logic which will eventually work find the transition to a disciplined approach in programming quite difficult. It has been the authors' experience in talking with instructors that many students are unable to break the bad habits acquired in their first programming course using the BASIC language.

Clearly, then, there is a real need for a book which teaches good programming methodology using the BASIC language. This textbook is designed to teach not only the BASIC language but also the proper and correct ways to design and write programs.

The book uses a problem-oriented approach; that is, the student is introduced to computer programming through the use of a series of sample programs that are completely designed and coded. From the first program, students are shown the proper way to design and code a program using the BASIC language. Trivial examples that have no relation to an application are avoided. Heavy emphasis is placed on using only the three logic control structures found in structured programming: the sequence logic structure, the if-then-else logic structure, and the looping logic structure. By using these structures, the design and coding of the program is made much simpler than when a shotgun, haphazard approach is used.

Each sample program is thoroughly documented with remarks. All coding is indented following coding standards to improve the readability of the program listing. These concepts, although not new, are seldom found in textbook programs. They reflect a professional approach to the task of programming in the same manner that other educational disciplines require adherence to certain standards and rules. Indeed, it is difficult to imagine that an English teacher would allow a term paper to be submitted in any form desired by the student; for example, with no title page and no sentence or paragraph structure. Yet this is what has been occurring in BASIC programming classes for many years. The approach has often been . . . write the program in any way you want just to get it to work. By following the standards introduced in this text, students will emerge with a firm foundation in program design and will be able to produce professional quality software.

The book is designed to be used in a one quarter or one semester course in BASIC programming. No prior knowledge of data processing or computer programming is required. The first chapter provides a brief overview of basic computer concepts. An explanation is also included of the concept of a stored program and the process of developing a computer program. Each of the remaining chapters contains an explanation of an application, the program design and program code for the application, and a detailed explanation of the program design and the program code. In addition, each chapter contains an explanation of other BASIC statements and programming techniques related to the class of problem being studied.

There are many well-defined concepts which must be taught in an introductory programming class. These include basic input/output operations, basic arithmetic operations, accumulating and printing totals, comparing, array processing, searching and sorting, string processing, file processing, and report generation. In addition, modern computer systems are centered around transaction-oriented or interactive processing. In this type of environment, the user enters data directly into the computer system, processing occurs, and the results are immediately conveyed back to the user. Interactive processing many times includes the use of a menu and the editing of data entered from the keyboard. The sample programs in this textbook are unique because they illustrate all of these important concepts.

At the conclusion of each chapter, review questions, debugging exercises, and student programming assignments are provided. The review questions use a variety of methods to test the student's understanding of the material covered in the chapter. The debugging exercises present, for student review, both syntax errors and errors occurring in the execution of a program. The programming assignments should be designed and coded using the standards recommended in the textbook. These assignments range from applications very similar to those shown in the sample program of the text to more difficult programs which require creative thinking on the part of the programmer to arrive at a solution to the problem.

Upon completion of this textbook, the student will have gained experience and practice in designing and writing a variety of programs covering important programming techniques applicable to all disciplines. The emphasis on good program design and coding will lay the foundation for the subsequent study of other programming languages, as well as providing the student with a model of good software which may be used in analyzing and evaluating packaged software systems.

Acknowledgements

As in every book, there are key people without whom the effort could not be completed. For this book, we owe a sincere debt of gratitude to some very important people. The quality of color found in this book is a result of the skill of Quality Graphics in Santa Ana, California. Max Loftin and Sue Davis from Quality Graphics made a significant contribution to this book. The book is printed by R. R. Donnelley & Sons. We literally would not have this book were it not for the superb efforts of John Conley, Bob Rochelle, and Jane Kaitson from Donnelley.

Our primary gratitude must go to our two colleagues at Anaheim who on every book perform above and beyond the call of duty. Marilyn Martin, who typeset the book and performed an important role as color consultant, and Michael Broussard, who transformed our scribblings into masterful drawings and illustrations and laid out the book, are two people who continually make contributions that only the authors can truly understand and appreciate. This book is as much a part of them as it is of us.

Finally, it is appropriate to thank our spouses — Kathleen Shelly, Francis Cashman, Val Martin, and Marcia Broussard — for their patience and encouragement. Each of them has lived with this book longer than should be expected and for that we thank them.

Gary B. Shelly
Thomas J. Cashman

Picture Credits

The following people and organizations have contributed to the text. We thank them for their generosity.

Cover photograph: Photograph by Melgar Photographers, Santa Clara, CA for Advanced Micro Devices, Sunnyvale, CA
Cover lettering: Lisa Martin
Chapter 1 Title Page: International Business Machines Corporation
Figure 1–1 National Semiconductor Corporation
Figure 1–2 International Business Machines Corporation
Figure 1–3 Hewlett-Packard Company
Figure 1–4 Burroughs Corporation
Figure 1–6 Raytheon Company
Figure 1–7 Data Electronics, Incorporated
Figure 1–8 Cado Systems Corporation

Figure 1–9 3M Company
Figure 1–10 Comshare Incorporated

Title Pages
Chapter 2 Radio Shack, A Division of Tandy Corporation
Chapter 3 NCR Corporation
Chapter 4 National Semiconductor Corporation
Chapter 5 Digital Equipment Corporation
Chapter 6 Apple Computer Incorporated
Chapter 7 Perkin-Elmer Corporation
Chapter 8 National Semiconductor Corporation
Chapter 9 Honeywell, Incorporated
Chapter 10 Apple Computer Incorporated

CHAPTER ONE

COMPUTERS AND COMPUTER PROGRAMMING

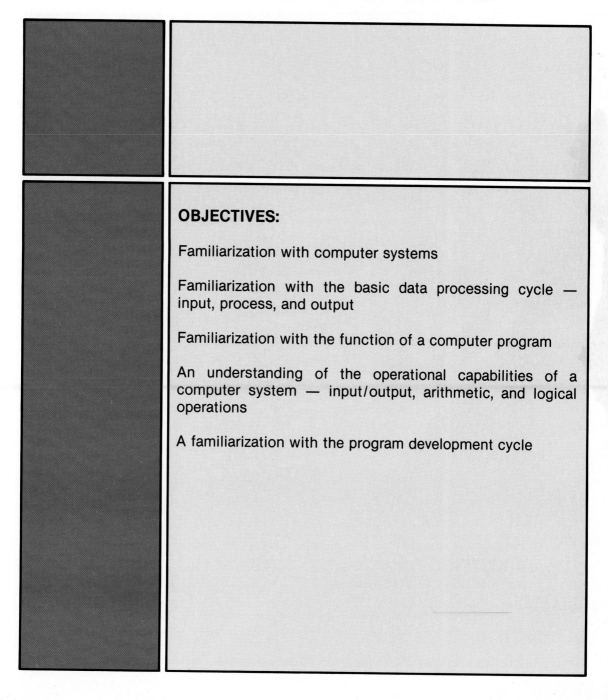

OBJECTIVES:

Familiarization with computer systems

Familiarization with the basic data processing cycle — input, process, and output

Familiarization with the function of a computer program

An understanding of the operational capabilities of a computer system — input/output, arithmetic, and logical operations

A familiarization with the program development cycle

CHAPTER ONE
COMPUTERS
AND COMPUTER
PROGRAMMING

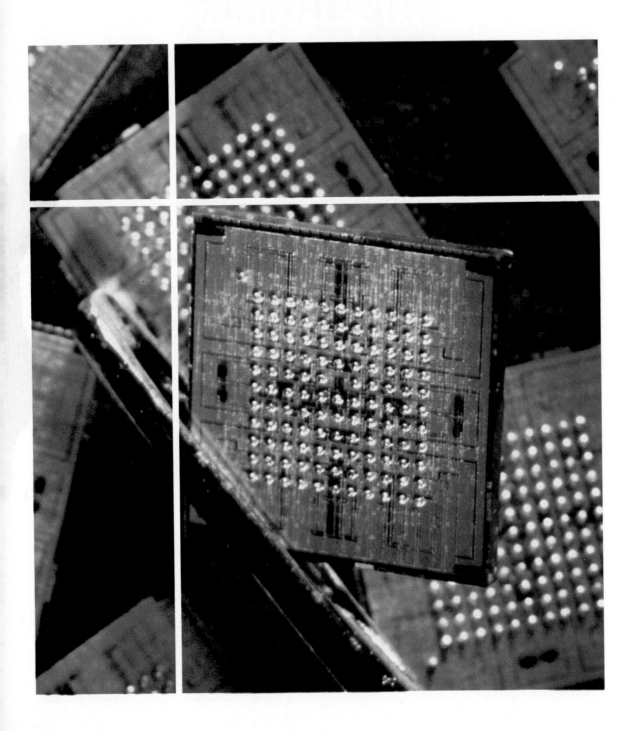

Today, the computer is an integral part of our daily lives. Airline reservations are made using a computer. A check used at the local department store may require computer verification. A bank teller is likely to use a computer terminal to find the balance in your account. Few aspects of our daily lives are left untouched by some type of computerized processing. With increasing frequency, children in elementary schools, students in high schools and colleges, and business executives everywhere are using the computer as a tool to assist in solving a variety of problems.

The ability to understand and use a computer system is rapidly becoming as important as the ability to read and write. People from all walks of life will routinely use computers in the future. The purpose of this book is to provide the ability to use many computer systems available today by teaching the BASIC computer programming language.

To most people, the computer is a mystery. This view may have arisen from the rapid manner in which the computer has entered our lives and the variety of computer systems that are found.

Computer systems of all sizes and capabilities are used today. Very small computer systems can be used to control electric appliances or regulate gas consumption in an automobile (Figure 1-1). Microcomputer systems are found in homes, businesses, and schools for a variety of uses (Figure 1-2). These machines provide new methods for learning, accessing information, and performing calculations.

Other computer systems, not much larger than an average desk, are found in thousands of businesses (Figure 1-3). They are used for business, scientific, and engineering applications.

Very large computer systems may be used to prepare thousands of telephone bills each day or to perform the millions of calculations required to make long-range weather forecasts. Such systems typically require large rooms housing what appears to be a bewildering array of electronic devices (Figure 1-4).

A computer is a device which can perform computations, including arithmetic and logic operations, without human intervention. To accomplish this, all computers perform basically the same functions regardless of their size. These functions are:

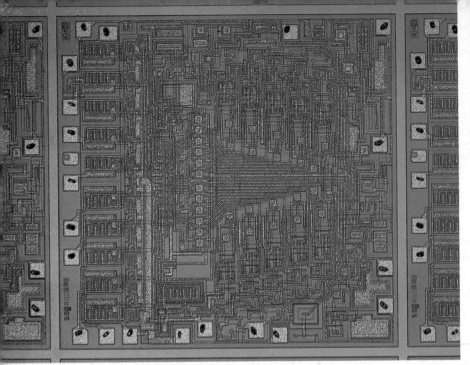

Figure 1-1 This small chip is a microprocessor capable of logical and arithmetic operations.

Figure 1-3 Desk-size computers from Hewlett-Packard are widely used by engineers, scientists, and business managers.

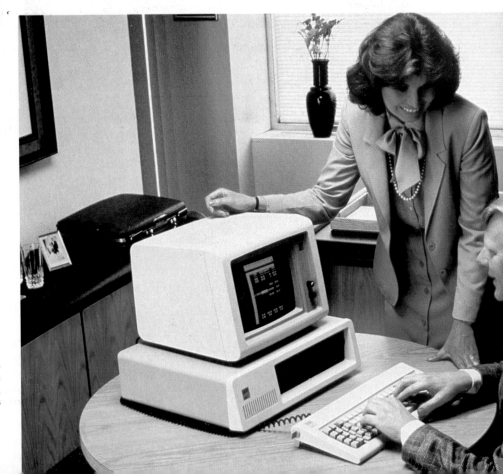

Figure 1-2 The IBM personal computer shown here can be used for home, school, and business applications.

Figure 1–4 This large Burroughs computer forms the backbone of a data processing network at Midland Bank in the United Kingdom. This network processes some 2.3 million items each day. Large computer systems such as this are used in applications which require the execution of millions of instructions each second.

1. Input/output operations, which involve accepting data for processing and causing the results of processing to be made available for use.
2. Arithmetic operations, which allow numeric data to be added, subtracted, multiplied, and divided.
3. Logical operations, which can, among other things, determine that one number is equal to, greater than, or less than another number.

These operations are relatively simple and straight-forward. The computer is unique because it can perform these operations very fast with no human intervention. For example, some computer systems can add two numbers in less than one-millionth of a second. These operations are carried out through the use of electronic circuits. Since electronic circuits are very reliable, the processing takes place rapidly and reliably.

What is data?   The three operations a computer performs all require data. Data is the representation of facts, concepts, or instructions in a formalized manner suitable for communication, interpretation, and processing by humans or automatic machines. For example, data is the balance in a bank account, the score a student receives on a test, or the cost of an item in a grocery store.

The purpose of a computer system is to accept data, process data, and as a result of the processing produce output in the form of useful information.

Input, processing, and output units   Three primary units are required on a computer system in order to process data (Figure 1–5). These units are:

1. Input Units
2. The Processor Unit
3. Output Units

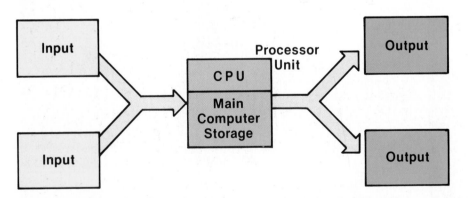

Figure 1–5 A basic computer system is composed of input units, the processor unit, and output units.

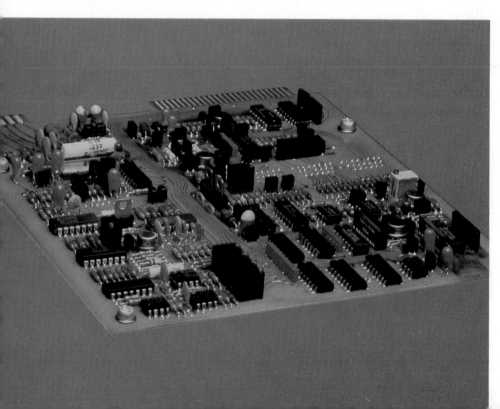

Figure 1-6 A keyboard is a typical input unit used to make data available to a computer for processing.

Input units make data available for processing. A typical input unit on many computer systems is a keyboard (Figure 1-6).

The processor unit is composed of two parts: the central processing unit (CPU) and main computer storage (Figure 1-7). The central processing unit contains the electronic circuits which actually cause processing to occur. The CPU interprets instructions to the computer, performs necessary logical and arithmetic operations, and causes the input and output operations to take place.

Main computer storage consists of electronic components which store letters of the alphabet, numbers, and special characters. Any data which is to be processed must be stored in main computer storage. The data stored in main computer storage is referenced by the CPU when the data is processed. Main computer storage is also used to store instructions which control the processing of the data.

Figure 1-7 This printed circuit board contains the central processing unit (CPU), main computer storage, and other electronic devices used for the processor unit of a computer system.

Figure 1-8 A printer is used to produce hard-copy output (left); and a CRT screen is used to display the results of computer processing.

Output units make information resulting from the processing of data available for use by either people or other machines. Typical output units include Cathode Ray Tube (CRT) screens and printers (Figure 1-8).

Computer programs

The input/output, arithmetic, and logical operations which are performed by a computer system are controlled by instructions collectively called a computer program. A computer program specifies the sequence in which operations are to occur in the computer system. There are many instructions which can be included in a computer program to control the computer system.

A computer program is written by an individual called a programmer (Figure 1-10). After the program has been written, it can be temporarily placed in main computer storage. Once in main computer storage, it is executed under the control of the central processing unit. After the program has been completed, another program can be placed in main computer storage for execution.

Auxiliary storage

In many computer applications, data must be stored for use at a later time. For example, test grade scores throughout a semester could be stored so that they could be averaged at the end of a semester. In addition, computer programs are frequently stored so that they can be recalled for placement in main computer storage and execution.

In order to store data or programs for subsequent use, auxiliary storage devices are used. The most widely used forms of auxiliary storage for small computer systems are cassette tapes and floppy disks (Figure 1-9).

Figure 1-9 This cut-away view of a floppy disk exposes the oxide-coated plastic disk on which data is electronically stored. Floppy disks are commonly found in two sizes — 5¼" and 8" in diameter.

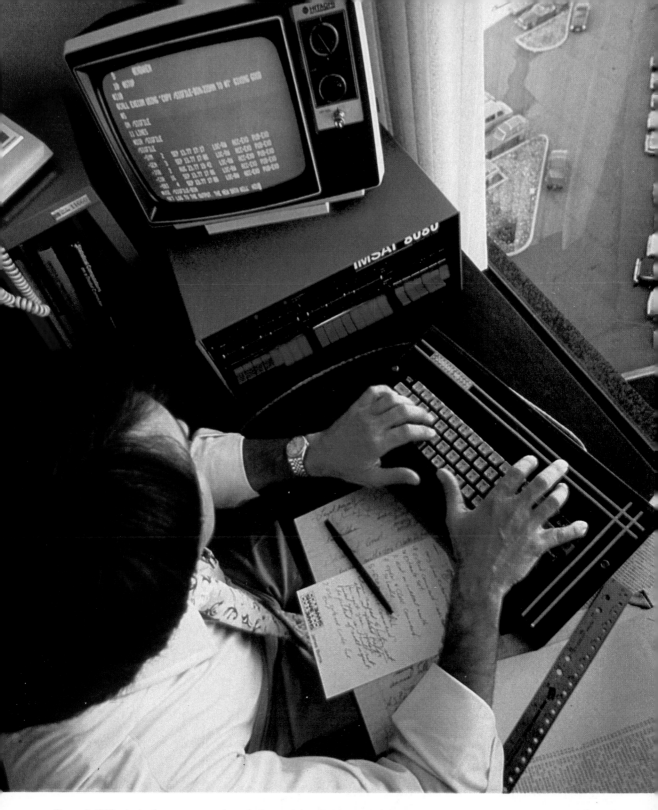

Figure 1–10 The task of a programmer is to design, code and implement programs which control operations on a computer system.

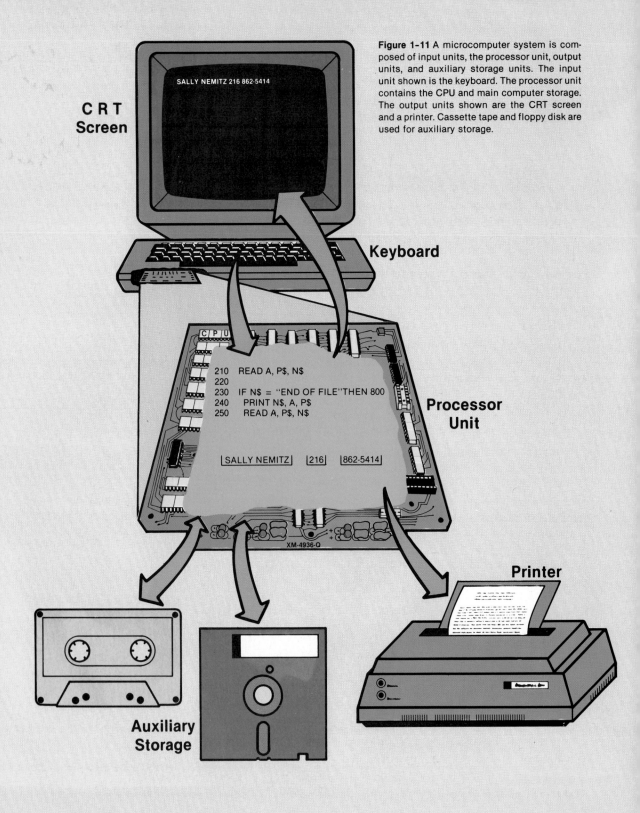

Figure 1-11 A microcomputer system is composed of input units, the processor unit, output units, and auxiliary storage units. The input unit shown is the keyboard. The processor unit contains the CPU and main computer storage. The output units shown are the CRT screen and a printer. Cassette tape and floppy disk are used for auxiliary storage.

Data or programs to be stored on auxiliary storage are transferred from main computer storage to the cassette tape or floppy disk. There, the data is recorded as a series of electronic spots. When required, the data or programs stored on auxiliary storage are transferred back to main computer storage for use.

The input, processing, output, and auxiliary storage units of a microcomputer system are illustrated in Figure 1-11. Input to the system occurs through the keyboard. As data is keyed on the keyboard, it is transferred to main computer storage. In addition, it is normally displayed on the CRT screen when keyed.

Components of a microcomputer system

The processor unit, which consists of main computer storage and the central processing unit, is contained on a printed circuit board within the keyboard housing. In addition to the CPU and main computer storage, this board also contains the electronic components which allow communication with the input, output, and auxiliary storage units.

Output from a microcomputer system may be printed on a low speed printer or may be displayed on the CRT. If the output is to be saved for future reference, it will normally be printed. Otherwise, the output will usually be displayed on the CRT screen.

Data is transferred from main computer storage to auxiliary storage and from auxiliary storage to main computer storage. As noted, cassette tape and floppy disk are the two primary means of auxiliary storage on a small computer system.

The previous examples have illustrated the input, output, auxiliary storage, and processor units. These hardware units are used in conjunction with a computer program to cause processing to occur on a computer system.

BASIC PROCESSING CONCEPTS

In order to understand how computer systems solve problems, it is necessary to examine in more detail the exact processing which takes place when a computer program is executed. This processing is explained below.

A computer program is a series of instructions which specifies the operations to be done by a computer. A program must be stored in main computer storage in order to be executed. When a program is placed in main computer storage, control is given to the program by the CPU. Instructions in the program are executed one at a time. These instructions can direct the computer system to perform the basic operations of input, output, arithmetic, and comparing.

Executing computer programs

After the program has completed processing, another program can be placed in main computer storage for execution. Therefore, a computer system can execute multiple programs. It executes whatever program is placed in main computer storage.

Input operations

One of the more common methods for entering data into a computer system is the use of a keyboard. The steps that occur when data is entered into computer storage by means of a keyboard are (Figure 1-12):

1. A computer program is stored in main computer storage. All processing on a computer system, including data input, occurs under the control of a program stored in main computer storage.
2. The input data is keyed on the keyboard. The data is displayed on the screen as it is keyed.
3. The keyed data is stored in main computer storage.

Once data is placed in main computer storage, it can be processed under program control to produce the required output. After the data has been completely processed, the program can request that more input data be entered from the keyboard. This cycle can continue until all input data has been entered and processed, and all output has been produced. At that time, the program will normally be terminated and another program loaded into main computer storage for execution.

Output operations

Output is produced by transferring data from main computer storage to a medium which can be used by people. The two most common forms of output are the CRT screen and the printed report. The example in Figure 1-13 illustrates displaying output on the CRT screen. The steps are:

1. As always, a program must be stored in main computer storage to control the operations of the computer system. In the example, the program specifies that the name, area code, and telephone number are to be displayed on the CRT screen.
2. When the instruction in the program to transfer data to the CRT screen is executed, the name, area code, and telephone number are electronically transferred to the CRT screen. The data remains in main computer storage when this transfer occurs. In reality, the data is duplicated on the CRT screen.

As with the input processing, the production of output from the computer system will occur so long as there is output to be produced. After all the output is produced, the program is terminated.

The operations of input and output are basic to all computer systems. Indeed, it is the ability to input data, process it in some manner, and create output which makes computer systems useful. It is important to understand the input/output operation because it is the foundation for many of the computer programs which will be written in this text.

Input

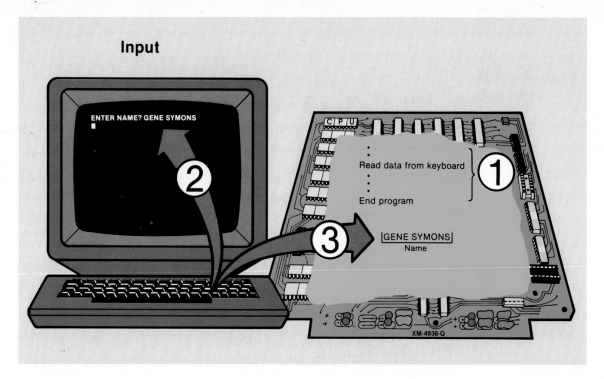

Figure 1-12 Data is transferred from the keyboard to main computer storage during the input operation.

Output

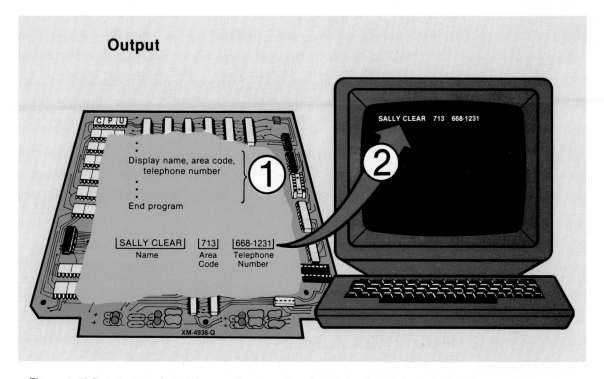

Figure 1-13 Data is transferred from main computer storage to the CRT screen in this output operation.

Basic arithmetic operations

Once data is stored in main computer storage by the input operation, it is normally processed in some manner. In many applications, arithmetic operations (addition, subtraction, multiplication, and division) are performed on numeric data to produce output. The ability to perform arithmetic operations rapidly and accurately is an important characteristic of computer systems.

Prior to any arithmetic being performed, the data to be used in the calculations must be stored in main computer storage. Then, statements in the program also stored in main computer storage can cause the numbers to be added, subtracted, multiplied, or divided. The answers from the arithmetic operations can be used in further calculations and processing or can be used as output from the program.

The diagram in Figure 1-14 illustrates the steps that occur in an application to calculate an average golf score. The average is calculated from three scores entered on the keyboard. These steps are:

1. The computer program to calculate the average score is stored in main computer storage.
2. The data required to calculate the average score is entered on the keyboard, causing it to be placed in storage. This data includes the name of the golfer and three golf scores.
3. The data which is entered on the keyboard is displayed on the CRT screen as it is entered.
4. The three scores are added together. The sum of the three scores is then divided by three, giving the average score. The average score is stored in main computer storage. These calculations are performed by instructions contained in the program.
5. The average score which has been calculated is then displayed on the CRT screen.

This example illustrates the use of both input/output operations and arithmetic operations. The data must first be entered into main computer storage via the input operation. The arithmetic operations are then performed to calculate the average golf score. Finally, the average score is displayed as output on the CRT screen.

The basic cycle of input, process, and output is fundamental to most applications performed on a computer system. In this case, the processing consisted of calculating the average golf score. Although many applications are much more complex than the one illustrated, arithmetic operations are commonly a part of the processing step.

Logical operations

It is the ability of a computer system to perform logical operations that separates it from other types of calculating devices. Computer systems are

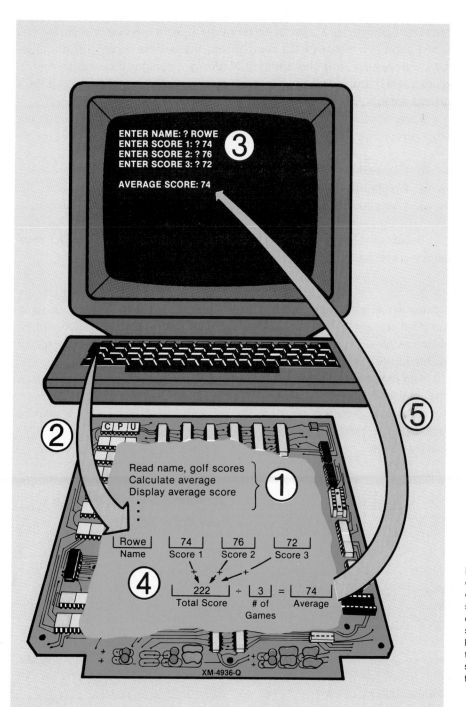

Figure 1-14 Arithmetic operations are used to calculate an average golf score. The average is calculated by adding the three scores entered from the keyboard and then dividing the sum by 3. The average score is then displayed on the CRT screen.

capable of comparing numbers, letters of the alphabet, and special characters. Based upon the results of the comparison, the computer can perform alternative processing. It is this ability that allows a computer system to control space flights, teach children to read, determine how much money is in a savings account, or predict presidential election results.

Three types of comparing operations are commonly performed under program control:

1. Comparing to determine if two values are equal.
2. Comparing to determine if one value is less than another value.
3. Comparing to determine if one value is greater than another value.

Based upon the results of these comparisons, the program in main computer storage can direct the computer system to take alternative actions.

Comparing — equal condition

Frequently, a computer program will compare two values stored in main computer storage to determine if they are equal. If the values are equal, one set of instructions will be executed; if they are not equal, another set of instructions will be executed.

The example in Figure 1–15 illustrates the use of an equal comparison. The name and marital status of a person has been entered into main computer storage. If the person is married, the taxes deducted will be for a married person. If the person is not married, the taxes will be deducted for a non-married person.

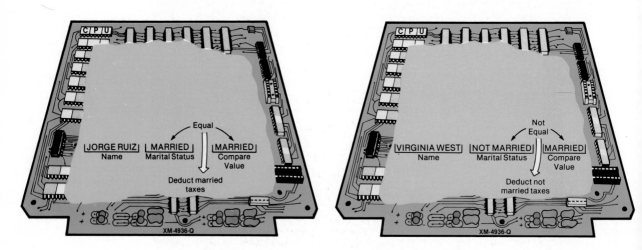

Figure 1–15 The marital status is compared to a fixed compare value field which contains the value MARRIED. The marital status of Jorge Ruiz is married; therefore, an equal condition results from the comparison and married taxes are deducted. Virginia West is not married. Thus, an unequal condition results when the comparison is made, and the program deducts not married taxes.

Since the marital status field for Jorge Ruiz contains the value MARRIED, an equal condition will occur when it is compared to the compare value. Based upon this equal result, taxes for a married person will be deducted.

The marital status for Virginia West is NOT MARRIED, resulting in an unequal condition. Therefore, taxes for a not married person will be deducted.

In this example, the program will execute different instructions based upon the result of the comparison. Comparing for an equal or not equal condition is commonly done in computer programs.

Applications also require comparing fields to determine if one value is less than another value. If so, one sequence of operations takes place. If, however, a value is equal to or greater than another value, then a different sequence of instructions is executed.

**Comparing —
less than condition**

For example, in an educational application, part-time students must be identified (Figure 1–16). Part-time students take fewer than 16 class units. Therefore, it is necessary to compare the number of units a student is taking to the value 16. If the number of units is less than 16, the student is identified as a part-time student. If the number of units is 16 units or more, the student is identified as a full-time student.

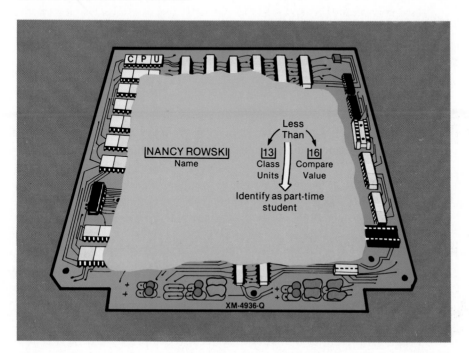

Figure 1–16 The class units for each student are compared to a constant value 16. If the class units are less than 16, instructions to identify the student as part-time are executed. If the class units are not less than 16 (they are 16 or greater), the student is identified as full-time. Nancy Rowski is taking 13 class units; therefore, she is a part-time student.

**Comparing —
greater than
condition**

The third type of comparing operation determines if one value is greater than another value. For example, in a payroll application, the hours an employee worked could be compared to 40. If the employee worked more than 40 hours, overtime pay would be calculated. If the employee worked 40 hours or less, no overtime pay would be calculated. This comparing operation is illustrated in Figure 1–17.

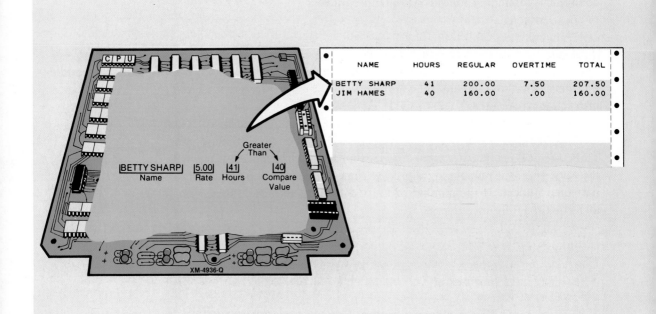

NAME	HOURS	REGULAR	OVERTIME	TOTAL
BETTY SHARP	41	200.00	7.50	207.50
JIM HAMES	40	160.00	.00	160.00

Figure 1–17 Betty Sharp worked 41 hours. Therefore, overtime pay is calculated because her hours are greater than 40.

In the example, the hours worked value for Betty Sharp is compared to the value 40. Since the hours worked value is greater than 40, overtime pay is calculated.

The ability of a computer system to compare values and perform alternative operations based upon the results of the comparison provides the computer with tremendous processing power to solve a variety of problems.

Summary

Input/output operations, arithmetic operations, and logical operations can be performed by all computer systems. When they are performed and what data is used in their performance is determined by the program controlling the computer system.

Programs to control a computer system are written by a computer programmer. The process of developing a computer program consists of specific steps to be accomplished by the programmer. This process is explained in the next section.

Programming a computer has been defined as one of the more precise of all human activities. Some programs for solving complex problems may involve hundreds and even thousands of individual instructions to the computer. Dr. John von Neumann, the individual credited with developing the concept of storing instructions in computer memory, stated over 30 years ago, "I am not aware of any other human effort where the result really depends on a sequence of a billion steps...and where furthermore it has the characteristic that each step really matters...yet precisely this is true of computing machines."

THE PROGRAM DEVELOPMENT CYCLE

Because of the precision required when writing computer programs, it is essential that the individual writing a program approach the problem in a systematic, disciplined manner. This systematic approach is called the program development cycle. It consists of the following steps:

1. Review of programming specifications.
2. Program design.
3. Program coding.
4. Program testing.
5. Program documentation.

When programming any problem, a complete description of the problem to be solved must be provided to the programmer. This description should include a definition of the input, an explanation of the processing that must be performed, and a definition of the output. The first step in the program development cycle is to review these programming specifications.

Review of programming specifications

It is extremely important that the programmer thoroughly understand all aspects of the problem to be solved. This understanding comes from the review of the programming specifications. After the review, the programmer should have no questions concerning the type and format of the output to be produced by the program. This understanding is the basis for designing and writing a program which will produce the correct results.

After reviewing and thoroughly understanding the programming specifications, the programmer procedes to the next step in the program development cycle — program design.

Just as the architect must design a building prior to actually beginning construction, so too must the programmer design a program before writing the actual instructions which the computer will execute. Designing a program means planning the logic and detailed steps which will lead to the solution of the problem.

Program design

When designing a program, the programmer should first examine the entire problem to determine the tasks which must be accomplished to solve the problem. Once these tasks are identified, the programmer will begin to define the precise sequence in which operations are to be performed by the computer system. To do this, the programmer must think through each of the individual steps required to solve the problem. These steps could include obtaining the input data, performing calculations or comparing operations, and producing the required output information.

Each individual step can be illustrated through the use of a flowchart. A flowchart is a series of symbols which graphically represents the solution to a problem. Some of the more commonly used flowcharting symbols are illustrated below.

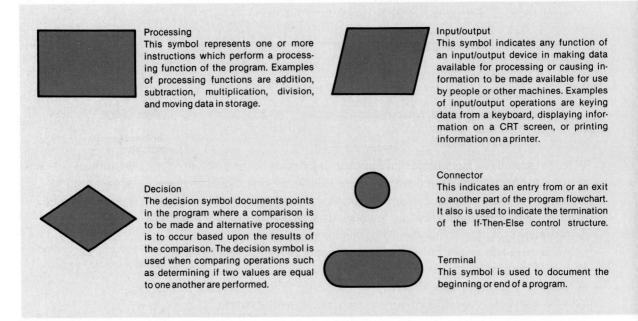

Processing
This symbol represents one or more instructions which perform a processing function of the program. Examples of processing functions are addition, subtraction, multiplication, division, and moving data in storage.

Input/output
This symbol indicates any function of an input/output device in making data available for processing or causing information to be made available for use by people or other machines. Examples of input/output operations are keying data from a keyboard, displaying information on a CRT screen, or printing information on a printer.

Decision
The decision symbol documents points in the program where a comparison is to be made and alternative processing is to occur based upon the results of the comparison. The decision symbol is used when comparing operations such as determining if two values are equal to one another are performed.

Connector
This indicates an entry from or an exit to another part of the program flowchart. It also is used to indicate the termination of the If-Then-Else control structure.

Terminal
This symbol is used to document the beginning or end of a program.

Figure 1-18 The symbols above are commonly used when flowcharting a program.

As the programmer determines each step to be performed by the program, the appropriate symbol is drawn. The task to be accomplished is then written inside the symbol. When the program design is completed, the flowchart will provide a graphic representation of the steps that are to occur to solve the problem.

The flowchart in Figure 1-19 illustrates the logic required to determine and display a sales commission. The input/output symbol is used when data is being accepted or displayed (1). The decision symbol is used when a comparison is made and alternative processing is to occur based upon the results of the comparison (2). The processing symbol is used when calculations are performed (3). The connector symbol shows the termination of the comparison operation (4); and the terminal symbol is used at the start and end of the program (5).

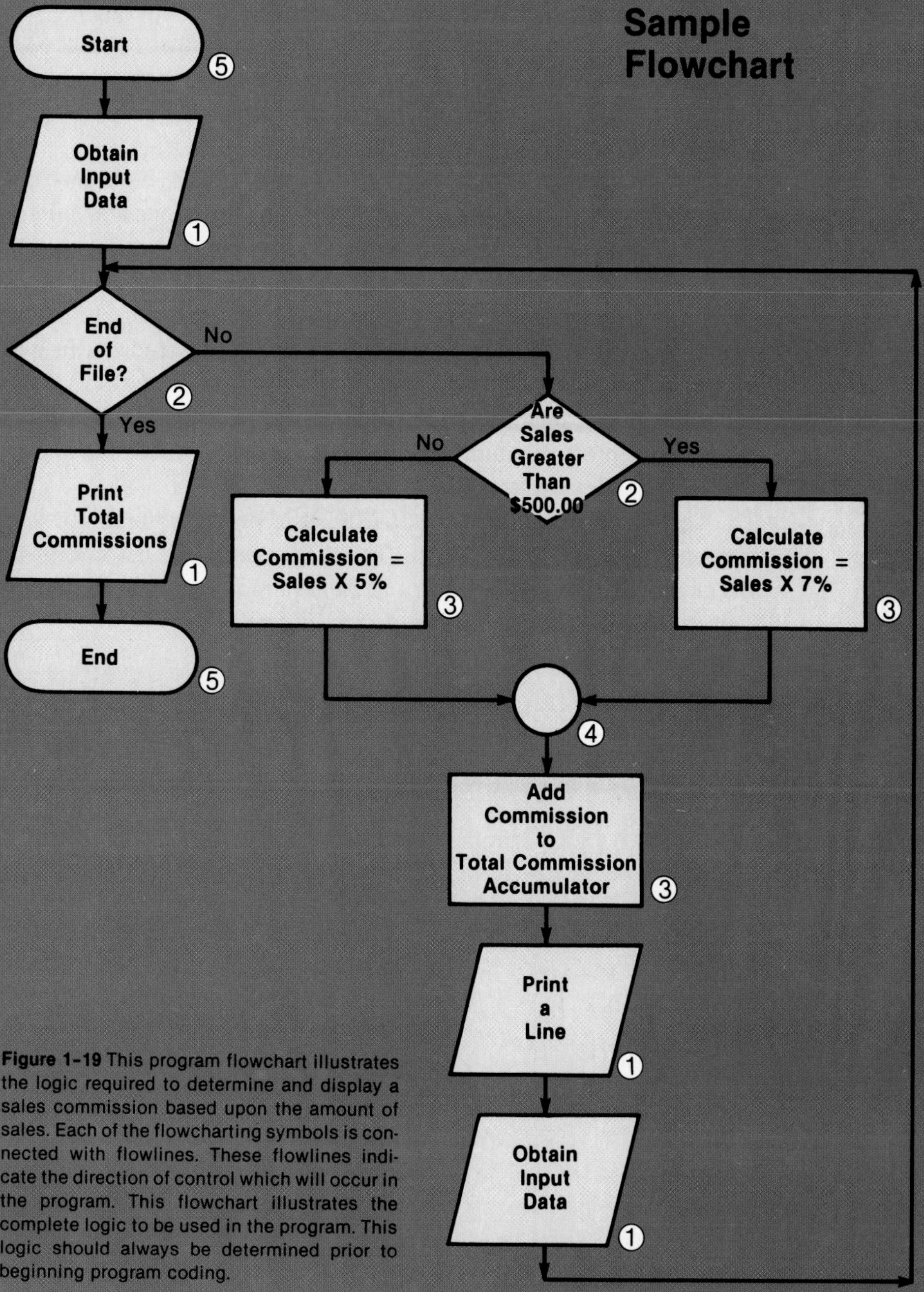

Sample Flowchart

Figure 1-19 This program flowchart illustrates the logic required to determine and display a sales commission based upon the amount of sales. Each of the flowcharting symbols is connected with flowlines. These flowlines indicate the direction of control which will occur in the program. This flowchart illustrates the complete logic to be used in the program. This logic should always be determined prior to beginning program coding.

Program coding

After the program has been designed, the program must be coded. Coding the program is the process of writing instructions in a programming language which define the data and implement the logic developed in the design phase of the program development cycle.

A programming language consists of a set of instructions which can be written by the programmer. These instructions direct the computer system to perform the operations that the programmer has determined are necessary to solve a problem.

A large number of programming languages have been developed during the past 35 years. Each has its own form of instructions and rules (called the language syntax). In this book, the programming language being used is BASIC.

BASIC, whose letters stand for Beginner's All-purpose Symbolic Instruction Code, was developed in 1965 at Dartmouth College by Dr. John Kemeny and Dr. Thomas Kurtz. It was designed to be used by students in an academic environment.

With the introduction of microcomputer systems using BASIC, it became a widely accepted programming language. Today, BASIC is used by thousands of students and programmers.

Figure 1-20 The BASIC program coding is written on a coding form. It implements the logic specified in the flowchart. The coding must follow the syntax rules of the programming language.

To code a program using BASIC, the programmer must write BASIC instructions on a coding form. These instructions must conform with the syntax of the BASIC language. The instructions written will implement the logic determined during program design (Figure 1–20).

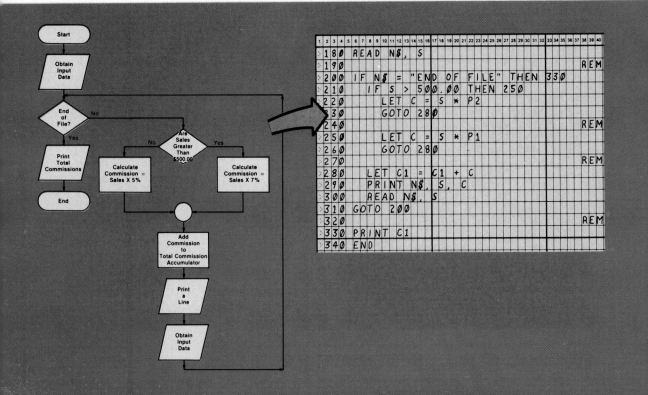

Coding a program is a very exact skill. The programmer must not only implement the program design in code but must also be very precise in the use of the programming language. The language syntax must be followed exactly. Even a single coding error can result in a program executing improperly. Therefore, it is mandatory that strict attention be paid to coding an error-free program.

Program reviews

Since program design and program coding require extreme precision, however, it is possible that a programmer may inadvertently violate a programming language syntax rule or commit a logic error in the program design. Thus, prior to entering the program into the computer system, it should be reviewed.

The review consists of examining the program logic represented by the flowchart and examining the code written by the programmer. The intent of the review is to discover any errors which have been made by the programmer. If errors are found, they should be corrected by the programmer prior to entering the program code into the computer system.

The program is reviewed by people other than the programmer who designed and wrote the program. In a classroom environment, this may consist of two or three classmates who closely look at the flowchart and coding. In an industrial environment, the review may be conducted by other programmers or even by quality control people whose task is to review programs. The important point of a review is to discover, prior to entering and executing the program, errors which have been accidentally made.

When a program review takes place, the programmer is not being critiqued. Rather, the program design and program coding are being reviewed. This distinction means that a programmer need not personally fear a program review. To the contrary, reviews should be encouraged because they offer the following advantages:

1. After the review, the program should contain no errors. Therefore, when it is entered into the computer system and executed, it will produce the correct output.
2. Since the program should contain no errors after the review, the programmer will spend little time in the frustrating process of testing and correcting the program.
3. The students or programmers reviewing the program will benefit by seeing alternative approaches to solving a problem. Additionally, the reviewers will probably not duplicate errors in their own programs which they find in the program being reviewed.

It has been stated that participating in a program review is as much a part of programming as coding. A program should always be reviewed prior to being entered into a computer system and executed.

Entering the program

After the program has been designed, coded, and reviewed, it must be entered and stored in main computer storage. This process is illustrated in Figure 1–21.

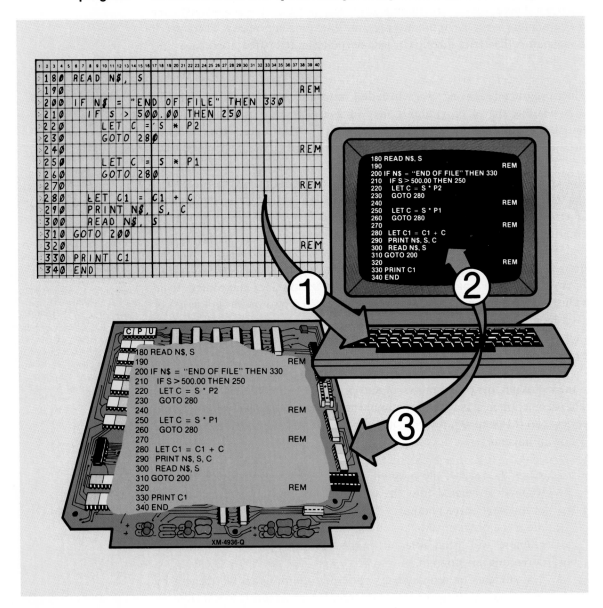

Figure 1-21 The program which has been coded is keyed on the keyboard (1). As it is keyed, it is displayed on the CRT screen (2) and stored in main computer storage (3).

To enter the program into main computer storage, the programmer keys the program on the keyboard. As it is keyed, two things happen: The program statements are displayed on the CRT screen, and the program statements are stored in main computer storage. Each program statement which has been coded by the programmer must be entered. After the entire program has been entered, it can be saved on auxiliary storage or it can be executed.

Most programs will be executed more than one time. Therefore, it is normally necessary to save a program so that it can be loaded into main computer storage at a later time. This eliminates the need to key in a program each time it is to be executed.

Auxiliary storage is used to store a program when it is to be saved for later execution. Cassette tape or floppy disk are used as auxiliary storage on microcomputer systems. The example in Figure 1-22 illustrates a program being stored on a cassette tape.

Saving the program

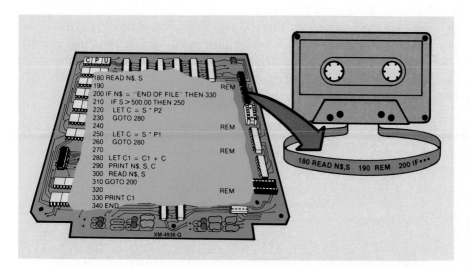

180 READ N$, S
190   REM
200 IF N$ = "END OF FILE" THEN 330
210   IF S > 500.00 THEN 250
220   LET C = S * P2
230   GOTO 280
240   REM
250   LET C = S * P1
260   GOTO 280
270   REM
280   LET C1 = C1 + C
290   PRINT N$, S, C
300   READ N$, S
310 GOTO 200
320   REM
330 PRINT C1
340 END

XM-4936-Q

Figure 1-22 The program statements which have been entered into main computer storage via the keyboard can be stored on auxiliary storage. Here, the statements are transferred from main computer storage to cassette tape. At a later time, the program stored on the tape can be entered back into main-computer storage for execution.

The program statements are stored on auxiliary storage (either cassette tape or disk) as a series of electronic spots. A command from the keyboard, such as Save, is usually keyed by the programmer to cause the program to be stored on auxiliary storage. After the program is stored, the cassette tape or floppy disk can be removed from the computer system and saved.

At a later time, the tape or disk can be placed on the appropriate device and the program can be read into main computer storage. After the program has been transferred from the tape or disk to main computer storage, it can be executed.

In a few cases, it is not necessary to save the program on auxiliary storage. In those cases, the program would be executed immediately after it is keyed into main computer storage.

When the program is stored in main computer storage, it can be executed. The program is placed in main computer storage either by entering it from the keyboard or by loading it from auxiliary storage. When the program is executed, each of the instructions in the program is executed, one at a time. As a result of the execution of the program, the desired output is produced.

Executing the program

Interpreting or compiling the program

A programmer writes a program in a programming language, such as BASIC, which can be understood by people. The statements used in the programming language, however, cannot be interpreted and executed by the electronics of the computer system. The central processing unit, which actually executes the instructions, can understand only machine language. Machine language is a series of numbers which indicates to the CPU which instruction to execute. A machine language instruction also specifies what data is to be processed.

Since only machine language can be executed by the CPU, the statements written by the programmer in a programming language must be translated to machine language prior to execution. On microcomputer systems, a translating program called an interpreter is normally supplied with the system. The function of a BASIC interpreter is to translate each BASIC statement in the program into machine language. After the statement is translated, it is passed from the interpreter to the CPU, where it is executed (Figure 1–23).

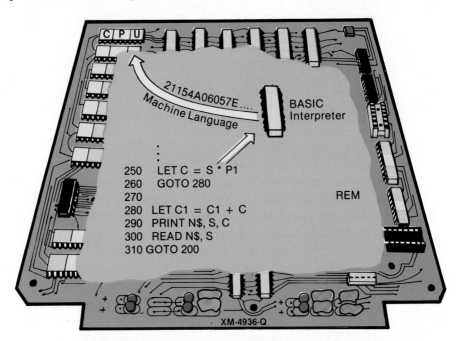

Figure 1-23 The statement on line 250 is translated by the BASIC interpreter into a series of machine language statements. A language such as BASIC, which requires multiple machine language instructions to implement a single statement, is called a high-level programming language.

The BASIC interpreter is often stored in a special type of memory called Read Only Memory (ROM). When stored in ROM, the BASIC interpreter is available for use at all times. On other systems the interpreter, which is a program whose function is to translate statements from BASIC to machine language, is stored on auxiliary storage. In this case, the interpreter must be loaded from auxiliary storage into main computer storage before the BASIC program can be executed.

On larger computer systems, a BASIC compiler is often used. A compiler is a program whose function is to translate the statements in a BASIC program into machine language. This is the same function as an interpreter. Instead of passing the machine language instruction onto the CPU for execution, however, the compiler creates an object program. An object program consists of the entire program in machine language format. When the program is to be executed, the object program is loaded into main computer storage. The CPU can then directly execute the machine language statements in the object program rather than requiring a BASIC statement to be translated and then executed.

Programs which have been compiled into an object program normally execute faster than those which use an interpreter. The use of an interpreter or a compiler is dependent upon the type of computer system being used and the available software.

Program testing

After a program has been designed, coded, and reviewed, it should run perfectly when it is loaded into main computer storage for execution. The programmer must approach the programming process with the attitude and intent that the program will be correct the first time it is executed. Errors should rarely occur.

In order to verify that the program has no errors, it must be tested. Testing involves loading the program into main computer storage for execution. The program will process test data to ensure that the correct output is produced.

If errors are found in a program despite the diligent attempt by the programmer to write an error-free program, they will normally be either syntax errors or logic errors. A syntax error occurs because of improper use of the programming language. A logic error occurs because the logic designed and coded will not process the data in the manner desired.

It is the responsibility of the programmer to adequately test the program to verify that no errors exist in the program. If inadvertent errors are found, the programmer must correct the errors.

**Program
documentation**

Program documentation is the recorded facts regarding a program. These facts should be documented in enough detail so that anyone can understand what the program is to accomplish and how it accomplishes it. Two levels of documentation are required for a program — documentation within the program itself and external documentation available to users of the program.

Documentation within the program itself is critical for a program. BASIC, as well as most other programming languages, allows comments to be written within the program. These comments explain the data being used, the processing which is to occur, and any other facts which will enable a programmer to understand what the program is doing and how it is doing it. Every well-written computer program contains comments which aid in the understanding of the program.

External documentation is information prepared about the program to aid in running or using the program. Typically, it would include operating instructions, data formats, error messages generated from the program, and similar information. External documentation can be prepared at various levels of detail, depending upon the requirements of the users of the program.

The preparation of program documentation occurs throughout the program development cycle. Beginning with the review of the programming specifications, the programmer should record the facts about the program. Particularly important is the documentation which takes place when the program is being coded. Comments within the program should always be present.

SUMMARY

The following points have been discussed and explained in this chapter.

1. Few aspects of our daily lives are left untouched by some type of computerized processing.

2. The ability to understand and use a computer system is rapidly becoming as important as the ability to read and write.

3. Computer systems can be very small or very large. Each size computer is capable of performing certain types of tasks.

4. A computer is a device which can perform computations, including arithmetic and logic operations, without human intervention.

5. A computer system performs three basic operations — input/output operations, arithmetic operations, and logical operations.

6. Data is the representation of facts, concepts, or instructions in a formalized manner suitable for communication, interpretation, and processing by humans or automatic machines.

7. Input units make data available for processing.

8. The processor unit consists of two parts: the central processing unit and main computer storage.

9. The central processing unit contains the electronic circuitry which actually causes processing to occur.

10. Main computer storage consists of electronic components which store letters of the alphabet, numbers, and special characters.

11. Output units make information resulting from the processing of data available for use.

12. A computer program contains instructions which specify the operations and sequence of operations which are to occur on a computer system. A computer program must be stored in main computer storage to be executed.

13. Auxiliary storage devices are used to store data and programs for subsequent use.

14. The keyboard is the primary input device for a microcomputer system.

15. Output from a microcomputer system may be printed on a low speed printer or displayed on the CRT screen.

16. Cassette tape and floppy disk are the two primary means of auxiliary storage on a small computer system.

17. The steps when using a keyboard for input to the computer system are: a) The program is stored in main computer storage and controls the input operation; b) The input data is keyed on the keyboard and is displayed on the CRT screen as it is keyed; c) The keyed data is stored in main computer storage.

18. Output is produced by transferring data from main computer storage to an output device. The steps are: a) The program is stored in main computer storage; b) Under control of the program, the output data is transferred from main computer storage to the output device.

19. Arithmetic operations are used to add, subtract, multiply, and divide numeric data. The data to be used in the calculations must be stored in main computer storage.

20. The three types of logical (comparing) operations which are commonly performed under program control are: a) Comparing to determine if two values are equal; b) Comparing to determine if one value is less than another value; c) Comparing to determine if one value is greater than another value.

21. In any comparison operation, if the condition being tested is true, the program will perform one set of operations; if the condition is not true, the program will perform an alternative set of operations.

22. The program development cycle consists of five steps: a) Review of programming specifications; b) Program design; c) Program coding; d) Program testing; e) Program documentation.

23. Programming specifications are a complete description of the problem to be solved. The programming specifications must be thoroughly reviewed and understood prior to beginning the design of the computer program.

24. Designing a program means planning the logic and detailed steps which will lead to the solution of the problem.

25. A flowchart can be used to graphically illustrate the steps required in the program.

26. Program coding involves writing the actual program instructions to implement the solution to a problem. Coding should take place only after the program has been designed.

27. A programming language consists of a set of instructions which can be written by the programmer. These instructions direct the computer system to perform the operations that the programmer has determined are necessary to solve a problem.

28. BASIC was developed at Dartmouth College in 1965. Today it is used by thousands of programmers and students.

29. The syntax of a programming language is the form of the instructions

and the rules which must be followed.

30. Coding is a very exact skill which requires precise attention to detail. Even a single coding error can result in a program executing improperly.

31. A program review consists of examining program logic and program code. The review is conducted by people other than the programmer who wrote the program. The intent of a review is to find any errors which have been inadvertently made by the programmer.

32. A program should always be reviewed prior to being entered into a computer system and executed.

33. To enter the program into main computer storage, the programmer keys the program on the keyboard. Each programming statement coded by the programmer must be entered.

34. After the program has been entered, it will normally be saved on auxiliary storage.

35. The program entered by the programmer must be translated from BASIC to machine language prior to being executed.

36. An interpreter translates a program one statement at a time into machine language and passes the machine language instruction to the CPU for execution.

37. A compiler translates all instructions in a computer program and creates an object program. An object program consists of machine language instructions which can be executed on the computer system.

38. A program should be documented as it is being designed, coded, and implemented. All programs should have comments within them to explain the processing which is accomplished within the program.

QUESTIONS AND EXERCISES

1. What is the definition of a computer?
2. What three operations can a computer perform?
3. What is the difference between the processor unit and the central processing unit?
4. What is a computer program?
5. Where must data be stored to be processed by a computer program?
6. Which of the following is classified as auxiliary storage: (a) Floppy disk; (b) Keyboard; (c) CPU; (d) CRT.
7. What are the three steps which take place when data is entered into main computer storage?
8. A _____ must always be stored in main computer storage before data can be entered from the keyboard.
9. A computer can compare data and determine that: (a) Two numbers are not equal; (b) One number is less than or equal to another number; (c) One number is equal to another number; (d) All of the preceding.
10. What are the five steps of the program development cycle?
11. Program specifications are the recorded facts regarding a program and should always be included as comments in the program (T or F).
12. Which of the following depict the correct sequence for the program development cycle: (a) Program coding, program design, program documentation; (b) Program documentation, program testing, program coding; (c) Program design, program coding, program testing; (d) Program design, program testing, program coding, program documentation.
13. A flowchart is used to graphically illustrate the steps required in a computer program (T or F).
14. What is a programming language? What is programming language syntax?
15. Coding a program is a very exact skill which requires precise attention to detail. If the program is not coded properly: (a) There is the possibility of harming the electronics of the computer system; (b) The program will not produce the desired output; (c) The computer system will always indicate to the programmer why the program is not correct; (d) It is likely not to matter because most computer systems are capable of self-correcting small errors.
16. The intent of a program review is to find errors in a program (T or F).
17. An _____ translates a program one statement at a time into machine language and passes the machine language instruction to the CPU for execution.
18. Programs with comments tend to be hard to read and understand (T or F).

CHAPTER TWO

INPUT/OUTPUT PROGRAMMING

OBJECTIVES:

An understanding of the program development and coding process

An understanding of the logic required to create a list of information using a simple loop

An understanding of and the ability to use the following BASIC statements: REM, DATA, READ, IF, PRINT, GOTO, and END

An understanding of and ability to use numeric and string variables and constants

An understanding and recognition of good programming techniques, including program comments and proper indentation of the source code

INPUT/OUTPUT PROGRAMMING

Computer programs can vary significantly in size. A simple program contains only a few statements. A complex program can contain hundreds and even thousands of statements. Regardless of the size of the program, the task of computer programming is one of the more precise of all human activities. A single error in a program can produce erroneous results. It is extremely important, therefore, that programming a computer be accomplished with precision. A careless, casual approach to programming can lead to frustration and anxiety. With a careful, precise approach to program design and coding, however, programming becomes an enjoyable, challenging experience that provides the user with access to and control over the most powerful tool ever developed.....the computer.

Thus, it is mandatory that a programmer consistently pay attention to detail, both in the program design and program coding. Programmers must always remember that each step in a program is critical. Again, one programming mistake can produce invalid output from the computer system. When designing and coding a program, the programmer should understand the programming rules and concentrate so that the rules are always followed. Every program should be error-free from its inception.

To teach computer programming using the BASIC language, each of the chapters in this textbook contains a problem to be programmed. After the problem is presented, the design of the program is illustrated by means of a flowchart. This is followed by an explanation of the statements in the BASIC program.

Upon completion of the textbook, a firm foundation in the methods of program design will have been gained, together with the ability to program the computer to solve a variety of problems encountered in one's personal and professional life. This ability will be applicable to large computer systems as well as microcomputer systems.

The input/output operation occurs in most computer applications. A common application using the input/output operation is displaying lists of information, such as names and telephone numbers, the names of students in a class, a list of the products produced by a company, and others. A program which lists information is one of the simpler computer programs which can be written in the BASIC language.

The process of producing a list of information consists of reading some type of input data and writing this data in the desired format.

The sample problem to illustrate the input/output operation involves creating a telephone number listing. The input, output, and processing to be accomplished are illustrated in the following sections.

Input   The input data contains the area code, telephone number, and the person's name. The data to be processed by the program is illustrated in Figure 2-1.

Four names, together with the corresponding area code and telephone number, are shown in Figure 2-1. The data, taken as a group, is called a file. The data about a single individual is called a record. Thus, the input data consists of a file of records.

Figure 2-1 The input file contains name and telephone number records. The last record is a trailer record. When it is read, all valid records have been processed.

AREA CODE	TELEPHONE NUMBER	NAME
714	749-2138	SAM HORN
213	663-1271	SUE NUNN
212	999-1193	BOB PELE
312	979-4418	ANN SITZ
999	999-9999	END OF FILE

Each record contains three fields. A field is defined as a unit of data. Each record contains an area code field, a telephone number field, and a name field (Figure 2-2).

Figure 2-2 A record is composed of fields. In the sample problem, the record contains the area code field, the telephone number field, and the name field.

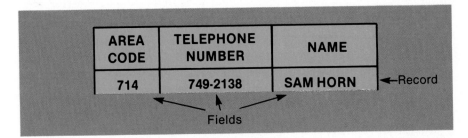

AREA CODE	TELEPHONE NUMBER	NAME	
714	749-2138	SAM HORN	◄—Record

Fields

The last record in Figure 2-1 is a trailer record. The trailer record is the last record in the input file. It indicates that all valid data records have been processed. When the trailer record is read by the program, the name field will contain the value END OF FILE. Through the comparing operation, the program can determine that when the name field contains this value, all data records have been processed. The area code and telephone number fields in the trailer record contain all 9's because all fields must contain data.

The output is a listing of each record in the input file (Figure 2–3).   **Output**

```
    SAM  HORN         714           749-2138
    SUE  NUNN         213           663-1271
    BOB  PELE         212           999-1193
    ANN  SITZ         312           979-4418

    END OF  TELEPHONE  LISTING
```

Figure 2-3 The output listing from the program con-
tains the name, area code,
and telephone number.

The first field for each line on the output listing is the name field, followed by the area code field, and then the telephone number field. This
sequence of fields on the output listing is different from the sequence in the input
file (Figure 2–1). After all records have been printed, the message END OF
TELEPHONE LISTING is printed. The program processing is then terminated.

After the specifications for the program have been studied and thoroughly   **Program design**
understood, the program must be designed. Designing the program means
determining the step-by-step processing which is necessary to solve the problem. In the sample problem in this chapter, the steps necessary to create the
telephone number listing must be determined. As noted previously, a program
contains the individual instructions to the computer system which will cause
the desired processing to occur. These instructions must be specified in exactly
the right sequence and be executed under the proper conditions. Therefore, the
design of the program is critical.

To begin the design of a program, the programmer should identify those
tasks which must be accomplished by the program. The tasks are then listed by
the programmer. The tasks required for the sample program are listed below.

Program Tasks

1. Read input records.
2. Print lines on the CRT screen.
3. Print END OF TELEPHONE LISTING on the CRT screen.

If the tasks specified above are completed, the telephone listing will be
properly prepared. It is important that all tasks which are required for the program are identified. It is from these tasks that the exact sequence of execution
will be determined. This sequence of execution will be documented through the
use of a flowchart.

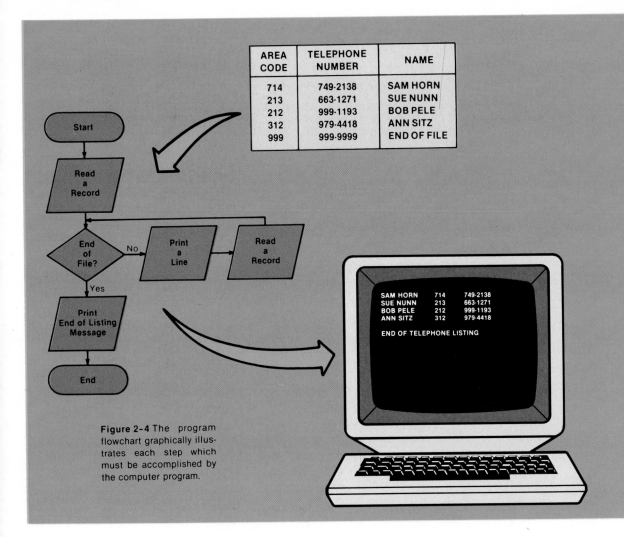

AREA CODE	TELEPHONE NUMBER	NAME
714	749-2138	SAM HORN
213	663-1271	SUE NUNN
212	999-1193	BOB PELE
312	979-4418	ANN SITZ
999	999-9999	END OF FILE

Figure 2-4 The program flowchart graphically illustrates each step which must be accomplished by the computer program.

Program flowchart

The flowchart illustrating the logic for the sample program is shown in Figure 2-4. The input data and output listing that will be produced by this logic are also contained in Figure 2-4. This flowchart uses three different symbols — the terminal symbol, the input/output symbol, and the decision symbol.

The terminal symbol is used to indicate the start and the end of the program. The input/output symbol is used for the operations of reading a record, printing a line on the output listing, and printing the end of listing message. The decision symbol indicates where the end of file decision is made.

In order to fully understand the logic presented in the flowchart, it is necessary to examine the step-by-step processing which will occur when the logic is implemented. Each of the steps is explained in the following examples.

Step 1: A record is read.

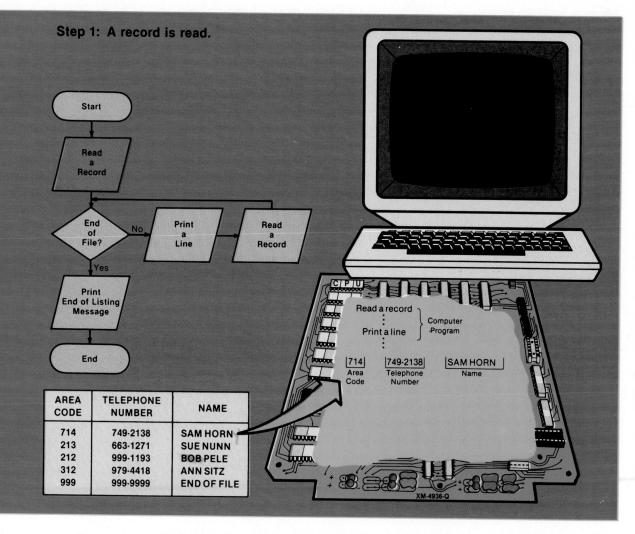

AREA CODE	TELEPHONE NUMBER	NAME
714	749-2138	SAM HORN
213	663-1271	SUE NUNN
212	999-1193	BOB PELE
312	979-4418	ANN SITZ
999	999-9999	END OF FILE

Figure 2-5 When a record is read, the data is placed in storage for use.

It must be recalled that all processing on a computer system takes place under the control of a computer program. Thus, for the processing shown in this step-by-step example to occur, the program must be stored in main computer storage. Once the program is stored in main computer storage, the operator initiates the execution of the program. The actual statements which are found in the program should not be of concern. Instead, in this example, it is the logic used by the program which is important. The BASIC language statements to implement the logic will be explained later in this chapter.

In step 1, the first input record is read. The value in each of the fields (area code, telephone number, and name) is placed in storage so that it can be referenced by instructions within the program.

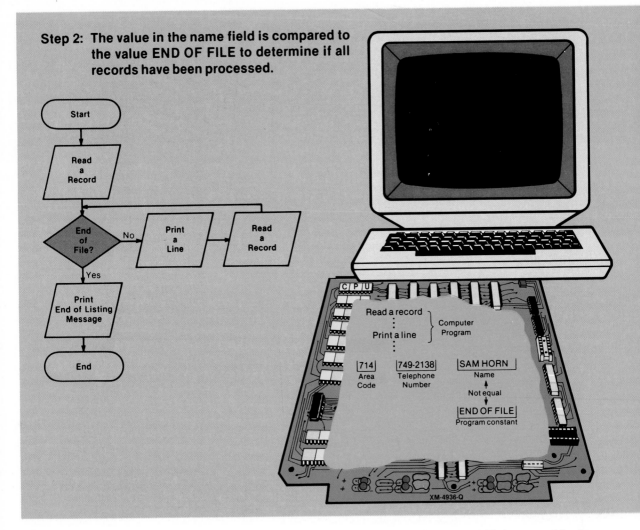

Step 2: The value in the name field is compared to the value END OF FILE to determine if all records have been processed.

Figure 2-6 The value in the name field is compared to the constant END OF FILE.

After an input record is read, it must be determined if the record is the trailer record (see Figure 2–1). If so, then all records have been processed. If not, then the input values must be printed and another record read. This decision is indicated by the question End of File? in the decision symbol.

To determine if the trailer record has been read, the value in the name field is compared to the value END OF FILE, which is defined within the program. If they are equal, the trailer record has been read. If they are not equal, the data from the record must be printed. In the example in Figure 2-6, the value in the name field is SAM HORN. Since this value is not equal to END OF FILE, the data in the record must be printed on the CRT screen. This processing is illustrated in Step 3 (Figure 2-7).

Step 3: The values are printed on the CRT screen.

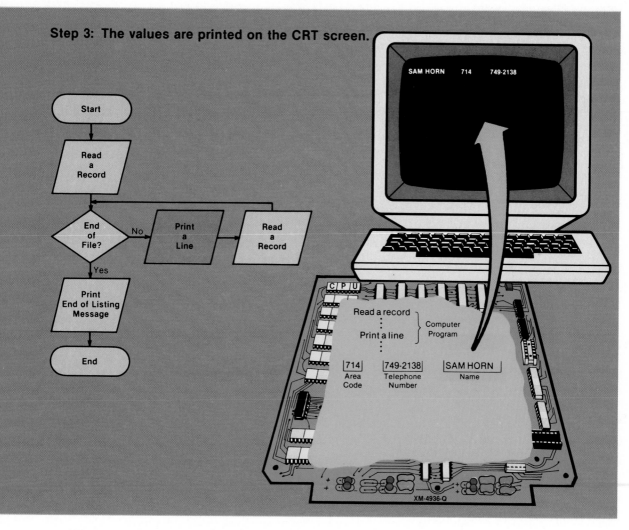

Figure 2-7 A line is printed on the CRT screen.

Since the record just read is not the trailer record, the data in the record is printed on the CRT screen. An instruction in the program will cause the data to be transferred from main computer storage to the screen. The sequence of the data printed on the screen (name, area code, and telephone number) is different from the sequence of the data in the input record (area code, telephone number, and name). The sequence in which the data is printed on the screen is determined by instructions within the program.

After the information is printed on the screen, the data in the input record has been completely processed. The program specifications state only that the data which is read is to be printed on the screen. The programmer must then ask, "What should occur after the data in a single record has been completely processed?" In this program, and in most programs, the answer is that more input data must be obtained. Therefore, the next step is to read another input record.

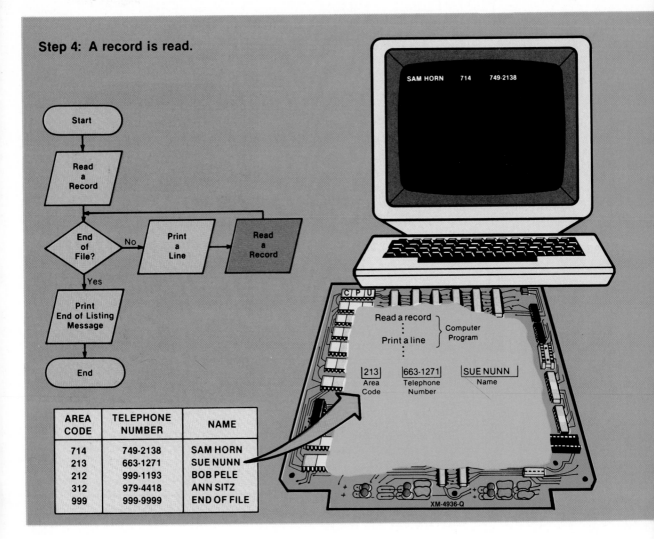

Step 4: A record is read.

AREA CODE	TELEPHONE NUMBER	NAME
714	749-2138	SAM HORN
213	663-1271	SUE NUNN
212	999-1193	BOB PELE
312	979-4418	ANN SITZ
999	999-9999	END OF FILE

Figure 2-8 When a record is read, data is stored in main computer storage.

In Figure 2–8, the values in the fields of the second record are read and are placed in main computer storage for use. These values can now be referenced by instructions within the computer program.

After the record has been read, it is again necessary to determine if the record read is the trailer record. Therefore, control returns to the decision symbol where end of file is checked (Step 5).

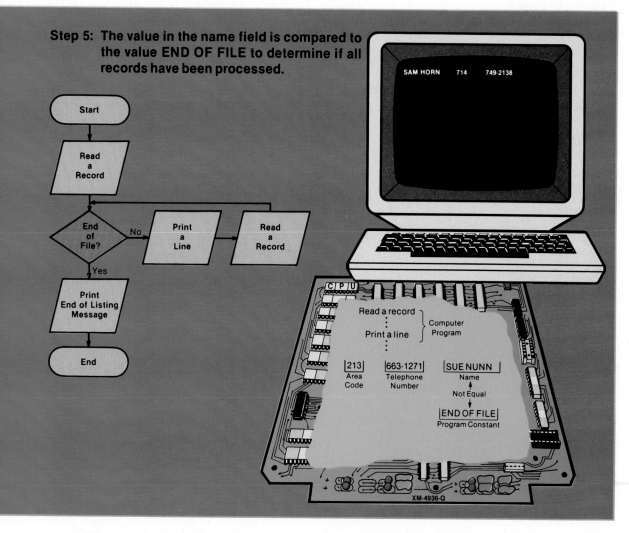

Step 5: The value in the name field is compared to the value END OF FILE to determine if all records have been processed.

Figure 2-9 The value in the name field is compared to the constant END OF FILE.

In Figure 2-9, the value in the name field (SUE NUNN) is compared to the constant END OF FILE. Since they are not equal, the trailer record has not been read. Instead, the data from the record must be printed on the screen.

This example illustrates several very important programming logic concepts. First, the decision to determine end of file will always be executed immediately after a record is read. If end of file has not been found, the instructions to print a line and read a record are repeated. They will be repeated so long as the record read is not the trailer record. Repeating a sequence of instructions multiple times is called looping. That is, a loop is established because a sequence of instructions is repeated until a particular condition occurs. In this case, the looping will continue until the trailer record is read. The concept of looping is quite important because one set of instructions can be written to process many records. The programmer need not write a set of instructions for each record which is to be processed.

The second important concept illustrated concerns the nature of a loop. Through research over the past thirty years, computer scientists have determined that good programming practice requires the first instruction in a loop to be the instruction which determines if the body of the loop should be executed. In this example, that instruction is the one which determines if the trailer record has been read (is it end of file?). Therefore, the first instruction in the loop should be the decision instruction. Any other instruction violates good programming practices which have been established through years of research and experimentation.

Because of this very important rule concerning loops, two read statements are required in this program. Passing control back to the first read statement violates this rule (Figure 2–10).

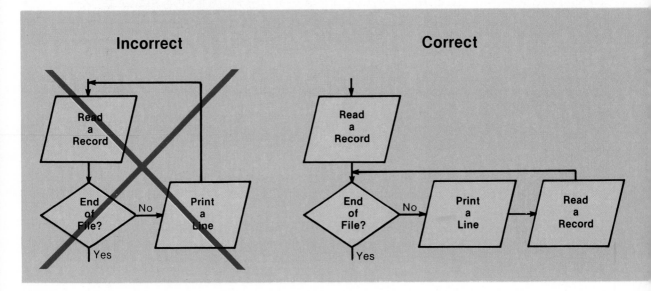

Figure 2-10 The first instruction in a loop should be the instruction which determines if the body of the loop will be executed. In the incorrect example, the first instruction in the loop is the read statement. This violates a rule for developing good program logic as specified by computer experts after years of research and experimentation.

In the incorrect example above, control is passed from the "print a line" statement to the first read statement. This means that the first statement in the loop is a read statement, not a decision statement.

In the correct example, after a line is printed a record is read. Control is then passed to the decision symbol where end of file is checked. If end of file is not found, the data from the record just read will be printed and then another record will be read. The first statement in the loop is the decision whether the print and read statements should be executed. The correct example follows the rule that the first statement in the loop should be the decision statement which determines whether the body of the loop will be executed.

Although the value of this rule may not be readily apparent in this example, more complex programs later in the text will illustrate the soundness of the rule. The rule will never be violated in well-designed programs.

After end of file has been checked and it is found that the trailer record has not been read, the data from the input record must be printed. This is shown in Step 6.

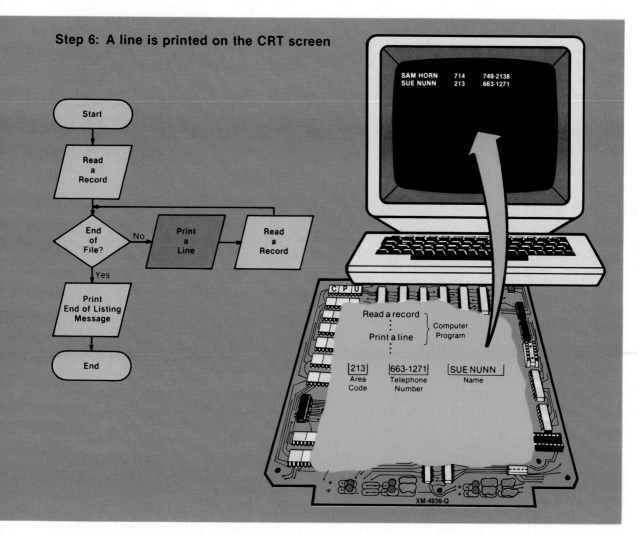

Step 6: A line is printed on the CRT screen

The data from the second record is printed on the CRT screen in the same manner as the data from the first record. After the data from the second record has been printed, the next record must be read (Step 7).

Figure 2-11 The data from the second record is printed on the CRT screen.

Step 7: The next record is read and end of file is checked.

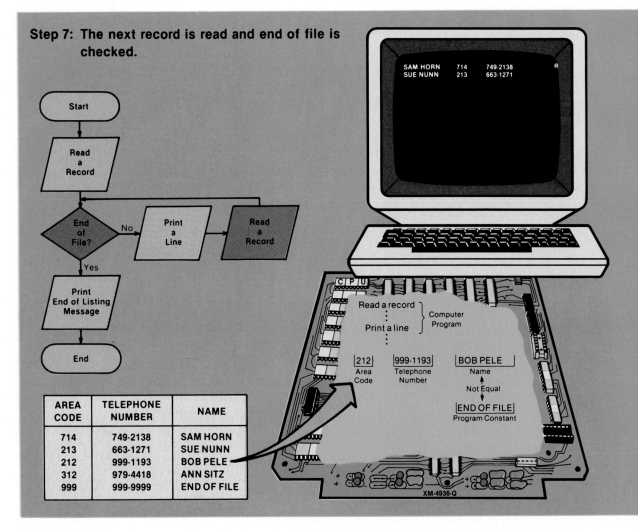

Figure 2-12 The next record is read and checked for end of file.

After the next record is read, the value in the name field is again compared to the program constant value END OF FILE. If the two values are equal, the trailer record has been read, and there are no more records to process. In Step 7, the value in the name field is BOB PELE, indicating the trailer record has not been read. The data in the input fields should, therefore, be printed.

This cycle of print the data, read a record, and check for end of file will continue until the trailer record is read. When this occurs, the statements within the loop will no longer be executed. Instead, the statements following the loop will be given control. This is shown in Step 8.

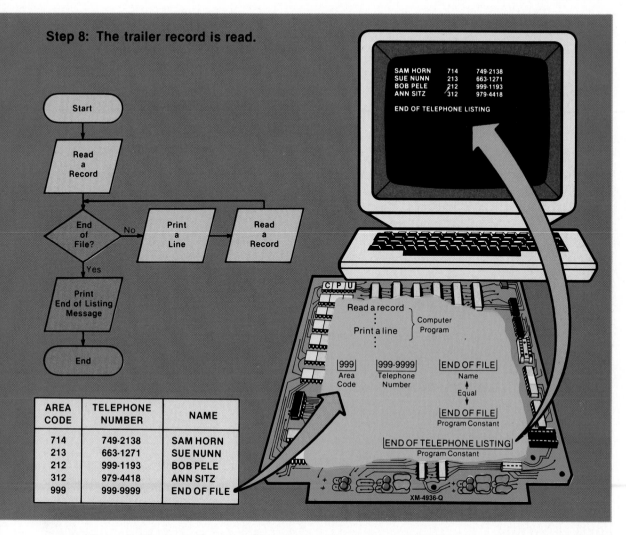

Step 8: The trailer record is read.

AREA CODE	TELEPHONE NUMBER	NAME
714	749-2138	SAM HORN
213	663-1271	SUE NUNN
212	999-1193	BOB PELE
312	979-4418	ANN SITZ
999	999-9999	END OF FILE

In Figure 2–13, the trailer record has been read (the name field contains END OF FILE). When the value in the name field is compared to the program constant, an equal condition occurs. Therefore, the loop is not entered. Instead, the "yes" leg of the decision is taken. The END OF TELEPHONE LISTING message is printed. The program is then terminated.

The previous examples have shown the step-by-step processing which takes place in a program whose function is to list data. This program, although simple in comparison to programs containing thousands of steps, illustrates the basic logic which is required for any program that obtains input data for processing — the looping operation of obtaining data, processing the data, and then obtaining more data until there is no more data to process. It is very important that this basic loop be well-understood, for it forms the basis of many computer programs.

Figure 2-13 When the trailer record is read, the statement following the loop prints the END OF TELEPHONE LISTING message.

THE BASIC PROGRAM   After the design has been completed, the program code is written. When coding, the programmer must implement the logic developed during the program design. This logic is specified by the program flowchart. Thus, the programmer will follow the sequence of operations which has been specified on the flowchart. The BASIC program to prepare the telephone number listing is illustrated below.

```
100 REM TELLIST            SEPTEMBER 22            SHELLY/CASHMAN
110                                                          REM
120 REM THIS PROGRAM DISPLAYS THE NAME, TELEPHONE AREA CODE
130 REM AND PHONE NUMBER OF INDIVIDUALS.
140                                                          REM
150 REM VARIABLE NAMES:
160 REM    A.....AREA CODE
170 REM    T$....TELEPHONE NUMBER
180 REM    N$....NAME
190                                                          REM
200 REM ***** DATA TO BE PROCESSED *****
210                                                          REM
220 DATA 714, "749-2138", "SAM HORN"
230 DATA 213, "663-1271", "SUE NUNN"
240 DATA 212, "999-1193", "BOB PELE"
250 DATA 312, "979-4418", "ANN SITZ"
260 DATA 999, "999-9999", "END OF FILE"
270                                                          REM
280 REM ***** PROCESSING *****
290                                                          REM
300 READ A, T$, N$
310                                                          REM
320 IF N$ = "END OF FILE" THEN 370
330    PRINT N$, A, T$
340    READ A, T$, N$
350 GOTO 320
360                                                          REM
370 PRINT " "
380 PRINT "END OF TELEPHONE LISTING"
390 END
```

Figure 2-14 The program contains the instructions required to implement the logic designed using the flowchart.

The program code consists of BASIC statements which direct the computer system to perform the operations required to produce the telephone number listing. The individual statements in the program are explained in the following paragraphs.

Statement numbers   Each BASIC statement begins with a unique number that identifies the statement. These numbers are assigned in an ascending sequence by the programmer. The number can begin with the value 1 and be incremented by one, if desired. A better way to assign the numbers, however, is to begin with the value 100 and increment the number by 10 (as shown in Figure 2–14).

Beginning with the number 100 allows a relatively large program to be written using a 3-digit number. This makes the program listing easy to read. Incrementing the numbers by 10 allows additional statements to be added to the program without changing any statements within the program (Figure 2–15).

```
150 LET P = A * M
155 LET F = T + P   ◄——— Statement
160 PRINT A, M, P, F        Added
```

Figure 2-15 Statement number 155 has been added to the program. Neither statement 150 nor statement number 160 were changed when the addition was made.

Sequence numbers are required for each BASIC statement. Following the number, a blank space should be specified. Although not required by the BASIC language, this blank space makes the program easier to read. After the blank space, an entry defining the operation to be performed is coded.

The remark statement

A quality program is well documented. This means the program contains information which helps a reader of the program understand it. Included in this documentation should be the name of the program, a brief explanation of what the program does, and a description of the data fields used in the program.

Documentation in a BASIC program is accomplished using the REM (remark) statement. The segment of the program using remark statements to document the program is illustrated in Figure 2–16.

```
100 REM TELLIST            SEPTEMBER 22            SHELLY/CASHMAN
110                                                            REM
120 REM THIS PROGRAM DISPLAYS THE NAME, TELEPHONE AREA CODE
130 REM AND PHONE NUMBER OF INDIVIDUALS.
140                                                            REM
150 REM VARIABLE NAMES:
160 REM    A.....AREA CODE
170 REM    T$....TELEPHONE NUMBER
180 REM    N$....NAME
190                                                            REM
```

Figure 2-16 The REM statement allows comments to be written in a BASIC program.

On the first line of the program, statement number 100 is followed by a single blank and then the entry REM. This entry identifies the entire statement as a remark. A remark statement causes no operation to be performed by the computer system. It is used merely to provide documentation within the program.

Following the REM entry is a single blank space and then the name of the program. This programmer-chosen name should be the name under which the program is saved on auxiliary storage. The rules for forming this name vary depending upon the computer system being used. In the sample program, an abbreviation of telephone listing, TELLIST, was chosen by the programmers.

This entry is followed by the date the program was written, centered on the line. The names of the authors of the program are entered in the rightmost positions of the line. The entries on line 100 of the program are not required by the BASIC language. It is strongly recommended, however, that the documentation and program formatting techniques illustrated in the sample programs be carefully followed, for these techniques reflect good documentation methods.

Line 110 contains a REM statement in the rightmost positions of the line. The REM statement should be placed in the rightmost positions when a blank line in the program listing is desired. The blank line is included to increase the readability of the program.

On lines 120 and 130, the REM statements are used to give a brief description of the processing accomplished by the program. These lines are again followed by a blank line at statement 140

The REM statements on lines 150 through 180 document the variable names used in the program. The variable names are indented two spaces. Variable names are names assigned by the programmer to fields in main computer storage which will be referenced by statements within the program. A detailed discussion of variable names can be found on page 2.19. Documenting the variable names is mandatory in any well-written program. Statement 190 is a blank line used to separate the introductory documentation statements from the rest of the statements in the program.

Documenting the program code is fundamental to writing a good program. Every program, regardless of size or complexity, should be well documented.

The data statement

The REM statements on lines 200 and 210 indicate that the next section of coding contains the definition of the data which will be processed by the program (Figure 2–17). The data is defined through the use of the data statement.

The data statements from the program and the data which they define are shown in Figure 2–17, together with the general format of the data statement. The first data statement defines the data to be processed as the first input record. The second data statement defines the data to be processed as the second input record, and so on.

The first entry in the data statement is a line number. All BASIC statements must be preceded by a line number. A single space follows the line number and then the word DATA is specified. This entry identifies the

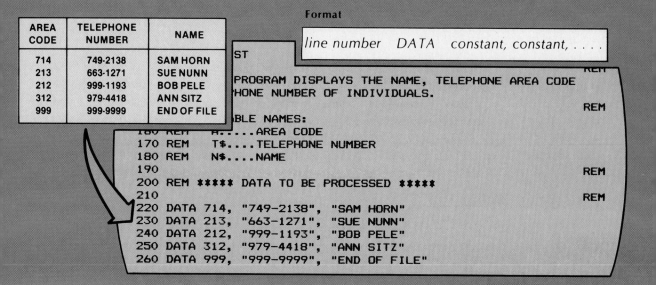

AREA CODE	TELEPHONE NUMBER	NAME
714	749-2138	SAM HORN
213	663-1271	SUE NUNN
212	999-1193	BOB PELE
312	979-4418	ANN SITZ
999	999-9999	END OF FILE

Format

line number   DATA   constant, constant, ...

```
ST
       ...PROGRAM DISPLAYS THE NAME, TELEPHONE AREA CODE     REM
       ...HONE NUMBER OF INDIVIDUALS.
                                                             REM
       ...BLE NAMES:
160 REM      A.....AREA CODE
170 REM      T$....TELEPHONE NUMBER
180 REM      N$....NAME
190                                                          REM
200 REM ***** DATA TO BE PROCESSED *****
210                                                          REM
220 DATA 714, "749-2138", "SAM HORN"
230 DATA 213, "663-1271", "SUE NUNN"
240 DATA 212, "999-1193", "BOB PELE"
250 DATA 312, "979-4418", "ANN SITZ"
260 DATA 999, "999-9999", "END OF FILE"
```

Figure 2-17 The data statement is used to define data within the program. String data is normally enclosed within double quotation marks while numeric constants do not use quotes The area code is a numeric constant, and the telephone number and name are string constants.

statement as a data statement. The word DATA is followed by a single blank.

The data to be defined is specified next. The first entry on line 220 is 714, the area code for the first record. It is followed immediately by a comma. The comma separates each entry in a data statement. The area code is a numeric constant, which means it contains only numbers.

The entry following the comma is the telephone number for the first record. The telephone number is an example of a string constant because it contains a non-numeric character (the hyphen). Any constant containing a non-numeric character is a string constant.

A string constant specified in a data statement should normally be enclosed within double quotation marks. It must be enclosed if the constant contains a comma, but good programming practice dictates that quotation marks always be used. Therefore, the telephone number is enclosed within double quotation marks.

The next entry, ''SAM HORN'', is the person's name. It is a string constant because it contains alphabetic characters. Therefore, it is enclosed within quotes.

The second data statement, on line 230, contains the data to be processed as the second record. The numeric constant 213 is specified as the area code. The next two entries are the telephone number and the person's name.

The remaining data statements contain the data to be processed as the third and fourth records.

The last data statement will be used in the program to indicate that all records have been processed and end of file has been reached.

The data statements in the sample program contain three constants each. A data statement must contain at least one constant. Each constant is separated from the other by a comma and a blank space. Again, string constants should be enclosed within double quotation marks; numeric constants are specified without quotation marks.

The read statement and variable names

After the initial documentation of the program is complete and the data to be processed by the program has been defined, the statements which will be executed in the program are specified. These statements are written based upon the logic expressed in the flowchart.

The first statement in the program is a read statement which transfers the data from the data statement to an area in main computer storage where the data can be referenced. The general format of the read statement, the read statement, and the associated entry in the flowchart are illustrated in Figure 2–18.

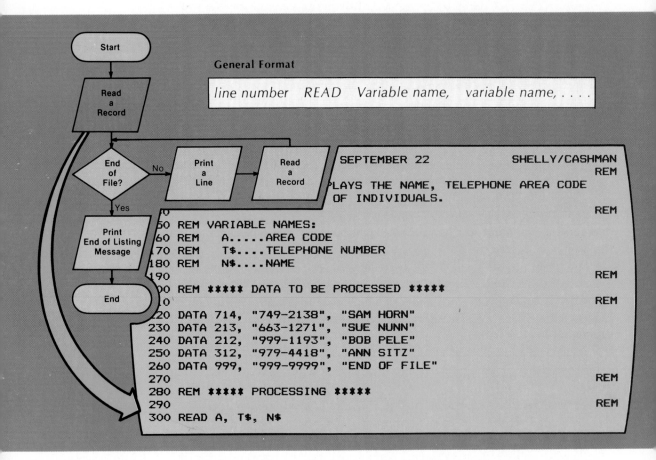

General Format

line number   READ   Variable name,   variable name, ...

```
                                        SEPTEMBER 22                    SHELLY/CASHMAN
                                                                                    REM
                                        PLAYS THE NAME, TELEPHONE AREA CODE
                                        OF INDIVIDUALS.
                                                                                    REM
150 REM VARIABLE NAMES:
160 REM    A.....AREA CODE
170 REM    T$....TELEPHONE NUMBER
180 REM    N$....NAME
190                                                                                 REM
200 REM ***** DATA TO BE PROCESSED *****
210                                                                                 REM
220 DATA 714, "749-2138", "SAM HORN"
230 DATA 213, "663-1271", "SUE NUNN"
240 DATA 212, "999-1193", "BOB PELE"
250 DATA 312, "979-4418", "ANN SITZ"
260 DATA 999, "999-9999", "END OF FILE"
270                                                                                 REM
280 REM ***** PROCESSING *****
290                                                                                 REM
300 READ A, T$, N$
```

Figure 2-18 The read statement causes data defined in a data statement to be placed in the fields identified by the variable names. The variable names must be specified in the same sequence as the related data in the data statement.

The read statement causes data defined in a data statement to be placed in the fields in main computer storage identified by the variable names following the word READ. The first entry for the read statement, as with all BASIC statements, is a line number. This value is followed by a blank space and then the word READ. A blank follows this word.

The next entries are variable names, which are chosen by the programmer to identify fields in main computer storage where data is to be stored. Variable names are used to identify numeric data fields and string data fields.

Variable names assigned to fields in a BASIC program must conform to the BASIC language syntax. All BASIC interpreters allow variable names according to the following rules:

1. Numeric variable names, which identify numeric fields, must begin with a letter of the alphabet (A – Z). The names can be one or two characters in length. If a second character is used, this character must be numeric (0 –9). Valid variable names include A1, V4, and Y7.

2. String variable names, which identify string fields, must begin with a letter of the alphabet (A – Z). This letter of the alphabet must be followed by a dollar sign ($). Valid string variable names include A$, P$, and N$.

On some computer systems, the syntax rules may allow variable names which contain more characters than specified above. The rules above, however, are valid for all BASIC interpreters.

In the read statement in Figure 2–18, the variable names A, T$, and N$ are specified following the word READ. The variable name A identifies the field where the area code will be stored when it is read. T$ identifies the field for the telephone number, and N$ identifies the field for the person's name. As a result of the read statement, data from the first data statement will be placed in the fields in main computer storage identified by these variable names (Figure 2–19).

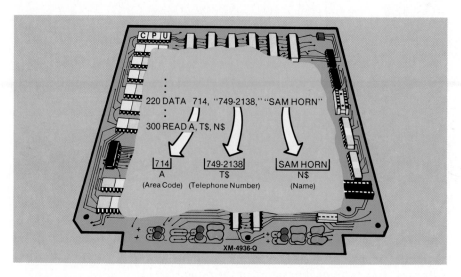

Figure 2-19 When the read statement is executed, values from the data statements are placed in fields identified by variable names in the read statement.

When the read statement is executed, the first constant in the data statement is placed in the main computer storage field identified by the first variable name in the read statement. Thus, in Figure 2–19, the first constant (714) is placed in the field identified by the first variable name (A) in the read statement. The second constant in the data statement, which is the telephone number, is placed in the second variable field (T$). Likewise, the third constant is placed in the third variable field (N$). After the read statement has been executed, an instruction referencing the variable name A will reference the value 714. Similarly, the use of the variable name T$ will reference the value 749-2138; and the variable name N$ will reference SAM HORN.

If statement

After the first read statement has been executed, a check must be performed to determine if end of file has been reached. A test for end of file should always immediately follow the reading of data. This test is implemented using the if statement. The flowchart, the general format of the if statement, and the if statement in the program are shown in Figure 2–20.

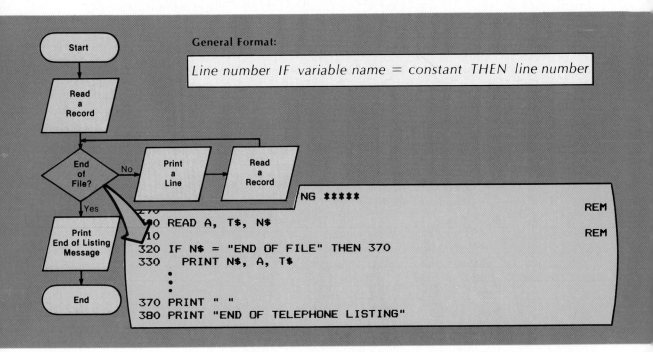

General Format:

Line number IF variable name = constant THEN line number

```
                                              NG *****
                                                                        REM
270
300 READ A, T$, N$
310                                                                     REM
320 IF N$ = "END OF FILE" THEN 370
330    PRINT N$, A, T$
       .
       .
       .
370 PRINT " "
380 PRINT "END OF TELEPHONE LISTING"
```

Figure 2-20 The if statement compares the value in the N$ field to the value END OF FILE to determine if all the data has been processed.

The if statement on line 320 begins the loop which will process all of the data in the program (see Figure 2–9). Because it is the start of the loop, the if statement is separated from the previous statement by a rem statement in the rightmost columns. This generates a blank line, allowing the start of the loop to be easily seen by someone examining the program.

Each if statement must be preceded by a line number, which in the sample program is 320. The line number is followed by a blank and then the word IF.

The variable name following the word IF identifies the field which contains the value to be compared. In the example, the value in the N$ field is to be compared. Therefore, N$ is specified as the first entry in the if statement.

The equal sign indicates that if the two values being compared are equal, then the condition being tested is considered true. If the two values being compared are not equal, the condition being tested is considered not true. Following the equal sign is the constant END OF FILE. Since it is a string constant (it contains alphabetic data), it is enclosed within quotation marks.

The word THEN is specified next, followed by the line number to which control will be transferred if the condition is true. As a result of the if statement, the value in N$ will be compared to the value END OF FILE. If they are equal, control is passed to statement 370 in the program; if they are not equal, control is passed to the statement immediately following the if statement (Figure 2–21).

Figure 2-21 The line number following the word THEN specifies the statement that will be executed if the condition is true. When the condition is not true, the statement immediately following the if statement is executed. In this example, if N$ contains the value END OF FILE, statement 370 is executed next; if not, statement 330 is executed next.

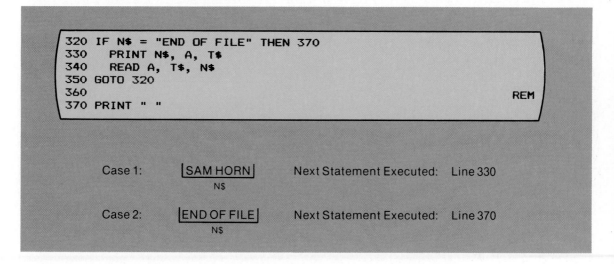

```
320 IF N$ = "END OF FILE" THEN 370
330    PRINT N$, A, T$
340    READ A, T$, N$
350 GOTO 320
360                                          REM
370 PRINT " "
```

Case 1: | SAM HORN | Next Statement Executed: Line 330
                    N$

Case 2: | END OF FILE | Next Statement Executed: Line 370
                    N$

In case 1 above, the value in N$, SAM HORN, is not equal to END OF FILE. Therefore, the statement on line 330 is the next statement executed.

In case 2, the value in N$ is equal to END OF FILE. Therefore, the condition tested by the if statement is considered true, and control is given to the statement at the line number following the THEN entry (line 370). When writing the if statement, the line number of the statement to receive control when the condition is true may not be known. In this case, the line number following the word THEN should be left blank when the if statement is coded. The number should be filled in when it is known.

Print statement

When end of file is not detected, the next statement to be executed is the print statement which displays a line on the CRT screen. The line to be displayed contains the name, the area code, and the telephone number from the input data. The flowchart, the general format of the print statement, and the print statement used in this program are shown in Figure 2–22.

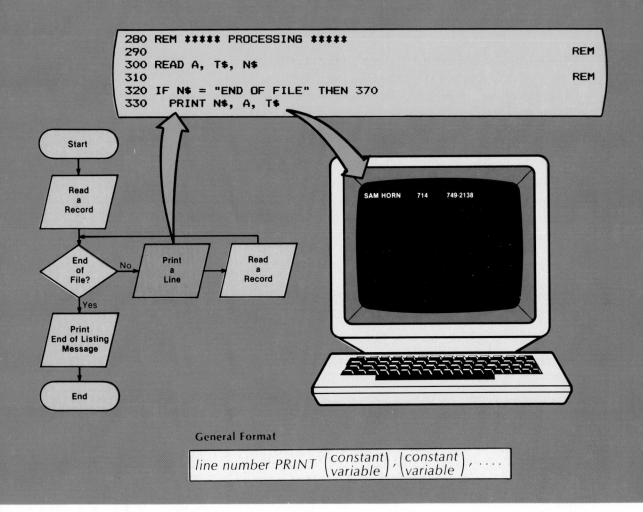

```
280 REM ***** PROCESSING *****
290                                                    REM
300 READ A, T$, N$
310                                                    REM
320 IF N$ = "END OF FILE" THEN 370
330   PRINT N$, A, T$
```

Start

Read a Record

End of File? No → Print a Line → Read a Record

Yes

Print End of Listing Message

End

SAM HORN   714   749-2138

General Format

line number PRINT $\left(\begin{array}{c}constant\\variable\end{array}\right)$, $\left(\begin{array}{c}constant\\variable\end{array}\right)$, ...

Figure 2-22 The print statement causes data identified by the variable names within the statement to be displayed on the CRT screen. Here, the name, area code, and telephone number are displayed.

A line number and then the word PRINT are the first entries in the print statement. In the example in Figure 2-22, the line number is followed by three blanks. These blanks indent the print statement two spaces from the beginning column of the if statement. This is done to identify statements within the loop. A general coding rule which will be followed throughout this text is that statements within a loop will be indented two spaces from the column where the if statement at the start of the loop begins. It is strongly suggested that this coding rule be followed in all programs which are written.

The word PRINT is followed by a blank space and the variable names of the fields to be printed. The variable names are specified in the sequence in which they will appear on the CRT screen. Thus, the value in N$ (the name) will appear first on the screen, followed by the value in A (the area code), and the value in T$ (the telephone number).

Each of the variable names in the print statement is separated by a comma and a blank. When a comma is used to separate variable names, each field will be displayed on the CRT screen in predetermined locations called zones.

These zones have varying sizes, ranging from 10 characters to 16 characters depending on the computer system being used. Regardless of the number of characters in each zone, spacing works in the manner illustrated in Figure 2–23.

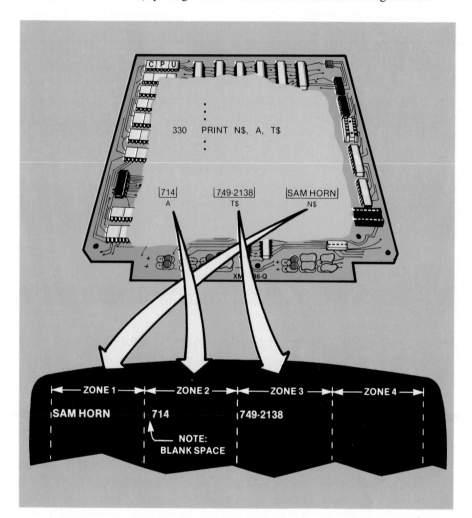

Figure 2-23 When variable names are separated by commas in the print statement, the values from each of the fields identified by the variable names are displayed in predefined printing zones on the CRT screen. Therefore the name (N$) is displayed in the first zone, the area code (A) in the second zone, and the telephone number (T$) in the third zone.

The example above illustrates four printing zones on the CRT screen. The value in the first variable of the print statement (N$) is placed in the first zone. Since the variable is a string variable, the first character in the field (S) is placed in the first position of the printing zone. Whenever a string field is printed in a printing zone, the first character in the field is placed in the first position of the zone.

The second variable in the print statement is the numeric variable for the area code, A. Therefore, the value in the field identified by the variable name A is displayed on the CRT screen. The numeric value in the example (714) is displayed in the second printing zone because the variable name A is separated from the previous name (N$) by a comma.

The first digit in the value is placed in the second position of the zone. On most computer systems, whenever a value in a numeric field is to be printed, the value will be preceded by a blank space if it is positive and by a negative sign (–) if it is negative. In the example, the value in the area code field (A) is positive; therefore, it is preceded by a blank space.

The third variable in the print statement (T$) will be printed in the third printing zone. Since the field is a string field, the first character in the field will appear in the first position of the third zone. The print statement is terminated after the third variable name. Therefore, no value is displayed in the fourth zone. When the next print statement is executed, the data will be displayed on the next line.

The print statement is the primary means for making information available from a BASIC program. The use of the statement and the output produced from the statement should be well understood.

GOTO statement

After the print statement is executed and the values from the first input data have been displayed on the CRT screen, the second set of input data must be read. This processing is accomplished using the read statement in the same manner as the first data was read.

After the second set of data has been read, control must be returned to the if statement at the beginning of the loop to determine if the body of the loop should be executed. The goto statement is used to transfer this control (Figure 2–24).

The format of the goto statement shows it begins with a line number. Following the line number is a blank space and then the word GOTO. Note that no blanks are allowed in this word. A blank follows the word GOTO and then a line number is specified. When the goto statement is executed, control is passed to the statement at the line number specified after the word GOTO. In Figure 2–24, the goto statement on line 350 will cause control to be passed to the statement at line 320. Therefore, after the execution of the goto statement, the next action performed by the program will be to compare the value in N$ to the constant value "END OF FILE."

The goto statement on line 350 is the last statement in the loop which obtains and processes the input data. Since it is the last statement, it is not indented. Instead, the word GOTO begins in the same vertical column as the word IF which determines if the body of the loop is to be executed. In this manner, the beginning and ending statements within the loop are easily identified when reading the program.

The loop which begins on line 320 and ends on line 350 will continue to process input data until the value END OF FILE is read into the N$ field. At that time, the end of file processing will occur.

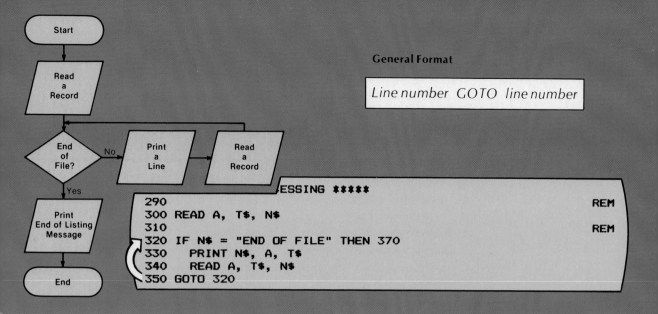

General Format

Line number GOTO line number

```
                                     ESSING *****
290                                                              REM
300 READ A, T$, N$
310                                                              REM
320 IF N$ = "END OF FILE" THEN 370
330    PRINT N$, A, T$
340    READ A, T$, N$
350 GOTO 320
```

The end of file processing begins at line 370 with a print statement (Figure 2–25). In the statement, the word PRINT is followed by a blank and then a blank within quotes. This statement will cause a blank line to be displayed on the screen. The next print statement displays the constant END OF TELEPHONE LISTING on the CRT screen. The constant is enclosed within quotes because it is a string constant. Whenever a string constant is used in a print statement, it must be enclosed within double quotation marks.

The last statement within the program is the end statement. This statement, consisting of a line number and the word END, terminates the program.

Figure 2-24 The goto statement is used to transfer control to a statement identified by its line number. The goto statement on line 350 transfers control to the if statement on line 320.

Figure 2-25 The print statement with a blank constant displays a blank line. Line 380 displays END OF TELEPHONE LISTING.

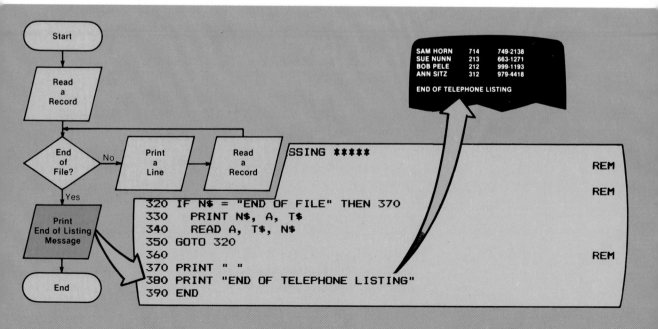

```
SAM HORN    714    749-2138
SUE NUNN    213    663-1271
BOB PELE    212    999-1193
ANN SITZ    312    979-4418

END OF TELEPHONE LISTING
```

```
                                     SSING *****
                                                                REM
                                                                REM
320 IF N$ = "END OF FILE" THEN 370
330    PRINT N$, A, T$
340    READ A, T$, N$
350 GOTO 320
360                                                             REM
370 PRINT " "
380 PRINT "END OF TELEPHONE LISTING"
390 END
```

Coding tips The following tips should be kept in mind when coding a program:

1. The programmer should expect a program to work properly the first time the program is entered and executed. For this to occur, much attention must be paid to detail when designing and coding the program. Indeed, programming is a very precise activity because one small error can cause a program to operate incorrectly. Each programming statement must be written with care and be reviewed carefully to ensure correctness.

2. Each statement in a BASIC program must be written using the proper language syntax. Punctuation must be included in the right places in a statement. All words must be spelled correctly. The variable names used must be consistent. For example, a programmer cannot use the variable name A for the area code in one part of the program and the variable name A1 for the area code in another part of the program.

3. Before using a program statement, the programmer must know how the statement works and what will result when the statement is executed. If this is not thoroughly understood, the programmer should consult reference material to ensure an understanding of the statement.

4. Spacing and indentation in a program are important so that the coding in the program will be understandable. Therefore, the standards which are established by the programs in this book should always be followed.

5. Rem statements should be a part of every program, regardless of size. These statements explain processing, identify the variables in a program and generally make the coding in the program more understandable. It is important, however, that the comments specified in rem statements always be accurate. Therefore, each rem statement must be carefully written and reviewed to ensure its accuracy.

6. Some typical areas where errors can be made in a program like the sample program in this chapter are:

   a. String values and constants must normally be enclosed within double quotation marks. Numeric values are not enclosed within quotes.

   b. Line numbers must be written in ascending sequence.

   c. All keywords, such as PRINT and READ, must be spelled correctly.

   d. Entries in the data statement must be separated by commas.

   e. The sequence of the variables specified in a read statement must be the same sequence as the related data in the data statement. The sequence of the variable names in a print statement must be the sequence in which the data is to be displayed on the CRT screen.

By following the tips presented in this section, the programmer will find that good programs which execute the first time they are entered into a computer system will be the normal way of doing things.

The listing of the sample program and the output generated from the program are illustrated in Figure 2–26.   **Sample program**

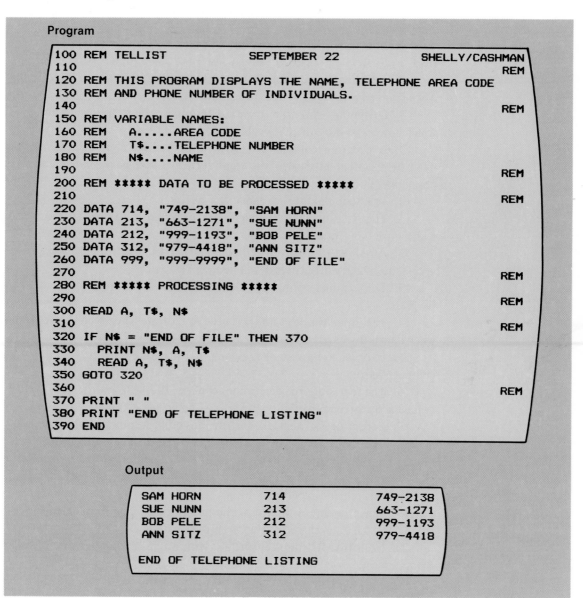

Program

```
100 REM TELLIST              SEPTEMBER 22           SHELLY/CASHMAN
110                                                              REM
120 REM THIS PROGRAM DISPLAYS THE NAME, TELEPHONE AREA CODE
130 REM AND PHONE NUMBER OF INDIVIDUALS.
140                                                              REM
150 REM VARIABLE NAMES:
160 REM    A.....AREA CODE
170 REM    T$....TELEPHONE NUMBER
180 REM    N$....NAME
190                                                              REM
200 REM ***** DATA TO BE PROCESSED *****
210                                                              REM
220 DATA 714, "749-2138", "SAM HORN"
230 DATA 213, "663-1271", "SUE NUNN"
240 DATA 212, "999-1193", "BOB PELE"
250 DATA 312, "979-4418", "ANN SITZ"
260 DATA 999, "999-9999", "END OF FILE"
270                                                              REM
280 REM ***** PROCESSING *****
290                                                              REM
300 READ A, T$, N$
310                                                              REM
320 IF N$ = "END OF FILE" THEN 370
330    PRINT N$, A, T$
340    READ A, T$, N$
350 GOTO 320
360                                                              REM
370 PRINT " "
380 PRINT "END OF TELEPHONE LISTING"
390 END
```

Output

```
SAM HORN          714           749-2138
SUE NUNN          213           663-1271
BOB PELE          212           999-1193
ANN SITZ          312           979-4418

END OF TELEPHONE LISTING
```

Figure 2-26 The complete program listing and the output produced by the program are shown in this figure.

SUMMARY   The following points have been discussed and explained in this chapter.

1. The task of computer programming is one of the more precise of all human activities.

2. Programming a computer must be accomplished with precision.

3. Every program should be error free from its inception.

4. Data, taken as a group, is called a file.

5. Data about a single entity, such as an individual in a telephone listing, is called a record.

6. A field is defined as a unit of data. Records consist of a series of fields.

7. A trailer record is the last record in a file and serves to indicate that, when read, all records have been processed.

8. Designing a program means determining the step-by-step processing which is necessary to solve the problem.

9. A program consists of instructions to the computer system which must be specified in exactly the right sequence and be executed under the proper conditions.

10. The design of the program is critical.

11. The first step when designing a program is to specify those tasks which must be accomplished by the program.

12. After the tasks are specified, a flowchart depicting the step-by-step processing which will occur is developed.

13. The terminal symbol in a flowchart illustrates the start and end of the program.

14. The input/output symbol is used to indicate when records are read or when data is displayed on the CRT screen.

15. In order to be executed, a computer program must be stored in main computer storage.

16. The decision to determine end of file will always be executed immediately after a record is read.

17. Repeating a sequence of instructions multiple times is called looping.

18. The first instruction in a loop should be the instruction which determines if the body of the loop should be executed. Any other instruction violates good programming practices which have been established through years of research and experimentation.

19. When coding a program, the programmer must implement in code the logic which is developed during the program design.

20. Each BASIC statement begins with a unique number that identifies the statement.

21. Line numbers can begin with the value 1 and be incremented by 1, but it is better programming to begin with 100 and increment by 10.

22. A quality program is well documented, meaning the program contains

information which aids in understanding it.

23. The REM (remark) statement allows remarks to be placed in a program.

24. The first line in a program should be a rem statement containing the program name, the date the program was coded, and the name of the programmer.

25. The variable names used in a program should be identified by rem statements at the beginning of the program.

26. The data statement can be used to define data which will be processed by the program. The statement begins with a line number, followed by the word DATA, and then the data itself.

27. Numeric data consists of numeric digits only. In a data statement, numeric data is not enclosed in quotation marks.

28. Any constant containing a non-numeric character is a string constant. A string constant should be enclosed within quotation marks.

29. Constants within a data statement must be separated by commas.

30. The read statement transfers data from a data statement to an area in main computer storage where the data can be referenced. A read statement begins with a line number, followed by the word READ, and then the variable names of the areas in main computer storage where the data is to be stored.

31. Numeric variable names, which define numeric fields, must begin with a letter of the alphabet (A – Z). The names can be one or two characters in length. If a second character is used, this character must be numeric (0 – 9).

32. String variable names, which identify string fields, must begin with a letter of the alphabet (A – Z). This letter of the alphabet must be followed by a dollar sign ($).

33. The if statement compares two values. When used as the first statement in a loop, it can compare a value in a record to a constant which indicates that the last record has been read. The if statement begins with a line number, followed by the word IF. The condition being tested and the fields and constant used in the comparison are then specified. The word THEN is next specified, followed by the line number of the statement which will receive control if the condition being tested is true. If the condition is not true, the statement immediately following the if statement will be executed.

34. The print statement displays a line on the CRT screen. The first entry in the print statement is a line number, followed by the word PRINT, and then the constants and variable names of the fields to be displayed.

35. When variable names or constants in a print statement are separated by commas, each variable or constant will be displayed in predefined printing zones on the CRT screen. When printing string constants or fields, the first character will be placed in the first position of the printing zone. When printing numeric constants or fields, the first digit will be placed in the second position of the printing zone. The first position of the printing zone will be blank if the numeric value is positive and will contain a minus sign if the value is negative.

36. The goto statement transfers control to the statement whose line number appears after the word GOTO.

37. The end statement consists of a line number and the word END. Program execution is terminated when the end statement is executed.

38. A program should be expected to work the first time it is entered into a computer system and executed. The program should be written with extreme precision and attention to detail to ensure its correctness.

39. Spacing, indentation, and documentation within the program are extremely important, for all programs regardless of size should be easily understood by anyone examining the program.

Chapter 2
QUESTIONS AND EXERCISES

1. In most cases, programs can be written quickly because a few mistakes are always expected (T or F).

2. Program design should be: a) Finished before program coding begins; b) Finished after program coding has been completed; c) Done at the same time program coding is taking place; d) Done by someone other than the programmer.

3. What is a flowchart? What is it used for?

4. The first instruction in a loop should be: a) The loop instruction; b) The instruction which determines if the body of the loop should be executed; c) The instruction which obtains data; d) A GOTO instruction.

5. Each BASIC statement must begin with a _____

6. Why should rem statements be included in a well-written program?

7. A string variable name must consist of two characters, one of which must be numeric (T or F).

8. B5: a) Could be used as a string variable name; b) Could be used as a string constant; c) Could be used as a numeric variable name; d) Could be used as a numeric constant.

9. Constants within a data statement are separated by: a) A period; b) A semicolon; c) A colon; d) A comma.

10. How does a read statement work? What other BASIC statement must be used in conjunction with a read statement?

11. The if statement can be used as the first statement in a loop to determine if the body of the loop should be executed (T or F).

12. When the variable names in a print statement are separated by a comma: a) They must all reference numeric data; b) They must all reference string data; c) They will be printed in predefined print zones; d) Each name will be printed on a separate line.

13. In the sample program in this chapter, write the print statement on line 330 which would cause the area code to be printed first, followed by the telephone number and then the name.

14. Which statements in the sample program in this chapter would have to be changed if the name of the variable containing the telephone number was changed from T$ to P$? Write the changed statements.

15. Write all statements which would be required to add the name JOE HELM, area code 313, and telephone number 776-0008 to the telephone listing produced by the sample program in this chapter.

16. Write the code to modify the sample program in this chapter to list each line except the end message twice on the CRT screen.

Chapter 2
DEBUGGING EXERCISES

The following lines of code contain one or more syntax errors. Circle each of the errors and write the coding to correct the errors.

1.
```
300 READ A, T, N
310                                                    REM
320 IF N$ = "END OF FILE" THEN 370
330    PRINT N, A, T
```

2.
```
300 READ A, T$, N$
310                                                    REM
320 IF N$ = END OF FILE THEN 370
330    PRINT N$, A, T$
340    READ A, T$, N$
```

3.
```
200 REM ***** DATA TO BE PROCESSED *****
210                                                    REM
220 DATA 714, "749-2138", "SAM HORN"
230 DATA 213, "663-1271", "SUE NUNN"
240 DATA 212, "999-1193", "BOB PELE"
250 DATA 312, "979-4418", "ANN SITZ"
260 DATA 999, "999-9999", "END OF FILE"
270                                                    REM
280 REM ***** PROCESSING *****
290                                                    REM
300 READ T$, A, N$
```

4.
```
320 IF N$ = "END OF FILE" THEN 370
330    PRINT N$, A, T$
340    READ A, T$ N$
350 GOTO 320
```

5.
Need REM
```
200 ***** DATA TO BE PROCESSED *****
210                                                    REM
220 DATA 714, "749-2138", "SAM HORN"
230 DATA 213, "663-1271", "SUE NUNN"
240 DATA 212, "999-1193", "BOB PELE"
250 DATA 312, "979-4418", "ANN SITZ"
260 DATA 999, "999-9999", "END OF FILE"
```

6.
```
370 PRINT
380 PRINT END OF TELEPHONE LISTING
390 END
```

Chapter 2
PROGRAM DEBUGGING

The following program was designed and written to produce a telephone listing in the format shown in Figure 2–3 (page 2.3). The output actually produced by this program is shown below. Analyze the output to determine if it is correct. If it is in error, circle the incorrect statement(s) in the program and write corrections.

Program

```
100 REM TELLIST              SEPTEMBER 22           SHELLY/CASHMAN
110                                                          REM
120 REM THIS PROGRAM DISPLAYS THE NAME, TELEPHONE AREA CODE
130 REM AND PHONE NUMBER OF INDIVIDUALS.
140                                                          REM
150 REM VARIABLE NAMES:
160 REM    A.....AREA CODE
170 REM    T$....TELEPHONE NUMBER
180 REM    N$....NAME
190                                                          REM
200 REM ***** DATA TO BE PROCESSED *****
210                                                          REM
220 DATA 714, "749-2138", "SAM HORN"
230 DATA 213, "663-1271", "SUE NUNN"
240 DATA 212, "999-1193", "BOB PELE"
250 DATA 312, "979-4418", "ANN SITZ"
260 DATA 999, "999-9999", "END OF FILE"
270                                                          REM
280 REM ***** PROCESSING *****
290                                                          REM
300 READ A, T$, N$
310                                                          REM
320 IF N$ = "END OF FILE" THEN 370
330    PRINT A, T$, N$
340    READ A, T$, N$
350 GOTO 320
360                                                          REM
370 PRINT " "
380 PRINT "END OF TELEPHONE LISTING"
390 END
```

Output

```
714              749-2138      SAM HORN
213              663-1271      SUE NUNN
212              999-1193      BOB PELE
312              979-4418      ANN SITZ

END OF TELEPHONE LISTING
```

Chapter 2
PROGRAMMING ASSIGNMENT 1

Instructions A list of names, birthdates, and current age of individuals is to be prepared. A program should be designed and coded in BASIC to produce the list.

Input Input consists of records that contain the current age of the individual, their date of birth, and their name. The input data is illustrated below.

AGE	BIRTH DATE	NAME
18	JULY 2	ANN OWNES
19	APRIL 5	BOB LASKY
16	MAY 19	SUE ALCO
21	JUNE 9	TOM RAIL

Output Output is a list of the input records containing the name, date of birth, and age. The format of the output is illustrated below. Spacing between fields should be based upon the standard zones provided by the BASIC language being used. After all records have been processed, the message END OF LIST should be printed.

```
ANN OWNES        JULY 2           18
BOB LASKY        APRIL 5          19
SUE ALCO         MAY 19           16
TOM RAIL         JUNE 9           21

END OF LIST
```

Chapter 2
PROGRAMMING ASSIGNMENT 2

A travel distance table is to be displayed. A program should be designed and coded in BASIC to produce the table.   **Instructions**

The table below should be used to obtain data used as input to the program.   **Input**

FROM	TO	MILES
CHICAGO	NEW YORK	806
CHICAGO	DALLAS	936
CHICAGO	BOSTON	958
CHICAGO	DETROIT	262

The format of the output is illustrated below. Spacing between fields should be based upon the standard zones provided by the BASIC language being utilized.   **Output**

```
CHICAGO TO:

NEW YORK        806
DALLAS          936
BOSTON          958
DETROIT         262

END OF TRAVEL TABLE
```

Chapter 2
SUPPLEMENTARY PROGRAMMING ASSIGNMENTS

Instructions   The following programming assignments contain an explanation of the problem and list suggested test data. The student should design the format of the output.

Program 3   A report is to be prepared listing the age at which individuals can marry with parental consent in selected states throughout the country. The input data is illustrated below. The state should appear in the leftmost column on the report. After all data has been processed, the message END OF REPORT should be printed.

MARRIAGE AGE MALE	MARRIAGE AGE FEMALE	STATE
14	14	ALABAMA
18	16	FLORIDA
16	16	NEVADA
14	14	UTAH

Program 4   A report is to be prepared of the lifetime batting averages of selected major league baseball players. The input data is illustrated below. The output should contain the player's name, the years played, and the batting average. After all data has been processed, the message END OF LIST should be printed.

PLAYER	BATTING AVERAGE	YEARS PLAYED
COBB	.367	24
WILLIAMS	.344	19
RUTH	.342	22
MUSIAL	.331	22

Program 5   An airline schedule report is to be prepared. The input data is illustrated below. After all data has been processed, the message END OF AIRLINE SCHEDULE should be printed.

FROM	TO	DEPARTURE TIME	MESSAGE
SF	SD	8:00 A.M.	ON TIME
SF	LAX	9:00 A.M.	CANCELLED
SF	SAC	9:30 A.M.	ON TIME
SF	LV	9:45 A.M.	ON TIME

A report is to be prepared listing national holidays for a company. The input is illustrated below. The output should print the date on one line followed by a description of the holiday on the next line. A blank line should be printed between the holidays. After all data has been processed, the message END OF LIST should be printed.

Program 6

DATE	HOLIDAY
JANUARY 1	NEW YEAR'S DAY
MAY 28	MEMORIAL DAY
JULY 4	INDEPENDENCE DAY
SEPTEMBER 6	LABOR DAY
NOVEMBER 26	THANKSGIVING
DECEMBER 25	CHRISTMAS

A list of names, addresses, cities, and zip codes of customers is to be prepared. The input is illustrated below. The output should print the name on one line, the address on the second line, and the city and zip code on the third line. The customers should be separated by a blank line. After all data has been processed, the message END OF LIST should be printed.

Program 7

NAME	ADDRESS	CITY	ZIP CODE
ACE COMPANY	111 PINE	LAMONT	90813
BROWN BROTHERS	981 ARROW	SEAVIEW	90915
DANDY WARES	773 SKY DRIVE	PARKVIEW	97812
GOGO FOODS	881 OAK	MONTCLARE	88811

A reference table containing commonly used formulas is to be prepared. The input data is illustrated below. The figure (such as circle) should appear on the first line and the formula on the second line. The report should be double spaced with an extra blank line between each symbol-formula combination. After all data has been processed, the message END OF REFERENCE TABLES should appear on the report.

Program 8

FIGURE	FORMULA
CIRCLE	CIRCUMFERENCE = 2 * Pi * R
SQUARE	AREA = S * S
RECTANGLE	AREA = L * W

CHAPTER THREE

ARITHMETIC OPERATIONS

OBJECTIVES:

A knowledge of the BASIC statements to perform arithmetic operations

An understanding of how to round numeric values

A knowledge of the print using statement for editing fields

A knowledge of the tab statement for controlling output

The ability to design a program requiring calculations, accumulations, and printing final totals

ARITHMETIC OPERATIONS

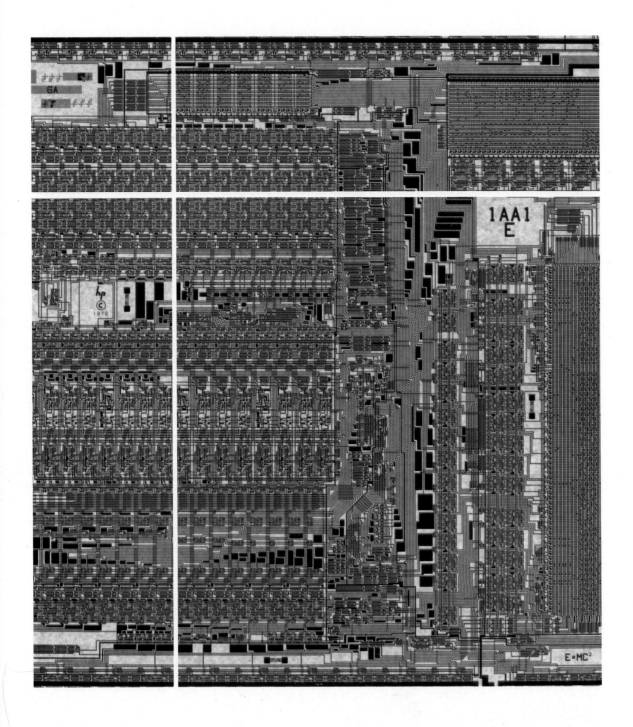

Many computer applications involve performing calculations, including the accumulation and printing of final totals. In addition, on most reports and screen displays, it is desirable to include formatted output and report and column headings to assist in identifying the output. These operations can easily be accomplished when programming in BASIC.

To illustrate the logic and BASIC instructions required to read data, accumulate and print totals, and prepare a listing with headings, a sample program is explained in this chapter.

The output to be produced from the program is a listing of checks which have been written during the month. The format of the output is illustrated below.

```
              CHECKING ACCOUNT

     DATE          NO.      NAME       AMOUNT

SEPTEMBER   1     501    JIM'S ART      85.60
SEPTEMBER   5     502    SEARS         424.23
SEPTEMBER  14     503    NORDSTROM     312.59
SEPTEMBER  22     504    BONDS          67.92
SEPTEMBER  25     505    ED'S AUTO     713.95

TOTAL NUMBER OF CHECKS    5
TOTAL AMOUNT OF CHECKS $1,604.29
```

Figure 3-1 This checking account report includes column headings and final totals.

The report heading, CHECKING ACCOUNT, serves to identify the report. A blank line follows the report heading. The column headings identify the date field, the check number field, the name to whom the check was written, and the check amount. These headings are also followed by a blank line.

The data fields contain the date, the check number, the name, and the check amount. The check amount contains a decimal point to indicate dollars and cents. After all of the detail data has been printed, the total number of checks written is printed together with the total amount of the checks. The total amount of the checks contains a dollar sign and a comma within the field to indicate thousands of dollars.

The logic and the BASIC coding required to produce this report are explained in this chapter.

BASIC ARITHMETIC OPERATIONS

In order to accumulate final totals, addition must be performed by the program. Arithmetic operations, including addition, subtraction, multiplication, division, and raising to a power (exponentiation) are accomplished in BASIC using arithmetic operators. These operators are very similar to those used in ordinary arithmetic (Figure 3–2).

Figure 3-2 These arithmetic operators are used in the BASIC language to accomplish arithmetic operations.

ARITHMETIC OPERATION	BASIC OPERATOR
Addition	+
Subtraction	—
Multiplication	*
Division	/
Raising to a Power	↑

Let statement

To perform arithmetic operations, the let statement is used. The general format of the let statement is illustrated in Figure 3–3.

Figure 3-3 The LET statement will cause the answer generated in the arithmetic expression to be stored in the field identified by the variable name to the left of the equal sign.

line number   LET   variable name   =   arithmetic expression

The first entry in the let statement is a line number. This entry is followed by a blank and then the word LET. The remainder of the let statement contains the entries to cause the arithmetic operation to occur. When the let statement is executed, the arithmetic expression on the right side of the equal sign is evaluated. The answer from the evaluation is placed in the field identified by the variable name on the left side of the equal sign. The arithmetic expression consists of constants, variable names, and arithmetic operators.

Addition

To illustrate the use of the let statement in an addition operation, the let statement in Figure 3–4 will cause the value in the field identified by the variable S1 to be added to the value in the field with the variable name S2. The answer is stored in the field with the name T.

In this example, the arithmetic expression consists of the variable name S1, the addition arithmetic operator (+), and the variable name S2. The evaluation of this arithmetic expression takes place by adding 125, the value in the field identified by the variable S1, to 25, the value in the field identified by the variable S2. The result, 150, is stored in the T field.

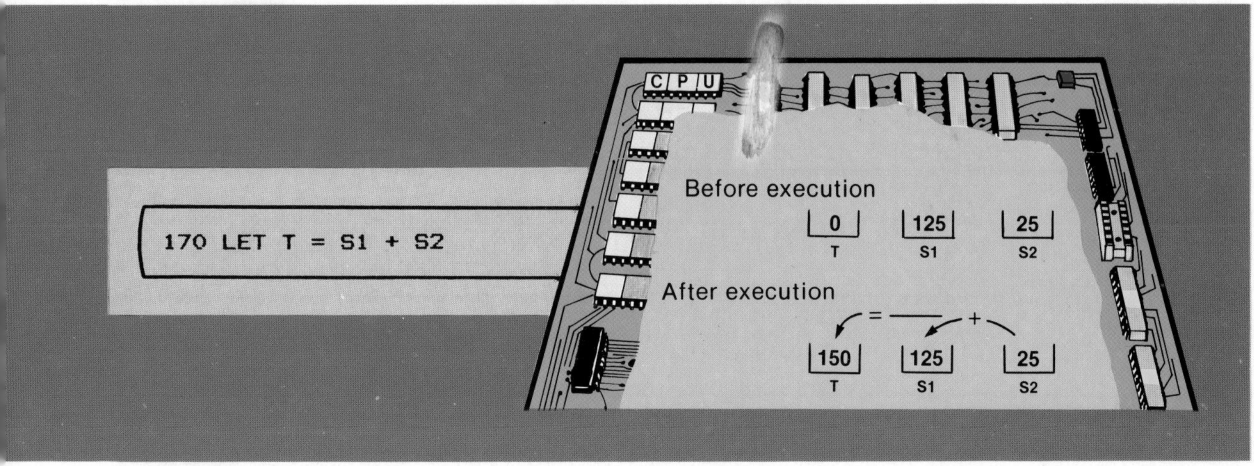

Before execution

| 0 | | 125 | | 25 |
| T | | S1 | | S2 |

170 LET T = S1 + S2

After execution

$$= \qquad +$$

| 150 | | 125 | | 25 |
| T | | S1 | | S2 |

The arithmetic expression in the example in Figure 3–4 contains two variable names and a single arithmetic operator. An arithmetic expression can contain multiple arithmetic operators. In the example in Figure 3–5, four variable names which require three addition arithmetic operators are used.

210 LET M5 = W1 + W2 + W3 + W4

When the let statement in Figure 3–5 is executed, the values in W1, W2, W3, and W4 will be added together and the sum placed in M5.

The arithmetic expression used in a let statement can also contain constant numeric values called literals. In Figure 3–6, the let statement contains a literal which is used in the compilation of the answer.

190 LET T4 = F3 + 2.75

In this example, the value in the field identified by the variable name F3 is added to the constant value 2.75. The constant, or literal, will remain the same in the calculation. The value in F3 can vary each time the let statement is executed.

In most applications, a literal should be used in a calculation only when there is little chance the value specified by the literal will be modified at a later time. If the value specified by the literal is likely to be modified, it is usually better to place the value in a field identified by a variable.

Subtraction

The let statement is used to cause all arithmetic operations to occur. In order to subtract one value from another, the subtraction operator (–) is placed in the arithmetic expression (Figure 3–7).

Figure 3-7 The subtraction operator (–) will cause the value in the field to the right of the minus sign to be subtracted from the value in the field to the left of the minus sign.

```
220 LET N1 = G1 - D1
```

In the example above, the value in the field identified by the variable name D1 is subtracted from the value in the field identified by the variable name G1. The answer is stored in the field with the name N1. If the value in D1 is greater than the value in G1, the answer stored in N1 is negative.

Use of arithmetic results

After the arithmetic has been performed by the let statement, the values used in the arithmetic operation together with the answer obtained can be used in subsequent arithmetic operations or for other purposes in the program. For example, the result of one calculation can be used in a subsequent calculation (Figure 3–8).

Figure 3-8 The result of the first calculation (the value in T1) can be used in a subsequent arithmetic expression or in any other statement where a numeric variable is allowed.

```
160 LET T1 = C1 + C2
170 LET T2 = T1 + M3
180 PRINT T1, T2
```

In Figure 3–8, the value in the field identified by the variable T1, which was calculated by the let statement on line 160, is used in the let statement on line 170 as a part of the arithmetic expression and on line 180 in the print statement. Whenever a value is stored in a field, it can be used in other statements within the program.

Decimal alignment

When two or more values are used in an addition or subtraction operation, the BASIC interpreter will generate instructions to align the decimal points within the numbers before the arithmetic operation takes place. For example, in Figure 3–7 if the value in G1 was 5.136 and the value in D1 was 2.76, the decimal points would be aligned and then the subtraction would take place. The answer stored in N1 would be 2.376.

Multiplication is accomplished through the use of the let statement and the multiplication operator (∗). The example in Figure 3-9 illustrates multiplying two numbers when using the BASIC language.

Multiplication

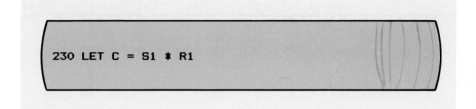

230 LET C = S1 ∗ R1

Figure 3-9 Multiplication is accomplished by using the multiplication operator (∗).

In the let statement in Figure 3-9, the value in the field S1 is multiplied by the value in R1. The product of the multiplication is stored in the field identified by the variable name C. When the multiplication takes place, the signs of the fields are considered. Therefore, if two positive numbers are multiplied, the answer is positive. If two negative numbers are multiplied, the answer is positive. If one negative and one positive number are multiplied, the answer is negative.

When two numbers are multiplied, the programmer should be aware of the size of the answer which could develop. The largest number of digits which can appear in a product of two numbers is the sum of the number of digits in each of the values being multiplied. Therefore, if a three digit number is multiplied by a two digit number, the maximum number of digits the product can contain is five digits.

Additionally, it should be noted that the number of digits to the right of the decimal point in a product will be the sum of the number of digits to the right of the decimal point in the multiplicand and the multiplier. Thus, if a number with two digits to the right of the decimal point is multiplied by a number with one digit to the right of the decimal point, the answer will have three digits to the right of the decimal point.

Division is accomplished in a let statement through the use of the division operation symbol (/). In the example in Figure 3-10, the value in M2 is divided by the value in M1. The result of the division is stored in R4.

Division

140 LET R4 = M2 / M1

Figure 3-10 The slash (/) is used as the division arithmetic operator. The value in the field to the left of the slash is divided by the value in the field to the right of the slash.

Exponentiation

Exponentiation means raising a number to a power. The value A^3 is the same as A*A*A. The example in Figure 3–11 illustrates the use of the exponentiation operator (⬆) in a let statement.

Figure 3-11 In this example, the value in A is cubed, and the result is stored in C3. The entry A⬇3 is equivalent to A*A*A.

```
260 LET C3 = A ↑ 3
```

As a result of the let statement in Figure 3–11, the value in A would be cubed and the answer stored in C3. The exponent used in the exponentiation operation can also be a fraction. If the exponent is a fraction, the root of the number is taken (Figure 3–12).

Figure 3-12 The cube root of the value in R5 is placed in R3. The fractional exponent must be enclosed within parentheses.

```
230 LET R5 = 64
240 LET R3 = R5 ↑ (1/3)
```

In the example above, the cube root of 64, which is 4, is stored in R3. Note in the example that the let statement is used to place a value in a field. That is, the value 64 is placed in the field R5 by the let statement on line 230. The value to the right of the equal sign in a let statement can be a single number as well as an arithmetic expression.

When the root of a number is taken using a fractional exponent, the number whose root is being taken cannot be negative. If it is, the program will normally be cancelled.

Multiple operations

In Figure 3–5, multiple variables were used in an addition operation. Multiple operations can be performed using all of the arithmetic operators. In Figure 3–13, the addition and subtraction operators are used to calculate the new balance in a savings account by adding the deposits to the old balance and then subtracting the withdrawals.

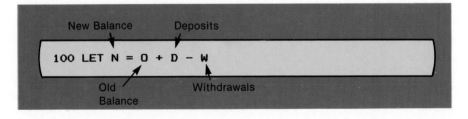

Figure 3-13 The addition and subtraction operations are carried out in the same arithmetic expression. Multiplication and division can be included as well.

When the let statement in Figure 3–13 is executed, the value in the O field will be added to the value in the D field, and the value in the W field will be subtracted from that sum. The calculations procede left to right through the arithmetic expression.

Hierarchy of operations

When multiple arithmetic operations are included in a single let statement, the sequence in which the calculations are performed is determined in accordance with the following rules:

1. Exponentiation is performed first.
2. Multiplication and division are performed next.
3. Addition and subtraction are performed last.
4. Within these three steps, calculations are performed left to right.

As a result of this predetermined sequence, the arithmetic expression A * B + C would result in the product of A * B being added to C. The arithmetic expression A + B / C would result in the value in B being divided by the value in C and this answer being added to A.

In some applications, this predetermined sequence of evaluation is not satisfactory. Consider, for example, the let statement in Figure 3–14 which is designed to calculate the average of three golf scores.

```
140 LET A = S1 + S2 + S3 / 3
```

Figure 3–14 The arithmetic expression will not calculate the average of S1, S2, and S3 because division takes place before addition.

In this example, according to the predetermined sequence of operations, the value in the field identified by the variable S3 would be divided by the value 3. That result would then be added to the values in the fields identified by S1 and S2. This sequence of operations would result in an incorrect answer. For example, if the value in S1 was 78, the value in S2 was 76, and the value in S3 was 72, the average golf score would be calculated as 178 (78 + 76 + 72/3).

To correct the statement in Figure 3–14, parentheses are used to dictate the sequence in which arithmetic operations will occur. The arithmetic operations within the parentheses will be evaluated before those outside the parentheses. The correct method of writing the statement to calculate the average golf score is illustrated in Figure 3–15.

```
140 LET A = (S1 + S2 + S3) / 3
```

Figure 3–15 Because of the parentheses, the values in S1, S2, and S3 will be added first in the arithmetic expression. The sum will then be divided by 3.

In Figure 3–15, the values in S1, S2, and S3 will be added together as the first operation to be performed because this operation is within parentheses. After these values are added, the sum will be divided by 3, giving the average golf score. In most cases, it is advisable to use parentheses around multiple arithmetic operations in an arithmetic expression even if the predetermined sequence of operations will produce the correct answer. In this way, the sequence of operations is explicitly clear.

Rounding Many arithmetic applications require a rounding operation to be performed. For example, in a retail sales application, the state tax must be computed each time a sale is made. This calculation will normally involve multiplying the sales amount by the sales tax percentage, as illustrated below.

$$54.79 \quad X \quad .06 \quad = \quad 3.2874$$

The sales tax should be expressed as dollars and cents. Therefore, in the example the value 3.2874 must be rounded to 3.29. A number can be rounded by adding 5 to the digit to the right of the digit which will be retained after rounding. If a number is expressed as dollars and cents, this means that the value 5 must be added to the third digit to the right of the decimal point, as illustrated in Figure 3–16.

Figure 3-16 When rounding for dollars and cents, the value .005 is added to the value to be rounded. The third digit to the right of the decimal point is then dropped from the number.

Rounding Up	Rounding Down
3.2874	3.2844
+ .005	+ .005
Rounded Value 3.29	Rounded Value 3.28

When the third digit to the right of the decimal point is less than 5, the second digit to the right of the decimal point remains the same. When the third digit to the right of the decimal point is 5 or greater, the number is rounded up.

When programming in BASIC, no explicit instruction is available to cause rounding. Instead, the programmer must write a series of instructions to round a number. The steps which are used to round the sales tax to dollars and cents are illustrated in the following examples.

Step 1: The value .005 is added to the sales tax which has been calculated.

$$3.2874 \quad + \quad .005 \quad = \quad 3.2924$$

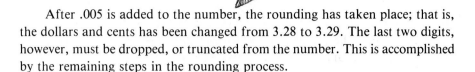

After .005 is added to the number, the rounding has taken place; that is, the dollars and cents has been changed from 3.28 to 3.29. The last two digits, however, must be dropped, or truncated from the number. This is accomplished by the remaining steps in the rounding process.

Step 2: The decimal point is moved two positions to the right.

$$3.2924 \quad * \quad 100 \quad = \quad 329.24$$

The value calculated in step 1 is multiplied by 100, which moves the decimal point in the value two positions to the right. After this step, the sales tax is expressed as an integer value (i.e., a whole number), not as dollars and cents. The next step is to truncate the two digits to the right of the decimal point.

Step 3: The two rightmost digits are truncated.

$$329.24 \quad \longrightarrow \quad 329$$

When the digits to the right of the decimal point are truncated, the rounded value for the sales tax is all that remains. The next, and last, step is to put the number back into a dollars and cents format. This is accomplished by dividing the number from step 3 by 100.

Step 4: Change the value to a dollars and cents format.

$$329 \quad / \quad 100 \quad = \quad 3.29$$

The result from step 4 is the rounded sales tax value.

In order to illustrate the BASIC instructions required to round a number, each of the above steps will be illustrated together with the BASIC instructions. In the following example, the field identified by the variable name T contains the tax value 3.2874.

Step 1: The value .005 is added to the sales tax which has been calculated.

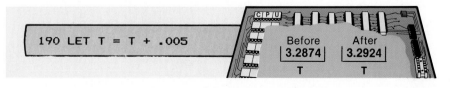

Figure 3-17 The let statement is used to add .005 to the value stored in T. The answer is then stored back in T. When a variable name is used on both sides of the equal sign in an arithmetic expression, the value in the field is modified and then stored back in the field.

The let statement in Figure 3-17 is used to add the literal .005 to the value in T.

After the let statement is executed, the value in T has been rounded. The low-order digits must be truncated, however.

Step 2: The decimal point is moved two digits to the right.

Figure 3-18 When the value in T is multiplied by 100, the decimal point is moved two positions to the right.

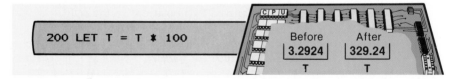

The let statement multiplies the value in T by the constant 100, thereby changing the sales tax to an integer value. The next step is to truncate the digits to the right of the decimal point.

Step 3: The digits to the right of the decimal point are truncated.

Figure 3-19 The integer function is used to truncate digits to the right of the decimal point.

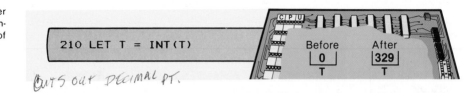

To truncate the digits, the int (integer) function is used. A function in BASIC is a prewritten set of instructions to accomplish a given task. These instructions can be called by a single word. A function can be used just like a variable in an arithmetic expression. The purpose of the int function is to return the next lowest integer from the value in the parentheses. Therefore, when the int function in Figure 3–19 is executed, the value 329 will be placed in the field T because 329 is the next lowest integer from the value 329.24.

It is important that the syntax of a function is followed exactly. For the int function, the variable name of the value from which the integer is obtained must be specified within parentheses. No spaces are allowed between the word INT and the parentheses. A violation of these syntax rules will produce an error in the program.

The next step is to change the value in T to a dollars and cents format.

Step 4: Change the value in T to a dollars and cents format.

Figure 3-20 When the value in T is divided by 100, the two rightmost digits are placed to the right of the decimal point, resulting in a dollars and cents format.

After division by 100, the value in T is equal to the rounded sales tax, which was the desired result.

Through the use of parentheses, the four steps shown in this example can be combined into a single let statement. This statement is illustrated in Figure 3–21.

All in one

```
290 LET T = INT((T + .005) * 100) / 100
```

Figure 3-21 All steps in rounding a number are performed in this single let statement. The sequence of operations is determined by the parentheses.

When the let statement in Figure 3–21 is analyzed, it is important to remember that the operations included in the innermost parentheses will be performed first. Therefore, the first step in the let statement execution is addition of the value .005 to the value in T. Next, the result of that calculation will be multiplied by 100, and the digits to the right of the decimal point in the answer will be truncated by the int function. Finally, the result of the int function will be divided by 100. This answer is stored in the field identified by the variable name T.

This example has illustrated rounding a positive number. A negative number can be rounded using essentially the same procedures except that the value .005 is subtracted instead of added, and the value 1 may have to be added to the result of the int function. The one is added because the int function returns the next lower integer. This process of rounding a negative number with the int function requires the use of the if statement discussed in Chapter 4.

REPORT EDITING

Information should be placed on a report or displayed on a CRT screen in a format which is easy to read and understand. For example, in the sample program in this chapter, the amount field is to be expressed as a dollars and cents field; and the total amount of the checks is to be printed with a comma and a dollar sign (see Figure 3–1). Preparing report information in this manner is called report editing.

Report editing can be performed on both numeric and string data. This is explained in the following sections.

Print using statement

Report editing is accomplished in the BASIC programming language through the use of the print using statement. It must be noted that this statement is not found in all BASIC interpreters. Without the print using statement, the editing to be discussed in this section cannot be accomplished.

Numeric editing

Editing with the print using statement is accomplished by using special characters to format the data. These special characters are specified within quotation marks in the format portion of the print using statement (Figure 3–22).

no colons

Figure 3-22 This print using statement is used to edit the numeric value in T2 with a dollar sign, comma, and decimal point. The # sign is specified in the print using format for each digit in T2. Special characters are included as they are to appear on the report.

```
260 PRINT USING "$#,###.##"; T2
```

When the print using statement above is executed, the value in the field indicated by the variable name T2 will be printed according to the editing format specified. The result is illustrated in Figure 3–23.

Figure 3-23 As a result of the print using statement, the edited results contain a dollar sign, comma, and decimal point.

DATA IN T2	PRINT USING FORMAT	PRINTED RESULTS
2453.98	$#,###.##	$2,453.98

The form of the print using statement is contained in Figure 3–24.

Figure 3-24 The general form of the print using statement is shown in this figure.

line number PRINT USING $\left(\begin{array}{c}\text{"format literal"}\\ \text{variable name}\end{array}\right); \left(\begin{array}{c}\text{variable name}\\ \text{literal}\end{array}\right)\ldots$

The print using statement, as all BASIC statements, begins with a line number. This is followed by one or more blanks and then the words PRINT USING. These words are followed by a blank and then the format portion of the print using statement. The format can be either a literal, such as in Figure 3–22, or the variable name of a field in which a print using format has been placed. If a literal is specified, the format must be enclosed within double quotation marks. If a variable name is used, no quotation marks are used. Following the format portion of the print using statement is a semicolon. The semicolon is followed by a blank and then the literals or variable name(s) of the fields which are to be edited by the print using statement. In the example in Figure 3–22, the field containing the data to be edited is T2.

The format portion of a print using statement consists of the special characters which are used to cause editing to occur. These special characters are described in the following paragraphs.

Numbers and the decimal point

The number sign (#) is used to represent numbers in the format portion of the print using statement. A decimal point specified in the format portion indicates where the decimal point of the number being edited is to be aligned. The examples in Figure 3-25 illustrate the use of the number sign and the decimal point.

DATA TO BE EDITED	PRINT USING FORMAT	PRINTED RESULTS
125.62	###.##	125.62
1268.9	####.##	1268.90
54.986	###.##	54.99
5.76	###.##	5.76
.65	###.##	0.65
−6.47	##.##	−6.47
142.98	##.##	%142.98

Figure 3-25 Numeric data is edited according to the print using format. Note that if the number to be edited contains more digits to the right of the decimal point than the print using format has room for, the number is rounded. Thus, the rounding sequence demonstrated previously need not be used if the rounded number is only going to be printed.

The number sign (#) represents each number that will appear in the printed results. When the editing takes place, the decimal points in the number to be edited and the print using format are aligned. The digits from the number being edited are then inserted in the format moving both directions from the decimal point. If there are not enough spaces to the right of the decimal point in the print using format (third example), the digits to the right of the decimal point are rounded and printed according to the format. If there are not enough positions to the left of the decimal point, the entire number is printed, but it is preceded by a percent sign (%) to indicate the number was too large (example 7). If there are more positions in the using format than digits in the number being edited, spaces are placed to the left of the decimal point (examples 3 and 4) and zeros are added to the right of the decimal point (example 2). If there are no digits to the left of the decimal point in the number being edited, a zero is placed immediately to the left of the decimal point (example 5). A negative number is printed with the minus sign. The print using format must contain enough positions for both the number and the minus sign.

When numeric values are equal to or greater than 1000, it is usually helpful to include commas to indicate each three digits (1,000). This is easily done in BASIC by specifying a comma in the print using format at the position where the comma is to appear (Figure 3-26).

Commas

DATA TO BE EDITED	PRINT USING FORMAT	PRINTED RESULTS
1208.78	#,###.##	1,208.78
986.05	#,###.##	986.05

Figure 3-26 A comma can be specified in the print using format at the position where it will be printed when one is desired in the printed results.

From the second example note that if the number to be edited contains no digits to the left of the comma position in the print using format, then the comma will be replaced by a blank.

Dollar signs

The dollar sign is often used when the field being edited is expressed in dollars and cents. When two dollar signs are placed in the leftmost positions of the using format, a dollar sign will be inserted to the left of and adjacent to the first significant digit in the number. This type of dollar sign is called a floating dollar sign. When a single dollar sign is placed in the leftmost position of the print using format, a single dollar sign will appear in the leftmost position of the printed results. The use of this editing character in the print using format is shown in Figure 3–27.

Figure 3-27 When two dollar signs are placed at the beginning of the print using format, a floating dollar sign is printed. When a single dollar sign is specified, the dollar sign is printed in the leftmost position.

DATA TO BE EDITED	PRINT USING FORMAT	PRINTED RESULTS
34.87	$$#,###.##	$34.87
3579.75	$$#,###.##	$3,579.75
.03	$$#,###.##	$0.03
45678.07	$$#,###.##	$45,678.07
561.93	$##,###.##	$ 561.93

The first example in Figure 3–27 contains two digits to the left of the decimal point. The dollar sign is immediately to the left of and adjacent to the first significant digit (3) in the printed result. In the second example, the number contains four digits to the left of the decimal point. Therefore, in addition to the dollar sign, a comma is contained in the printed results.

If there are no digits to the left of the decimal point in the data to be edited, a zero will be printed immediately to the left of and adjacent to the decimal point with the dollar sign to the left of the zero (example 3). Even if the digit to the right of the decimal point is zero, as in the example, the decimal point will be printed, and all of the digits to the right of the decimal point will be printed.

In the fourth example, the number to be edited contains five digits to the left of the decimal point. This is the maximum number of digits to the left of the decimal point for which the print using format in the example has room. There must always be one position in the format for the dollar sign.

Plus and minus signs

Plus and minus signs can also be included in the print using format to edit numeric data. A plus sign at the beginning or end of the format string will cause the sign of the number (plus or minus) to be printed before or after the number. A minus sign at the end of the format will cause negative numbers to be printed with a trailing minus sign. If the number being edited is positive, no sign will be printed. The use of the plus and minus signs when editing numeric data is illustrated in Figure 3-28.

DATA TO BE EDITED	PRINT USING FORMAT	PRINTED RESULTS
+ 142	+ ###	+142
– 532	+ ###	–532
+ 749	### +	749+
– 518	### +	518–
+ 915	### –	915
– 429	### –	429–

Figure 3-28 A plus or minus sign can be included in the printed results by using the appropriate print using format.

A double asterisk at the beginning of the print using format causes leading spaces in the numeric field to be filled with asterisks. This editing feature is commonly used when writing financial documents such as payroll checks where no spaces should appear before the number.

The asterisk can be used with the dollar sign to produce a floating dollar sign preceded by the asterisks. The use of the asterisk with and without the dollar sign is shown in Figure 3-29.

Asterisk fill characters

floats asterisks just like $ signs

DATA TO BE EDITED	PRINT USING FORMAT	PRINTED RESULTS
34.36	* * ##,.##	***34.36
361.49	* * ##,.##	**361.49
5732.08	* * ##,.##	5,732.08
5.78	* * $##,.##	****$5.78
636.35	* * $##,.##	**$636.35
4289.67	* * $##,.##	$4,289.67

Figure 3-29 In these examples, the comma is placed immediately to the left of the decimal point. When the print using statement is executed, the comma will be placed in the proper position if there are four significant digits to the left of the decimal point. If there are not, the comma is replaced by an asterisk. If the number being edited is large enough to contain two commas, then two commas must be specified to the left of the decimal point. This method of specifying commas can be used in all formats of the print using statement.

From the examples above, note that asterisks are used as fill characters when the number being edited does not contain as many digits as can be placed in the print using format. It should also be noted that when a comma appears in a format, it occupies one position. If there are three or fewer characters to the left of the decimal point, the comma's position is replaced by an asterisk (examples 1 and 2). Whether or not an asterisk is used, the comma always accounts for one position in the print using format.

The previous examples have edited numeric data. String data can be edited with the print using statement as well. The examples in Figure 3-30 illustrate

String editing

string editing with the print using statement.

DATA TO BE EDITED	PRINT USING FORMAT	PRINTED RESULTS
PROGRAM	"\ \"	PROGRAM
PROGRAMMING	"\ \"	PROGRAM
PRO	"\ \"	PRO
UP	"\\"	UP
* *	"!"	*

Figure 3-30 In the first three print using formats, there are five spaces separating the backward slashes. The data is edited accordingly.

The using format for string editing is enclosed in double quotation marks the same as with numeric editing. The format illustrated begins with a backward slash (\ ). On some computer systems, the character may be a percent sign (%) or other character. The beginning character accounts for one character in the data to be edited. The trailing backward slash accounts for a second character. Therefore, the minimum number of characters which can be edited with the backward slash is two characters (example 4). Between the backward slashes are blanks. These blanks account for the remainder of the characters in the field to be edited.

When the number of characters in the field to be edited is equal to the number of positions in the using format, each character in the field is placed in the corresponding position in the using format (example 1). If the number of characters in the field to be edited is greater than the number of positions in the using format (example 2), the rightmost characters of the field being edited are truncated.

If the number of characters is fewer than the positions in the using format, the characters from the field being edited are placed in the leftmost positions of the using format, and the remaining positions are filled with blanks (example 3).

The last example in Figure 3-30 illustrates the use of the exclamation point editing character (!). When this character is specified in the print using format, the first character of the field being edited will be placed in the output line where the exclamation point appears. Thus, in the last example, a single asterisk appears on the output line because it is the first character of the data being edited.

Building a report line

The print using format can specify space for more than one field. In addition, the format specified in the print using statement can be for numeric data, string data, or a combination of the two. Using this feature, it is possible to format the entire print line with a single print using statement.

In the sample program, the checking account report is produced. The detail report line contains the check date, the check number, the name of the party to whom the check is made out, and the amount of the check. A sample of the report together with a printer layout form for the detail line is illustrated in Figure 3–31.

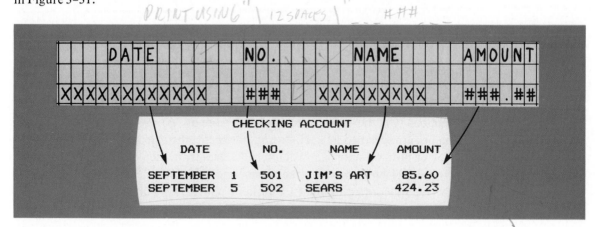

Figure 3-31 The printer layout form is used to design the format of the printed line.

The format of the print line is shown on the printer layout form. String fields are represented by X's, and numeric fields are represented by the character #. Punctuation is placed in the numeric fields where it will appear in the actual printed report or display. Spaces between each of the fields are designated by blanks on the printer spacing form. From Figure 3–31 it can be seen that the layout on the printer spacing form corresponds exactly to the report which is produced.

The print using format to specify this report line is shown below, together with the report format.

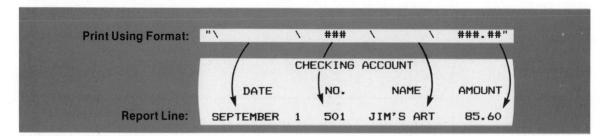

Figure 3-32 The print using format specifies where data will be printed and the type of editing that will be performed on the data.

In the example above, the print using format is specified between double quotation marks. Within the quotes are the editing symbols to specify the detail line on the report. As can be seen, these symbols correspond to the fields which actually appear on the report. As a result of the print using format in Figure 3–32, the entire detail line on the report has been defined, including the spacing which is to occur between each of the fields and the editing that is to be performed on the data to be printed.

The entire print using statement that could be used in the sample program is illustrated in Figure 3-33.

```
210 PRINT USING "\          \    ###    \        \    ###.##"; D$, C, N$, A
```

Figure 3-33 Variable names of the fields to be printed follow the semicolon in the print using statement.

In the example above, the format is specified in the print using statement as a constant. The variable names which follow are for the date (D$), the check number (C), the name (N$), and the amount (A). When multiple variable names are specified in a print using statement, they are separated by commas. The print using statement will insert the data from each of the fields identified by the variable names into the corresponding format fields. Thus, the data in the field identified by the first variable name (D$) will be placed in the first field in the print using format (\   \). The data in the field identified by the second variable name (C) will be placed in the second field in the format (###). This processing continues for the entire line.

The print using statement in Figure 3-33 is quite long and somewhat difficult to read. Since the print using format is nothing more than a string constant, one way to overcome a long print using statement is to place the format in a string field through the use of a let statement. The variable name of the field is then specified in the print using statement. This technique is shown in Figure 3-34.

Figure 3-34 The print using format can be placed in a field and then the variable name of the field is specified in the print using statement.

```
410 LET F1$ = "\          \    ###    \        \    ###.##"
    :
    :
570    PRINT USING F1$; D$, C, N$, A
```

The let statement on line 410 places the print using format constant into a field with the variable name F1$. In the print using statement, this variable name is specified in place of the format constant. The results of the print using statement on line 570 will be the same as if the print using format had been specified as a constant in the statement. Generally, it is good practice to place the format constant in a field and then use the variable name of the field in the print using statement.

The print using statement is a powerful tool for the BASIC programmer. It can be used to increase the readability of output produced from a program.

The variety of editing formats that are available with the print using statement should be well understood by the programmer.

Further formatting of a printed line can be obtained through the use of the tab function in the print statement and the use of the semicolon in the print statement. For those BASIC interpreters that do not support the print using statement, the tab function and the semicolon provide a way in which a print line can be formatted when not using the standard BASIC printing zones.

Tab function

The tab function is used to specify the column in which a constant or value in a field is to begin printing. In the example below, the tab function is used to indicate that the constant CHECKING ACCOUNT is to be printed beginning in column 12 of the report.

Figure 3-35 The tab function is used to specify the beginning column where a value is to be printed. Here, the constant CHECKING ACCOUNT will begin in column 12 of the printed output.

```
470 PRINT TAB(12) "CHECKING ACCOUNT"
```

The word TAB follows the word PRINT, separated by a space. Immediately following the word TAB, with no intervening spaces, is a left parenthesis. Within the parentheses is the number specifying the column where the value is to begin printing. Following the number is a right parenthesis. The value to be printed follows.

When using the tab function, the programmer must know the number of the leftmost column on a report. Some BASIC interpreters assign the number zero to the leftmost column while others begin the numbering with 1. Since the value in the tab function specifies the column where the value is to begin printing, when the value 12 is specified, some BASIC interpreters will cause 12 spaces to appear before the constant while others will cause only 11 spaces to appear. This is illustrated in Figure 3-36.

Figure 3-36 When the beginning column is zero, the function TAB(12) will cause twelve spaces from the left edge of the printed results. When the beginning column is one, only eleven spaces will be present.

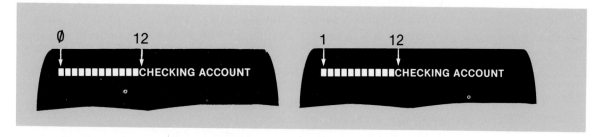

In the example above, note that if the leftmost column is numbered zero, then the entry TAB(12) will cause twelve spaces. If the leftmost column is numbered one, the entry TAB(12) will cause eleven spaces. Again, the programmer must know the numbering scheme of the BASIC interpreter being used in order to properly use the tab function.

Multiple tab functions can be included in a single print statement, as illustrated in Figure 3-37.

Figure 3-37 In this example, NAME begins in col-
umn 5, ADDRESS in column
15, and CITY in column 25.

```
350 PRINT TAB(5) "NAME" TAB(15) "ADDRESS" TAB(25) "CITY"
```

In the example above, the constant NAME would print beginning in column 5. The constant ADDRESS would begin in column 15, and the constant CITY would begin in column 25. In the print statement in Figure 3-37, there is no punctuation between the constant and the word TAB. This is the preferred way of writing a print statement which uses multiple tab functions.

The entry specifying the column in the tab function need not always be a numeric constant. It can be a variable name or even an arithmetic expression, as shown in Figure 3-38.

Figure 3-38 A numeric
value in any form (literal,
variable, or arithmetic expression) may be used
with the tab function.

```
420 LET N = 12
430 LET P = 22
440 PRINT TAB(N) "START" TAB(P) "MIDDLE" TAB(N + P) "END"
```

When an arithmetic expression is used with the tab function, there is a possibility that the value in the expression is less than a previous value in the same print statement. For example, if statements 420 and 430 were not included in Figure 3-38, there is a possibility that the value in P could be less than the value in N. When this occurs, the various versions of BASIC handle it in one of two ways. On some systems, the tab statement is ignored, and the data is printed beginning in the next column. On other systems, the tab function is honored by printing in the specified column on the next line. Thus, if the value in N was equal to 22 and the value in P was equal to 12, on some systems the word MIDDLE would begin in column 28 (22 + five characters in START + 1); and on other systems, it would begin in column 12 on the next line. The line position cannot be moved backwards by the tab function. The programmer should be aware of the method found on the computer system being used.

Semicolon Spacing across the line when using a print statement can also be controlled by the punctuation placed between the variable names or constants in the print statement. It will be recalled from Chapter 2 that a comma between the variable names or constants in a print statement will cause each of the fields to begin in a predefined print zone.

A semicolon can be used in a print statement in place of a comma to specify the printing between fields. The use of a semicolon and the output received as a result of using this punctuation is illustrated in Figure 3–39.

Print Statement

```
120 PRINT "ABC"; "DEF"
130 PRINT "NUMBER IS"; 6
140 PRINT "NUMBER IS"; -6
150 PRINT 7; "IS THE NUMBER"
160 PRINT 6; "+"; 6; "="; 12
170 PRINT 8; 5; -9
```

Printed Results

```
ABCDEF
NUMBER IS 6
NUMBER IS-6
 7 IS THE NUMBER
 6 + 6 = 12
 8  5 -9
```

Figure 3-39 The semicolon is used to control spacing between all types of data. The rules for spacing between numeric fields using the semicolon can vary between computer systems. For example, on some systems, a positive numeric value will not be preceded by a space.

When a semicolon follows a string variable or string constant (example 1), there are no spaces placed after the value. Similarly, in example 1, when a semicolon precedes a string variable or string constant, there are no spaces placed in front of the value when it is printed.

When a numeric variable or constant follows a string variable or constant (example 2), a space is always placed in front of the numeric value when it is printed if the value is positive. When the numeric value is negative, however, the minus sign is printed immediately preceding the number and no space is printed (example 3).

When a numeric constant or variable name is followed by a semicolon (examples 4 and 5), there will be a single space following the numeric value which is printed. In example 6, the numeric value 8 is followed by a semicolon in the print statement. When it is printed, the value 8 is followed by a space. Since the next numeric value, 5, is positive, it is preceded by a space. Therefore, in the printed results, the numbers 8 and 5 are separated by two spaces. A space follows the 5, but a space does not precede the negative 9 value because it is negative. Instead, the minus sign is printed. Thus, the 5 and negative 9 are separated by a single space.

Although it may appear that the same printing results can be obtained from the use of a semicolon as from the print using statement, in many cases this is not true. The print using statement places the numeric digits into the using format while the print statement with the semicolon prints the numeric value as it is found and merely controls the spacing between the values. The following examples illustrate the results obtained from both the print statement with a semicolon and the print using statement.

Print Statement

```
PRINT 23.6; 5.97        yields        23.6  5.97
PRINT 3.8; 6.40         yields        3.8  6.4
PRINT 124.01; 3.0       yields        124.01  3
```

Print Using Statements

```
PRINT USING "###.##  #.##"; 23.6, 5.97    yields    23.60  5.97
PRINT USING "###.##  #.##"; 3.8, 6.40     yields     3.80  6.40
PRINT USING "###.##  #.##"; 124.01, 3.0   yields   124.01  3.00
```

Figure 3-40 When numeric values are printed with a semicolon, there is no decimal point alignment. Instead, all values are aligned to the left. In addition, zeros to the right of the decimal point do not print.

From Figure 3-40, it can be seen that the printed results from a print statement with the semicolon separating numeric constants are different from those obtained with the print using statement. The print using statement allows more flexibility when formatting an output line on a CRT screen or a printer. Generally, if it is available, the print using statement should be used when formatting an output line.

SAMPLE PROGRAM

As noted previously, the sample program in this chapter creates a checking account report. The format of the report and the input data to be used for the program are shown in Figure 3-41.

Output

```
              CHECKING ACCOUNT

     DATE        NO.      NAME       AMOUNT

SEPTEMBER  1     501    JIM'S ART     85.60
SEPTEMBER  5     502    SEARS        424.23
SEPTEMBER 14     503    NORDSTROM    312.59
SEPTEMBER 22     504    BONDS         67.92
SEPTEMBER 25     505    ED'S AUTO    713.95

TOTAL NUMBER OF CHECKS    5
TOTAL AMOUNT OF CHECKS $1,604.29
```

Input

DATE	CHECK NUMBER	NAME	CHECK AMOUNT
SEPTEMBER 1	501	JIM'S ART	85.60
SEPTEMBER 5	502	SEARS	424.23
SEPTEMBER 14	503	NORDSTROM	312.59
SEPTEMBER 22	504	BONDS	67.92
SEPTEMBER 25	505	ED'S AUTO	713.95

Figure 3-41 The format of the output and the input data are illustrated here. The report contains final totals of the number of checks processed and the total amount of all of the checks.

The first step in designing the program is to specify the tasks which must be accomplished within the program. These are specified below.

Program design

Program Tasks

1. Set counters and accumulators to zero.
2. Read input records.
3. Accumulate total number of checks and total amount of checks.
4. Print lines on the report.
5. Print total number of checks and total check amount.

The flowchart of the logic to implement these tasks is shown in Figure 3-42.

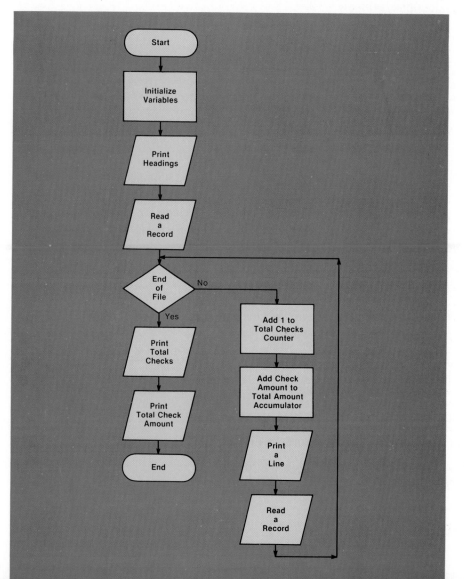

Figure 3-42 The flowchart for the sample program shows that all of the records are processed in a loop. A line will be printed on the report for each record that is read.

Program documentation

The first statements in the sample program are rem statements used to document the program. The program documentation, which specifies the name of the program, the date it was written, the programmers, the function of the program, and the variable names is illustrated in Figure 3-43.

```
100 REM CHECKACT           NOVEMBER 19          SHELLY/CASHMAN
110                                                          REM
120 REM THIS PROGRAM PREPARES A LIST OF CHECKS WRITTEN DURING
130 REM THE MONTH. AFTER ALL CHECKS ARE PROCESSED, THE TOTAL
140 REM NUMBER OF CHECKS WRITTEN AND THE TOTAL AMOUNT OF THE
150 REM CHECKS ARE PRINTED.
160                                                          REM
170 REM VARIABLE NAMES:
180 REM    D$....DATE
190 REM    C.....CHECK NUMBER
200 REM    N$....NAME
210 REM    A.....AMOUNT
220 REM    T1....FINAL TOTAL - NUMBER OF CHECKS
230 REM    T2....FINAL TOTAL - AMOUNT OF CHECKS
240 REM    F1$...PRINT USING FORMAT FOR THE DETAIL LINE
250 REM    F2$...PRINT USING FORMAT FOR CHECK NUMBER TOTAL LINE
260 REM    F3$...PRINT USING FORMAT FOR CHECK AMOUNT TOTAL LINE
```

Figure 3-43 Documentation of a program is very important. The variable names especially must be accurately and completely documented.

The name of the program is CHECKACT. It was written November 19 by Shelly and Cashman. The remarks on lines 120 – 150 indicate the function of the program. The variable names are described on lines 170 – 260. It is very important that all of the variable names are included in this portion of the documentation and that they are accurately described. The listing of the variable names is one of the more valuable pieces of documentation in a program listing.

Data to be processed

The next program entries are the data statements which define the data to be processed in the program (Figure 3-44).

```
270                                                          REM
280 REM ***** DATA TO BE PROCESSED *****
290                          '                              REM
300 DATA "SEPTEMBER  1", 501, "JIM'S ART", 85.60
310 DATA "SEPTEMBER  5", 502, "SEARS", 424.23
320 DATA "SEPTEMBER 14", 503, "NORDSTROM", 312.59
330 DATA "SEPTEMBER 22", 504, "BONDS", 67.92
340 DATA "SEPTEMBER 25", 505, "ED'S AUTO", 713.95
350 DATA "END", 999, "END OF FILE", 99.99
360                                                          REM
```

Figure 3-44 Data statements are used to define data to be processed in the program. String data must be enclosed within quotation marks.

Data statements are used to define the data to be processed. Each entry in the data statement is separated by a comma. String variables are placed within double quotation marks while numeric variables are not placed within quotation marks. The last data statement, on line 350, is the trailer record which indicates that there are no more records to process.

After the data has been defined, the variables within the program should be initialized before the actual processing of the data begins. In the sample program, there are two sets of variables which must be initialized — the fields used for final totals and the fields used for the print using formats. The let statements to initialize the variables are shown in Figure 3–45.

Initialization of variables

```
                                                                    REM
370 REM ***** INITIALIZATION OF VARIABLES *****
380                                                                 REM
390 LET T1 = 0
400 LET T2 = 0
410 LET F1$ = "\               \    ###    \           \    ###.##"
420 LET F2$ = "TOTAL NUMBER OF CHECKS ###"
430 LET F3$ = "TOTAL AMOUNT OF CHECKS $$,###.##"
440                                                                 REM
```

Start

Initialize
Variables

Figure 3-45 Fields used for totals must be initialized to zero. The print using formats are placed in string fields.

The let statement on line 390 places the value 0 in the field identified by the variable name T1. Similarly, the let statement on line 400 sets the field used for the total amount of the checks, T2, to the value 0. Whenever a field is to be used for a total, it should be initialized to the value zero.

The let statements on lines 410 – 430 place the print using formats into fields identified by the variable names F1$, F2$, and F3$. The fields used for the formats must be string fields. Therefore, the variable names must be followed by a dollar sign.

The print using formats placed in the fields and the corresponding output produced on the report are illustrated in Figure 3–46.

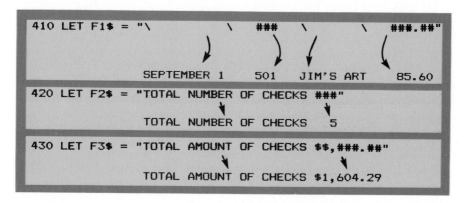

Figure 3-46 Note that the output produced reflects the editing specified in the print using format. The print using formats for F2$ and F3$ contain the actual constants that are to be printed. Constant values which will never change can be placed directly in the print using format.

Printing headings

The output produced from the sample program contains report and column headings. In this program, they are printed one time at the start of the report. The coding required to print the headings in this program is shown below.

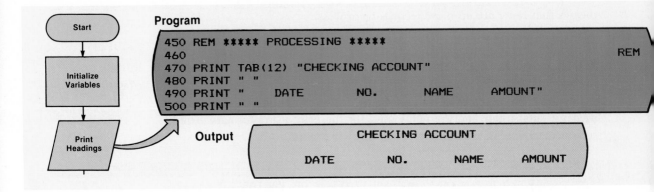

Program

```
450 REM ***** PROCESSING *****
460                                                    REM
470 PRINT TAB(12) "CHECKING ACCOUNT"
480 PRINT " "
490 PRINT "     DATE      NO.       NAME      AMOUNT"
500 PRINT " "
```

Output

```
                    CHECKING ACCOUNT

             DATE        NO.        NAME       AMOUNT
```

Figure 3-47 Headings serve to identify information on the report. The use of a blank line makes the headings easier to read.

The print statement on line 470 causes the constant CHECKING ACCOUNT to be printed beginning in column 12 of the report. The print statement on line 480, with a single blank specified as the value to be printed, will cause a blank line to be printed on the report. When blank lines are required on a report, a print statement with a single blank is the way in which to print them.

Line 490 contains the print statement to print the column headings. The constant, consisting of each of the column headings, is printed. The spacing between the words is determined from the printing chart which is developed for the program (Figure 3-48).

Figure 3-48 The printing chart is used to indicate where fields are to appear on the report line. The programmer will normally follow the printing chart when writing both the headings and the print using formats.

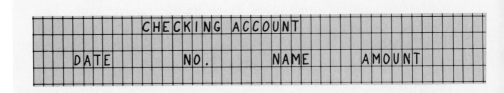

The printing chart above indicates the exact columns where the report and column headings are to appear. The print statement on line 490 reflects this. The last print statement on line 500 prints a blank line following the column headings.

Reading an input record

The next step in the program logic is to read an input record. The flowchart and related coding for this operation are shown in Figure 3-49.

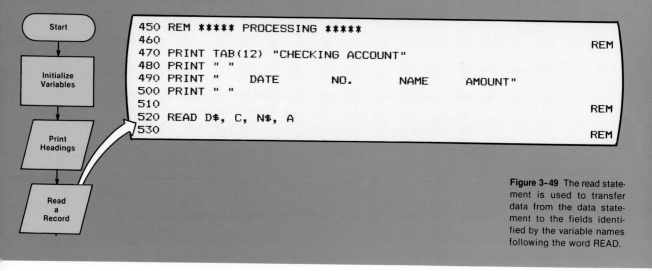

```
450  REM ***** PROCESSING *****
460                                                          REM
470  PRINT TAB(12) "CHECKING ACCOUNT"
480  PRINT " "
490  PRINT "      DATE          NO.        NAME       AMOUNT"
500  PRINT " "
510                                                          REM
520  READ D$, C, N$, A
530                                                          REM
```

Figure 3-49 The read statement is used to transfer data from the data statement to the fields identified by the variable names following the word READ.

The read statement on line 520 places data in the date field (D$), the check number field (C), the name field (N$), and the check amount field (A). The data is acquired from the first data statement (see Figure 3–44).

After the first read statement, the main processing loop is entered. The first statement in the loop checks for end of file to determine if the statements within the loop should be executed (Figure 3–50).

Main processing loop

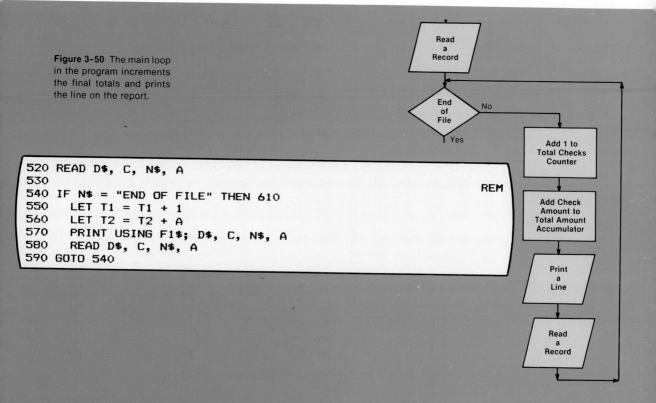

Figure 3-50 The main loop in the program increments the final totals and prints the line on the report.

```
520  READ D$, C, N$, A
530                                                          REM
540  IF N$ = "END OF FILE" THEN 610
550     LET T1 = T1 + 1
560     LET T2 = T2 + A
570     PRINT USING F1$; D$, C, N$, A
580     READ D$, C, N$, A
590  GOTO 540
```

The if statement on line 540 compares the value in the field identified by the N$ variable name to the value END OF FILE. If they are equal, it indicates the trailer record has been read and all records have been processed. If the values are not equal, the trailer record has not been read and the loop is entered.

The first statement in the loop (line 550) adds the value 1 to the value already in the field T1. The let statement is executed as follows: a) The value 1 is added to the value in T1; b) The result of the arithmetic is placed in the T1 field. This processing for the first two records is illustrated below.

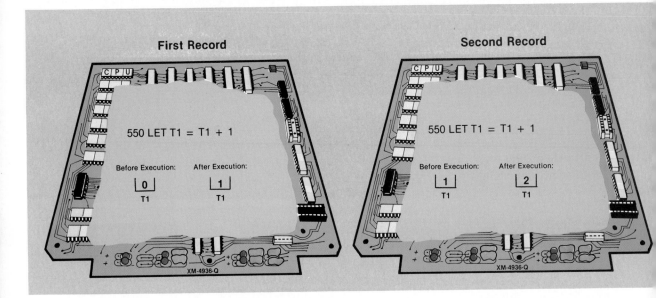

First Record

550 LET T1 = T1 + 1

Before Execution: | 0 | T1

After Execution: | 1 | T1

XM-4936-Q

Second Record

550 LET T1 = T1 + 1

Before Execution: | 1 | T1

After Execution: | 2 | T1

XM-4936-Q

Figure 3-51 The counter, T1, is incremented by 1 each time a record is processed. In the let statement, the arithmetic expression on the right of the equal sign is evaluated, and the answer is placed in the field identified by the variable to the left of the equal sign.

For the first record, the value in T1 is zero. This value was placed there when the field was initialized (Figure 3-45). After the statement on line 550 has been executed for the first record, the value 1 is stored in T1. This value is calculated by adding the initial value in T1 (0) to the constant 1 and storing the result in T1. When the second record is processed, the value in T1 (1) is added to the constant 1, and the result (2) is stored in T1.

The field identified by variable name T1 is called a counter because it is being used to store a count — in this case, a count of the number of checks which have been written.

The next let statement in the program, on line 560, is used to accumulate the total amount of the checks written (Figure 3-52). When the statement is executed for the first record, the value in the field identified by the variable name A is added to the initial value in T2, which is zero as a result of the initialization processing (Figure 3-45). Therefore, after the first record is processed, the value in T2 is equal to the check amount for the first check. When the second record is processed, the check amount for the second check is added

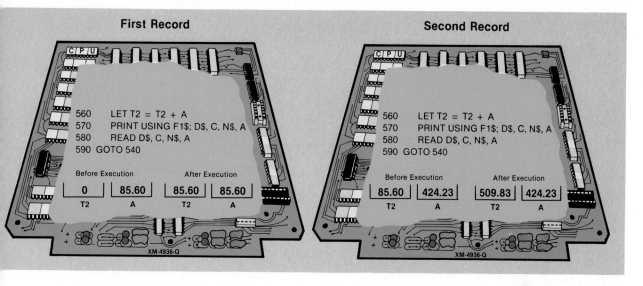

First Record

```
560   LET T2 = T2 + A
570   PRINT USING F1$; D$, C, N$, A
580   READ D$, C, N$, A
590 GOTO 540
```

Before Execution   After Execution

| 0 | 85.60 | 85.60 | 85.60 |
| T2 | A | T2 | A |

Second Record

```
560   LET T2 = T2 + A
570   PRINT USING F1$; D$, C, N$, A
580   READ D$, C, N$, A
590 GOTO 540
```

Before Execution   After Execution

| 85.60 | 424.23 | 509.83 | 424.23 |
| T2 | A | T2 | A |

XM-4936-Q

to the value in T2. Therefore, after the second record is processed, the value in T2 (509.83) is the sum of the amounts in the first and second checks.

The T2 field is called an accumulator because it is being used to accumulate a value — in this case the sum of the check amounts. Both counters and accumulators are widely used in computer programming, and their use should be well understood.

After the counter and accumulator have been updated, the print using statement on line 570 prints the detail line which contains the date, the check number, the name, and the check amount. Another record is then read and the goto statement on line 590 passes control back to the if statement on line 540. This loop will continue until the trailer record is read, at which time the end of file processing will occur.

Figure 3-52 Each time the value in A is added to the value in T2, the value in T2 reflects the total amount of all checks which have been processed.

After all of the records have been read and processed, the final totals must be printed. The flowchart and statements to implement this processing are illustrated in Figure 3-53.

Printing final totals

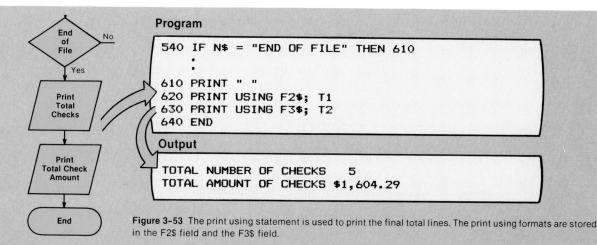

Program

```
540 IF N$ = "END OF FILE" THEN 610
        .
        .
610 PRINT " "
620 PRINT USING F2$; T1
630 PRINT USING F3$; T2
640 END
```

Output

```
TOTAL NUMBER OF CHECKS   5
TOTAL AMOUNT OF CHECKS $1,604.29
```

Figure 3-53 The print using statement is used to print the final total lines. The print using formats are stored in the F2$ field and the F3$ field.

Coding tips   The following tips should be kept in mind when coding a program:

1. Documentation of the variable names in a program is probably the most important documentation which can be written in the coding. When it is necessary to review the program, the use of the variable names used in the program must be known.

2. Certain characters can sometimes cause confusion. For example, many times it is difficult to distinguish between a zero and the letter of the alphabet O. Therefore, on many computer systems, the zero is written with a slash through it (Ø), and the letter of the alphabet is written without a slash (O). Other characters which might cause confusion are the number 1 and the letter I, and the number 2 and the letter Z. Errors which are caused by misusing characters can be extremely difficult to find, so care must be taken both when writing these characters and when entering them into the computer system.

3. Some typical areas where errors can be made in a program like the sample program in this chapter are:

   a. All variable names specified in a read statement must correspond to the type of data which is defined in a data statement. Thus, if the data in a data statement is defined as string data (enclosed in quotes), the variable name must be a string variable name (followed by a dollar sign).

   b. Total counters and accumulators must be initialized to zero prior to being used for counting or accumulating values. Many BASIC interpreters will automatically set numeric variables to zero when they are first encountered in the program. To ensure compatibility between varying BASIC interpreters, however, it is recommended that the variables used for totals be explicitly initialized.

   c. When using the tab function, the programmer must be aware of the numbering system used for the vertical columns. Some BASIC interpreters begin numbering with column 0 while others begin numbering with column 1.

   d. Generally, the using format specified for a numeric or string field should specify enough positions for the largest value to be edited. If the number of positions in the using format is less than the number of characters or digits to actually be edited, unpredictable results may occur. The only exception is if the print using statement is used to round a number. In that case, the number of positions specified to the right of the decimal point in the print using format should be the number of digits which will appear in the number after rounding takes place.

The listing of the sample program is illustrated below.   **Sample program**

```
100 REM CHECKACT              NOVEMBER 19            SHELLY/CASHMAN
110                                                              REM
120 REM THIS PROGRAM PREPARES A LIST OF CHECKS WRITTEN DURING
130 REM THE MONTH. AFTER ALL CHECKS ARE PROCESSED, THE TOTAL
140 REM NUMBER OF CHECKS WRITTEN AND THE TOTAL AMOUNT OF THE
150 REM CHECKS ARE PRINTED.
160                                                              REM
170 REM VARIABLE NAMES:
180 REM    D$....DATE
190 REM    C.....CHECK NUMBER
200 REM    N$....NAME
210 REM    A.....AMOUNT
220 REM    T1....FINAL TOTAL - NUMBER OF CHECKS
230 REM    T2....FINAL TOTAL - AMOUNT OF CHECKS
240 REM    F1$...PRINT USING FORMAT FOR THE DETAIL LINE
250 REM    F2$...PRINT USING FORMAT FOR CHECK NUMBER TOTAL LINE
260 REM    F3$...PRINT USING FORMAT FOR CHECK AMOUNT TOTAL LINE
270                                                              REM
280 REM ***** DATA TO BE PROCESSED *****
290                                                              REM
300 DATA "SEPTEMBER  1", 501, "JIM'S ART", 85.60
310 DATA "SEPTEMBER  5", 502, "SEARS", 424.23
320 DATA "SEPTEMBER 14", 503, "NORDSTROM", 312.59
330 DATA "SEPTEMBER 22", 504, "BONDS", 67.92
340 DATA "SEPTEMBER 25", 505, "ED'S AUTO", 713.95
350 DATA "END", 999, "END OF FILE", 99.99
360                                                              REM
370 REM ***** INITIALIZATION OF VARIABLES *****
380                                                              REM
390 LET T1 = 0
400 LET T2 = 0
410 LET F1$ = "\             \   ###   \        \   ###.##"
420 LET F2$ = "TOTAL NUMBER OF CHECKS ###"
430 LET F3$ = "TOTAL AMOUNT OF CHECKS $$,###.##"
440                                                              REM
450 REM ***** PROCESSING *****
460                                                              REM
470 PRINT TAB(12) "CHECKING ACCOUNT"
480 PRINT " "
490 PRINT "    DATE        NO.      NAME      AMOUNT"
500 PRINT " "
510                                                              REM
520 READ D$, C, N$, A
530                                                              REM
540 IF N$ = "END OF FILE" THEN 610
550    LET T1 = T1 + 1
560    LET T2 = T2 + A
570    PRINT USING F1$; D$, C, N$, A
580    READ D$, C, N$, A
590 GOTO 540
600                                                              REM
610 PRINT " "
620 PRINT USING F2$; T1
630 PRINT USING F3$; T2
640 END
```

Figure 3-54 The listing for the sample program illustrates the coding rules, including spacing and indentation, which should always be followed.

SUMMARY   The following points have been discussed and explained in this chapter.

1. Many computer applications involve performing calculations, including the accumulation and printing of final totals.

2. Formatted output and report and column headings are commonly found.

3. Arithmetic operations, including addition, subtraction, multiplication, division, and exponentiation are accomplished in BASIC using arithmetic operators.

4. The arithmetic operators are: + (addition), — (subtraction), * (multiplication), / (division), and ↑ (exponentiation).

5. To perform arithmetic operations, the let statement is used.

6. The let statement to perform arithmetic operations consists of a line number, the word LET, and an arithmetic expression.

7. An arithmetic expression consists of constants, variable names, and arithmetic operators.

8. An arithmetic expression can contain multiple arithmetic operators.

9. A numeric literal, which is a constant numeric value, can be used in an arithmetic expression.

10. In most applications, a literal should be used in a calculation only when there is little chance the value specified by the literal will be modified later.

11. After the arithmetic has been performed by the let statement, the values used in the arithmetic operation together with the answer obtained can be used in subsequent arithmetic operations or for other purposes in the program.

12. When two or more values are used in an addition or subtraction operation, the BASIC interpreter will generate instructions to align the decimal points within the numbers before the arithmetic operation occurs.

13. When multiplication takes place, the signs of the numbers are considered. If two positive or two negative numbers are multiplied, the answer is positive. If a negative and a positive number are multiplied, the answer is negative.

14. The largest number of digits which can appear in a product of two numbers is the sum of the number of digits in each of the values being multiplied.

15. The number of digits to the right of the decimal point in a product is the sum of the number of digits to the right of the decimal point in the multiplicand and the multiplier.

16. Exponentiation means raising a number to a power.

17. The value to the right of the equal sign in a let statement can be a number as well as an arithmetic expression.

18. When the root of a number is taken using a fractional exponent, the number whose root is being taken cannot be negative. If it is, the program will normally be cancelled.

19. When multiple arithmetic operations are included in a single let statement, the sequence in which the operations are performed is determined in accordance with the following rules: a) Exponentiation is performed first; b) Multiplication and division are performed next; c) Addition and subtraction are performed last; d) Within these three steps, calculations are performed left to right.

20. Arithmetic operations specified within parentheses in an arithmetic expression will be evaluated before those outside the parentheses.

21. In most cases, it is advisable to use parentheses around multiple arithmetic operations even if the predetermined sequence of operations will produce the correct answer.

22. To round a dollars and cents field, the following steps are taken: a) The value .005 is added to the value to be rounded; b) The decimal point is moved two positions to the right by multiplying the number by 100; c) The digits to the right of the decimal point are truncated; d) The value is changed to a dollars and cents format by dividing by 100.

23. A function in BASIC is a prewritten set of instructions to accomplish a given task. These instructions can be called by a single word. A function can be used just like a variable in an arithmetic expression.

24. The purpose of the int function is to return the next lowest integer from the number being examined.

25. The syntax of a function must be followed exactly.

26. Placing report data in a format which is easy to read and understand by using special characters such as the dollar sign and decimal point is called report editing.

27. Report editing can be performed on both numeric data and string data.

28. Report editing is accomplished in the BASIC language through the use of the print using statement.

29. Editing with the print using statement is accomplished by using special characters to format the data.

30. The print using statement consists of a line number, the words PRINT USING, the print using format, and the data to be edited and printed.

31. A semicolon is used to separate the print using format from the variable names or constants to be edited and printed.

32. The number sign (#) is used to represent numbers in the format portion of the print using statement.

33. A decimal point in the format portion of the print using statement indicates where the decimal point of the number being edited is to be aligned.

34. A comma is included in the print using format where it is to appear in the printed result. If the number being edited does not contain a digit to the left of the position where the comma appears in the print using format, the comma will be replaced by a blank in the printed results.

35. When two dollar signs are placed in the leftmost positions of the print

using format, a dollar sign will be inserted to the left of and adjacent to the first significant digit in the number being edited. When one dollar sign is in the format, it will be printed in its fixed position.

36. Plus and minus signs can also be included in the using format to edit numeric data.

37. A double asterisk at the beginning of the print using format causes leading spaces in the numeric field to be filled with asterisks.

38. The asterisk can be used with the dollar sign to produce a floating dollar sign preceded by the asterisks.

39. String data can be edited. The print using format begins and ends with the backward slash on many computer systems. On some systems, the percentage sign or other character may be used.

40. If the number of characters in the string field to be edited is greater than the number of positions in the print using format, the rightmost characters in the field being edited are truncated. If the number of characters is fewer than the positions in the print using format, the characters from the field are placed in the leftmost positions, and the remaining positions are filled with blanks.

41. The print using format can specify space for more than one field. Therefore, the entire print line can be formatted with one print using statement.

42. The let statement can be used to place the print using format into a string field. The variable name of the string field is then specified in the print using statement.

43. The tab function is used to specify the column in which a constant or value in a field is to begin printing.

44. The column where printing is to begin is specified in parentheses immediately following the word TAB when using the tab function.

45. Some BASIC interpreters begin numbering columns with the value zero while others begin with one.

46. Multiple tab functions can be included in a single print statement.

47. A semicolon can be used in a print statement to specify the printing between fields. When used with a string variable, there are no spaces before or after the value. A numeric value preceded by a semicolon will have a space before it if the value is positive and a minus sign (–) before it if the value is negative. A numeric variable or constant followed by a semicolon will always have a space following it when it is printed.

48. Generally, if it is available, the print using statement should be used when formatting an output line.

49. The listing of the variable names in the program documentation is probably the most important documentation in the program.

50. Variable initialization should take place prior to entering the main processing of a program.

51. A counter is a field used to store a count that is kept in the program.

52. An accumulator is used to accumulate a value in a program.

1. The arithmetic operators are: a) Addition _____; b) Subtraction _____; c) Multiplication _____; d) Division _____; e) Exponentiation _____.

2. An arithmetic expression consists of _____, _____, and _____.

3. The sequence of execution in an arithmetic operation is: a) _____; b) _____; c) _____.

4. In most cases, it is advisable to use parentheses around multiple arithmetic operations in an arithmetic expression (T or F).

5. What is a function in BASIC? How is it implemented?

6. What is report editing? How is it accomplished in BASIC?

7. Which of the following symbols represents numbers in the print using statement: a) /; b) %; c) #; d) &.

8. How is a comma specified in the using format of a print using statement? Where does it appear in the edited number?

9. Which of the following using formats will produce the edited result $5,987.87 from the value 5987.87 a) #,#$$.$$; b) $$,###.##; c) $$*,*##.##; d) $,$$$.$$.

10. If the number of characters in a string field to be edited is greater than the number of positions in the using format, the rightmost characters in the field being edited are truncated (T or F).

11. An entire print line can be edited with one print using statement (T or F).

12. The tab function is used to: a) Specify the number of the line on which data is to be printed; b) Specify the column in which a constant or value in a field is to begin printing; c) Specify the number of characters which are to be printed for a numeric or string constant; d) Set tabs in the same manner as a typewriter.

13. When a semicolon is specified between two numeric variable names in a print statement, the values in the two fields will be separated by: a) One blank space; b) Two blank spaces; c) Two blank spaces if both the numbers are negative; d) One blank space if the second number is negative.

14. Make the appropriate changes to the sample program in this chapter to print the check amount for each check with a floating dollar sign.

15. The sample program in this chapter must be changed to accomodate a check amount up to a maximum of $9,999.99. Make the appropriate changes in the sample program to accomodate this requirement. Note that this change will require the total amount for all checks to be a maximum of $99,999.99.

16. Make the changes in the sample program in this chapter to calculate the average amount of all the checks processed and print this amount with the identifier AVERAGE AMOUNT OF CHECKS after the total check amount line.

Chapter 3
DEBUGGING EXERCISES

The following lines of code contain one or more syntax errors. Circle each of the errors and write the coding to correct the errors.

1.
```
390 LET T1 = 0
400 LET T2 = 0
410 LET F1$ = \        \    ###    \        \    ###0##
```

2.
```
470 PRINT TAB (12) "CHECKING ACCOUNT"
480 PRINT " "
```

3.
```
280 REM ***** DATA TO BE PROCESSED *****
290                                                              REM
300 DATA SEPTEMBER  1, 501, JIM'S ART, 85.60
310 DATA SEPTEMBER  5, 502, SEARS, 424.23
320 DATA SEPTEMBER 14, 503, NORDSTROM, 312.59
330 DATA SEPTEMBER 22, 504, BONDS, 67.92
340 DATA SEPTEMBER 25, 505, ED'S AUTO, 713.95
```

4.
```
410 LET F1 = "\           \    ###    \        \    ###.##"
420 LET F2 = "TOTAL NUMBER OF CHECKS ###"
430 LET F3 = "TOTAL AMOUNT OF CHECKS $$,###.##"
```

5.
```
540 IF N$ = "END OF FILE" THEN 610
550    LET T1 = T1 + 1
560    LET T2 = T2 + A
570    PRINT USING F1$; D$, C, N$, A
580    READ D$, C, N$, A
590 GO TO 540
```

6.
```
550    LET T1 = T1 + 1
560    LET T2 = T2 + A
570    PRINT USING F1$, D$, C, N$, A
580    READ D$, C, N$, A
```

7.
```
610 PRNT " "
620 PRINT USING "F2$"; T1
630 PRINT USING "F3$"; T2
```

Chapter 3
PROGRAM DEBUGGING

The following program was designed and written to produce a checking account listing in the format shown in Figure 3–1 (page 3.1). The output actually produced by this program is shown on the following page. Analyze the output to determine if it is correct. If it is in error, circle the incorrect statement(s) in the program and write corrections.

```
100 REM CHECKACT              NOVEMBER 19            SHELLY/CASHMAN
110                                                              REM
120 REM THIS PROGRAM PREPARES A LIST OF CHECKS WRITTEN DURING
130 REM THE MONTH. AFTER ALL CHECKS ARE PROCESSED, THE TOTAL
140 REM NUMBER OF CHECKS WRITTEN AND THE TOTAL AMOUNT OF THE
150 REM CHECKS ARE PRINTED.
160                                                              REM
170 REM VARIABLE NAMES:
180 REM    D$....DATE
190 REM    C.....CHECK NUMBER
200 REM    N$....NAME
210 REM    A.....AMOUNT
220 REM    T1....FINAL TOTAL - NUMBER OF CHECKS
230 REM    T2....FINAL TOTAL - AMOUNT OF CHECKS
240 REM    F1$...PRINT USING FORMAT FOR THE DETAIL LINE
250 REM    F2$...PRINT USING FORMAT FOR CHECK NUMBER TOTAL LINE
260 REM    F3$...PRINT USING FORMAT FOR CHECK AMOUNT TOTAL LINE
270                                                              REM
280 REM ***** DATA TO BE PROCESSED *****
290                                                              REM
300 DATA "SEPTEMBER  1", 501, "JIM'S ART", 85.60
310 DATA "SEPTEMBER  5", 502, "SEARS", 424.23
320 DATA "SEPTEMBER 14", 503, "NORDSTROM", 312.59
330 DATA "SEPTEMBER 22", 504, "BONDS", 67.92
340 DATA "SEPTEMBER 25", 505, "ED'S AUTO", 713.95
350 DATA "END", 999, "END OF FILE", 99.99
360                                                              REM
370 REM ***** INITIALIZATION OF VARIABLES *****
380                                                              REM
390 LET T1 = 0
400 LET T2 = 0
410 LET F1$ = "\            \    ###    \        \    ###.##"
420 LET F2$ = "TOTAL NUMBER OF CHECKS ###"
430 LET F3$ = "TOTAL AMOUNT OF CHECKS $$,###.##"
440                                                              REM
450 REM ***** PROCESSING *****
460                                                              REM
470 PRINT TAB(12) "CHECKING ACCOUNT"
480 PRINT " "
490 PRINT "    DATE        NO.      NAME      AMOUNT"
500 PRINT " "
```

```
510                                                          REM
520 READ D$, C, N$, A
530                                                          REM
540 IF N$ = "END OF FILE" THEN 610
550    LET T1 = T1 + 1
560    LET T2 = T2 + 1
570    PRINT USING F1$; D$, C, N$, A
580    READ D$, C, N$, A
590 GOTO 540
600                                                          REM
610 PRINT " "
620 PRINT USING F2$; T1
630 PRINT USING F3$; T2
640 END
```

Output

```
                    CHECKING ACCOUNT

        DATE          NO.      NAME        AMOUNT

    SEPTEMBER  1      501    JIM'S ART       85.60
    SEPTEMBER  5      502    SEARS          424.23
    SEPTEMBER 14      503    NORDSTROM      312.59
    SEPTEMBER 22      504    BONDS           67.92
    SEPTEMBER 25      505    ED'S AUTO      713.95

    TOTAL NUMBER OF CHECKS      5
    TOTAL AMOUNT OF CHECKS       $5.00
```

Chapter 3
PROGRAMMING ASSIGNMENT 1

A monthly budget listing of the expenses of an individual is to be prepared. A program should be designed and coded in BASIC to produce the required output.

Instructions

Input consists of records that contain a description of the item in the budget and the amount of the monthly expense. The input data is illustrated below.

Input

ITEM	EXPENSE AMOUNT
RENT	495.23
FOOD	120.75
VISA CARD	39.84
AUTOMOBILE	92.13

Output is a list of the monthly expenses. The format of the output is illustrated below. Report and column headings are to be printed. After all records have been processed, the total number of bills and the total monthly expenses are to be printed.

Output

```
                    MONTHLY BUDGET

                              EXPENSE
        ITEM                  AMOUNT

     RENT                     495.23
     FOOD                     120.75
     VISA CARD                 39.84
     AUTOMOBILE                92.13

     TOTAL BILLS    4
     TOTAL MONTHLY EXPENSES $747.95
```

Chapter 3
PROGRAMMING ASSIGNMENT 2

Instructions A report of the yardage gained by football players on a football team is to be prepared. A program should be designed and coded in BASIC to produce the report.

Input Input consists of records containing the name of the football player, his position, the number of times he carried the ball and the total yards he gained. The input data is illustrated below.

NAME	POSITION	TIMES CARRIED	YARDS GAINED
JIM HAYNES	QB	3	39
HANK WALLAMS	RB	38	231
IKE NEUMAN	RB	59	326
DEAM IMSKI	FB	19	64

Output Output is a list of the players containing their name, position, times they carried the ball, the yards gained, and the average yards gained per carry. The average yards gained per carry is calculated by dividing the yards gained by the times carried. After all records have been read and processed, the total number of players, the total yards gained, and the average yards per carry for all players are to be printed. The format of the output is illustrated below.

```
                    ATLANTA WARRIORS

                          TIMES        YARDS      AVERAGE YARDS
     NAME       POSITION  CARRIED       GAINED      PER CARRY

JIM HAYNES        QB         3           39          13.00
HANK WALLAMS      RB        38          231           6.08
IKE NEUMAN        RB        59          326           5.53
DEAM IMSKI        FB        19           64           3.37

TOTAL PLAYERS     4
TOTAL YARDS GAINED    660 YARDS
AVERAGE YARDS PER CARRY  5.55 YARDS
```

Chapter 3
PROGRAMMING ASSIGNMENT 3

A snowfall report for the water conservation commission is to be prepared. A **Instructions**
program should be designed and coded in BASIC to produce the report.

Input consists of records containing the amount of snowfall in inches for a six **Input**
hour period of time. The input data is illustrated below.

CITY	TIME	SNOW	TIME	SNOW	TIME	SNOW	TIME	SNOW	TIME	SNOW	TIME	SNOW
NEW YORK	1 AM	.6	2 AM	.35	3 AM	.89	4 AM	1.76	5 AM	.97	6 AM	.31
SYRACUSE	1 AM	.9	2 AM	1.65	3 AM	1.16	4 AM	.81	5 AM	.68	6 AM	.95

The output is a listing of the snowfall by city and time. For each city, the **Output**
snowfall at each hour is to be printed. In addition, for each city the total
snowfall should be printed. After all cities have been printed, the average
snowfall per city should be printed. The average snowfall is calculated by
adding the inches of snow for each city and dividing the total by the number of
cities. The format of the output is illustrated below.

```
                    SNOWFALL REPORT
        CITY     TIME   SNOWFALL   TIME    SNOWFALL

     NEW YORK  1 AM        .60     4 AM      1.76
               2 AM        .35     5 AM       .97
               3 AM        .89     6 AM       .31
     TOTAL SNOWFALL FOR NEW YORK: 4.88 IN.


     SYRACUSE  1 AM        .90     4 AM       .81
               2 AM       1.65     5 AM       .68
               3 AM       1.16     6 AM       .95
     TOTAL SNOWFALL FOR SYRACUSE: 6.15 IN.

     AVERAGE SNOWFALL PER CITY: 5.52 INCHES
```

Chapter 3
SUPPLEMENTARY PROGRAMMING ASSIGNMENTS

Instructions   The following programming assignments contain an explanation of the problem and list suggested test data. The student should design the format of the output.

Program 4   A report is to be prepared listing doctor names, patient names, and charges. Report and column headings should appear on the report. After all records have been processed, the total number of patients and total charges should be printed.

DOCTOR	PATIENT	CHARGES
JOHNSON	MURRAY	143.97
GOLDSTEIN	JUAREZ	56.70
NICHOLS	HALLERIN	45.00
HARRISON	TASS	321.60

Program 5   A report is to be prepared which summarizes the number of males and females enrolled in various classes in a school. The input data is illustrated below. Each line of the output should contain the class identification, the number of males, the number of females, and the total number of students in the class. Report and column headings should appear on the report. After all records have been processed, the total number of classes and the average number of students per class should be printed.

CLASS ID	MALES	FEMALES
DP 101	25	29
BUS 132	17	8
ART 7	12	10
BUS 276	9	14

Program 6   A report is to be prepared of the average monthly temperatures during January from cities across the United States. Temperature readings are taken once a week. The input data is shown below. The report should contain the city, the temperatures for each of the weeks, and the average temperature for the city during January. Report and column headings should appear on the report. After all records have been processed, the total number of cities analyzed should be printed.

CITY	WEEK 1	WEEK 2	WEEK 3	WEEK 4
CHICAGO	18.9	15.9	10.6	12.3
DALLAS	48.9	32.5	34.5	40.6
MIAMI	70.4	65.7	69.9	54.8
SEATTLE	44.8	33.7	42.5	39.8

A report of the scores of participants in a gymnastics meet is to be prepared. The input data is illustrated below. The report line should contain the gymnast's name and the average score. This average score is calculated by adding the three scores and dividing by 3. The report should contain report and column headings. After all records have been processed, the total number of gymnasts and the overall average score should be printed.   **Program 7**

GYMNAST	JUDGE 1 SCORE	JUDGE 2 SCORE	JUDGE 3 SCORE
JEAN HANSON	9.5	9.4	9.5
NANCY MILLER	8.9	9.1	9.3
JAMES MILBURN	8.6	8.9	8.8
WILLIAM ROWE	9.4	9.4	9.4

A mileage report for sales people is to be prepared. The input data is illustrated below. The report should contain the salesperson's name, the beginning mileage, the ending mileage, the total miles (ending mileage – beginning mileage), and the mileage allowance ($.20 x total mileage)). After all records have been processed, the total number of sales people, the total mileage for all people, and the total mileage allowance should be printed. The report should contain report and column headings.   **Program 8**

SALESPERSON'S NAME	BEGINNING MILEAGE	ENDING MILEAGE
HARRIET HILL	13505	13607
EUGENE JACKSON	26482	27101
HARVEY MUMM	32598	32690
JULIE SIMPSON	15444	16748

A computer time usage report is to be prepared. The input data is shown below. The report should contain the application identification, the description of the application, the number of seconds the computer run took, and the number of minutes the computer run took. After all records have been processed, the total number of applications run, the total number of minutes of processing, and the average number of minutes for each application should be printed. The report should contain report and column headings.   **Program 9**

DUE THURS

NO FLOWCHART

APPLICATION I.D.	DESCRIPTION	COMPUTER TIME (SECONDS)
C–015	C.A.I.	632
P–0097	PAYROLL	533
I–9	INVENTORY	325
AP–086	ACCOUNTS PAYABLE	128

CHAPTER FOUR

COMPARING

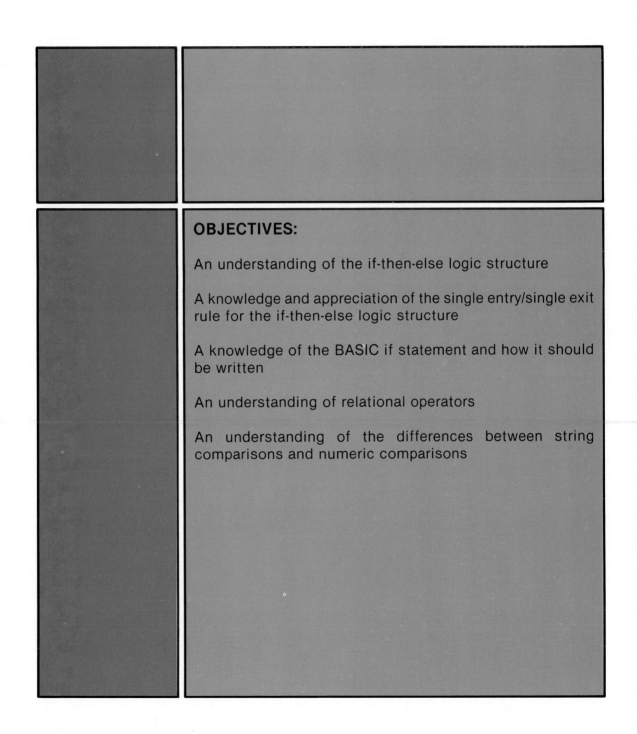

OBJECTIVES:

An understanding of the if-then-else logic structure

A knowledge and appreciation of the single entry/single exit rule for the if-then-else logic structure

A knowledge of the BASIC if statement and how it should be written

An understanding of relational operators

An understanding of the differences between string comparisons and numeric comparisons

CHAPTER FOUR   **COMPARING**

One of the more powerful features of any programming language is the ability to compare numbers or letters of the alphabet and perform alternative operations based upon the results of the comparison. When programming in the BASIC language, comparing is accomplished through the use of the if statement.

To illustrate comparing operations, a sample program in this chapter is designed and coded to prepare a report of the members of a health club listing their membership dues. The report is illustrated below.

```
                    HEALTH CLUB
                 MEMBERSHIP DUES

       NAME          AGE  MONTHS      DUES

    SID BARNES        16     3        59.85
    LYNN DAVIES       18     8       159.60
    KEVIN GALLEY      19    48     1,197.60
    KIM KALLEN        21    36       898.20
    LARRY MOONEY      32     3        74.85

    TOTAL - NEW MEMBERS    5
    TOTAL - MEMBERSHIP DUES $2,390.10
```

The report contains the names of the new members of the club, their age, the number of months for which they have enrolled, and their total dues. Total dues are calculated as follows: If a person is over 18 years of age, membership dues are $24.95 per month. If a person is 18 years of age or younger, the dues are $19.95 per month.

Figure 4-1 The report contains the name, age, months, and dues of people joining a health club.

To produce the report, the new member's age must be compared to the value 18. If the age is 18 or less, the membership dues are calculated by multiplying the number of months for which the person is enrolled by $19.95. If the age is greater than 18, the membership dues are calculated by multiplying the number of months for which the individual has enrolled by $24.95. After all of the records have been processed, the total number of new members and the total membership dues are to be printed.

The program required to produce this report is explained in this chapter.

A standardized logic structure is used for any comparing operation. This logic structure is commonly called the if-then-else structure, or the selection structure. A generalized flowchart of this logic structure and an example of its use is illustrated in Figure 4–2.

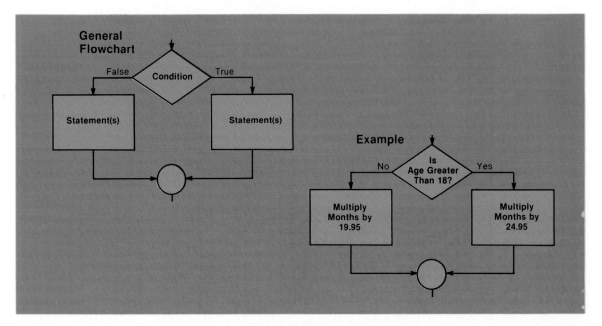

Figure 4-2 The if-then-else logic structure consists of the condition being tested, the statements which are executed when the condition is true, and the statements which are executed when the condition is false.

The flowchart on the left illustrates the general format of the if-then-else logic structure. This flowchart specifies that a condition is to be tested (the diamond-shaped decision symbol). If the condition is true, one statement or series of statements will be executed. If the condition being tested is false, a different statement or series of statements will be executed.

To illustrate this, in the example on the right, the condition begin tested is, "Is the age greater than 18?" If the age is greater than 18, then the leg to the right is taken, and the number of months is multiplied by the value 24.95. If the age is not greater than 18 (that is, the age is less than or equal to 18), the number of months is multiplied by 19.95.

This statement is commonly referred to as the if-then-else structure because it can be read, "IF the condition is true THEN do one set of instructions ELSE do another set of instructions." In the example on the right in Figure 4–2, if the age is greater than 18 then the months are multiplied by 24.95 else the months are multiplied by 19.95.

An important characteristic of the if-then-else logic structure is that there is a single entry point into the logic structure and a single exit point from the logic structure. The entry into the logic structure must be through the decision that is the first statement of the structure. Therefore, the only time any of the statements within the logic structure will be executed is after the condition has been tested at the entry point of the structure. The flowchart illustrated in Figure 4–3 represents poor programming because it violates the single entry rule.

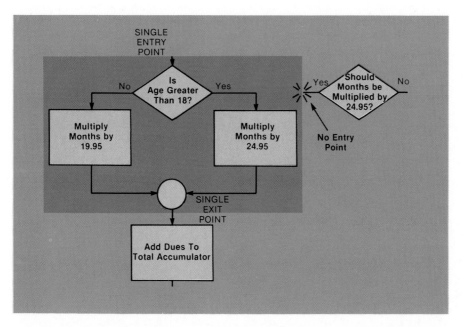

SINGLE
ENTRY
POINT

Is Age Greater Than 18?   No / Yes

Should Months be Multiplied by 24.95?   Yes / No

Multiply Months by 19.95

Multiply Months by 24.95

No Entry Point

SINGLE EXIT POINT

Add Dues To Total Accumulator

Figure 4-3 The if-then-else logic structure must have a single entry point and a single exit point. None of the statements within the structure can be executed unless the decision which marks the entry point has been executed first.

In the example in Figure 4–3, the if-then-else structure explained for Figure 4–2 is again illustrated. The entry point to the structure is the decision which tests if the age is greater than 18. The statements within the if-then-else structure should be executed only after this decision has been made because this is the single entry point to the structure.

In Figure 4–3, however, an attempt is made to have a second entry point into the if-then-else structure by the decision symbol outside the logic structure. If this were allowed, the statement which multiplies the months by 24.95 could be reached from any point in the program. Allowing this violates the basic rule of one entry point/one exit point in the if-then-else structure. Therefore, in a well-designed program, no statement within the structure will be executed unless the decision which marks the single entry point into the structure has been executed first.

The if-then-else structure also is required to have a single exit point. In the example in Figure 4–3, the point of exit is noted by the circle in the flowchart. The statement which adds the dues to the total accumulator will ALWAYS be the next statement executed after the statements within the if-then-else structure have been executed. Control should not be passed from any statement within the control structure to anywhere in the program except to the single exit point. If this rule is violated, it leads to programs which are virtually impossible to read and understand.

An understanding of the if-then-else logic structure and the single entry/single exit rule is important. All well-written programs use this structure and rule when alternative processing is to occur based upon a condition in the program.

**Forms of the
if-then-else
structure**

The if-then-else logic structure can take several forms within the rules just presented. For example, an if-then-else structure can be developed in which no processing will occur when the condition is true; or, on the other hand, no processing when the condition is false. These two variations are illustrated below.

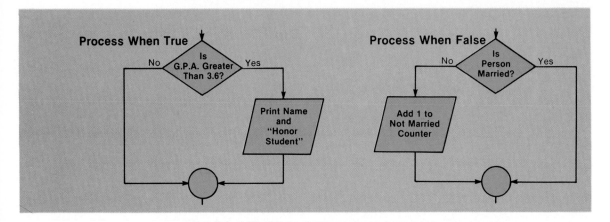

Figure 4-4 Both true and false conditions do not require statements.

In the example on the left in Figure 4-4, if the grade point average (G.P.A.) is greater than 3.6, the student's name and the constant "Honor Student" are to be printed. If the G.P.A. is not greater than 3.6, no processing will occur based on that fact. In this instance, there is processing to occur if the condition tested is true, but none if the condition is false.

In the example on the right, if a person is married, no processing is to take place. If, however, the person is not married, the value 1 is added to the not married counter. In this case, processing is to occur when the condition is false, but nothing is done if the condition is true.

It is allowable to have multiple statements following the decision statement. In addition, there need not be the same number of statements for the true processing as there are for the false processing (Figure 4-5).

Figure 4-5 Multiple statements can be executed when the condition is true or when the condition is false.

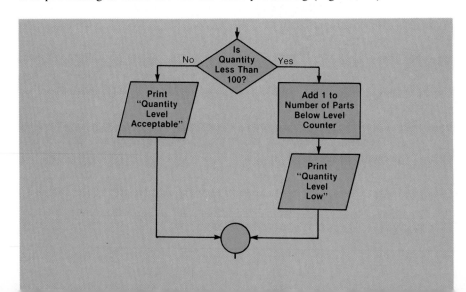

The use of proper logic structures is essential to a well-designed program. The following example illustrates a segment of a flowchart in which no consideration is given to the proper design of the program. Even in this very simplified example, it becomes obvious that a poorly designed program is very difficult to understand.

Invalid logic structures

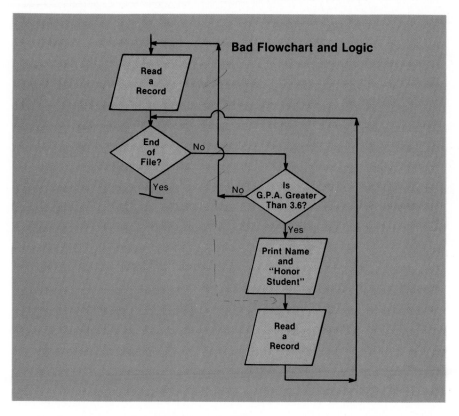

Bad Flowchart and Logic

Figure 4-6 The poor structure of this flowchart makes it very difficult to read because it violates the if-then-else logic structure rules. Logic which does not follow these rules should never be developed.

In the segment of the flowchart in Figure 4-6, no consideration was given to designing the program using the proper logic structure for comparing. The rule of a single entry is followed for the decision which determines if the G.P.A. is greater than 3.6, but there are multiple exits (one to the read statement and one to the end of file decision). In addition, flowlines cross one another, and it is difficult to read the logic from the top of the flowchart to the bottom of the flowchart.

Although the logic illustrated would produce the correct results, such poor program design results in programs that are very difficult to understand. In larger programs, with hundreds or even thousands of statements, it becomes nearly impossible to trace the original logic if standardized logic structures are not used. The if-then-else structure and its accompanying rules should always be used when comparing and performing alternative operations based upon the results of the comparison.

If statement   To perform comparing operations in a program, the if statement is used. The general format of the if statement, the logic which it implements, and an example of the if statement are illustrated in Figure 4–7.

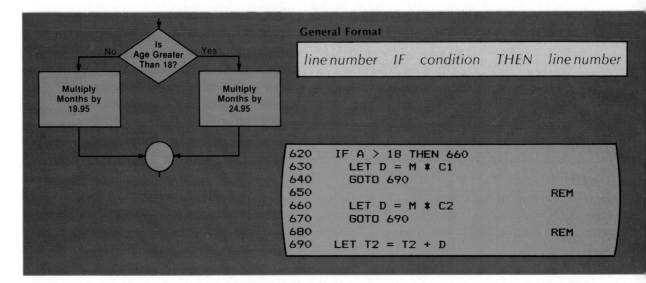

Figure 4-7 The if statement implements the if-then-else logic structure. The spacing and indentation illustrated here should always be followed so the statement is easy to read. The symbol **>** on line 620 means greater than.

In the if statement on line 620, the value in the field identified by the variable name A is compared to the value 18. The if statement corresponds to the decision symbol in the flowchart. If the value in A is greater than 18, the condition tested is considered true, and the statement at the line number following the word THEN will be given control. Therefore, in the example, if the value in A is greater than 18, control will be passed to the let statement on line 660.

If the value in A is not greater than 18, the statement immediately following the if statement is given control. Thus, if the value in A is not greater than 18, the let statement on line 630 will be executed.

The goto statements on lines 640 and 670 both transfer control to the statement on line 690. This means that regardless of whether the condition being tested is true or false, the statement on line 690 will be the statement executed after the processing within the logic structure is completed. This accomplishes the single exit requirement of the if-then-else structure.

The goto statement on line 670 is not required because, without it, control would pass from statement 660 to statement 690. It should be included, however, to generate an explicit transfer of control to the single exit point from the if-then-else logic structure.

Relational operators   In BASIC, six types of comparing operations can be performed. These comparing operations are performed through the use of relational operators.

Relational operators are symbols used within an if statement to compare numeric or string variables and constants. The chart below summarizes these symbols, their meaning, and illustrates how they might be used within an if statement.

RELATIONAL OPERATOR	INTERPRETATION	EXAMPLE
=	equal to	300 IF A = A3 THEN 350
<	less than	330 IF C < 21 THEN 490
>	greater than	370 IF M$ > "A" THEN 410
<=	less than or equal to	650 IF L <= 3 THEN 720
>=	greater than or equal to	690 IF X >= 81 THEN 800
<>	not equal to	750 IF A$ <> B$ THEN 920

The values placed on either side of the relational operator in an if statement can be numeric or string variables and constants. In addition, they can be arithmetic expressions. The following examples illustrate a variety of if statements with different types of values being compared.

Values which can be compared

Example 1: Numeric variable compared to numeric literal.

```
230 IF A1 > 255 THEN 270
```

Example 2: Numeric variable compared to arithmetic expression.

```
150 IF C1 <= (4 * S) + (4 * T) THEN 220
```

Example 3: Arithmetic expression compared to arithmetic expression.

```
270 IF 3.14 * (R1↑2) = 3.14 * (R2↑2) THEN 300
```

Example 4: String variable compared to string constant.

```
430 IF Q$ <> "CODE A" THEN 560
```

Example 5: String variable compared to string variable.

```
490 IF L$ >= P$ THEN 540
```

Comparing numeric variables and constants

Numeric data must always be compared to numeric data and string data must always be compared to string data. The manner in which they are compared is different because of the nature of the data.

A numeric comparison is one in which numeric constants or fields referenced by numeric variable names are compared. A numeric comparison is based upon the algebraic values of the numbers being compared. This means that not only the value of the number but also the sign of the number being compared is considered. In the example below, two temperature readings are compared. One reading represents 10 degrees above zero (+ 10) while the other represents 15 degrees below zero (–15).

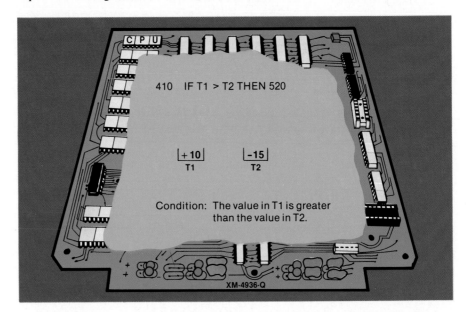

Figure 4-9 When numeric values are compared, the comparison is based on the algebraic value of the numbers. Therefore, positive numbers are greater than negative numbers. Here, positive 10 is greater than negative 15.

When the value stored in the area identified by the variable T1 (+ 10) is compared to the value in the area identified by the variable T2 (–15), a numeric comparison is taking place because the variable names are both numeric. Therefore, the signs of the numbers are considered in the comparison. As a result, the value in T1 is considered greater than the value in T2 because a positive number is always greater than a negative number. Since the value in T1 is greater than the value in T2, the statement at line number 520 will be the next statement to be executed in the program.

When numeric values with digits to the right of the decimal point are compared, there may be occasions when one value has more characters to the right of the decimal point than another value. For example, the value 23.879 could be compared to the value 23.8786. In deciding which value is greater, the BASIC interpreter will internally insert zeros to the right of the decimal point in the number with fewer digits until each number has the same number of digits to the right of the decimal point. The numbers are then compared.

Therefore, in the example the interpreter would insert a zero in the value 23.879, giving the equivalent number 23.8790. This number is then compared to the value 23.8786. In the comparison, 23.8790 is greater than 23.8786 even though it has fewer digits to the right of the decimal point.

Comparing string values

When string variables or constants are compared, the comparison takes place from left to right a character at a time. As soon as a character in one field is less than a character in another field, the comparison terminates, and the field with the lower value is considered less than the other field.

The determination of which characters are less than others is based upon the code used to store data in main computer storage. On many computer systems, the ASCII code (American Standard Code for Information Interchange) is used. The characters in the ASCII code and their relative values (called the collating sequence) are shown below.

(blank)	Low	4	Low	H	Low
!		5		I	
"		6		J	
#		7		K	
$		8		L	
%		9		M	
&		:		N	
'		;		O	
(		<		P	
)		=		Q	
*		>		R	
+		?		S	
,		@		T	
-		A		U	
.		B		V	
/		C		W	
0		D		X	
1		E		Y	
2		F		Z	
3	High	G	High	_	High

Figure 4-10 The ASCII code is commonly used to represent characters on computer systems. The collating sequence of ASCII shown here is important because when string values are compared, it is this sequence which determines that one value is greater than another value.

From the table above, note that some special characters are considered less than the numbers and some are greater than the numbers. The numbers are less than the letters of the alphabet. Note also that the blank is considered less than all other characters illustrated in Figure 4-10.

To illustrate string comparing, in the following example, two names which are stored in fields identified by string variables are compared.

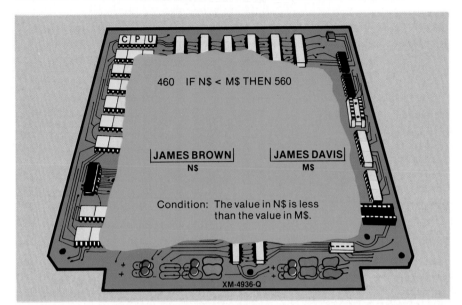

Figure 4-11 A string comparison proceeds from the leftmost character to the right, one character at a time, until an inequality occurs. Here, the first inequality is when the B in BROWN is compared to the D in DAVIS. Since the B is less than the D, the field JAMES BROWN is considered less than JAMES DAVIS.

In the example, the name JAMES BROWN, stored in the field identified by the variable name N$, is compared to the name JAMES DAVIS, stored in the field identified by the variable name M$. The comparison proceeds left to right, one character at a time. Thus, the first characters compared are the J's in the two names. Since these characters are equal, the next characters to the right, the A's in the two names, are compared. Because these characters are equal, the next characters to the right are compared. This process continues until an unequal condition occurs. As can be seen, this will occur when the first characters of the last names (B in Brown and D in Davis) are compared.

When an unequal condition occurs, the field with the lower character in the collating sequence is considered the lower field. In this example, the B is less than the D (see Figure 4-10). Therefore, the name JAMES BROWN is considered less than the name JAMES DAVIS, and statement 560 is the next statement to be executed.

When string fields or constants are compared, they will not always contain the same number of characters. When the number of characters in the two fields being compared is different, the field with the smaller number of characters is considered less than the field with more characters when all of the characters in the shorter field are equal to the first characters in the longer field (Figure 4-12).

When the value in N$ (BOB MAN) is compared to the value in M$ (BOB MANLEY), the first seven characters are equal. When this occurs, the shorter field is considered less than the longer field. Therefore, the value in N$ is considered less than the value in M$, and the next statement to be executed is the statement at line 560.

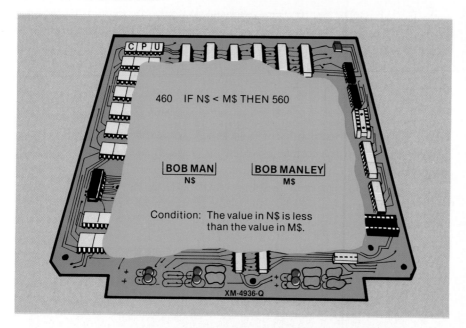

Figure 4-12 When all of the characters in a shorter field are equal to the left-most characters in a longer field, the shorter field is considered less than the longer field.

When numbers in a string variable field or constant are compared, only their relative position within the collating sequence is considered. Numbers are considered less than letters of the alphabet. The example in Figure 4-13 illustrates an application in which a part number that contains all numbers is compared to a part number which begins with a letter of the alphabet.

Comparing numeric values in strings

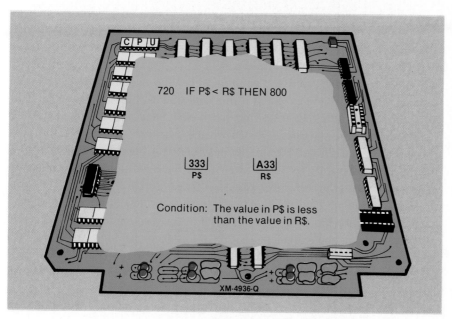

Figure 4-13 In the ASCII collating sequence, numbers are less than letters of the alphabet.

In Figure 4–13, a string comparison takes place because the fields being compared are string fields. Therefore, the comparison begins with the first character in each field. Since the first character in P$ (3) is lower in the collating sequence than the first character in R$ (A), the data in the P$ field is considered less than the data in the R$ field. Thus, the next instruction to be executed is the one at line 800.

Writing the if statement

In the example in Figure 4–7, the if statement was explained. It is important, however, to review the format in which the if statement is written. Programs which contain clearly written if statements are generally easy to read and understand while programs without clearly written if statements can be impossible to read and understand. The if statement below illustrates the format which should be used for an if statement.

Figure 4-14 The indentation and spacing standards for the if statement illustrated here should always be followed. They produce a program which is easy to read and understand.

```
620    IF A > 18 THEN 660
630        LET D = M * C1        Executed if not true
640        GOTO 690
650                                          REM
660        LET D = M * C2        Executed if true
670        GOTO 690
680                                          REM
690    LET T2 = T2 + D    Single-exit point
```

Note that all statements which are to be executed based upon the condition tested by the if statement (is the value in A greater than 18) are indented two vertical columns from the column where the if statement begins. The statements which will be executed if the condition is not true (lines 630 – 640) are specified immediately following the if statement. These statements are separated from the statements which will be executed when the condition is true (lines 660 – 670) by a blank line on line 650. A blank line should always separate the statements to be executed when the condition is false from the statements executed when the condition is true.

The statement on line 690 will be executed regardless of the result of the if statement. It represents the single exit point of the if statement. This statement is separated from the statements within the if-then-else logic structure by a blank line (line 680). In addition, the statement on line 690 begins in the same vertical column as the if statement, indicating its execution is not dependent upon the results of the if statement.

All if statements implementing the if-then-else logic structure should be written in the manner shown in Figure 4–14.

Some BASIC interpreters have implemented the actual if-then-else statement. **If-then-else**
An example of this statement, together with the flowchart and the general **statement**
format is shown in Figure 4–15.

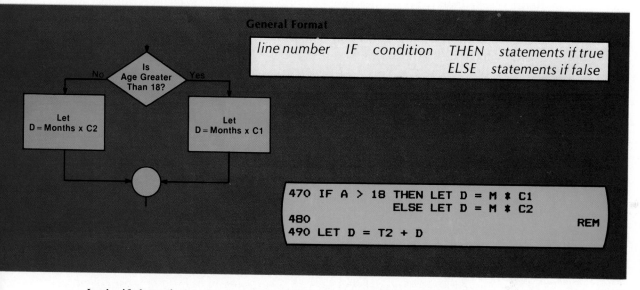

In the if-then-else statement, the condition is tested in the same manner as
the if statement. The statement(s) following the word THEN will be executed
when the condition is true. The statement(s) following the word ELSE will be
executed when the condition is false. Thus, in the example in Figure 4–15, if
the value in A is greater than 18, the value in M will be multiplied by the value
in C1. If the value in A is not greater than 18, the value in M will be multiplied
by the value in C2.

Regardless of the statements executed within the if-then-else statement,
the next statement executed is on line 490. Therefore, a single exit exists for the
if-then-else statement.

The entire if-then-else statement comprises a single statement with one
line number. Thus, when entering the statement on a computer system, the
ENTER or RETURN key should be used only for the last line. The cursor
control should be used to allow the statement to be placed on multiple lines.

Figure 4–15 The if-then-else statement can directly implement the if-then-else logic structure. Because most BASIC interpreters limit the number of characters in any statement to 255 characters including the spaces, care must be taken when writing the if-then-else statement not to exceed this maximum.

The sample program in this chapter illustrates the design and coding of a pro- **SAMPLE**
gram to prepare a health club membership report. If the individual joining the **PROGRAM**
health club is above 18 years of age, membership dues are calculated by
multiplying the months enrolled by $24.95. If the age of the new member is 18

or less, dues are calculated by multiplying the months enrolled by 19.95. After all records have been processed, the total number of new members and the total membership dues are printed. The sample report is shown in Figure 4–1 on page 4.1.

Input   The input consists of a series of records for the new members of the health club. Each record contains the name of the new member, the age of the new member, and the number of months the member enrolled. The format of the input is illustrated below.

Figure 4-16 The input consists of the name, age, and months enrolled of the new health club members.

NAME	AGE	MONTHS ENROLLED
SID BARNES	16	3
LYNN DAVIES	18	8
KEVIN GALLEY	19	48
KIM KALLEN	21	36
LARRY MOONEY	32	3

Program design   The program design begins by specifying the tasks which must be accomplished in the program. These are listed below.

Program Tasks

1. Read input records.
2. Determine membership dues.
3. Accumulate final totals.
4. Print report lines.
5. Print final totals.

These tasks must be carefully designated to reflect the requirements of the program. After they are defined, the flowchart to implement them must be developed.

Flowchart   The flowchart for the sample program is shown in Figure 4–17. After the variables are initialized and the heading for the report printed, a record is read. The main loop of the program is then entered. The looping will continue until end of file is reached.

Within the loop, the total members counter is incremented by 1, and then the if-then-else logic structure is entered to determine the total dues. After the dues are calculated, they are added to the final total accumulator and a line is

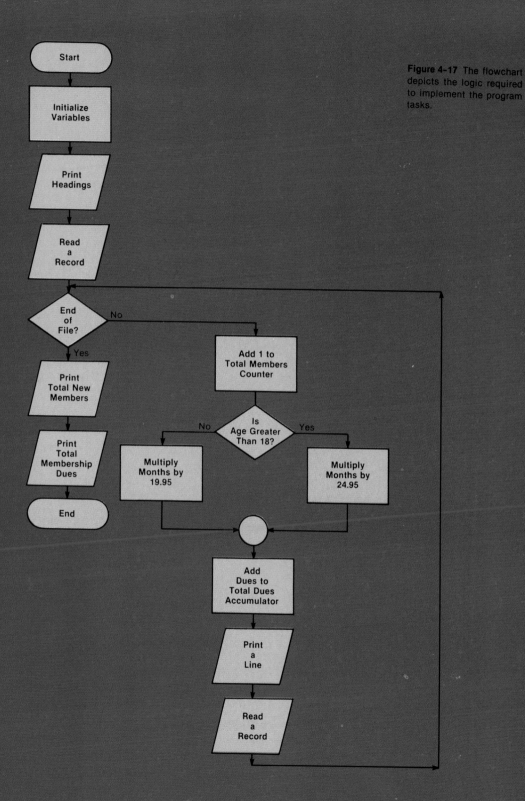

Figure 4-17 The flowchart depicts the logic required to implement the program tasks.

printed. A record is then read, and the looping continues until there are no more records to process. At that point, the loop is terminated, the total number of members and total dues amount are printed, and the program is ended.

The logic expressed in the program flowchart should be well-understood prior to examining the program code, which is explained in the following paragraphs.

The BASIC program   The code which documents the program and defines the data to be processed is illustrated below.

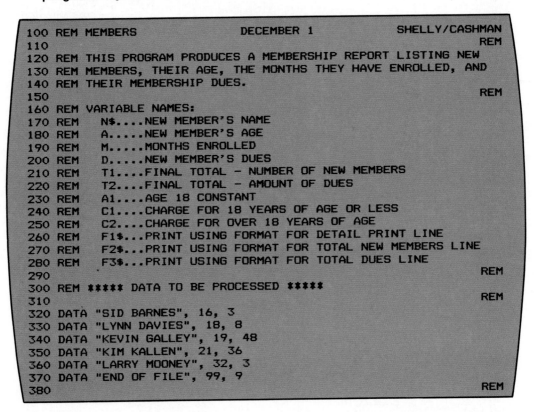

```
100 REM MEMBERS                    DECEMBER 1              SHELLY/CASHMAN
110                                                                  REM
120 REM THIS PROGRAM PRODUCES A MEMBERSHIP REPORT LISTING NEW
130 REM MEMBERS, THEIR AGE, THE MONTHS THEY HAVE ENROLLED, AND
140 REM THEIR MEMBERSHIP DUES.
150                                                                  REM
160 REM VARIABLE NAMES:
170 REM     N$....NEW MEMBER'S NAME
180 REM     A.....NEW MEMBER'S AGE
190 REM     M.....MONTHS ENROLLED
200 REM     D.....NEW MEMBER'S DUES
210 REM     T1....FINAL TOTAL - NUMBER OF NEW MEMBERS
220 REM     T2....FINAL TOTAL - AMOUNT OF DUES
230 REM     A1....AGE 18 CONSTANT
240 REM     C1....CHARGE FOR 18 YEARS OF AGE OR LESS
250 REM     C2....CHARGE FOR OVER 18 YEARS OF AGE
260 REM     F1$...PRINT USING FORMAT FOR DETAIL PRINT LINE
270 REM     F2$...PRINT USING FORMAT FOR TOTAL NEW MEMBERS LINE
280 REM     F3$...PRINT USING FORMAT FOR TOTAL DUES LINE
290                                                                  REM
300 REM ***** DATA TO BE PROCESSED *****
310                                                                  REM
320 DATA "SID BARNES", 16, 3
330 DATA "LYNN DAVIES", 18, 8
340 DATA "KEVIN GALLEY", 19, 48
350 DATA "KIM KALLEN", 21, 36
360 DATA "LARRY MOONEY", 32, 3
370 DATA "END OF FILE", 99, 9
380                                                                  REM
```

Figure 4-18 Clear documentation is the mark of any well-written program. The data statements define the data to be processed by the program.

As with previous programs, the documentation at the beginning of the program specifies what the program is to accomplish and also identifies the variable names used in the program. Documenting the variable names is a critical part of the program coding.

The data to be processed is defined using the data statement. Each data statement represents a single input record. The name is a string constant, so it is contained within quotes. The age and months enrolled are numeric constants, so they are not within quotes.

The code to initialize the variables in the program and print the headings is shown in Figure 4-19.

Variable initialization and headings

```
390 REM ***** INITIALIZATION OF VARIABLES *****
400                                                    REM
410 LET A1 = 18
420 LET C1 = 19.95
430 LET C2 = 24.95
440 LET T1 = 0
450 LET T2 = 0
460 LET F1$ = "\             \    ##      ##      #,###.##"
470 LET F2$ = "TOTAL - NEW MEMBERS ###"
480 LET F3$ = "TOTAL - MEMBERSHIP DUES $$,###.##"
490                                                    REM
500 REM ***** PROCESSING *****
510                                                    REM
520 PRINT TAB(13) "HEALTH CLUB"
530 PRINT TAB(11) "MEMBERSHIP DUES"
540 PRINT " "
550 PRINT "    NAME        AGE  MONTHS      DUES"
560 PRINT " "
570                                                    REM
```

Figure 4-19 Placing numeric values into fields identified by variable names and using the variable names in subsequent statements is a good programming practice.

The entries on lines 410 - 430 are used to assign constants which are required within the program to fields identified by variable names. The age to be compared (18) is placed in the field A1. The membership dues rates are placed in C1 and C2. It is good programming practice to use this technique rather than specifying the actual numeric values in the statements where they are required within the program because it greatly facilitates program maintenance.

Maintenance refers to the process of making changes to the program at some future date. For example, if the age requirement is changed from 18 to 21, the statement on line 410 could easily be changed to read LET A1 = 21 rather than searching through the entire program to determine where the value 18 should be changed to the value 21.

The total accumulators (T1 and T2) are initialized to zero by the statements on lines 440 - 450. The print using formats are placed in F1$, F2$, and F3$ by the statements on lines 460 - 480. The initialization is then completed.

The headings are printed on the report by the statements on lines 520 - 560.

Main processing   The main processing in the program is shown in Figure 4–20.

```
580 READ N$, A, M
590                                            REM
600 IF N$ = "END OF FILE" THEN 740
610    LET T1 = T1 + 1
620    IF A > A1 THEN 660
630       LET D = M * C1
640       GOTO 690
650                                            REM
660       LET D = M * C2
670       GOTO 690
680                                            REM
690    LET T2 = T2 + D
700    PRINT USING F1$; N$, A, M, D
710    READ N$, A, M
720 GOTO 600
730                                            REM
740 PRINT " "
750 PRINT USING F2$; T1
760 PRINT USING F3$; T2
770 END
```

Figure 4-20 Indentation and physical layout of the program code are important when reading the program. All programs should be written using the techniques shown in this program.

The read statement on line 580 reads the first set of data from the data statement and places the data in the fields identified as N$ (name), A (age), and M (months). The if statement on line 600 is the entry point to the loop which will process the data. If end of file has been reached, the statement at line 740 will be given control. Otherwise, the statement on line 610 will increment the total members counter by 1.

The statement on line 620 implements the if-then-else logic structure to determine what the dues should be. If the age is greater than 18, the statement at line 660 is given control, where the months (M) are multiplied by the value in C2 (see Figure 4–19) and the result is stored in D. Control is then passed to statement 690, where the dues amount is added to the final total accumulator (T2), and a line is printed on the report. Another record is then read, and control is passed to the start of the loop at statement 600.

If the age is not greater than 18, the statement on line 630 will multiply the number of months by the value in C1 and store the result in D. Control is then passed to the statement at line 690 where processing is the same as when the age is greater than 18.

Once again, note the format of the if statement and the statements that are executed in the if-then-else logic structure (statements 620 – 670). An if statement should always be written as illustrated in this program.

After all of the records have been processed, the end of file record will be read, and the if statement at the start of the loop at line 600 will transfer control to statement 740. There, a blank line is printed, and then the final totals of the number of new members and the membership dues are printed. The program is then terminated.

The complete listing for the sample program is illustrated below and on the following page.   **Sample program**

```
100 REM MEMBERS                DECEMBER 1              SHELLY/CASHMAN
110                                                              REM
120 REM THIS PROGRAM PRODUCES A MEMBERSHIP REPORT LISTING NEW
130 REM MEMBERS, THEIR AGE, THE MONTHS THEY HAVE ENROLLED, AND
140 REM THEIR MEMBERSHIP DUES.
150                                                              REM
160 REM VARIABLE NAMES:
170 REM    N$....NEW MEMBER'S NAME
180 REM    A.....NEW MEMBER'S AGE
190 REM    M.....MONTHS ENROLLED
200 REM    D.....NEW MEMBER'S DUES
210 REM    T1....FINAL TOTAL - NUMBER OF NEW MEMBERS
220 REM    T2....FINAL TOTAL - AMOUNT OF DUES
230 REM    A1....AGE 18 CONSTANT
240 REM    C1....CHARGE FOR 18 YEARS OF AGE OR LESS
250 REM    C2....CHARGE FOR OVER 18 YEARS OF AGE
260 REM    F1$...PRINT USING FORMAT FOR DETAIL PRINT LINE
270 REM    F2$...PRINT USING FORMAT FOR TOTAL NEW MEMBERS LINE
280 REM    F3$...PRINT USING FORMAT FOR TOTAL DUES LINE
290                                                              REM
300 REM ***** DATA TO BE PROCESSED *****
310                                                              REM
320 DATA "SID BARNES", 16, 3
330 DATA "LYNN DAVIES", 18, 8
340 DATA "KEVIN GALLEY", 19, 48
350 DATA "KIM KALLEN", 21, 36
360 DATA "LARRY MOONEY", 32, 3
370 DATA "END OF FILE", 99, 9
380                                                              REM
390 REM ***** INITIALIZATION OF VARIABLES *****
400                                                              REM
410 LET A1 = 18
420 LET C1 = 19.95
430 LET C2 = 24.95
440 LET T1 = 0
450 LET T2 = 0
460 LET F1$ = "\             \      ##      ##      #,###.##"
470 LET F2$ = "TOTAL - NEW MEMBERS ###"
480 LET F3$ = "TOTAL - MEMBERSHIP DUES $$,###.##"
490                                                              REM
500 REM ***** PROCESSING *****
510                                                              REM
520 PRINT TAB(13) "HEALTH CLUB"
530 PRINT TAB(11) "MEMBERSHIP DUES"
540 PRINT " "
550 PRINT "    NAME        AGE   MONTHS        DUES"
560 PRINT " "
570                                                              REM
```

Figure 4-21 Sample Program (Part 1 of 2)

```
580 READ N$, A, M
590                                                                    REM
600 IF N$ = "END OF FILE" THEN 740
610   LET T1 = T1 + 1
620   IF A > A1 THEN 660
630     LET D = M * C1
640     GOTO 690
650                                                                    REM
660     LET D = M * C2
670     GOTO 690
680                                                                    REM
690   LET T2 = T2 + D
700   PRINT USING F1$; N$, A, M, D
710   READ N$, A, M
720 GOTO 600
730                                                                    REM
740 PRINT " "
750 PRINT USING F2$; T1
760 PRINT USING F3$; T2
770 END
```

Figure 4-22 Sample program (Part 2 of 2)

Output

```
                    HEALTH CLUB
                 MEMBERSHIP DUES

         NAME         AGE  MONTHS      DUES

      SID BARNES       16     3        59.85
      LYNN DAVIES      18     8       159.60
      KEVIN GALLEY     19    48     1,197.60
      KIM KALLEN       21    36       898.20
      LARRY MOONEY     32     3        74.85

      TOTAL - NEW MEMBERS      5
      TOTAL - MEMBERSHIP DUES $2,390.10
```

Figure 4-23 Program Output

The following points have been discussed and explained in this chapter.   **SUMMARY**

1. One of the more powerful features of any programming language is the ability to compare numbers or letters of the alphabet and perform alternative operations based upon the results of the comparison.

2. A standardized logic structure called the if-then-else structure is used for any comparing operation.

3. In the if-then-else logic structure, a diamond-shaped flowchart symbol indicates the condition to be tested. If the condition is true, one leg of the decision symbol is given control. If the condition is false, the other leg of the decision symbol is given control.

4. There is a single entry point and a single exit point for the if-then-else logic structure.

5. The entry into the if-then-else logic structure is the decision which tests the condition.

6. The only time any of the statements within the if-then-else logic structure will be executed is after the condition has been tested at the entry point of the structure.

7. Control should not be passed from any statement within the if-then-else logic structure to anywhere in the program except to the single exit point.

8. An if-then-else structure can be developed which has no processing to occur when the condition being tested is true; or no processing when the condition is false.

9. Multiple statements can follow the decision symbol for either the true leg or the false leg, or both.

10. The use of proper logic structures is essential to a well-designed program.

11. To perform comparing operations in a program, the if statement is used.

12. The if statement corresponds to a decision symbol in a flowchart.

13. The word IF in an if statement is followed by a condition. If the condition is true, the statement at the line number following the word THEN is given control. If the condition is false, the next statement in the program is given control.

14. Although not required by the BASIC language, a goto statement which passes control to the common exit point should be included after both the true and the false processing in an if-then-else logic structure.

15. Comparing operations are performed through the use of relational operators.

16. Relational operators are symbols used within an if statement to compare numeric or string variables and constants.

17. The symbols are: $=$ (equal); $<$ (less than); $>$ (greater than); $< =$ (less than or equal to); $> =$ greater than or equal to); $< >$ (not equal).

18. Five types of comparisons are: numeric variable to numeric literal; numeric variable to arithmetic expression; arithmetic expression to arithmetic expression; string variable to string constant; string variable to string variable.

19. A numeric comparison is one where numeric constants or fields referenced by numeric variable names are compared.

20. A numeric comparison is based upon the algebraic values of the numbers being compared.

21. When string variables or constants are compared, the comparison takes place left to right one character at a time based upon the collating sequence of the code used on the computer system.

22. The ASCII code (American Standard Code for Information Interchange) is used on many computer systems.

23. In the ASCII code, numbers are considered less than letters of the alphabet.

24. In a string comparison, when an unequal condition occurs between two characters in the strings, the field with the lower character in the collating sequence is considered the lower field.

25. When a string comparison takes place and one field contains a smaller number of characters than another field, the field with the smaller number of characters is considered less than the field with more characters when all of the characters in the shorter field are equal to the first characters in the longer field.

26. When implementing the if-then-else logic structure, all statements which are to be executed based upon the condition tested by the if statement are indented two vertical columns from the column where the if statement begins.

27. A blank line should always separate the statements which are executed when a condition is false from the statements which are executed when the condition is true.

28. A blank line should always separate the statements executed as a result of a condition being true or not true from those that follow the if-then-else logic structure.

29. Some BASIC interpreters have implemented the if-then-else statement. The condition is tested following the word IF. If the condition is true, the statements following the word THEN are executed. If the condition is false, the statements following the word ELSE are executed.

30. Program maintenance is the process of making changes to a program at some future date after the program is originally written.

31. For program maintenance purposes, it is generally a good practice to place program constants in fields identified by variable names so that if the values must be changed, they can be changed at only one place in the program.

1. Standardized logic structures are usually too simple to use (T or F).
2. The if-then-else logic structure is used to implement: a) Looping; b) Comparing; c) Programming; d) Structuring.
3. In an if-then-else logic structure, there is a single _____ and a single _____.
4. The only time any statement in the if-then-else logic structure will be executed is after the condition has been tested at the entry point of the structure (T or F).
5. Should the if-then-else logic structure always be used? Why?
6. In an if statement, the line number following the word THEN is: a) The line number of the last statement in the if-then-else logic structure; b) Where control is passed if the condition is false; c) Where control is passed if the condition is true; d) Only required if the condition tested is false.
7. Match the following relational operators with their use:

   Symbol = matches _____   a. Not equal
   Symbol < > matches _____   b. Less than
   Symbol < = matches _____   c. Less than or equal to
   Symbol > = matches _____   d. Equal
   Symbol > matches _____   e. Greater than or equal to
   Symbol < matches _____   f. Greater than

8. Which of the following is an invalid comparison: a) Numeric variable to numeric variable; b) String variable to string variable; c) Arithmetic expression to arithmetic expression; d) String variable to numeric variable.
9. When numeric fields are compared, the sign of the number has no meaning (T or F).
10. What is ASCII? What is its relevance to comparing?
11. Which of the following is incorrect: a) @ < Y; b) A > 6; c) % > O; d) 9 > 1.
12. A field with the value BASIC stored in it is less than a field with which of the following values in it: a) BASIC PLUS; b) APPLE; c) 12345; d) ASCII.
13. What are the format rules when writing an if statement? Why should these be followed?
14. When using the if-then-else statement available on some BASIC interpreters, only the if statement should contain a line number (T or F).
15. It is good programming practice to place constant values in fields identified by variable names because: a) There is less code to write; b) It facilitates program maintenance; c) String constants cannot be specified in a let statement; d) Numeric constants cannot be specified in the let statement.

Chapter 4
DEBUGGING EXERCISES

The following lines of code contain one or more coding errors. Circle each of the errors and write the coding to correct the errors.

1.

```
410 LET A1 = "18"
420 LET C1 = "19.95"
430 LET C2 = "24.94"
440 LET T1 = "O"
450 LET T2 = O"
```

2.

```
600 IF N$ = "END OF FILE" THEN 720
610    LET T1 = T1 + 1
620    IF A > A1 THEN 660
630       LET D = M * C1
640       GOTO 690
650                                              REM
660       LET D = M * C2
670       GOTO 690
680                                              REM
690    LET T2 = T2 + D
700    PRINT USING F1$; N, A, M, D
710    READ N$, A, M
720 GOTO 600
730                                              REM
740 PRINT " "
750 PRINT USING F2$; T1
760 PRINT USING F3$; T1
770 END
```

3.

```
620    IF A > A1 THEN 660
630       LET D = M * C1
640       GOTO 660
650                                              REM
660       LET D = M * C2
670       GOTO 690
680                                              REM
690    LET T2 = T2 + D
```

4.

```
620    IF A > A1 THEN 690
630       LET D = M * C1
640       GOTO 690
650                                              REM
660       LET D = M * C2
670       GOTO 690
680                                              REM
690    LET T2 = T2 + D
```

Chapter 4
PROGRAM DEBUGGING

The following program was designed and written to produce the membership listing in the format shown in Figure 4–1 (page 4.1). The output actually produced by the program is illustrated on page 4.26. Analyze the output to determine if it is correct. If it is in error, circle the errors and write corrections.

```
100 REM MEMBERS                     DECEMBER 1              SHELLY/CASHMAN
110                                                                    REM
120 REM THIS PROGRAM PRODUCES A MEMBERSHIP REPORT LISTING NEW
130 REM MEMBERS, THEIR AGE, THE MONTHS THEY HAVE ENROLLED, AND
140 REM THEIR MEMBERSHIP DUES.
150                                                                    REM
160 REM VARIABLE NAMES:
170 REM     N$....NEW MEMBER'S NAME
180 REM     A.....NEW MEMBER'S AGE
190 REM     M.....MONTHS ENROLLED
200 REM     D.....NEW MEMBER'S DUES
210 REM     T1....FINAL TOTAL - NUMBER OF NEW MEMBERS
220 REM     T2....FINAL TOTAL - AMOUNT OF DUES
230 REM     A1....AGE 18 CONSTANT
240 REM     C1....CHARGE FOR 18 YEARS OF AGE OR LESS
250 REM     C2....CHARGE FOR OVER 18 YEARS OF AGE
260 REM     F1$...PRINT USING FORMAT FOR DETAIL PRINT LINE
270 REM     F2$...PRINT USING FORMAT FOR TOTAL NEW MEMBERS LINE
280 REM     F3$...PRINT USING FORMAT FOR TOTAL DUES LINE
290                                                                    REM
300 REM ***** DATA TO BE PROCESSED *****
310                                                                    REM
320 DATA "SID BARNES", 16, 3
330 DATA "LYNN DAVIES", 18, 8
340 DATA "KEVIN GALLEY", 19, 48
350 DATA "KIM KALLEN", 21, 36
360 DATA "LARRY MOONEY", 32, 3
370 DATA "END OF FILE", 99, 9
380                                                                    REM
390 REM ***** INITIALIZATION OF VARIABLES *****
400                                                                    REM
410 LET C1 = 19.95
420 LET C2 = 24.95
430 LET T1 = 0
440 LET T2 = 0
450 LET F1$ = "\             \    ##      ##     #,###.##"
460 LET F2$ = "TOTAL - NEW MEMBERS ###"
470 LET F3$ = "TOTAL - MEMBERSHIP DUES $$,###.##"
480                                                                    REM
490 REM ***** PROCESSING *****
500                                                                    REM
510 PRINT TAB(13) "HEALTH CLUB"
520 PRINT TAB(11) "MEMBERSHIP DUES"
530 PRINT " "
540 PRINT "    NAME        AGE  MONTHS      DUES"
550 PRINT " "
560                                                                    REM
```

```
570 READ N$, A, M
580                                                    REM
590 IF N$ = "END OF FILE" THEN 730
600    LET T1 = T1 + 1
610    IF A > A1 THEN 650
620      LET D = M * C1
630      GOTO 680
640                                                    REM
650      LET D = M * C2
660      GOTO 680
670                                                    REM
680    LET T2 = T2 + D
690    PRINT USING F1$; N$, A, M, D
700    READ N$, A, M
710 GOTO 590
720                                                    REM
730 PRINT " "
740 PRINT USING F2$; T1
750 PRINT USING F3$; T2
760 END
```

Output

```
                HEALTH CLUB
                MEMBERSHIP DUES

        NAME        AGE  MONTHS      DUES

    SID BARNES       16     3        74.85
    LYNN DAVIES      18     8       199.60
    KEVIN GALLEY     19    48     1,197.60
    KIM KALLEN       21    36       898.20
    LARRY MOONEY     32     3        74.85

    TOTAL - NEW MEMBERS    5
    TOTAL - MEMBERSHIP DUES $2,445.10
```

Chapter 4
PROGRAMMING ASSIGNMENT 1

A bar association dues report is to be prepared. Design and code the BASIC program to produce the report. **Instructions**

The input to the program consists of records containing the name and the number of years the attorney has been a member of the bar. The input data is illustrated below. **Input**

NAME	YEARS
HARVEY HILL	6
JAMES NUTT	5
HORACE LECINC	7
JANE ST. CLAIR	3
DORIS VILLAMY	13

The output from the program is the bar association dues report. The report contains the attorney's name, the number of years the attorney has been a member of the bar, and the bar association dues. The dues are calculated as follows: If the attorney has been a member of the bar more than five years, the dues are $200.00. If the attorney has been a member of the bar five years or less, the dues are $75.00. After all records have been processed, totals should be printed for the number of attorneys, the attorneys of more than five years, the number of attorneys for five years or less, and the total membership dues. The format of the output is illustrated below. **Output**

```
                BAR ASSOCIATION REPORT
        NAME              YEARS              DUES

     HARVEY HILL            6              200.00
     JAMES NUTT             5               75.00
     HORACE LECINC          7              200.00
     JANE ST. CLAIR         3               75.00
     DORIS VILLAMY         13              200.00

     TOTAL ATTORNEYS     5
     TOTAL MORE THAN 5 YEARS    3
     TOTAL LESS THAN OR EQUAL  TO 5 YEARS   2
     TOTAL MEMBERSHIP DUES $     750.00
```

Chapter 4
PROGRAMMING ASSIGNMENT 2

Instructions A traffic citation report is to be prepared. Design and code the BASIC program to produce the report.

Input Input consists of records containing the name of the person receiving the traffic citation, an indicator whether the citation was for a moving (code = M) or non-moving (code = N) violation, and the number of citations for that person over the past three years. The input data is illustrated below.

NAME	TYPE OF VIOLATION	NUMBER OF VIOLATIONS
JUNIOR HAINES	M	2
TOM JULION	N	6
JUNE RHODES	M	4
DALE SMEARS	N	1

Output Output is a traffic citation report. The report contains the name of the person receiving the citation, the fine ($30.00 if a moving violation, $10.00 if a non-moving violation), a penalty (none if 3 or fewer violations, $20.00 if more than 3 violations), and the amount due (fine + penalty). After all records have been processed, the total tickets, total moving violations, total non-moving violations, total fines, total penalties, and total amount due should be printed. The format of the report is illustrated below.

```
              TRAFFIC CITATION REPORT

        NAME          FINE      PENALTY      AMOUNT

    JUNIOR HAINES    30.00        0.00       $30.00
    TOM JULION       10.00       20.00       $30.00
    JUNE RHODES      30.00       20.00       $50.00
    DALE SMEARS      10.00        0.00       $10.00

    TOTAL TICKETS     4
    TOTAL MOVING VIOLATIONS      2
    TOTAL NON-MOVING VIOLATIONS      2
    TOTAL FINES    $80.00
    TOTAL PENALTIES    $40.00
    TOTAL AMOUNT DUE      $120.00
```

Chapter 4
PROGRAMMING ASSIGNMENT 3

A credit union deductions report is to be prepared. Design and code the BASIC program to produce the report.

Instructions

Input to the program consists of records containing the name of the employee, the weekly pay for the employee, and the percentage of the weekly pay the employee wishes to deduct for deposit in the credit union. The input data is illustrated below.

Input

NAME	WEEKLY PAY	PERCENTAGE
HARRY BAILY	243.90	20%
IRVING LICHTNER	346.50	7%
NORMA MILLS	320.75	8%
MARTHA RIIZ	280.40	8%

The output is a report listing the employee's name, the weekly pay, and the amount deducted from the pay for deposit in the credit union. Company rules specify that the maximum amount that can be deducted from the weekly pay of an employee is $25.00. Therefore, if the amount the employee requests (calculated by multiplying the weekly pay by the percentage in the input data) is greater than 25.00, then 25.00 is deducted. This condition can occur because overtime pay for employees can make their weekly pay higher than normal. If it does occur, three asterisks should be printed by the 25.00 to indicate that the maximum was taken. After all records have been processed, the number of employees, the total amount of all deductions, and the average deduction for all employees should be printed. The format of the output is illustrated below.

Output

```
            CREDIT UNION DEDUCTIONS

      NAME              WEEKLY PAY          DEDUCTION

   HARRY BAILY           243.90              25.00 ***
   IRVING LICHTNER       346.50              24.26
   NORMA MILLS           320.75              25.00 ***
   MARTHA RIIZ           280.40              22.43

   NUMBER OF EMPLOYEES    4
   TOTAL DEDUCTIONS      $96.69
   AVERAGE DEDUCTION/EMPLOYEE $24.17
```

Chapter 4
SUPPLEMENTARY PROGRAMMING ASSIGNMENTS

Instructions The following programming assignments contain an explanation of the problem and list suggested test data. The student should design the format of the output.

Program 4 A shipping report is to be prepared. The input data, illustrated below, contains the city from where the package is being shipped, the city to which the package is being shipped, and the weight of the package. If the package weighs more than 50 pounds, it is shipped via truck. If it weighs 50 pounds or less, it is shipped via UPS. The report should contain the shipped from city, the destination city, the weight, and the way the package is shipped.

SHIPPED FROM	SHIPPED TO	WEIGHT
CHICAGO	NEW YORK	50
DALLAS	ATLANTA	51
SAN DIEGO	PROVIDENCE	35
SEATTLE	MEMPHIS	63

Program 5 A discount report is to be prepared which lists an item number, the item price, the item discount, and the net price (item price – discount). If the item price is more than $100.00, then the discount is 30% of the item price. If the item price is $100.00 or less, the discount is 20% of the item price. After all records have been processed, the total item price, the total discount, and the total net price should be printed. The input data is illustrated below.

ITEM NUMBER	ITEM PRICE
A908-91	121.98
C887009-P	99.98
F00988-KK0	342.89
G332-LM9	100.99

Program 6 An airlines baggage report containing the passenger name, the flight number, and the baggage charge is to be prepared. The input data consists of the passenger name, the flight number, and the baggage weight. If the weight is 40 pounds or less, there is no baggage charge (the words NO CHARGE should be printed on the report). If the baggage weighs more than 40 pounds, there is a $3.00 service charge plus $.75 for each pound over 40. Therefore, a baggage weight of 45 pounds would incur a baggage charge of $6.75 (3.00 + (.75 x 5)).

After all data has been printed, the total passengers and the total baggage charges should be printed.

PASSENGER NAME	FLIGHT	BAGGAGE WEIGHT
JAMES HARLOW	273	40
HILMAN JENSYN	273	42
NANCY MILLER	421	44
HARRIET NORME	421	35

Program 7

A payroll report containing the employee name, regular hours pay, overtime hours pay, and total pay is to be prepared. The input data consists of the employee name, the employee's hourly pay rate, and the number of hours the employee worked. The pay is calculated as follows: If the employee works 40 hours or less, regular pay is hours times rate. There is no overtime pay, and the total pay is equal to the regular pay. If the employee works more than 40 hours, regular pay is equal to 40 times the hourly pay rate. Employees receive time and one half for overtime, so overtime pay equals the number of hours worked greater than 40 times the pay rate times 1.5. Total pay is equal to the sum of regular pay plus overtime pay. After all records have been printed, the totals for regular, overtime, and total pay should be printed.

NAME	PAY RATE	HOURS WORKED
NANCY JABLONSKI	7.59	43
RAY WERSHING	6.75	38
TRACY YUBLEIN	8.90	40
JEFF ZERRTUIK	7.23	41

Program 8

A wheat production listing is to be prepared. The input to the program contains a field number from where the wheat was harvested and the tonnage produced. The report contains the field number and the tons of wheat produced. After all records have been printed, the total number of tons which were produced should be printed, together with the field number and tons of the field which produced the most wheat and the field number and tons of the field which produced the least wheat.

FIELD NUMBER	TONS OF WHEAT
65-009	280
65-010	463
67-221	196
67-348	564
68-110	392

CHAPTER FIVE

MORE ON COMPARING

OBJECTIVES:

An understanding of the nested if-then-else logic structure

An understanding of the logical operators AND, OR, and NOT

A familiarization with the manner of internally storing numeric data and considerations when comparing this data

A familiarization with the TRON, TROFF, STOP, and CONT debugging statements

MORE ON COMPARING

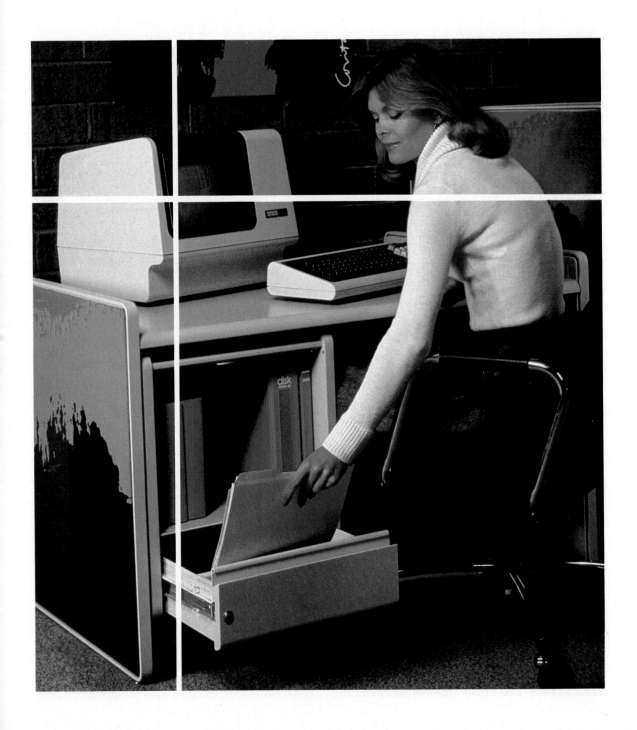

The if-then-else logic structure and the BASIC if statement presented in Chapter 4 form an important basis for much of the programming that is performed on a computer system. The use of this structure can take several forms, depending upon the application being processed. In the sample program in this chapter, the if-then-else structure is used in a nested configuration; that is, an if-then-else structure is contained within an if-then-else structure.

This chapter will also illustrate the use of the logical operators AND, OR, and NOT. Additional uses of the BASIC if statement are illustrated as well. Finally, the testing and debugging aids trace on, trace off, stop, and continue, which are available with most BASIC interpreters, will be examined.

The sample program in this chapter creates a camping fees report. An example of the report is illustrated in Figure 5–1.

```
                    DESERT STATE PARK

        NAME           RESIDENCY     DAYS   FEES

     JACK HENRY        RESIDENT        3    23.85
     DON JAMES         RESIDENT        8    61.60
     BILL DONALD       NON-RESIDENT    9    89.55
     RALPH ADAM        UNKNOWN
     MURRAY FRANK      RESIDENT        7    55.65


     TOTAL CAMPERS     5
     TOTAL FEE AMOUNT     $230.65
```

Figure 5-1 The report created by the sample program calculates the camping fees for resident and non-resident campers. After all records have been processed, the total number of campers and the total fee amount are printed.

The report contains the camper's name, the residency (whether the camper is a resident of the state or is not a resident of the state), the days the camper is staying in the park, and the camping fees. The camping fees are determined as follows: If the camper is a state resident, the cost for the first seven days is 7.95 per day. After seven days, the cost drops to 5.95 per day. If the camper is a non-resident of the state, the cost is 9.95 per day, regardless of the number of days. If there is an error in the input record and the residency code contains neither an R (resident) nor an N (non-resident), the value UNKNOWN is printed in the residency column.

After all records have been printed, the total number of campers and the total fee amount are printed.

In order to create this report, a nested if-then-else structure is required. This structure is explained in the following sections.

Nested if-then-else structure

In order to understand the nested if-then-else structure, it is mandatory to understand the if-then-else structure itself. The if-then-else structure is reviewed in Figure 5–2.

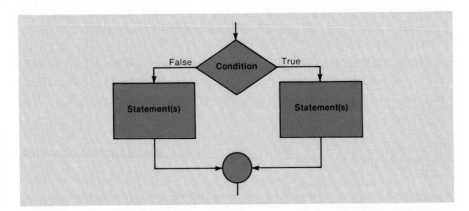

Figure 5-2 When the condition in the if-then-else structure is tested, one set of statements is executed when the condition is true, and another set is executed when the condition is false.

When the condition being tested in the if-then-else structure is true, one set of instructions is executed. If the condition is false, another set of instructions is executed. The instructions which are executed when a condition is true or a condition is false can be any instructions available on the computer system. It is perfectly allowable, therefore, that the set of instructions executed when a condition is true or a condition is false can include another if-then-else structure. When this occurs, the second if-then-else structure is said to be nested within the first if-then-else structure. This is illustrated in Figure 5–3.

Note in Figure 5–3 that the instructions to be executed when the first condition is true include another if-then-else structure. This nested if-then-else structure will be executed only if the first condition is true.

It will be recalled that all if-then-else structures have a single entry point and a single exit point. A nested if-then-else structure is no exception. Therefore, as can be seen in Figure 5–3, the nested if-then-else has a single entry point and a single exit point.

An example of a nested if-then-else structure is the logic required in the sample program to determine the camping fees. This logic is shown in Figure 5–4.

The first condition statement tests if the camper is a resident. If so, a further check must be made to determine how many days the camper is staying because the calculation of the camping fee for residents is based upon the

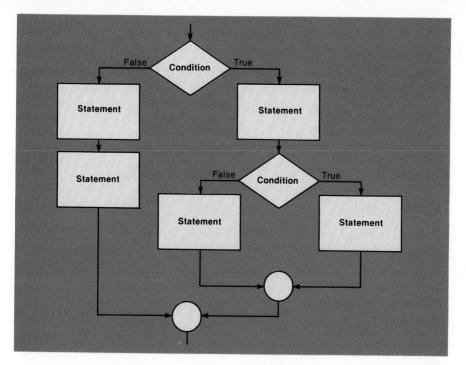

Figure 5-3 A nested if-then-else structure is one which is executed only after a prior condition has been tested. In this general example, if the first condition tested is true, a statement will be executed and then a second condition will be tested. The second condition tested is the entry point for the second if-then-else structure.

number of days the camper is staying. If the days are greater than 7, the fee is calculated by multiplying 7.95 times 7 for the first seven days, and the number of days greater than 7 by 5.95. This is an example of a nested if-then-else structure because the conditional statement testing for number of days will be executed only if the camper is a resident.

If the camper is not a resident, the fees are calculated by multiplying the number of days by 9.95. A nested if-then-else structure is not required here because the calculation of non-resident fees does not depend upon the number of days the camper is staying.

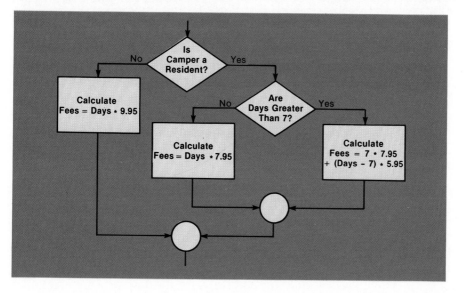

Figure 5-4 In this example, if the camper is a resident, the nested if-then-else logic structure which tests the number of days is executed. The test for the number of days will occur only after the test for residency finds that the camper is a resident.

Nested if-then-else structures can be used when the condition is false as well as when the condition is true. In addition, a nested if-then-else structure may itself contain an if-then-else structure. Figure 5–5 contains an example of this.

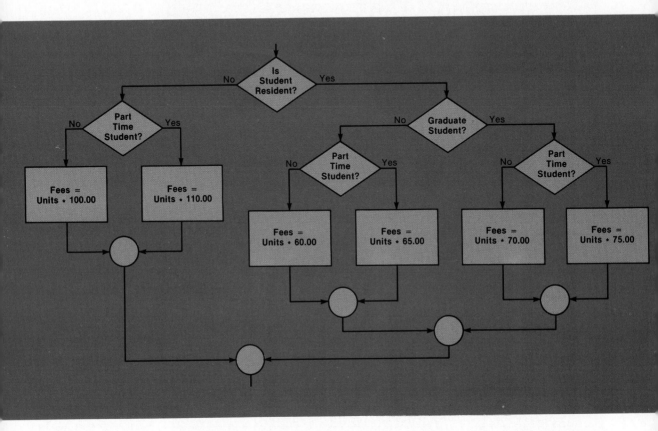

Figure 5-5 In this example, both the true and false conditions have a nested if-then-else structure. The nested if-then-else structure on the true side itself contains nested if-then-else structures.

In Figure 5–5, when the student is a resident, a check is performed to determine if the student is part-time after the graduate status is determined. This is an example of a nested if-then-else structure within a nested if-then-else structure. So long as each if-then-else structure has a single entry point and a single exit point, the structures will be easy to read and understand.

It is vital that the rule for single entry and single exit be followed when writing nested if-then-else structures. The example in Figure 5–6 illustrates a violation of this rule.

The logic in Figure 5–6 is designed to find the largest of three values, A, B, or C. If A is greater than B, then A is compared to C. If A is not greater than C, then C is the largest number.

If A is not greater than B, then C is compared to B. If C is greater than B, then C is the largest number. In Figure 5–6, the statement which prints "C is largest" is entered from two different decision symbols. Therefore, the

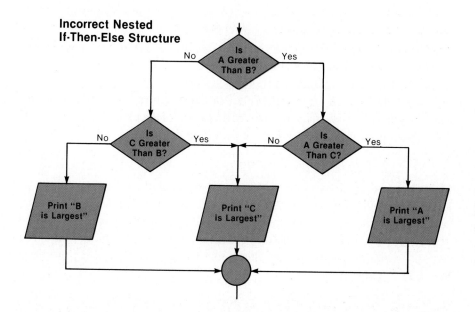

Figure 5-6 These nested if-then-else structures contain multiple entry points and multiple exit points.

single entry rule is violated because that statement should be executed from only one decision symbol. In addition, there is no single unique exit point for the two nested if-then-else structures. The exit point is shared by both. The structure illustrated in Figure 5–6, therefore, is an incorrect nested if-then-else structure and should be avoided. The correct structure is shown in Figure 5–7.

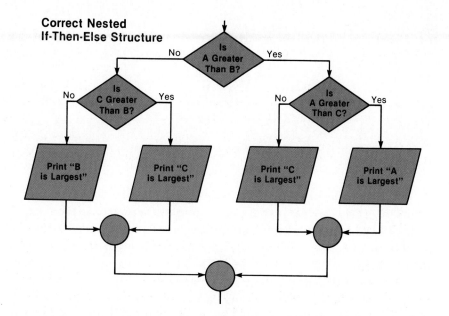

Figure 5-7 All if-then-else structures in this example contain one entry point and one exit point. The duplicate task "Print C is Largest" is required to ensure the integrity of the logic structures. The one entry point-one exit point rule should never be violated.

In Figure 5–7, each if-then-else structure has a single entry point and a single exit point. The statement which prints "C is largest" is found twice. This is necessary to preserve the proper structure of the program and presents no problems either logically or when the structure is implemented in BASIC code.

It is very important that programs be developed using proper control structures which exactly follow the rules for the structure. If this does not happen, programs very quickly become difficult to read, understand, and use. There is no excuse for violating these programming rules.

Implementing nested if-then-else structures

The nested if-then-else structure is implemented using the BASIC if statement. The if statement format is exactly the same as shown in Chapter 4. There are, however, several coding conventions which are used with nested if-then-else structures that should be followed in order to achieve maximum legibility. The coding in Figure 5–8 illustrates these conventions by expressing the logic shown in Figure 5–7.

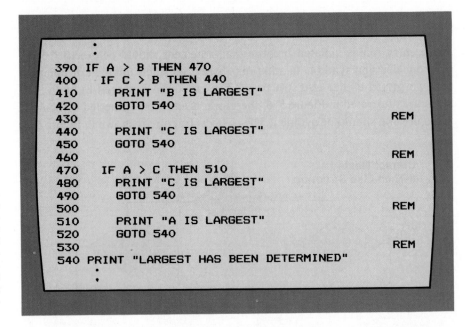

```
   .
   .
   .
390 IF A > B THEN 470
400   IF C > B THEN 440
410     PRINT "B IS LARGEST"
420     GOTO 540
430                                          REM
440     PRINT "C IS LARGEST"
450     GOTO 540
460                                          REM
470   IF A > C THEN 510
480     PRINT "C IS LARGEST"
490     GOTO 540
500                                          REM
510     PRINT "A IS LARGEST"
520     GOTO 540
530                                          REM
540 PRINT "LARGEST HAS BEEN DETERMINED"
   .
   .
```

Figure 5-8 The coding to implement a nested if-then-else structure should follow certain conventions so that it is easy to read and understand. The conventions shown in this example should always be used when writing if statements to implement nested if-then-else structures.

The if statement on line 390 corresponds to the first decision symbol in Figure 5–7. If A is greater than B, then control is transferred to the statement on line 470. If A is not greater than B, then control passes to the statement on line 400. In both cases, note that the statement on line 400 and the statement on line 470 are indented two spaces. This is because they are to be executed only after the if statement on line 390 is executed.

The statements on lines 410 – 450 are indented two columns from the if statement on line 400 because these statements will be executed only after the if statement on line 400 is executed. Similarly, the statements on lines 480 – 520 are indented two vertical columns from the if statement on line 470 because they will be executed only after the if statement on line 470. As in Chapter 4, blank lines are placed after each segment of processing which is accomplished as a result of a condition being true or not true.

The exit point of the first if-then-else structure (implemented by the if statement on line 390) is at line 540; that is, the statement on line 540 will be executed regardless of the results of conditions tested within the if-then-else structure. As can be seen from the flowchart in Figure 5–7, the nested if-then-else structures pass control to the same point of exit. Therefore, in the coding on lines 420, 450, 490, and 520, the statement GOTO 540 is used to transfer control to this common exit point.

In many applications, exit from the structure can be accomplished as shown in Figure 5–8. Some applications, however, require slightly different logic, and therefore, slightly different coding. Such an application is illustrated in Figure 5–9.

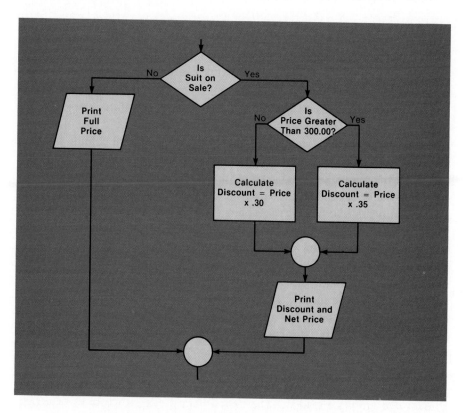

Figure 5-9 In this example, if a suit is on sale, the price is checked to determine the discount. If the price is greater than 300.00, the discount is 35%. Otherwise, the discount is 30%. Regardless of the discount, after it is calculated the discount and net price are printed. This logic is slightly different from that used in previous examples.

In Figure 5–9, the statement which prints the discount and net price after the discount has been calculated will be executed regardless of the size of the discount. Therefore, it is the exit point of the nested if-then-else structure.

When this nested if-then-else structure is implemented in code, control must be passed to the print statement after the discount has been calculated. The coding to do this is shown below.

```
720 IF S$ = "S"  THEN 760
730     PRINT P
740     GOTO 860
750                                              REM
760     IF  P > 300.00 THEN 800
770       LET D = P * .30
780       GOTO 830
790                                              REM
800       LET D = P * .35
810       GOTO 830
820                                              REM
830     PRINT D, P - D
840     GOTO 860
850                                              REM
860 PRINT "DISCOUNT PROCESSING COMPLETE"
```

Figure 5-10 The coding here implements the logic in Figure 5-9. The indentation and coding conventions used in this example should be used with all nested if-then-else structures coded in the BASIC language.

If the suit is on sale (that is, the value in S$ is equal to S), control is passed to the statement on line 760. There, the price of the suit (P) is compared to 300.00. If the price is greater than 300.00, control is passed to line 800; otherwise, the discount is calculated on line 770. Regardless of whether the discount is calculated on line 770 or line 800, control is passed to the print statement on line 830, where the discount and the net price (P – D) are printed. Note that the print statement on line 830 will be executed regardless of the size of the discount. Therefore, this statement begins in the same vertical column as the if statement on line 760 because it is not dependent upon the if statement on line 760. After the print statement is executed, the goto statement on line 840 passes control to line 860, which is the single exit point for the if statement on line 720.

It is important to be able to recognize the various forms of nested if-then-else structures which can occur and be able to implement them in BASIC code. Another form which can occur is when one or more statements must be executed before the nested if-then-else structure is coded. The flowchart and accompanying code in Figure 5–11 illustrate a form where a statement must be executed prior to the second condition's being tested. In this case, if the student is a graduate student, the constant GRADUATE is printed. Then, a test is made to determine if the student is a Masters or Ph. D. candidate. This is also printed on the report. Note that the constant GRADUATE is printed on one line, and the words MASTERS or PH. D. are printed on the next line.

In the example, the print statement on line 690 will be executed when the student is a graduate student. The nested if-then-else structure to determine masters or Ph.d. is then executed.

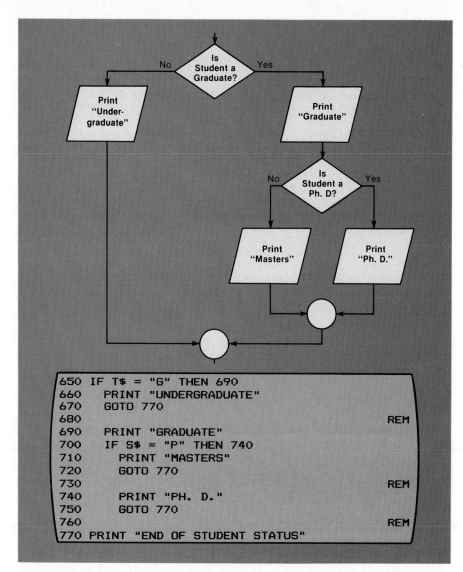

```
650 IF T$ = "G" THEN 690
660    PRINT "UNDERGRADUATE"
670    GOTO 770
680                                          REM
690    PRINT "GRADUATE"
700    IF S$ = "P" THEN 740
710       PRINT "MASTERS"
720       GOTO 770
730                                          REM
740       PRINT "PH. D."
750       GOTO 770
760                                          REM
770 PRINT "END OF STUDENT STATUS"
```

Figure 5-11 The nested if statement need not be the first statement executed after the first condition is tested. Here, the word GRADUATE is printed prior to the execution of the nested if statement. If the field identified by the variable name T$ contains the value G, the student is a graduate student. If the S$ field contains the value P, the student is a Ph.D candidate.

In addition to being able to design and code a nested if-then-else structure, a programmer must be able to recognize when one is required. Two general rules specify when a nested if-then-else structure is required.

The need for a nested if-then-else structure

RULE 1: If a given condition must be tested only when a previous condition has been tested, AND alternative actions are required for one or more of the conditions, then a nested if-then-else structure is required.

Rule 1 is illustrated by an example to calculate the camping fees (Figure 5–12, next page). In this example, the test for days being greater than 7 is done only after it is determined that the camper is a resident. Therefore, the first part of the rule is satisfied. Alternative actions are required for both conditions tested. That is, if the camper is a resident, one set of actions is taken; if

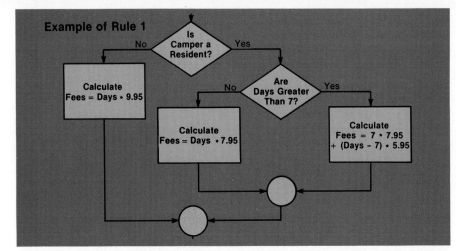

Figure 5-12 In this example, the test for the number of days occurs only after it is determined a camper is a resident. In addition, both tests have alternative operations. Therefore, a nested if-then-else structure is required.

the camper is a non-resident, another set of actions is taken. Similarly, if the days are greater than 7, one set of actions is taken; while if the days are not greater than 7, another set of actions is taken. Therefore, this logic problem requires the use of a nested if-then-else structure.

RULE 2: If a given condition must be tested only when a previous condition has been tested, AND one or more statements are to be executed before or after the second if-then-else structure, then a nested if-then-else structure is required.

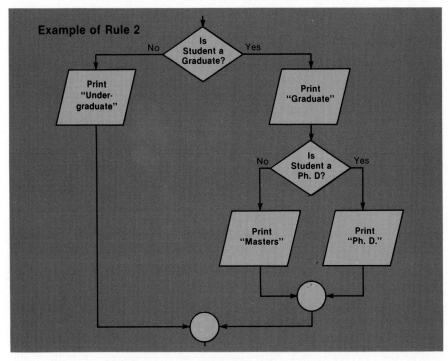

Figure 5-13 If the student is a graduate, the word GRADUATE is printed prior to determining if the student is a Ph.D. student. Thus, one statement must be executed before the second if-then-else structure, satisfying rule 2.

In the example above, which has also been seen before, the test for

Masters or Ph.D. takes place only after it has been determined that the student is a graduate student. Therefore, the first part of rule 2 is satisfied. The word GRADUATE is to be printed on the report before the second if-then-else structure, satisfying the second part of the rule. Thus, a nested if-then-else structure is required.

These rules should be well understood so that they can be applied to problems specified in program specifications.

Logical operators are used to combine conditions in an if statement. The logical operators which are available in BASIC include AND and OR.

Logical operators

The word AND is used to mean both when two or more conditions are specified in an if statement (Figure 5–14).

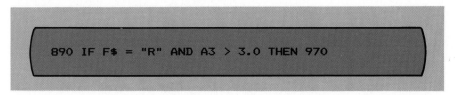

```
890 IF F$ = "R" AND A3 > 3.0 THEN 970
```

Figure 5-14 The word AND means both when used to combine logical operators. Here, both the field F$ must contain the value R and the value in A3 must be greater than 3.0 for the if statement to be considered true.

In the example above, the value in F$ is compared to R, and the value in A3 is compared to 3.0. If BOTH the conditions are true, then the entire if statement is considered true, and control is passed to the statement on line 970. If, however, the value in F$ is not equal to R or the value in A3 is not greater than 3.0, then control will pass to the statement following the if statement. Thus, it must be remembered that when the word AND is used to join conditions in an if statement, all conditions specified must be true in order for the statement on the line number following the word THEN to be given control.

The or logical operator is used to indicate that if EITHER or BOTH conditions are true, then the if statement is considered true. The use of the or logical operator is illustrated in Figure 5–15.

```
650 IF A$ = "END" OR B = 99 THEN 860
```

Figure 5-15 The word OR means either or both in an if statement. In this example, if A$ contains the word END, the if statement is considered true. Also, if the field B contains the value 99, the if statement is considered true.

In the example, the word OR is used to separate the conditions tested in the if statement. Therefore, if either A$ contains the word END or the field identified by the variable name B contains 99, then control will be passed to the statement on line 860. Otherwise, the statement following the if statement on line 650 will be executed. Again, when the word OR is used to combine conditions, it means either condition or both conditions.

The logical operators AND and OR can be combined into a single if statement (Figure 5–16).

Figure 5-16 When the operators AND and OR are combined, the conditions combined by the AND operator are evaluated prior to those combined by the OR logical operator.

```
820 IF C = 9 OR D = 76 AND R$ = "INV" THEN 970
```

When logical operators are combined within an if statement, they are evaluated according to a predefined priority. The conditions combined by the AND logical operator are evaluated first, and then those combined by the OR logical operator are evaluated. Therefore, in Figure 5–16, the if statement will be evaluated as follows:

C	OR	D	AND	R$	Result
9		65		INV	True
8		76		INV	True
9		76		INV	True
7		62		INV	False
9		76		ACC	True
9		81		ACC	True
7		76		ACC	False

Figure 5-17 This table containing the evaluation of the if statement in Figure 5-16 should be reviewed carefully so that the OR and AND logical operators are thoroughly understood.

The AND portion of the if statement is evaluated first. Then it is combined with the OR portion to determine if the condition tested is true. In the first example, since C contains 9, one portion of the OR condition is true, and therefore, the entire condition is true. In the second example, D contains 76 and R$ contains INV, so the AND condition is true, making the entire condition true. In the third example, both sides of the OR condition are true, so the entire condition is true.

In the fourth example, neither C, nor D and R$ satisfy one of the OR conditions. Therefore, even though R$ contains INV, the entire condition is not true. The same evaluations can be applied to the remaining examples.

The predefined priority for evaluating combined if statements can be altered through the use of parentheses. Those conditions specified within parentheses will be evaluated first, followed by those outside the parentheses. Thus, the if statement in Figure 5–16 could be written in the following manner.

Figure 5-18 The conditions specified within the parentheses are evaluated prior to those conditions outside the parentheses.

```
820 IF (C = 9 OR D = 76) AND R$ = "INV" THEN 970
```

In Figure 5-18, the condition within the parentheses will be evaluated first, followed by the condition outside the parentheses. Therefore, in order for the if statement to be true, R$ will have to contain the value INV. If it does not, the AND portion of the condition will never be satisfied. From Figure 5-17, the first example is true because R$ contains INV and C contains 9. The second example is true because D contains 76 and R$ contains INV. The third example is true because all conditions tested for are true.

The fourth example is false because C does not contain 9 nor does D contain 76. In the fifth example, the entire condition is false because R$ does not contain INV. The sixth and seventh examples are false for the same reason. Whenever a condition is combined using the AND logical operator, each side of the AND must be true for the entire condition to be true.

As can be seen, the meaning of the combined conditions can change based upon the parentheses. It is recommended that parentheses always be used even when the predefined priority would yield the correct result. In this manner, there will be no confusion regarding the processing to take place.

The not logical operator may be encountered in some programs. The use of the not logical operator is shown in Figure 5-19.

Not logical operator

```
450 IF NOT (A = B AND C < 7) THEN 580
```

Figure 5-19 The NOT logical operator is difficult for people to evaluate. It should normally be avoided.

In the example above, the conditions specified within the parentheses are evaluated. When the conditions within the parentheses are true, the if statement is considered false. When, on the other hand, the conditions within the parentheses are false, the if statement is considered true. Therefore, when the value in A is equal to the value in B and the value in C is less than 7, the if statement will be considered false and the statement following statement 450 will be given control. When the value in A is not equal to the value in B or the value in C is equal to or greater than 7, then the if statement will be considered true, and the statement on line 580 will be given control.

Research has shown that human beings have difficulty evaluating "not" logic. Therefore, unless it is absolutely mandatory, it is suggested that the not logical operator be avoided when designing programs.

When an if statement containing a relational operator is executed, the internal circuitry of the computer system will compare the two values. The result of the comparison is either that the condition tested is true, or the condition tested is

Evaluation of if statements

false. When the condition tested is true, the internal circuitry returns the value -1. When the condition is false, the internal circuitry returns the value 0. The if statement then checks the value returned. When the value is not zero, the condition is considered true. When the value returned is zero, the condition is deemed false by the if statement. This is illustrated in Figure 5-20.

Figure 5-20 When a condition is evaluated, the CPU returns the value -1 if the condition is true and the value 0 is the condition is false.

A	B	RELATIONAL OPERATOR	VALUE RETURNED	EVALUATION
15	15	A = B	-1	True
10	15	A = B	0	False
10	15	A > B	0	False
10	15	A < B	-1	True

When the if statement evaluates the condition specified, any non-zero value is considered true, and any zero value is considered false. Therefore, an if statement could be encountered in a program which merely has a variable name specified rather than a relational operator (Figure 5-21).

Figure 5-21 If the value in C is zero, the statement following line 790 is executed. If the value in C is not zero, the statement on line 900 is given control.

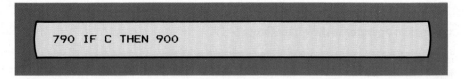

```
790 IF C THEN 900
```

In the example above, when the value in C is zero, the if statement considers the condition tested false, and the statement following the if statement will be executed. When the value in C is not zero, the if statement is considered true, and control will be passed to the statement on line 900.

Although this form of the if statement is not widely used, there are occasions when programs will use it. The BASIC programmer should be aware of this use of the if statement.

DEBUGGING THE IF STATEMENT

When writing programs containing if statements, some logical problems can become quite complex. When this is the case, it can be useful to trace exactly what processing is taking place in the program to ensure that the correct logic is being implemented. In addition, if a program is found to contain an error, tracing the exact steps which occur may aid in finding the error. The following sections will examine tools that are available with most implementations of BASIC which allow the programmer to follow exactly what is occurring in the program.

One very helpful aid when debugging a program is the ability to trace exactly which lines in a program have been executed. This process can be implemented through several different means, depending upon the BASIC interpreter being used. A common means is the TRON (TRace ON) instruction (Figure 5-22).

Tracing program steps

Program

```
430  TRON
440  IF C < 23 THEN 480
450     PRINT "COUNT IS OVER MINIMUM"
460     GOTO 510
470                                                    REM
480     PRINT "COUNT IS UNDER MINIMUM"
490     GOTO 510
500                                                    REM
510  TROFF
```

Output (C> = 23)

```
[440][450]COUNT IS OVER MINIMUM
[460][510]
```

Output (C < 23)

```
[440][480]COUNT IS UNDER MINIMUM
[490][510]
```

Figure 5-22 The TRON instruction turns on the BASIC trace mechanism. It prints each line number which is executed in the program. The TROFF instruction halts the printing of the line numbers.

In the example above, the TRON instruction is specified on line 430. This instruction turns on the mechanism within the BASIC interpreter which will print the line number of each instruction that is executed. This action will continue until the TROFF (TRace OFF) instruction is encountered.

The output generated when C is greater than or equal to 23 is shown on the left. The number within the square brackets (440) is the first line number executed after the trace mechanism is turned on by the tron instruction. The second number within brackets (450) is the next instruction executed. As a result of the execution of the print statement on line 450, the message COUNT IS OVER MINIMUM is printed and the report is spaced one line. The next instruction executed is on line 460, followed by the instruction on line 510. The troff instruction on line 510 will turn the trace mechanism off.

The output generated when the value in C is less than 23 is similar except that, as would be expected, different statements are executed. The tron statement and the troff statement can be placed anywhere in the program where they might be helpful. Once the trace mechanism is turned on, it will remain on until it is turned off by the troff instruction. It should be noted that these instructions are placed in the program during testing and debugging, but they are normally removed from the program once the program is working properly.

Stop and cont instructions

Another helpful debugging aid available with most BASIC interpreters is the ability to stop the program, examine the values in fields within the program, and then continue the execution of the program. This can be accomplished through the use of the stop and cont (continue) instructions together with the print statement.

The stop statement is specified in the program at a point where it is desired to temporarily halt the execution. Generally, it will be placed in the program when it is important to examine a value in a field. For example, if a calculation were performed based upon a certain condition, it may be desirable to examine the result of the calculation. This is illustrated in Figure 5–23.

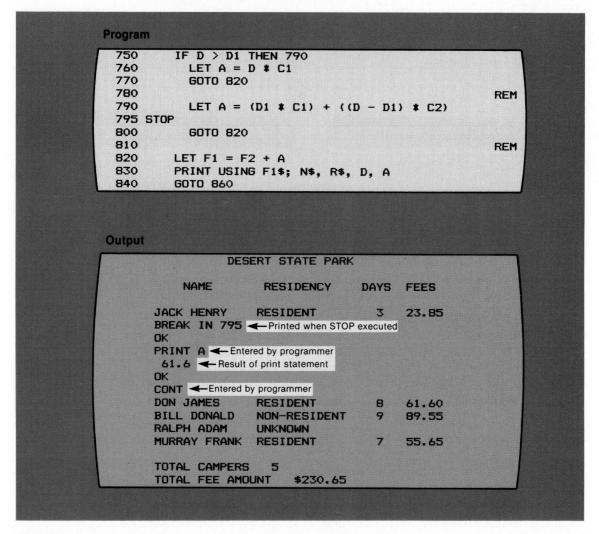

Program

```
750        IF  D  >  D1  THEN  790
760            LET  A  =  D  *  C1
770            GOTO  820
780                                              REM
790            LET  A  =  (D1  *  C1)  +  ((D  -  D1)  *  C2)
795 STOP
800            GOTO  820
810                                              REM
820            LET  F1  =  F2  +  A
830            PRINT  USING  F1$;  N$,  R$,  D,  A
840            GOTO  860
```

Output

```
                    DESERT  STATE  PARK

           NAME          RESIDENCY      DAYS   FEES

    JACK  HENRY      RESIDENT           3    23.85
    BREAK  IN  795  ◄─ Printed when STOP executed
    OK
    PRINT  A  ◄─ Entered by programmer
     61.6  ◄─ Result of print statement
    OK
    CONT  ◄─ Entered by programmer
    DON  JAMES       RESIDENT           8    61.60
    BILL  DONALD     NON-RESIDENT       9    89.55
    RALPH  ADAM      UNKNOWN
    MURRAY  FRANK    RESIDENT           7    55.65

    TOTAL  CAMPERS      5
    TOTAL  FEE  AMOUNT     $230.65
```

Figure 5-23 The STOP instruction will halt the program at the line where the instruction is encountered. The CONT instruction, entered by the operator, will resume the program at the statement which follows the stop instruction. The stop instruction is not indented so that it will be easy to spot when it must be removed from the program.

When the stop statement is encountered on line 795, the program execution will stop and the message BREAK IN 795 is printed. When the program is stopped, the values in the fields in the program can be examined using the print statement. The print statement is written without a line number (see example in Figure 5–23). When it is written without a line number, it is executed immediately. Therefore, the line following the statement PRINT A contains the value of A when the program was stopped. As can be seen, the value in A when the program was stopped was 61.6.

When a BASIC statement is written without a line number, it will be executed immediately. This mode is variously called the direct mode, the command mode, the immediate-execution mode, and other terms by different computer manufacturers. Most BASIC statements which do not require the use of a line number can be written in this mode. Statements which do require a line number, such as the goto statement, cannot be written in this mode. This mode is also referred to as the calculator mode because a calculation can be performed and the results displayed immediately. For example, the statement PRINT (456/43) * 91 + 319 can be entered, and the result (1284.023) will be printed immediately.

After the value of A has been printed, the remainder of the program should be executed. The CONT (continue) statement is used. This statement is not placed in the program. Rather, it is entered from the keyboard by the computer operator. When it is entered, the execution of the program is resumed at the point it was stopped by the stop statement. In Figure 5–23, the first statement executed when the program is resumed will be line 800. The execution of the program will continue until another stop statement is encountered or the end of the program is reached. Note in Figure 5–23 that the stop statement on line 795 is executed only one time because the program is halted only one time. Therefore, the condition which led to the execution of line 795 occurred only once.

Comparing numeric fields

Computer systems store numbers in which a decimal point appears (a real number) in a form called floating point. This method of representing numbers does not always produce the exact value of the number. For example, the number 7.98 could be stored as 7.9799999. The floating point form of representing numbers internally in main computer storage can sometimes lead to results when comparing numbers that would not be expected. For example, in the code in Figure 5–24 on page 5.18, the value in the field identified by the variable name A is not equal to the value in the field identified by the variable name B.

When the calculation on line 360 takes place, the answer stored in the field identified by the variable name A is 7.9799999. When this number is compared to the value 7.98 stored in the field named B, these numbers are not equal.

Program

```
360 LET A = 7.00 + .98
370 LET B = 7.98
380 IF A = B THEN 420
390    PRINT "FIELDS ARE NOT EQUAL"
400    GOTO 450
410                                              REM
420    PRINT "FIELDS ARE EQUAL"
430    GOTO 450
440                                              REM
450 PRINT "END OF COMPARISON"
```

Output

```
FIELDS ARE NOT EQUAL
END OF COMPARISON
```

Figure 5-24 Because of the way real numbers are stored internally in main computer storage, the value in A is not equal to the value in B.

Again, this is due to the manner in which numbers which contain digits to the right of the decimal point are stored internally in main computer storage.

When writing programs which compare real numbers (numbers with digits to the right of the decimal point), the programmer should be aware that although numerically the value should be equal to another number, it may not be when it is compared. This problem can be overcome, if required in the application, by writing an if statement which tests against a range of values. An if statement to compare the value in A to the value in B is shown in Figure 5–25.

Program

```
360 LET A = 7.00 + .98
370 LET B = 7.98
380 IF ABS(A - B) < .00001 THEN 420
390    PRINT "FIELDS ARE NOT EQUAL"
400    GOTO 450
410                                              REM
420    PRINT "FIELDS ARE EQUAL"
430    GOTO 450
440                                              REM
450 PRINT "END OF COMPARISON"
```

Output

```
FIELDS ARE EQUAL
END OF COMPARISON
```

Figure 5-25 The ABS (absolute) function is used to obtain the absolute value of the numbers being compared. This difference is then compared to a relative error amount to determine if the difference is because of the numeric representation or because the numbers are actually not equal.

In the example in Figure 5-25, the if statement on line 380 is used to test if the value in A is very close to the value in B. If so, the difference between them is attributed to the representation of the numbers, and they are considered equal.

This test is conducted as follows: 1) The value in the B field is subtracted from the value in the A field; 2) The absolute value of this result, which is the value of the number disregarding the sign, is obtained through the use of the ABS (ABSolute) function; 3) The ABS function returns the absolute value of the number or arithmetic expression which is contained within the parentheses immediately following the letters ABS. The absolute value of a number is always positive. The absolute value is required because it is not known whether the difference between A and B will be positive or negative, and a positive number is needed for the comparison.

When the comparison is made, the if statement determines if the difference between the two numbers being compared is less than a relative error amount. If it is, then the numbers are considered equal. In the example in Figure 5-25, this amount is .00001. If the difference between the two numbers is less than .00001, then the numbers in this application are considered equal.

The relative error amount which is specified in this comparison can vary depending upon the application and the number of positions to the right of the decimal place in the numbers being compared. When dollars and cents are being compared, it has been found that .00001 is a good number to use.

The programmer would normally write the code in the program as shown in Figure 5-25. When the program is listed, however, it will likely appear in a different format because of the very problem being discussed; that is, the numbers are not represented exactly. The listing of the code shown in Figure 5-25 is illustrated in Figure 5-26.

```
360 LET A = 7! + .9799999
370 LET B = 7.98
380 IF ABS(A - B) < 9.999999E-06 THEN 420
390    PRINT "FIELDS ARE NOT EQUAL"
400    GOTO 450
410                                          REM
420    PRINT "FIELDS ARE EQUAL"
430    GOTO 450
440                                          REM
450 PRINT "END OF COMPARISON"
```

Figure 5-26 Numbers can be represented as approximations and also in the scientific notation.

The two statements which appear different from when coded are on lines 360 and 380. On line 360, instead of the value 7.00, the interpreter prints 7!. The exclamation point following the number specifies that the number is a real number stored as a single precision number. A single precision number contains seven or fewer digits. The constant .98 has been changed to .9799999, which is the approximation of .98 obtained when the number is stored as a floating point number internally in main computer storage. It is because of these approximations that this special technique must be used when comparing real numbers.

The if statement on line 380 illustrates another method which is used by the BASIC interpreter to print numbers. It is called scientific notation. When it is used, a number with one position to the left of the decimal point is printed together with an exponent value which indicates the value to the base 10 to which the number is raised. The table in Figure 5–27 illustrates the use of the exponent in scientific notation.

ACTUAL NUMBER	EXPONENT	SCIENTIFIC NOTATION
100.00	1×10^{2}	1.0E + 2
1000000.00	1×10^{6}	1.0E + 6
.01	1×10^{-2}	1.0E − 2
.000001	1×10^{-6}	1.0E − 6

Note from Figure 5–27 that the value following the letter E in the scientific notation corresponds to the power of ten to which the number must be raised. Depending upon the characteristics of the BASIC interpreter, scientific notation will be used to print numbers greater than and less than a certain value. On many computer systems, a number of the size one million or greater will be printed using scientific notation, and a number equal to or less than .00001 will be printed using scientific notation.

In the example in Figure 5–25, the number coded was .00001. The number printed by the interpreter was 9.999999E-06. This is an example of both the approximation used for a number and scientific notation. The interpreter approximated .00001 with the value .000009999999. In addition, the number was printed in scientific notation.

Integer comparisons

The previous examples of comparing numeric values has applied to real numbers; that is, numbers with a value to the right of the decimal point. The difficulties presented do not apply to integers, or whole numbers. When integers, which contain no digits to the right of the decimal point, are compared, the exact values of the numbers will be used, and the approximations as illustrated in Figure 5–26 are not required.

Summary of if statement debugging

The previous examples have indicated some of the areas where the use of the if statement may cause difficulties and some of the tools which can be used to discover errors. It should be remembered, however, that errors in a program should be extremely rare. If the program is designed and coded properly, with a knowledge of how the comparing process works, the need for debugging aids should seldom occur.

The sample program in this chapter uses a nested if-then-else structure to produce a state park camping report. The input to the program and the output produced from the program are illustrated below.

NAME	RESIDENCY CODE	DAYS CAMPING
JACK HENRY	R	3
DON JAMES	R	8
BILL DONALD	N	9
RALPH ADAM	F	6
MURRAY FRANK	R	7

```
                DESERT STATE PARK

        NAME          RESIDENCY   DAYS   FEES

    JACK HENRY      RESIDENT        3    23.85
    DON JAMES       RESIDENT        8    61.60
    BILL DONALD     NON-RESIDENT    9    89.55
    RALPH ADAM      UNKNOWN
    MURRAY FRANK    RESIDENT        7    55.65

    TOTAL CAMPERS   5
    TOTAL FEE AMOUNT    $230.65
```

Figure 5-28 From the input data, the camping fee report is produced by the sample program.

It will be recalled that the camping fees are calculated as follows: 1) If the camper is a state resident, the cost is 7.95 per day for the first seven days and 5.95 per day for all days after 7; 2) If the camper is not a state resident, the cost is 9.95 for all days; 3) If the residency code in the input record is not equal to N or R, then the message UNKNOWN is printed in the residency column on the report.

The first step in the program design is to designate the tasks which must be

Program design

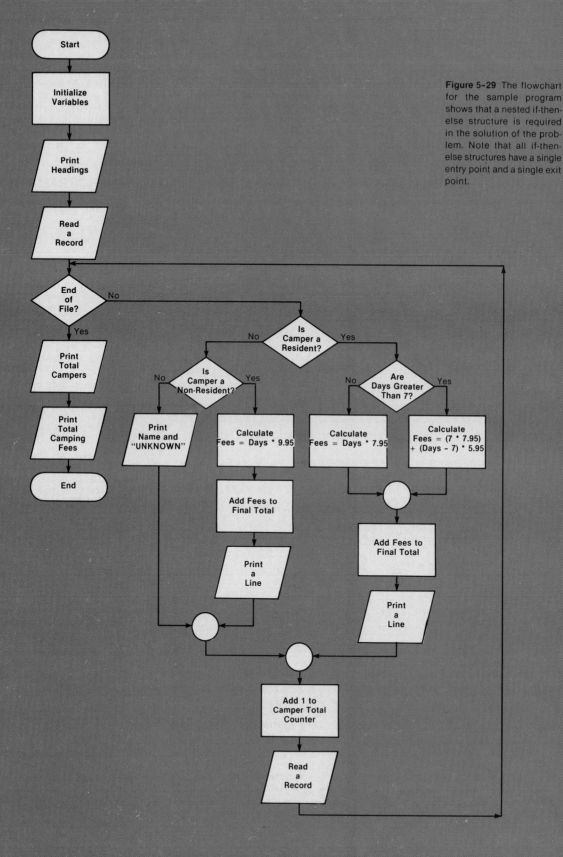

Figure 5-29 The flowchart for the sample program shows that a nested if-then-else structure is required in the solution of the problem. Note that all if-then-else structures have a single entry point and a single exit point.

accomplished within the program. These tasks are specified below.

Program Tasks

1. Read input records.
2. Calculate camping fees.
3. Accumulate final totals.
4. Print lines on the CRT screen.
5. Print the final totals.

As noted in previous chapters, it is important to define those tasks which must be accomplished in the program in order to produce the required output from the given input.

Once the program tasks have been defined, the logic to accomplish the tasks is designed using the flowchart (Figure 5-29). The flowchart indicates that nested if-then-else structures are used to prepare the line printed on the screen. The flowchart should be reviewed and understood prior to examining the code in the program.

Flowchart

The code in the sample program begins with the documentation of the program (Figure 5-30).

Program code

Figure 5-30 Program remarks

```
100 REM CAMPFEE              DECEMBER 7              SHELLY/CASHMAN
110                                                              REM
120 REM THIS PROGRAM PRODUCES A CAMPING FEES REPORT FOR
130 REM DESERT STATE PARK. THE FEES ARE BASED UPON
140 REM RESIDENCY AND LENGTH OF STAY. FINAL TOTALS FOR
150 REM THE NUMBER OF CAMPERS AND THE FEE AMOUNTS ARE PRINTED.
160                                                              REM
170 REM VARIABLE NAMES:
180 REM    N$....CAMPER NAME
190 REM    C$....RESIDENCY CODE
200 REM    D.....DAYS CAMPING
210 REM    A.....FEE AMOUNT
220 REM    T1....FINAL TOTAL - NUMBER OF CAMPERS
230 REM    T2....FINAL TOTAL - FEE AMOUNTS
240 REM    D1....NUMBER OF DAYS FOR RATE CHANGE
250 REM    C1....RATE FOR RESIDENTS UNTIL RATE CHANGE
260 REM    C2....RATE FOR RESIDENTS AFTER RATE CHANGE
270 REM    C3....RATE FOR NON-RESIDENTS PER DAY
280 REM    R$....RESIDENT CONSTANT
290 REM    O$....OUT OF STATE (NON-RESIDENT) CONSTANT
300 REM    U$....UNKNOWN RESIDENT CONSTANT
310 REM    F1$...DETAIL LINE PRINT USING FORMAT
320 REM    F2$...TOTAL CAMPERS LINE PRINT USING FORMAT
330 REM    F3$...TOTAL FEE AMOUNT LINE PRINT USING FORMAT
340                                                              REM
```

The documentation, as in previous programs, indicates the function of the program and also specifies the use of the variable names in the program. After the documentation, the data to be processed in the program and the initialization of the variables is coded (Figure 5-31).

```
350 REM ***** DATA TO BE PROCESSED *****
360                                                              REM
370 DATA "JACK HENRY", "R", 3
380 DATA "DON JAMES", "R", 8
390 DATA "BILL DONALD", "N", 9
400 DATA "RALPH ADAM", "F", 6
410 DATA "MURRAY FRANK", "R", 7
420 DATA "END OF FILE", "E", 9
430                                                              REM
440 REM ***** INITIALIZATION OF VARIABLES *****
450                                                              REM
460 LET D1 = 7
470 LET C1 = 7.95
480 LET C2 = 5.95
490 LET C3 = 9.95
500 LET T1 = 0
510 LET T2 = 0
520 LET R$ = "RESIDENT"
530 LET O$ = "NON-RESIDENT"
540 LET U$ = "UNKNOWN"
550 LET F1$ = "\           \ \              \  ##   ###.##"
560 LET F2$ = "TOTAL CAMPERS ###"
570 LET F3$ = "TOTAL FEE AMOUNT $$,###.##"
580                                                              REM
```

Figure 5-31 The variables are initialized with the values stated in the program specifications. If a change of these values is required at a later time, the only place they will be changed is in the variable initialization portion of the program.

The data to be processed contains the name, the residency code, and the days camping. The variable fields are initialized according to the program specifications. Thus, D1 (the number of days for a rate change) is initialized to 7, while the camping rates are initialized to 7.95 (resident — first seven days), 5.95 (resident — rate after seven days), and 9.95 (non-resident rate). If the rates or time for a rate change are ever changed in this program, the only place in the program where changes will have to be made is in the variable initialization area. No changes will have to be made to the processing portion of the program.

The processing coding within the program, except for final total printing, is shown in Figure 5-32. The headings are printed first, followed by the reading of the first input record (line 660). The name field (N$) is then checked for the value END OF FILE to determine if the trailer record has been read. If it has not been read, the next test, on line 690, is to determine if the input record is for a resident of the state. If it is, control is passed to line 790; while if it is not, control passes to line 700.

At line 700, a test is made to determine if the camper is a non-resident camper (value N in C$). It should be noted that this test is made even though the if statement on line 690 determined that the camper was not a resident. The reason is that when checking the values in input fields (which is called editing

```
590 REM ***** PROCESSING *****
600                                                        REM
610 PRINT TAB(11) "DESERT STATE PARK"
620 PRINT " "
630 PRINT "     NAME        RESIDENCY    DAYS    FEES"
640 PRINT " "
650                                                        REM
660 READ N$, C$, D
670                                                        REM
680 IF N$ = "END OF FILE" THEN 940
690   IF C$ = "R" THEN 790
700     IF C$ = "N" THEN 740
710       PRINT USING F1$; N$, U$
720       GOTO 900
730                                                        REM
740       LET A = D * C3
750       LET T2 = T2 + A
760       PRINT USING F1$; N$, O$, D, A
770       GOTO 900
780                                                        REM
790     IF D > D1 THEN 830
800       LET A = D * C1
810       GOTO 860
820                                                        REM
830       LET A = (D1 * C1) + ((D-D1) * C2)
840       GOTO 860
850                                                        REM
860     LET T2 = T2 + A
870     PRINT USING F1$; N$, R$, D, A
880     GOTO 900
890                                                        REM
900   LET T1 = T1 + 1
910   READ N$, C$, D
920 GOTO 680
```

the input fields), the programmer must never assume that if one value is not found in the field, another value will be. Thus, the fact that the value R was not found in the C$ field does not mean that the value N will be found there. The test on line 700 is made to ensure that the non-resident code is properly in the input record. If it is, control is passed to line 740 where the non-resident camping fees are calculated and printed.

If, however, the value N is not found in C$, then the input record contains an error. This is noted on the report by printing the word UNKNOWN in place of the residency (see Figure 5-28). When editing input records, it is important that any error be recorded on the report. Since the residency is not known, the camping fees cannot be calculated, so after the line is printed, control is passed to line 900, where the camper total counter is incremented by 1 and another record is read.

If the camper is a resident, as determined by the if statement on line 690, control is passed to statement 790. There, a test is made to determine the number of days the resident is camping. If the days camping (D) is greater

Figure 5-32 The coding in the processing portion of the program implements the logic developed in the flowchart in Figure 5-29. Note in this program the manner in which nested if-then-else structures are coded. These coding conventions should be used for all BASIC programs.

than the rate change days (D1), then the let statement on line 830 will calculate the camping fees. Otherwise, the statement on line 800 calculates the fees. On line 860, the camping fee final total accumulator is updated by whatever the camping fees were (A), and then the line is printed on the report. At line 900, the camper total accumulator is incremented by 1, and another record is read.

This main loop will continue until the trailer record is read. At that time, control is passed to the statement at line 940 for the printing of the final totals (Figure 5-33).

Figure 5-33 The final totals are printed through the use of the print using statement.

```
940 PRINT " "
950 PRINT USING F2$; T1
960 PRINT USING F3$; T2
970 END
```

After a blank line is printed, the print using statements on lines 950 and 960 print the final totals. The program is then terminated.

Coding tips

The following tips should be kept in mind when coding programs containing if statements:

1. When designing the program, great care must be taken to ensure that the proper values are being compared and that the correct action will be taken when the if statement is executed. A common error is that, for example, the condition greater than is tested for when actually the condition tested should have been equal to or greater than.

2. When designing test data for a program, always have data which will test for "off by one" errors. For example, if a value in a record is tested to determine if it is greater than 7, then test a record with a value 7 in the field and a record with the value 8 in the field. In this manner, it is unlikely that an "off by one" error will occur.

3. Always use the spacing and indentation standards illustrated in the programs in this book for if statements. It is very important that if statements be easily read and understood.

4. When real numbers are to be compared in the program, remember the potential problem when attempting to determine if two numbers are equal. Always consider using a test as shown in this chapter as opposed to an exactly equal test.

The coding for the entire sample program is illustrated below and on the following page.   **Sample program**

```
100 REM CAMPFEE              DECEMBER 7              SHELLY/CASHMAN
110                                                                REM
120 REM THIS PROGRAM PRODUCES A CAMPING FEES REPORT FOR
130 REM DESERT STATE PARK. THE FEES ARE BASED UPON
140 REM RESIDENCY AND LENGTH OF STAY. FINAL TOTALS FOR
150 REM THE NUMBER OF CAMPERS AND THE FEE AMOUNTS ARE PRINTED.
160                                                                REM
170 REM VARIABLE NAMES:
180 REM    N$....CAMPER NAME
190 REM    C$....RESIDENCY CODE
200 REM    D.....DAYS CAMPING
210 REM    A.....FEE AMOUNT
220 REM    T1....FINAL TOTAL - NUMBER OF CAMPERS
230 REM    T2....FINAL TOTAL - FEE AMOUNTS
240 REM    D1....NUMBER OF DAYS FOR RATE CHANGE
250 REM    C1....RATE FOR RESIDENTS UNTIL RATE CHANGE
260 REM    C2....RATE FOR RESIDENTS AFTER RATE CHANGE
270 REM    C3....RATE FOR NON-RESIDENTS PER DAY
280 REM    R$....RESIDENT CONSTANT
290 REM    O$....OUT OF STATE (NON-RESIDENT) CONSTANT
300 REM    U$....UNKNOWN RESIDENT CONSTANT
310 REM    F1$...DETAIL LINE PRINT USING FORMAT
320 REM    F2$...TOTAL CAMPERS LINE PRINT USING FORMAT
330 REM    F3$...TOTAL FEE AMOUNT LINE PRINT USING FORMAT
340                                                                REM
350 REM ***** DATA TO BE PROCESSED *****
360                                                                REM
370 DATA "JACK HENRY", "R", 3
380 DATA "DON JAMES", "R", 8
390 DATA "BILL DONALD", "N", 9
400 DATA "RALPH ADAM", "F", 6
410 DATA "MURRAY FRANK", "R", 7
420 DATA "END OF FILE", "E", 9
430                                                                REM
440 REM ***** INITIALIZATION OF VARIABLES *****
450                                                                REM
460 LET D1 = 7
470 LET C1 = 7.95
480 LET C2 = 5.95
490 LET C3 = 9.95
500 LET T1 = 0
510 LET T2 = 0
520 LET R$ = "RESIDENT"
530 LET O$ = "NON-RESIDENT"
540 LET U$ = "UNKNOWN"
550 LET F1$ = "\            \ \              \  ##  ###.##"
560 LET F2$ = "TOTAL CAMPERS ###"
570 LET F3$ = "TOTAL FEE AMOUNT $$,###.##"
580                                                                REM
```

Figure 5-34 Sample program (Part 1 of 2)

```
590 REM ***** PROCESSING *****
600                                                        REM
610 PRINT TAB(11) "DESERT STATE PARK"
620 PRINT " "
630 PRINT "    NAME        RESIDENCY   DAYS   FEES"
640 PRINT " "
650                                                        REM
660 READ N$, C$, D
670                                                        REM
680 IF N$ = "END OF FILE" THEN 940
690   IF C$ = "R" THEN 790
700     IF C$ = "N" THEN 740
710       PRINT USING F1$; N$, U$
720       GOTO 900
730                                                        REM
740       LET A = D * C3
750       LET T2 = T2 + A
760       PRINT USING F1$; N$, O$, D, A
770       GOTO 900
780                                                        REM
790     IF D > D1 THEN 830
800       LET A = D * C1
810       GOTO 860
820                                                        REM
830       LET A = (D1 * C1) + ((D-D1) * C2)
840       GOTO 860
850                                                        REM
860     LET T2 = T2 + A
870     PRINT USING F1$; N$, R$, D, A
880     GOTO 900
890                                                        REM
900   LET T1 = T1 + 1
910   READ N$, C$, D
920 GOTO 680
930                                                        REM
940 PRINT " "
950 PRINT USING F2$; T1
960 PRINT USING F3$; T2
970 END
```

Figure 5-35 Sample program (Part 2 of 2)

The following points have been discussed and explained in this chapter.   SUMMARY

1. The if-then-else logic structure and the BASIC if statement form an important basis for much of the programming that is performed on computer systems.

2. A nested if-then-else structure is one which is contained within another if-then-else structure.

3. When a condition being tested in the if-then-else structure is true, one set of instructions is executed. When the condition is false, another set of instructions is executed.

4. A nested if-then-else structure will be executed only after the preceding if statement has been executed.

5. All if-then-else structures have a single entry point and a single exit point. This holds true for nested if-then-else structures as well.

6. Nested if-then-else structures can be executed when the previously tested condition is true and when the previously tested condition is false.

7. A nested if-then-else structure can be contained within another nested if-then-else structure.

8. It is very important that programs be developed using proper control structures that exactly follow the rules for the structure. If this does not happen, programs very quickly become difficult to read, understand, and use.

9. The nested if-then-else structure is implemented in BASIC using the if statement.

10. Coding conventions, including spacing and indentation, should always be followed for if and nested if statements.

11. Nested if-then-else structures can have statements precede them or follow them.

12. The first general rule for needing a nested if-then-else structure is: If a given condition must be tested only when a previous condition has been tested, AND alternative actions are required for one or more of the conditions, then a nested if-then-else structure is required.

13. The second general rule for needing a nested if-then-else structure is: If a given condition must be tested only when a previous condition has been tested, AND one or more statements are to be executed before or after the second if-then-else structure, then a nested if-then-else structure is required.

14. Logical operators are used to combine conditions in an if statement.

15. The word AND is used to mean both when two or more conditions are specified in an if statement.

16. When the word AND is used to join conditions in an if statement, all conditions specified must be true or the if statement is considered false.

17. The OR logical operator is used to indicate that if either or both conditions are true, then the if statement is considered true.

18. When logical operators are combined within an if statement, they are

evaluated according to a predefined priority. The conditions combined by the word OR are evaluated first and then those combined by the word AND are evaluated. (And is First - not or)

19. The predefined priority for evaluating combined if statements can be altered through the use of parentheses. Those combinations specified within parentheses will be evaluated first, followed by those outside the parentheses.

20. It is recommended that parentheses always be used with combined if statements even when the predefined priority would yield the correct results. In this manner, there will be no confusion regarding the processing to take place.

21. The not logical operator may be encountered in some programs. However, since research has shown that human beings have difficulty evaluating "not" logic, it is suggested that the not logical operator be omitted from programs.

22. When a condition being evaluated is true, the internal circuitry of the computer system returns the value –1. When the condition is false, the value 0 is returned. The if statement is able to test these values to determine what action to take.

23. An if statement can be written with just a variable name in it, not a set of values separated by a relational operator. If this is done, the if statement will be considered true if the value in the field is non-zero. If the value is zero, the if statement is considered false.

24. It can be useful to trace exactly what processing is taking place in a program to ensure that the correct logic is being implemented.

25. Tracing the processing within a program can be implemented through the use of the TRON (TRace ON) instruction.

26. Tracing is turned off by using the TROFF (TRace OFF) instruction.

27. When tracing is turned on, the line numbers which are executed are displayed on the screen while the program is running.

28. The trace instructions can be placed in the program during testing and debugging, but they are normally taken out of the program once the program is working properly.

29. The execution of a program can be halted by the stop instruction. When executed, the stop instruction causes the program to be halted. The program is resumed at the instruction following the stop instruction when the computer operator types the word CONT on the keyboard.

30. When a BASIC instruction is written without a line number, it is executed immediately.

31. Computer systems store numbers in which a decimal point appears (real numbers) in a form called floating point. This method of representing numbers does not always produce the exact value of the number.

32. When real numbers are compared, results may not be what are expected. Therefore, when writing programs which compare real numbers, the programmer should be aware that although numerically the value should be

equal to another number, it may not be when it is compared.

33. To overcome the inexactness of real numbers, a statement can be written which tests against a range of values. If the difference between two numbers is very small, the difference is attributed to the representation of the numbers, and they are considered equal.

34. The ABS (ABSolute) function returns the absolute value of the number or arithmetic expression which is contained within the parentheses immediately following the letters ABS.

35. An exclamation point following a numeric literal indicates that the number is a real number stored as a single precision number. A single precision number contains seven or fewer digits.

36. When scientific notation is used, a number with one position to the left of the decimal point is printed together with an exponent value which indicates the value to the base 10 to which the number is raised.

37. When integers, which are numbers that contain no digits to the right of the decimal point, are compared, the exact values of the numbers will be used. The approximations required with real numbers are not used.

38. When checking the values in the input fields (which is called editing the fields), the programmer must never assume that if one value is not found in a field, another value will be.

39. When editing input records, it is important that any error in the input data be recorded on the report.

40. When designing test data for a program, always have data which will test for "off by one" errors. For example, if a value in a record is tested to determine if it is greater than 20, then test a record with the value 20 in the field and a record with the value 21 in the field.

41. Always use the spacing and indentation standards illustrated in the text.

1. What is a nested if-then-else structure? When is it used?
2. If-then-else structures have single entry and single exit points, but nested if-then-else structures must have multiple exit points (T or F).
3. The word AND in a combined if statement means: a) And; b) Either or both; c) Both; d) Neither.
4. The word OR in a combined if statement means: a) Or; b) Either or both; c) Both; d) Neither.
5. The logical operators AND and OR are evaluated left to right in a combined if statement (T or F).
6. Parentheses: a) Cannot be used with logical operators; b) Should never be used with logical operators; c) Normally should be used with logical operators; d) Must be used or a syntax error will occur.
7. Explain the use of the NOT logical operator. Is it recommended that this operator be used? Why?
8. The TRON and TROFF statements are used to: a) Trace the interpretation of the program; b) Trace the value in the variable name specified following the TRON statement; c) Translate the values in variable fields into real numbers; d) Trace the line numbers which are executed.
9. When a BASIC statement is written without a line number: a) The statement is executed immediately; b) A syntax error occurs; c) The statement is merged into the program at the beginning; d) The statement is merged into the program at the end.
10. The execution of a program can be halted through the use of the: a) Halt instruction; b) Cease instruction; c) Stop instruction; d) Cont instruction.
11. Real numbers are stored in a format which does not always produce the exact value of the number (T or F).
12. What process can be used to overcome the problem of comparing real numbers?
13. What is the absolute function? What role does it play when one real number is subtracted from another real number prior to comparing the two numbers?
14. The number $1.00078E + 4$ is represented in: a) BASIC notation; b) Scientific notation; c) Real number notation; d) Integer notation.
15. Modify the sample program in this chapter to print a final total of the number of resident campers and the number of non-resident campers in addition to the totals currently printed.
16. The state has changed the camping fees at Desert State Park to the following: If a resident stays 1 — 10 days, the charge is 8.95 per day. If a resident stays more than 10 days, the charge is 6.96 per day. If a non-resident stays 1 — 14 days, the charge is 12.95 per day. If a non-resident stays more than 14 days, the charge is 10.95 per day. Modify the sample program in this chapter to process these changes.

Chapter 5
DEBUGGING EXERCISES

The following lines of code contain one or more coding errors. Circle each
of the errors and write the coding to correct the errors.

1.
```
610 PRINT TAB (11) "DESERT STATE PARK"
620 PRINT " "
630 PRINT "     NAME        RESIDENCY   DAYS  FEES"
640 PRINT " "
```

2.
```
680 IF N$ = "END OF FILE" THEN 940
690    IF C$ = "R" THEN 740
700       IF C$ = "N" THEN 740
710          PRINT USING F1$; N$, U$
720          GOTO 860
730                                                    REM
740          LET A = D * C3
750          LET T2 = T2 + A
760          PRINT USING F1$; N$, O$, D, A
770          GOTO 860
780                                                    REM
790       IF D > D1 THEN 830
800          LET A = D * C1
810          GOTO 860
820                                                    REM
830          LET A = (D1 * C1) + ((D-D1) * C2)
840          GOTO 860
850                                                    REM
860       LET T2 = T2 + A
870       PRINT USING F1$ N$, R$, D, A
880       GOTO 900
890                                                    REM
900    LET T1 = T1 + 1
910    READ N$, C$, D
920 GOTO 680
930                                                    REM
940 PRINT " "
```

3.
```
680 IF N = "END OF FILE" THEN 940
690    IF C = "R" THEN 790
700       IF C = "N" THEN 740
```

Chapter 5
PROGRAM DEBUGGING

The following program was designed and written to produce the camping fee report in the format shown in Figure 5-1 (page 5.1). The output actually produced by the program is illustrated on page 5.35. Analyze the output to determine if it is correct. If it is in error, circle the errors and write corrections.

Program

```
100 REM CAMPFEE            DECEMBER 7              SHELLY/CASHMAN
110                                                            REM
120 REM THIS PROGRAM PRODUCES A CAMPING FEES REPORT FOR
130 REM DESERT STATE PARK. THE FEES ARE BASED UPON
140 REM RESIDENCY AND LENGTH OF STAY. FINAL TOTALS FOR
150 REM THE NUMBER OF CAMPERS AND THE FEE AMOUNTS ARE PRINTED.
160                                                            REM
170 REM VARIABLE NAMES:
180 REM    N$....CAMPER NAME
190 REM    C$....RESIDENCY CODE
200 REM    D.....DAYS CAMPING
210 REM    A.....FEE AMOUNT
220 REM    T1....FINAL TOTAL - NUMBER OF CAMPERS
230 REM    T2....FINAL TOTAL - FEE AMOUNTS
240 REM    D1....NUMBER OF DAYS FOR RATE CHANGE
250 REM    C1....RATE FOR RESIDENTS UNTIL RATE CHANGE
260 REM    C2....RATE FOR RESIDENTS AFTER RATE CHANGE
270 REM    C3....RATE FOR NON-RESIDENTS PER DAY
280 REM    R$....RESIDENT CONSTANT
290 REM    O$....OUT OF STATE (NON-RESIDENT) CONSTANT
300 REM    U$....UNKNOWN RESIDENT CONSTANT
310 REM    F1$...DETAIL LINE PRINT USING FORMAT
320 REM    F2$...TOTAL CAMPERS LINE PRINT USING FORMAT
330 REM    F3$...TOTAL FEE AMOUNT LINE PRINT USING FORMAT
340                                                            REM
350 REM ***** DATA TO BE PROCESSED *****
360                                                            REM
370 DATA "JACK HENRY", "R", 3
380 DATA "DON JAMES", "R", 8
390 DATA "BILL DONALD", "N", 9
400 DATA "RALPH ADAM", "F", 6
410 DATA "MURRAY FRANK", "R", 7
420 DATA "END OF FILE", "E", 9
430                                                            REM
440 REM ***** INITIALIZATION OF VARIABLES *****
450                                                            REM
460 LET D1 = 7
470 LET C1 = 7.95
480 LET C2 = 5.95
490 LET C3 = 9.95
500 LET T1 = 0
510 LET T2 = 0
520 LET R$ = "RESIDENT"
530 LET O$ = "NON-RESIDENT"
540 LET U$ = "UNKNOWN"
```

```
550 LET F1$ = "\              \  \              \  ##   ###.##"
560 LET F2$ = "TOTAL CAMPERS ###"
570 LET F3$ = "TOTAL FEE AMOUNT $$,###.##"
580                                                              REM
590 REM ***** PROCESSING *****
600                                                              REM
610 PRINT TAB(11) "DESERT STATE PARK"
620 PRINT " "
630 PRINT "    NAME          RESIDENCY   DAYS  FEES"
640 PRINT " "
650                                                              REM
660 READ N$, C$, D
670                                                              REM
680 IF N$ = "END OF FILE" THEN 940
690   IF C$ = "R" THEN 790
700     IF C$ = "N" THEN 740
710       PRINT USING F1$; N$, U$
720       GOTO 900
730                                                              REM
740       LET A = D * C3
750       LET T2 = T2 + A
760       PRINT USING F1$; N$, O$, D, A
770       GOTO 900
780                                                              REM
790     IF D > D1 THEN 830
800       LET A = D * C1
810       GOTO 900
820                                                              REM
830       LET A = (D1 * C1) + ((D-D1) * C2)
840       GOTO 900
850                                                              REM
860     LET T2 = T2 + A
870     PRINT USING F1$; N$, R$, D, A
880     GOTO 900
890                                                              REM
900   LET T1 = T1 + 1
910   READ N$, C$, D
920 GOTO 680
930                                                              REM
940 PRINT " "
950 PRINT USING F2$; T1
960 PRINT USING F3$; T2
970 END
```

Part 2 of 2

Output

```
                    DESERT STATE PARK

           NAME          RESIDENCY   DAYS  FEES

        BILL DONALD   NON-RESIDENT    9    89.55
        RALPH ADAM    UNKNOWN

        TOTAL CAMPERS   5
        TOTAL FEE AMOUNT    $89.55
```

Chapter 5
PROGRAMMING ASSIGNMENT 1

Instructions   A country club dues report is to be prepared. A program should be designed and coded in BASIC to produce the table.

Input   Input consists of records containing the country club member's name, the type of membership, and the years the member has belonged. The value F in the membership type field indicates a family membership. The value I indicates an individual membership. The input data is illustrated below.

NAME	MEMBERSHIP TYPE	YEARS
HARVEY HANLEY	F	9
WILMA LITT	F	7
EUGENE MITTER	F	2
WALL PITT	I	6
EUNICE PONNIR	I	8

Output   Output is a list of the country club members containing the member's name, the membership type (FAMILY or INDIVIDUAL), the years the member has belonged, and the country club dues. The dues are calculated as follows: If the member is a family member and has been a member more than six years, the dues are $1,200.00. If the member is a family member and has been a member six years or less, the dues are $1,600.00. If the member is an individual member and has been a member longer than 6 years, the country club dues are $800.00. If the member is an individual member and has been a member 6 years or less, the dues are $1,100.00. After all records have been printed, totals for the number of members, the number of individual members, the number of family members, and the total dues are to be printed. The format of the output is illustrated below.

```
              COUNTRY CLUB DUES

       NAME           TYPE       YEARS     DUES

   HARVEY HANLEY   FAMILY         9    $1,200.00
   WILMA LITT      FAMILY         7    $1,200.00
   EUGENE MITTER   FAMILY         2    $1,600.00
   WALLY PITT      INDIVIDUAL     6    $1,100.00
   EUNICE PONNIR   INDIVIDUAL     8    $  800.00

   NUMBER OF MEMBERS      5
   NUMBER OF INDIVIDUALS      2
   NUMBER OF FAMILIES      3
   TOTAL DUES   $5,900.00
```

Chapter 5
PROGRAMMING ASSIGNMENT 2 (10)

A hospital billing report is to be prepared. A program should be designed and coded in BASIC to produce the report.

Instructions

The input consists of the patient's name, the number of days the patient was in the hospital, the type of accomodations, and a code for special services. The value I in the accomodations field indicates intensive care. The value P indicates a private room, while the value D indicates a double room. In the special services field, the value N indicates a special private nurse, which is available only in intensive care; and the value T indicates a T.V., which is available only in the double room. A private room always has a T.V. The input data is illustrated below.

Input

PATIENT'S NAME	DAYS	ROOM ACCOMODATION	SPECIAL SERVICES
HILDA AYALE	6	P	
MILDRED MAS	12	I	
HOWARD NETT	3	I	N
GEENA PITT	6	D	
NORMAN RUSS	18	D	T

Output is a hospital billing report containing the patient's name, the type of room (INTENSIVE, PRIVATE, or DOUBLE), and the total room bill. The daily room rate is calculated as follows: If the room was intensive care, the rate is $398.00 per day. A special nurse adds $100.00 per day to the cost of the room. If a private room was used, the cost is $260.00 per day. If a double room was used, the cost is $135.00 per day. The use of a T.V. adds $40.00 per day to the cost of the room. The total bill is calculated by multiplying the daily rate by the number of days of the stay in the hospital. The totals to be accumulated and the format of the report are shown below.

Output

```
                HOSPITAL BILLING

        NAME            ROOM              BILL

    HILDA AYALE     PRIVATE           1,560.00
    MILDRED MAS     INTENSIVE         5,976.00
    HOWARD NETT     INTENSIVE         1,194.00
    GEENA PITT      DOUBLE              810.00
    NORMAN RUSS     DOUBLE            3,150.00

    TOTAL INTENSIVE PATIENTS    2
    TOTAL PRIVATE PATIENTS    1
    TOTAL DOUBLE PATIENTS    2
    TOTAL BILLING AMOUNT $12,690.00
```

Chapter 5
SUPPLEMENTARY PROGRAMMING ASSIGNMENTS

Instructions   The following programming assignments contain an explanation of the problem and list suggested test data. The student should design the format of the output.

Program 3   A client discount report is to be prepared which lists the client name, the amount of the sale, the discount amount allowed, and the net price. If a client receives a special discount (an "S" in the discount code of the input record), a 12% discount is given if the sales amount is greater than $500.00 and a 10% discount if the sales amount is $500.00 or less. If the client does not receive a special discount ("N" in the discount field), a 3% discount is given if the sales amount is greater than $500.00, and a 2% discount is given if the sales amount is less than or equal to $500.00. After all records have been processed, the total sales amount, discount amount, and net price should be printed.

CLIENT NAME	SALES AMOUNT	DISCOUNT CODE
COLLUM MFG. CO.	2678.90	S
EDAW TOOL AND DIE	499.97	N
FOLSUM BAR CO.	500.75	N
GYRO CO.	321.89	S

Program 4   A stock brokerage commission report is to be prepared. The input contains the name of the salesperson, the amount of the stock purchase or sale, an indicator that the transaction was a purchase or sale ("P" or "S" in the indicator field), and an indicator of the exchange where the transaction took place (N = New York Stock Exchange; A = American Stock Exchange; O = Over the Counter). The report contains the name of the salesperson, the amount of the purchase or sale of stock, the word PURCHASE or SALE, and the commission amount. The commission amount is calculated as follows: If the transaction was a purchase on the New York Stock Exchange (NYSE), the commission is 2.5% of the transaction amount. If the purchase was on the American Stock Exchange (AMEX), the commission is 2.9% of the purchase price. Otherwise, the commission is 3% of the purchase price. If the transaction was a sale on the NYSE, the commission is 1.3% of the sale price; otherwise, the commission is 1.6% of the sales price. After all records have been processed, the total commissions should be printed.

NAME	AMOUNT	TRANSACTION TYPE	EXCHANGE
NEVA NELSON	43009.07	S	A
HELGA OLSON	231.00	P	N
JAMES TURNER	5000.00	S	N
LOIS UNITAN	700.00	P	A
ALBERT VIX	8000.00	S	O
ALLEN YOUNG	900.00	S	O

Program 5

A computer rental report is to be prepared. The input record contains the client's name, the number of hours the system was used, and fields indicating what type of computer was used (Mainframe or Minicomputer), whether disk was used, and whether the printer was used. If the mainframe was used, the field will contain the value Y (Yes). If the minicomputer was used, the field contains the value N (No). If the disk was used, the value Y is in the field; otherwise the value N is in the field. If the printer was used, the value Y is in the field; otherwise, the value N is in the field. The report contains the client's name, the hours the machine was used, the billing rate, and the total amount due (hours x billing rate). The billing rate is calculated as follows: If the mainframe, the printer, and the disk were used, the cost is 192.00 per hour. If the mainframe and disk only were used, the cost is 183.00 per hour. If the mainframe and printer but not the disk were used, the cost is 186.00 per hour. If the mainframe was used without the disk or printer, the cost is 140.00 per hour. If the minicomputer and printer were used, the rate is 93.00 per hour. If the minicomputer is used without the printer, the rate is 49.00 per hour. Disk is used on the minicomputer at no extra charge. After all records have been processed, the total number of hours used for the mainframe, for the minicomputer, for the disk, and for the printer, together with the total amount billed, should be printed.

CLIENT NAME	HOURS	MAINFRAME	DISK	PRINTER
HAINES MFG. CO	12	Y	Y	Y
JEWELL JEWELS	10	Y	Y	N
KRAANK INC.	11	Y	N	Y
LOOM CO.	8	Y	N	N
MIKKE CO.	17	N	Y	Y
NUMM INC.	4	N	N	N

LOOPING — INTERACTIVE PROGRAMMING

OBJECTIVES:

A familiarization with interactive processing

The ability to use the input statement with appropriate prompting

A detailed knowledge of looping and the loop logic structure

The ability to use the for and next statements for looping

LOOPING — INTERACTIVE PROGRAMMING

Programs in the previous chapters have illustrated applications in which looping was used to process input records until end of file was detected. There are many other applications in which looping is of value. Indeed, looping can be used in any problem which requires repetitive actions until a given condition occurs. BASIC provides a set of instructions called For and Next which can be used to implement looping for certain types of applications.

The previous programs have also used the read instruction together with the data statement to provide data for processing. An alternative method for entering data for processing is to enter it from a keyboard or other input device as it is needed. The data is immediately processed by the program. The program then requests more data. This processing can continue indefinitely, so long as the user has more data to enter. This type of entering and processing data is variously called interactive processing, transaction-oriented processing, or real time processing.

This chapter discusses both looping and interactive processing in detail.

Introduction

The sample program in this chapter illustrates both interactive processing and looping by generating an investment chart based upon an amount and interest rate entered by the user. The output of the program is illustrated below.

Sample program

```
DO YOU WANT TO PERFORM AN INVESTMENT CALCULATION?
ENTER YES OR NO: ? YES
```

```
ENTER AMOUNT TO BE INVESTED: ? 1000
ENTER INTEREST RATE: ? 8
```

```
INVESTMENT CHART FOR   $1,000.00 AT   8.00% INTEREST

          YEAR              AMOUNT
           1              $1,080.00
           2              $1,166.40
           3              $1,259.71
           4              $1,360.49
           5              $1,469.33
           6              $1,586.87
           7              $1,713.82
           8              $1,850.93
           9              $1,999.01
          10              $2,158.93

DO YOU WANT TO PERFORM ANOTHER CALCULATION?
ENTER YES OR NO: ?
```

Figure 6-1 The output from the program is an investment chart. The data used for the calculation of the investment chart is entered by the user, as indicated by the ? colored entries.

INTERACTIVE PROGRAMS

In Figure 6-1, the program first asks the user if an investment calculation is to be performed. The user can answer yes or no. If the answer is no, the program is terminated. If the answer is yes, the program displays on the screen the message ENTER AMOUNT TO BE INVESTED:. The user then enters the amount to be used in the investment calculations. Next, the program asks the person to enter the interest rate. After the interest rate is entered, the program calculates and prints the value of the investment for each of ten years using the interest rate.

The user is then asked if another calculation is to be performed. If so, the same sequence of events is followed. If not, the program is terminated. In this program, the data to be processed is entered from the keyboard of the terminal or computer system, not from data statements in the program. In addition, when the data is entered it is immediately acted upon. For example, when the user indicates that yes, another calculation is to be performed, the program immediately responds by asking the amount of the investment. This is a characteristic of interactive programs — they respond immediately to entries made by the user and immediately process the data entered by the user.

The messages printed by the program which ask for data, such as ENTER INTEREST RATE:, are called prompts because they prompt the person to enter data. Prompts are widely used in interactive programming to help the user. Prompts should clearly state the action to be taken by the person using the program.

When data is entered from the terminal or computer keyboard, there is the possibility that invalid data will be entered. The program must, therefore, check the data entered to ensure that it conforms to the program requirements. This process of checking input data is called data editing. In the sample program, the answer to the question DO YOU WANT TO PERFORM AN INVESTMENT CALCULATION? must be either YES or NO. Any other answer will cause an error message to be printed (Figure 6-2).

Figure 6-2 Editing input data in an interactive program is mandatory if the program is to operate properly.

```
DO YOU WANT TO PERFORM AN INVESTMENT CALCULATION?
ENTER YES OR NO: ? YAS
        INVALID RESPONSE - PLEASE ENTER YES OR NO: ?
```

In Figure 6-2, the keyboard operator entered the value YAS in response to the prompt. This answer is invalid. Therefore, the program responds with a message indicating an invalid response and asks the operator to enter the word yes or the word no.

To enable data to be entered in an interactive environment, the BASIC language contains the Input statement. This statement is explained in the following section.

The input statement causes the program to halt operation until the user has entered one or more values or characters through the computer or terminal keyboard. The data entered via the keyboard is displayed on the CRT screen and is stored in main computer storage. Once stored in main computer storage, it is available for processing as required.

The general format of the input statement is illustrated below.

$$\text{line number} \quad INPUT \left\{ \begin{array}{l} \textit{numeric variable,...} \\ \textit{string variable,...} \end{array} \right\}$$

Input statement

Figure 6-3 When the input statement is written, a numeric variable or a string variable can be specified. The input statement allows data to be entered from a computer or terminal keyboard.

The input statement begins with a line number. The line number is followed by one or more spaces and then the word INPUT. The word INPUT is followed by one or more spaces and then one or more numeric and/or string variable names.

As noted, when the input statement is executed, the program is halted while the user enters data on the keyboard. The data is stored in main computer storage in the field or fields identified by the variable names following the word INPUT. When the enter or return key is depressed, program execution then continues. This process is illustrated in Figure 6-4.

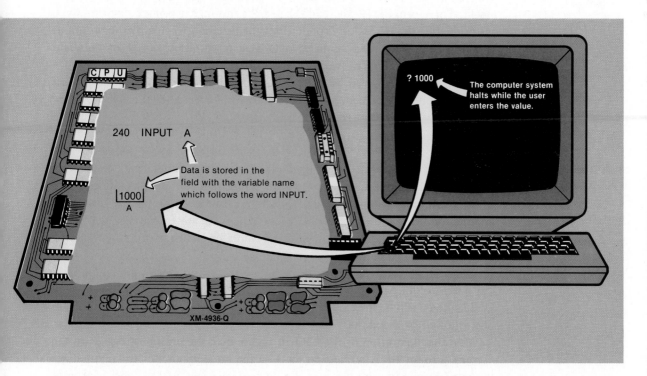

240 INPUT A

Data is stored in the field with the variable name which follows the word INPUT.

1000
A

? 1000

The computer system halts while the user enters the value.

XM-4936-Q

Figure 6-4 When the input statement is executed, the computer system halts while the user enters the data. The data is stored in the field identified by the variable name in the input statement.

In Figure 6-4, when the input statement is executed, a question mark (?) is displayed on the CRT screen and the program execution is halted. The question mark indicates to the user that the program is waiting for an entry to be made from the keyboard. The operator in the example entered the value 1000 and depressed the enter or return key. The value entered is stored in the field identified by the variable name A. When the key is depressed, program execution is continued with the next statement in the program.

In the input statement in Figure 6-4, the numeric variable name A is specified following the word INPUT. Therefore, numeric data must be entered by the user. The numeric data can consist of numbers, a decimal point, and a plus or minus sign. If any other character is entered when the variable name is numeric, the computer system will issue an error message, and the data will have to be reentered (Figure 6-5).

Figure 6-5 An error message is issued when non-numeric data is entered for a numeric variable. The actual message varies between computer systems. Other messages could be ? REDO, ? REENTER, or similar wording.

```
?  10M0.00
?  REDO FROM START
?  1000.00
```

In Figure 6-5, the operator inadvertently entered the letter M in place of a zero. The BASIC interpreter will not allow a string character in the numeric field. Therefore, the REDO FROM START message is printed. This message is printed by the BASIC interpreter, not the program written by the programmer. When the correct numeric data is entered, it is stored in the field identified by the numeric variable and execution continues.

String variables can be used with the input statement as well. When a string variable is specified, any characters may be entered by the operator. The data entered will be stored in the field identified by the string variable name.

Input statement prompts

A prompt message can be included within the input statement. The general format of the input statement with a prompt together with an example are shown in Figure 6-6. The string constant is placed within double quotation marks following the word INPUT. When the input statement is executed, the message within the quotation marks is printed prior to the program's halting for the data to be entered.

The string constant within the quotation marks is, in the example, followed by a semicolon. After the semicolon is the variable name of the field where the data entered will be stored. On some computer systems, the string constant can be followed by a comma.

In the illustration of the CRT in Figure 6-6, the prompt message on the screen is followed by a question mark in the same manner as the input statement without a prompt message. On some computer systems, when a prompt message is printed no question mark is printed by the input statement. On

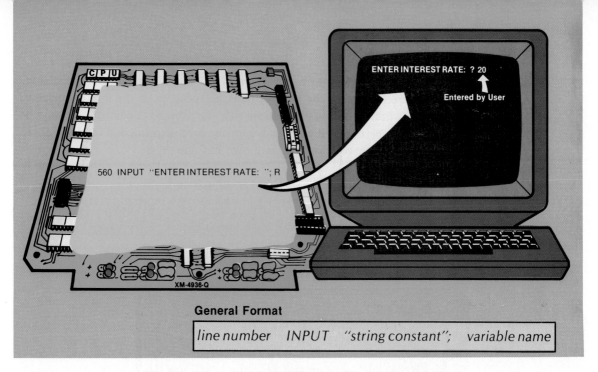

560 INPUT "ENTER INTEREST RATE: "; R

ENTER INTEREST RATE: ? 20

Entered by User

General Format

| line number   INPUT   "string constant";   variable name |

Figure 6-6 The message specified in the input statement — ENTER INTEREST RATE: — is printed before program execution is halted. The question mark is printed immediately following the message and the program is halted.

others, a question mark is printed if the string constant is followed by a semicolon; whereas if the string constant is followed by a comma, no question mark is printed. The programmer should examine the exact rules for the computer system being used.

The print statement can be used in place of or together with the prompt message in the input statement for further prompting (Figure 6-7).

Prompting with the print statement

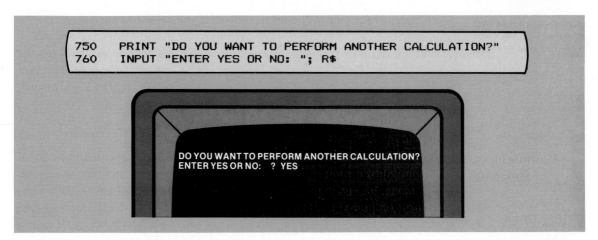

```
750    PRINT "DO YOU WANT TO PERFORM ANOTHER CALCULATION?"
760    INPUT "ENTER YES OR NO: "; R$
```

DO YOU WANT TO PERFORM ANOTHER CALCULATION?
ENTER YES OR NO: ? YES

Figure 6-7 The print statement prompt is used with the input statement prompt when two lines are required for the prompt message.

The print statement on line 750 in Figure 6-7 displays a prompt message on the screen prior to the prompt message specified in the input statement. When two lines of messages are required, the print statement must always be used. It may be required when only one line is to be printed if variables are to be printed on the prompt line, as shown in Figure 6-8.

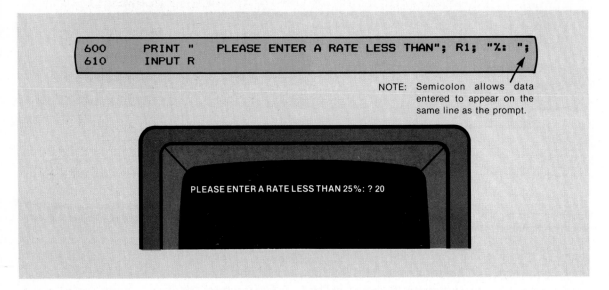

```
600     PRINT "    PLEASE ENTER A RATE LESS THAN"; R1; "%: ";
610     INPUT R
```

NOTE: Semicolon allows data entered to appear on the same line as the prompt.

PLEASE ENTER A RATE LESS THAN 25%: ? 20

Figure 6-8 Whenever a value in a field identified by a variable name is to appear in a prompt message, the print statement must be used for the prompt message. In this example, the print statement ends with a semicolon (;). Therefore, the interest rate which is entered (20) appears on the same line as the prompt message.

In the example above, the print statement on line 600 contains a message constant, the variable R1, and the constant %. The value in R1 is printed as part of the prompt message when the print statement is executed. The print statement must be used in this example even though only a single prompt line is produced because a variable, such as R1, cannot be used in the prompt message used with an input statement. Only a constant value can be used in an input statement prompt. Therefore, whenever the value in a variable field is to appear in a prompt, the print statement must be used to print the prompt.

The semicolon at the end of the print statement on line 600 will keep the cursor on the same line as the prompt message. Therefore, when the input statement on line 610 is executed, the interest rate entered by the user will appear on the same line as the prompt message.

Multiple input variables

More than one numeric or string variable name may be specified in an input statement. If more than one variable name is included in an input statement, the names are separated by a comma in the statement (Figure 6-9). When the data is entered from the keyboard, the values for each variable must be separated by commas. Thus, in the example, the entry JOHN SLOAN will be placed in the field identified by the variable name N$, and the entry 18 will be placed in the field identified by the variable name A. Note that both the

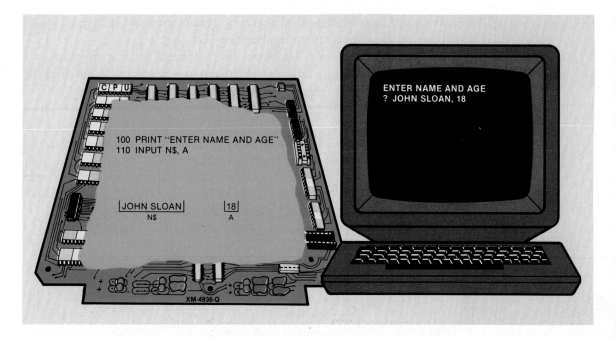

```
100  PRINT "ENTER NAME AND AGE"
110  INPUT N$, A
```

JOHN SLOAN
N$

18
A

XM-4936-Q

variable names and the entries by the user on the keyboard are separated by commas.

If the return or enter key is depressed before all values have been entered in response to an input statement with multiple variable names, different computer systems will react in different ways. On many computer systems, the BASIC interpreter will type two question marks (??), and the user will continue to enter values until all variables have been accounted for. On other computer systems, entering fewer values than the number of variable names in the input statement will cause the BASIC interpreter to print an error message. The user will then be required to reenter all of the values. The programmer should determine the response found on the computer system being used.

When a comma is placed in the data being entered on the keyboard, the input statement interprets it as a sentinel indicating that another value is to be entered. If, however, a string constant being entered is supposed to contain a comma, then the string constant entered on the keyboard must be enclosed within double quotation marks when entered. In this manner, the input statement can distinguish between a comma used to separate values being entered and a comma which is a part of a value. Similarly, if the value being entered contains a semicolon or a colon, the value must be enclosed within double quotation marks.

If more values are entered than there are variable names specified in the input statement, different computer systems handle the situation in different ways. On some systems, a message such as EXTRA IGNORED will be printed and execution of the program will continue. On other systems, an error

Figure 6-9 When multiple variable names are specified in the input statement, the names are separated by commas in the statement. The data entered is also separated by commas. Numeric and string variables can both be used in a single input statement.

message will be printed, and the user must reenter the same number of values as there are variable names in the input statement.

The input statement provides the primary means for users to enter data into a computer system in an interactive program. An understanding of its use is important when designing and writing interactive BASIC programs.

LOOPING

Applications frequently involve performing certain operations until a condition occurs. These types of applications are particularly well suited for a computer since a single set of instructions can be executed many hundreds or even thousands of times. When operations are to be repeated until a given condition occurs, a looping logic structure should be used.

The flowchart below illustrates the basic elements of the looping structure.

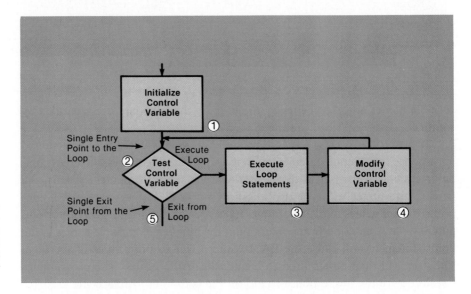

Figure 6-10 The five elements of a loop are: 1) Initialize the control variable; 2) Test the control variable; 3) Execute loop statements; 4) Modify the control variable; 5) Exit from the loop.

Every loop which is used in a computer program will possess the five elements of a loop illustrated in Figure 6-10. These elements are:

1. Initialize the control variable: This step involves setting an initial value which can be tested in step #2. In many applications, a variable field will be initialized to a given value in this step. The field can be initialized using any instruction appropriate, such as a let statement or a read statement.

2. Test the control variable: This step is the first step in the actual loop processing. It is the single entry point into the loop. When the control variable is tested, a determination is made concerning whether the body of the loop should be executed. This determination is made based upon the requirements of the program. For example, if there are more records to process or if the value in a field is not equal to a required

value, the loop could be entered; otherwise, an exit from the loop would occur.

3. Execute loop statements: The processing statements within the loop are executed when the loop is entered. These statements can be a single print statement or thousands of statements which themselves implement other looping structures within the structure illustrated in Figure 6–10. The statements can also implement the if-then-else logic structure within the loop. The only restriction on the statements within the loop is that control cannot be passed to statements outside the loop. To allow an instruction to pass control to a statement outside the loop violates the single entry-single exit rule for the loop logic structure. The only way an exit from the loop logic structure can occur is when the condition is tested in step #2, and a determination is made that the loop should be exited.

4. Modify control variable: During or after the execution of the instructions within the loop, an instruction or instructions must be executed which will modify the control variable that is checked in step #2. The variable will not necessarily be modified each time the body of the loop is executed, but it must be modified at some point so that the decision in step #2 will be to exit from the loop, not to enter the loop again. If the variable is not modified, an endless loop will occur because the decision in step #2 will always be to enter the loop.

5. Exit from the loop: At some point in the processing, after the control variable is modified in step #4, the decision will be to exit from the loop, not to enter the loop for further processing. This decision must be made in step #2. When the exit from the loop occurs, the statement in the program immediately following the decision statement is executed.

The loops used in previous programs to read data from a data statement and process the data until the trailer record is read contain all the elements of a loop just discussed. This is illustrated in Figure 6–11.

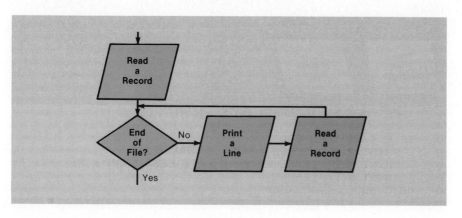

Figure 6–11 This loop which has been used in previous programs to read and process data contains all the elements of the loop illustrated in Figure 6–10.

The first statement which reads a record in Figure 6-11 acts as the control variable initialization because the control variable is the field containing the value END OF FILE. This value is placed in the field by a read statement. The end of file question tests the control variable. If the field contains END OF FILE, an exit from the loop will occur. Otherwise, the body of the loop is entered. As can be seen, it is possible that the loop will never be entered because the first record read could conceivably contain the value END OF FILE.

If the first record contains a value other than END OF FILE, the body of the loop is entered, and a line is printed. The printing of the line corresponds to step #3 — the execution of the loop statements. In some programs in previous chapters, this processing has been considerably more complex than printing a line on the screen. Regardless of the complexity of the processing within the loop, however, the loop logic structure remains the same.

After the print statement is executed, a read statement is performed. This statement corresponds to step #4 — modifying the control variable — because it will place a new value in the field which may contain the value END OF FILE. After the read statement is executed, control is passed back to the end of file decision, which corresponds to step #2 in the loop. If the field being checked indicates end of file, an exit from the loop will occur. Otherwise, the loop will be entered again for further processing. Thus, the basic loop which has been seen in all previous programs contains all of the elements of the loop logic structure.

In the sample program, the user will enter an interest rate which is used in calculating the values of the investment. The program specifications state the interest rate must be less than 25%. The logic and coding to implement this checking is shown in Figure 6-12.

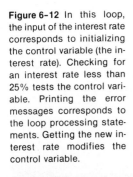

Figure 6-12 In this loop, the input of the interest rate corresponds to initializing the control variable (the interest rate). Checking for an interest rate less than 25% tests the control variable. Printing the error messages corresponds to the loop processing statements. Getting the new interest rate modifies the control variable.

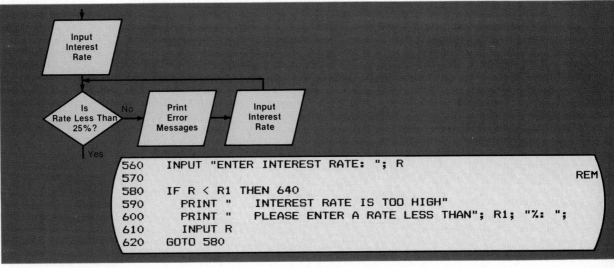

```
560     INPUT "ENTER INTEREST RATE: "; R
570                                                                    REM
580     IF R < R1 THEN 640
590         PRINT "    INTEREST RATE IS TOO HIGH"
600         PRINT "    PLEASE ENTER A RATE LESS THAN"; R1; "%: ";
610         INPUT R
620     GOTO 580
```

The loop illustrated in Figure 6–12 is identical in structure to that shown in Figure 6–11 even though the function performed by the loop is entirely different. The basic loop logic structure will always be the same, regardless of the function of the loop and the processing which occurs within the loop.

In Figure 6–12, the interest rate is entered by the user. This step is the control variable initialization step. The control variable testing step then determines if the interest rate entered is less than 25%. If it is, the body of the loop is never entered. Instead, the statement following the decision is executed. In this case, it can be clearly seen how it is possible for a loop to never be entered. If the control value is initialized with an interest rate less than 25%, the body of the loop will not be processed.

Within the loop, the error messages are printed and then another interest rate is entered. When another interest rate is entered, the control variable is modified. This corresponds to step #4 in the loop logic structure. The interest rate entered is then checked again. This processing will continue until an interest rate less than 25% is entered.

The coding to implement the loop is quite similar to the coding used in previous programs to read and process data. The input statement on line 560 initializes the control variable (the field R). The if statement on line 580 then determines if the value entered is less than the value in R1 (25). If it is, control is passed to the statement on line 640 and the loop is never entered.

If, on the other hand, the value in R is not less than the value in R1, the body of the loop is entered. The print statements on lines 590 and 600 print the error messages. The input statement on line 610 then obtains another interest rate, which modifies the control variable for the loop (the field R). Control is then returned to the if statement on line 580 to determine if the loop should be entered again.

It is important in this example and other looping examples in this chapter to realize why a loop is the appropriate logic structure to be used in the program. A loop should be used whenever a series of instructions is to be repeated until a given condition occurs. In this example, the instructions which indicate that an invalid interest rate has been entered are to be repeated until a valid interest rate is entered. Therefore, this problem should be solved with a loop.

The programmer should always examine the problem to be solved to determine the proper logic structure to be used. For those problems in which one set of instructions is to be executed if a condition is true and another set of instructions is to be executed if a condition is false, the if-then-else logic structure is appropriate. If a set of instructions is to be repeatedly executed until a condition is true, the loop logic structure is appropriate. Close examination may be required to determine which structure should be used. This determination is very important when properly designing a program.

For and next statements

The if and goto statements have been utilized in previous examples to implement the looping logic structure. The if statement determines whether the loop should be entered, and the goto statement transfers control to the if statement after the processing in the loop has been completed.

In some applications, a loop will be executed based upon the value in a counter. For example, in the sample program the investment values for one to ten years are to be calculated and printed. This application requires the use of a loop because a repetitive set of instructions (the calculation and printing of the investment value) is to be repeated for each of the years. The loop will be repeated for year one, year two, and so on, based upon a counter beginning at year one and continuing through year 10. When a loop is to be executed based upon the uniform incrementing of a counter, the For and Next statements in BASIC provide a convenient and easy to use method for controlling the execution of the loop. A for-next loop executes the statements between the words FOR and NEXT a specified number of times as controlled by the entries in the for statement. The general formats of the for and next statements together with an example of these statements are illustrated below.

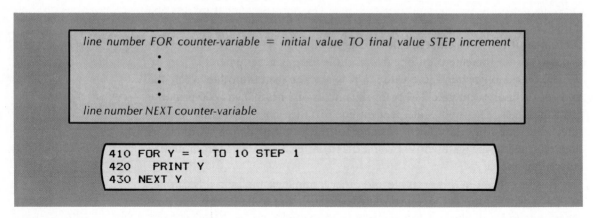

```
line number FOR counter-variable = initial value TO final value STEP increment
   .
   .
   .
line number NEXT counter-variable
```

```
410 FOR Y = 1 TO 10 STEP 1
420    PRINT Y
430 NEXT Y
```

Figure 6-13 When a loop is to be executed based upon the uniform incrementing of a counter, the for-next loop is used. The counter-variable field is set to the initial value and is incremented by the step increment until it is greater than the final value, at which time the loop is terminated. The effect of the code in this example is to print the numbers 1 through 10, which will be the values in the counter-variable Y.

The for statement begins with a line number and then the word FOR. The for statement is the first statement in the loop. The counter-variable is any numeric variable field. It is used to store the counter which is incremented and which is the control variable for the loop. In the example, the field identified by the variable name Y is used for the counter-variable.

The equal sign must be specified next, followed by the initial value which is to be placed in the counter-variable field by the for statement. In the example, the value 1 will be placed in Y by the for statement. This occurs before any processing within the loop takes place.

The word TO must then be specified, followed by the final value. When the value in the counter-variable field is greater than the final value specified in the for statement, the for-next loop will be terminated. Thus, in the example, when the value in Y is greater than 10, the for-next loop will be ended.

The optional STEP entry is next. It specifies the value which will be added to the value in the counter-variable field after the for-next loop is executed each time. In the example, after the loop has been executed once, the value 1 will be added to the value in Y. If the optional step entry is omitted from the for statement, the value 1 will automatically be added to the counter-variable field.

The Next statement consists of a line number, the word NEXT, and the variable name of the counter-variable. The next statement signifies the end of the for-next loop. All statements between the for statement and the next statement are considered part of the for-next loop.

The for-next loop operates in one of two ways, depending upon the BASIC interpreter being used. Some interpreters will cause the statements within the loop to be executed one time regardless of the initial value in the counter-variable field. Other interpreters will check the value in the counter-variable field prior to entering the loop. If it is greater than the final value, then the statements within the for-next loop will not be executed even one time. The flowcharts below illustrate the two ways in which the for-next statement in Figure 6–13 could be implemented.

Figure 6-14 Version 1 of the for-next loop will execute the statements within the loop one time regardless of the initial value placed in the counter-variable. Version 2 of the for-next loop will check the initial value of the counter-variable. If it is greater than the final value, the loop will never be entered. Version 2 of the for-next loop corresponds exactly to the general form of the loop logic structure shown in Figure 6–10.

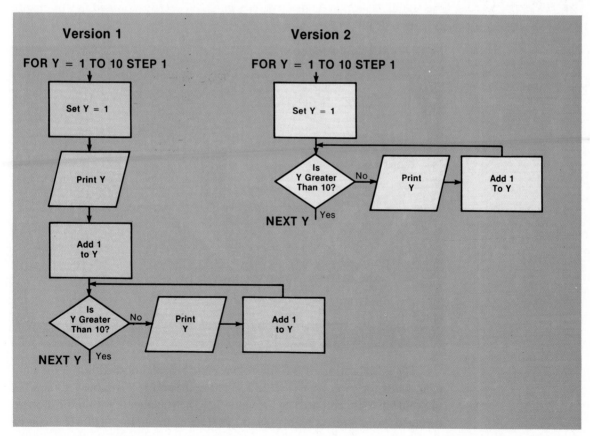

Version 1 in Figure 6–14 is the flowchart for the implementation of the for-next statement where the instructions within the loop are executed one time regardless of the initial value in the counter-variable field. Thus, the field identified by the variable name Y is set to the value 1, the value in Y is printed, and the value 1 is added to the value in Y. After the loop has been executed one time, the value in Y is compared to the final value, which is ten. If the value in Y is greater than ten, the loop will be terminated. Otherwise, the value in Y is printed, the value in Y is incremented by 1, and the test is performed again. This looping will continue until the value in Y is greater than 10.

In version 2, the initial value is set and then the value in the counter-variable field, Y, is compared to the final value. If the value in the counter-variable field is greater than the final value, the loop is terminated. If the value in Y is equal to or less than ten, then the loop is entered, and the instructions within the loop are executed. The last statement in the logic, which is accomplished by the for statement, is to increment the value in Y by 1. Then, the value in Y is again compared to the final value, 10. This loop will continue until the value in Y is greater than 10.

Version 2 of the implementation of the for-next statements corresponds to the standard looping logic structure which has been examined in this chapter (Figure 6–15).

Figure 6-15 The standard loop logic structure, which has been described previously, corresponds to the for-next loop.

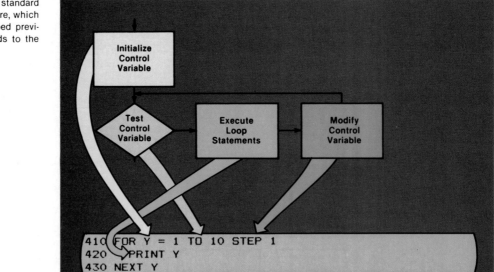

The initialization of the control variable is accomplished in the for statement when the value in Y is set to 1. Testing the control variable is done when the value in Y is compared to the value 10. The statements within the loop are executed, as represented by the print statement on line 420. The control variable is modified when the value in Y is incremented by the value specified following the word STEP. The exit from the loop occurs when the value in Y is greater than 10.

All properly designed loops have a single entry point and a single exit point. This includes loops implemented using the for-next statements. With the for-next loop, the entry point into the loop is the for statement and the exit point from the loop is the next statement. The example below illustrates a violation of the single entry rule.

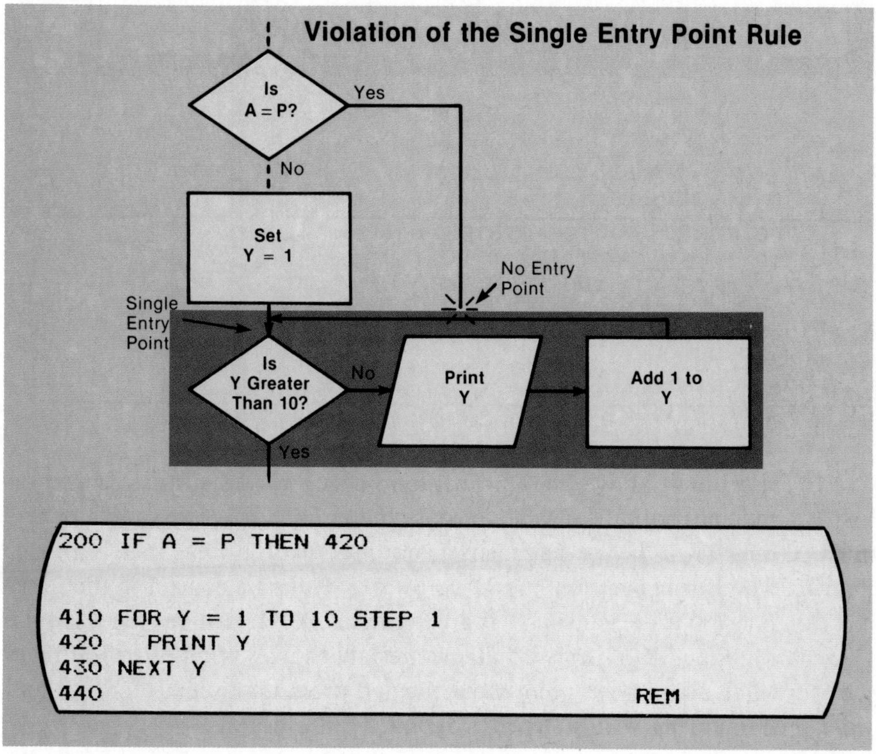

Single entry point and single exit point

Figure 6-16 Any loop, including a for-next loop, should have only one entry point. In this example, the if statement on line 200 will transfer control to the print statement on line 420 if the value in A is equal to the value in P. Transferring control to a statement within a loop establishes a second entry point, which violates good program design when using the loop logic structure.

In the example above, the for and next statements on lines 410 and 430 are the beginning and end of the loop. The for statement on line 410 provides the only valid entry point into the loop. The statements within the for-next loop should be executed only after the for statement has been executed. In the example, the if statement on line 200 will transfer control to the statement on line 420 if the value in A is equal to the value in P. This violates the single entry rule because the for statement on line 410 is not executed prior to executing an instruction within the loop. In addition, executing the next statement on line 430 without executing the for statement on line 410 first is, when using some BASIC interpreters, an error which will cause the program to be terminated.

The example in Figure 6–17 illustrates a violation of the single exit rule when using a for-next loop.

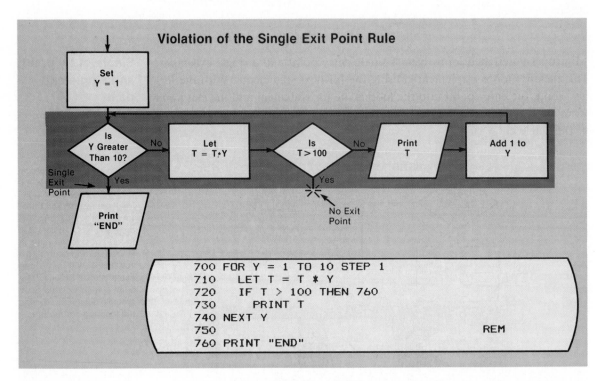

Violation of the Single Exit Point Rule

```
700 FOR Y = 1 TO 10 STEP 1
710     LET T = T * Y
720     IF T > 100 THEN 760
730         PRINT T
740 NEXT Y
750                                    REM
760 PRINT "END"
```

Figure 6-17 The if statement on line 720 will transfer control out of the loop if the value in T is greater than 100, violating the single exit point rule for a loop logic structure. The only time an exit from a for-next loop should occur is when the for statement determines that the value in the counter-variable field is greater than the final value.

In the example above, the for-next loop begins with the for statement on line 700 and ends with the next statement on line 740. This loop should be terminated only when the for statement determines that the value in Y is greater than 10. The if statement on line 720, however, will pass control to the statement on line 760 if the value in T is greater than 100. As can be seen from the flowchart in Figure 6–17, this if statement establishes a second exit point from the loop. This second exit point violates good program design standards and will not be found in a well-designed program.

Step incrementing

The initial value placed in the counter-variable of a for statement need not be the value 1. In addition, the step increment in a for statement need not be the value 1. Any integer or arithmetic expression may be used. The only criteria is that the value specified for the step increment must at some time produce a value greater than the final value specified in the for statement.

The example in Figure 6–18 illustrates an application in which an hourly wage is projected for weekly, monthly, and yearly wages, assuming a forty hour week. Note that the beginning value for the counter-variable is 4.25 and the increment is .5 (50 cents).

Program

```
100 LET F1$ = "  #.##   ###.##   #,###.##   ##,###.##"
110 PRINT "HOURLY WEEKLY    MONTHLY     YEARLY"
120 PRINT " "
130                                                        REM
140 FOR W = 4.25 TO 9.75 STEP .5
150    LET W1 = W * 40
160    LET M = ((W * 40) * 52) / 12
170    LET Y = (W * 40) * 52
180    PRINT USING F1$; W, W1, M, Y
190 NEXT W
```

Output

HOURLY	WEEKLY	MONTHLY	YEARLY
4.25	170.00	736.67	8,840.00
4.75	190.00	823.33	9,880.00
5.25	210.00	910.00	10,920.00
5.75	230.00	996.67	11,960.00
6.25	250.00	1,083.33	13,000.00
6.75	270.00	1,170.00	14,040.00
7.25	290.00	1,256.67	15,080.00
7.75	310.00	1,343.33	16,120.00
8.25	330.00	1,430.00	17,160.00
8.75	350.00	1,516.67	18,200.00
9.25	370.00	1,603.33	19,240.00
9.75	390.00	1,690.00	20,280.00

After the headings are printed in this example, the for statement on line 140 places the initial value of 4.25 in the counter-variable W. Since the value in W is not greater than 9.75, the loop is entered. There, the weekly, monthly, and yearly salaries are calculated using the value in the counter variable W as the hourly wage. It is quite common in a for-next loop for the value in the counter-variable to be used in calculations within the loop.

After the wages are printed, the value in the counter-variable will be incremented by the step increment. In this example, the value .5 will be added to the value in W. The result is tested against the final value; since it is not greater than 9.75, the loop will again be executed, this time with the value 4.75 in W. This loop will continue until the value in W is greater than 9.75.

Figure 6-18 The initial value in the for statement on line 140 is 4.25. The final value is 9.75, and the step increment is .5. The loop will be executed until the value in W exceeds 9.75.

A negative value may be specified as a step increment. To print the output illustrated in Figure 6-18 beginning with the highest value, the following for-next loop could be used.

Negative step increment

```
140 FOR W = 9.75 TO 4.25 STEP -.5
    .
    .
    .
190 NEXT W
```

Figure 6-19 When the step increment is negative, the value specified is subtracted from the value in the counter-variable field. The loop is ended when the value in W is less than 4.25.

When the for statement on line 140 in Figure 6–19 is executed, the value 9.75 will be placed in the field identified by the variable name W. When a negative step increment is specified in the for statement, the test performed by the for statement is to determine if the value in the counter-variable is less than the final value. Therefore, the value in W, 9.75, is compared to the final value, 4.25, to determine if it is lower. Since the value in W is greater than the final value, the loop will be entered.

After the processing in the loop is completed and the next statement on line 190 is encountered, the value .5 will be subtracted from the value in W, giving the result 9.25. Since this value is not less than the final value, the loop will again be entered. This processing will continue until the value in W is less than the final value, 4.25.

Again, it should be noted that if the step increment is negative, this value is subtracted from the original value placed in the counter-variable field. The loop is terminated when the value in the counter-variable field is less than the final value.

Omitting the step increment

It is not required that the step increment be specified in the for statement. If it is not, the value plus 1 is assumed. In Figure 6–20, the for-next loop is used to control raising the number 2 to the next higher power.

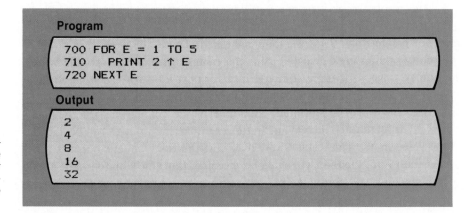

Program

```
700 FOR E = 1 TO 5
710    PRINT 2 ↑ E
720 NEXT E
```

Output

```
2
4
8
16
32
```

Figure 6-20 The default value plus 1 is used as the step increment in the for statement on line 700 because it contains no step increment.

The for statement on line 700 does not contain a step increment. Therefore, each time the for statement is executed, the default value of 1 is added to the counter-variable field E. When the value in E is greater than 5, the loop will be terminated.

Variable names in the for statement

Variable names of fields may be used in the for statement as the initial value, the final value, and the incremental value. The example in Figure 6–21 illustrates the use of variables in the for statement.

```
280 LET C = A1 * B2
290 LET F = A2 * B2
300 LET I = B4
310                                    REM
320 FOR Y = C TO F STEP I
    •
    •
450 NEXT Y
```

Figure 6-21 Fields identified by numeric variable names can be used as the initial value, the final value, and the step increment. In this example, if the value in the field identified by the variable name C is greater than the value in the field identified by the variable name F, the loop will be executed one time by some BASIC interpreters and zero times by other BASIC interpreters.

In Figure 6-21, the counter-variable Y is set to an initial value based upon the value in the variable field C. The final value is the value in the field identified by the variable F, while the step increment is the value in the variable field I.

Note that if the value in A1 is greater than the value in A2 in the example above, the initial value will be greater than the final value. As explained previously, depending upon the BASIC interpreter being used, the statements in the loop would not be executed or would be executed one time.

In many cases, the use of variables in a for statement is preferable to the use of literals for the same reasons as noted in previous programs. The major reason is for maintenance purposes. If a variable set in a program and used in the for statement must be modified, it can be changed at only one place instead of searching the program to find the applicable for statement. In addition, when the values used in a for statement will change dynamically, such as in Figure 6-21, a variable must be used.

Nested for-next loops

For-next loops can be nested within one another to provide the ability to loop within a loop. The example in Figure 6-22 illustrates nested for-next statements.

Program

```
340 FOR I = 1 TO 2 STEP 1      -loop
350    PRINT "GROUP"; I
360    FOR K = 1 TO 2           -loop
370       PRINT USING "   #:"; K
380    NEXT K
390 NEXT I
```

Output

```
GROUP  1
   1:
   2:
GROUP  2
   1:
   2:
```

Figure 6-22 A nested for-next loop will be executed in its entirety for each pass through the outer for-next loop. Here, the for-next loop on lines 360 – 380 will be executed for K = 1 and K = 2 when I = 1 and when I = 2.

In Figure 6-22, the first for-next loop begins with the for statement on line 340 and ends with the next statement on line 390. The next statement on line 390 ends the first loop because it contains the same counter-variable (I) as the for statement on line 340. The inner, or nested, for-next loop begins on line 360 and ends on line 380. The next statement on line 380 contains the same counter-variable (K) as the for statement on line 360.

When the statements on lines 340 – 390 are executed, the processing occurs as follows:

Figure 6-23 The chart in this example traces the value in the variable fields and the printed output which will occur as the statements in the loops are executed. Tracing the execution of portions of a program using a chart such as this can be quite useful in both understanding the processing which will occur and in determining the results which should occur when the program is executed.

```
340 FOR I = 1 TO 2 STEP 1
350    PRINT "GROUP"; I
360    FOR K = 1 TO 2
370       PRINT USING "  #:"; K
380    NEXT K
390 NEXT I
```

LINE EXECUTED	VALUE IN I	VALUE IN K	OUTPUT	NEXT STATEMENT
Line 340	1	0		Line 350
Line 350	1	0	GROUP 1	Line 360
Line 360	1	1		Line 370
Line 370	1	1	GROUP 1 1:	Line 380
Line 380	1	1		Line 360
Line 360	1	2		Line 370
Line 370	1	2	GROUP 1 1: 2:	Line 380
Line 380	1	2		Line 360
Line 360	1	3		Line 390
Line 390	1	3		Line 340
Line 340	2	3		Line 350
Line 350	2	3	GROUP 1 1: 2: GROUP 2	Line 360
Line 360	2	1		Line 370
Line 370	2	1	GROUP 1 1: 2: GROUP 2 1:	Line 380
Line 380	2	1		Line 360
Line 360	2	2		Line 370
Line 370	2	2	GROUP 1 1: 2: GROUP 2 1: 2:	Line 380
Line 380	2	2		Line 360
Line 360	2	3		Line 390
Line 390	2	3		Line 340
Line 340	3	3		End

By tracing the processing which occurs when the nested for-next statements are executed, it can be seen that the "inner" loop is executed through its entirety for each pass through the "outer" loop. Thus, when I = 1, the inner loop will process for K = 1 and K = 2. After the inner loop has completed processing, the counter-variable for the outer loop is incremented by the value in the step increment, and the inner loop will again be executed in its entirety. Therefore, when I = 2, the inner loop is processed for K = 1 and K = 2. The example in Figure 6–23 should be understood because nested for-next statements can be quite useful in some applications.

The programmer must be careful when using nested for-next statements to follow the single entry-single exit rule. Also, an inner for-next loop must be entirely contained within the outer for-next loop. The following example illustrates coding which violates this BASIC rule and is, therefore, invalid.

```
Invalid Coding

600 FOR K = Q TO T STEP 2
610    FOR L = 9 TO R3 STEP P
620       PRINT L, L * T
630 NEXT K
640 PRINT T - L
650 NEXT L
```

Figure 6-24 A BASIC rule is that a nested for-next loop must be entirely contained within the outer loop. Here, the rule is violated because the loop begun by the for statement on line 610 is terminated by the next statement on line 650, which is outside the loop begun by the for statement on line 600 and ended by the next statement on line 630.

In the example above, the loop begun by the for statement on line 600 ends on line 630 with the next statement. The loop begun by the for statement on line 610 ends with the next statement on line 650. Clearly, the inner loop, which is begun by the for statement on line 610, is not within the outer loop because the outer loop terminates before the inner loop. This violates a BASIC language rule concerning nested for-next loops and should never occur.

Looping is a very important logic structure for computer programming. The for-next statements in BASIC provide an easy implementation of the looping logic structure for certain types of applications. Both looping and the for-next statements should be well understood by the programmer.

The sample program in this chapter is designed to create an investment chart for an amount and interest rate entered by the user of the program. The output of the program is illustrated on page 6.1 in Figure 6–1. The input data to the program is entered by the user and cannot, therefore, be listed prior to the execution of the program.

SAMPLE PROGRAM

The program design begins with the specification of the program tasks which must be accomplished in this program. These tasks are listed on the next page.

Program design

Program Tasks

1. Obtain investment amount and interest rate.
2. Calculate investment value for ten years.
3. Print investment value.
4. Edit all input data.

Program flowchart

The flowchart illustrating the logic to accomplish these program tasks is shown in Figures 6-25 and 6-26.

Figure 6-25 Program flowchart (Page 1 of 2). This flowchart contains the logic to solve the sample program. It consists of a large processing loop similar to those shown in previous chapters. The main loop begins at the decision symbol asking if the answer entered by the user is NO. If the answer is NO, the loop is terminated, the ending message is printed, and the program is terminated. If the answer is YES, the main processing loop is entered. The loop continues on the second page of the flowchart in Figure 6-26.

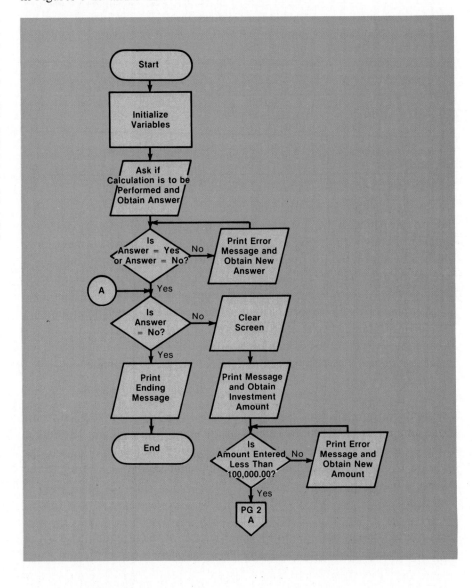

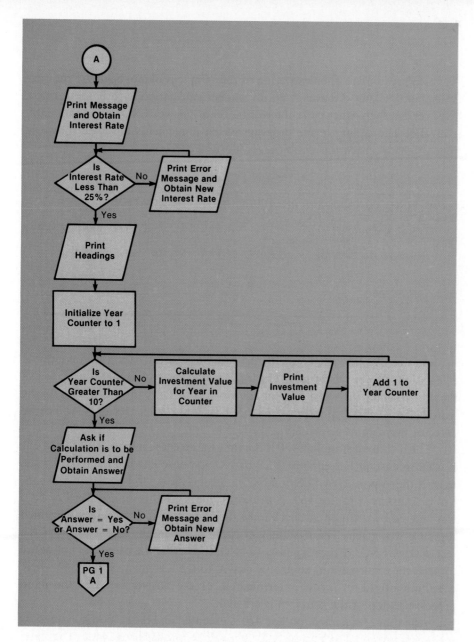

Figure 6-26 Program flow-chart (Page 2 of 2). This is a continuation of the flow-chart in Figure 6-25. The flowchart logic is entered at the connector symbol position A. It transfers control back to page 1 of the flowchart at the bottom, using the off-page connector.

The flowchart in Figures 6-25 and 6-26 illustrates the logic used in the program to produce the investment chart. Since the flowchart requires two pages, there must be an indication where control is passed from the logic on one page to the logic on another page. The page connector (▽) is used for this purpose. In Figure 6-25, the last statement will pass control to page 2, connector A. In Figure 6-26, this point is at the top of the flowchart, as indicated by the on-page connector symbol (◯).

When the logic in the flowchart in Figure 6-26 is complete, it passes control back to connector A on page 1. Through the use of on-page and off-page connectors, flowcharts can be multi-page documents.

Input editing   As noted previously, when execution of the sample program begins, a message is displayed asking the user if an investment calculation is to be performed. The user can then either enter the word YES or the word NO. Any other entry is invalid. The coding in the program which implements the logic shown in Figure 6–25 to check this condition is illustrated below.

```
390 PRINT "DO YOU WANT TO PERFORM AN INVESTMENT CALCULATION?"
400 INPUT "ENTER YES OR NO: "; R$
410                                                              REM
420 IF R$ = "YES" OR R$ = "NO" THEN 460
430    INPUT "   INVALID RESPONSE - PLEASE ENTER YES OR NO: "; R$
440 GOTO 420
450                                                              REM
460 IF R$ = "NO" THEN 840
470    CLS
```

Figure 6-27 A loop is the appropriate logic structure to use when editing input data because the checking will continue until valid data is entered. Note in this example the REM statements on lines 410 and 450, which generate blank lines. Blank lines should always precede and follow a loop so that the loop is easy to see in the coding.

On line 390, the print statement is used to ask the user if an investment calculation is to be performed. The input statement on line 400 is used to ask the user to enter the word YES or the word NO. Only the word YES or the word NO are valid responses — any other response, such as Y or N, will cause an error message to be printed.

The if statement on line 420 is the first statement in a loop. This statement is used to ensure that either a YES or NO response has been entered by the user. If the response is a YES or a NO, control is passed to line 460. When control is transferred to line 460, it is known that a valid response (YES or NO) was entered by the user. A check must then be performed to determine which response was given. The if statement on line 460 checks to determine if the response was NO. If the response was NO, indicating the user does not desire to perform a calculation, control is passed to the statement at line 840 where execution of the program is terminated. If the answer is YES, the main processing loop of the program is entered.

When the if statement on line 420 is executed and the response entered by the user is not equal to YES or NO, an invalid entry has been made. The statement on line 430 is then executed. The input statement on line 430 prints an invalid response message and allows the user to make another entry. The goto statement on line 440 returns control to the if statement on line 420 where the entry made by the user is again checked for YES or NO. This looping continues until a valid response has been entered.

The use of a loop is appropriate in this situation because a certain action (printing the error message and getting a new response) will be executed over and over until a given condition occurs (the user enters YES or NO). Whenever a set of instructions is to be executed multiple times until a given condition occurs, a loop is the proper logic structure to use.

In the loop in Figure 6–27, it should be noted that the loop processing may never be entered; that is, the user may (indeed, will likely) enter the correct response the first time. Thus, as with any loop, it is possible that the loop processing will not be executed, depending upon the condition tested at the start of the loop.

Editing for reasonableness

In most interactive applications, it is desirable to perform a check on data entered by the user to ensure that the value is reasonable; that is, the value is not below or above values which have been designated as reasonable. In the sample program, it has been determined that the amount entered by the user should be less than $100,000.00, and that the interest rate should be less than 25%.

When designing the logic of the program, the programmer must examine each processing requirement to determine the proper logic structure. Here, the user must enter a value less than $100,000.00. At first glance, this may appear to be an if-then-else logic structure problem; that is, if the value is less than 100,000.00, then an error message should be written. Otherwise, processing continues. This analysis is in error, however, because after the error message is written, another response must be entered, and this new response must be checked for reasonableness. Thus, a loop is required because the response must be checked each time until the amount entered is less than $100,000.00. When designing a program, the programmer must always ask if the processing is to be repeated until a given condition occurs. If so, then a loop is required.

The coding to check the amount entered and the interest rate entered is shown in Figure 6–28.

Figure 6-28 Reasonableness checks are quite common when editing input data. The use of the variable names A1 and R1 to contain the acceptable values means that if these values are changed at a later time, only the initialization statements must be changed. The statements in these editing routines need not be changed.

```
480      INPUT "ENTER AMOUNT TO BE INVESTED: "; A
490                                                              REM
500      IF A < A1 THEN 560
510         PRINT "    AMOUNT ENTERED IS TOO HIGH"
520         PRINT "    PLEASE ENTER AN AMOUNT LESS THAN"; A1;
530         INPUT A
540      GOTO 500
550                                                              REM
560      INPUT "ENTER INTEREST RATE: "; R
570                                                              REM
580      IF R < R1 THEN 640
590         PRINT "    INTEREST RATE IS TOO HIGH"
600         PRINT "    PLEASE ENTER A RATE LESS THAN"; R1; "%: ";
610         INPUT R
620      GOTO 580
630                                                              REM
640      CLS
```

In Figure 6–28, the input statement on line 480 asks the user to enter an amount to be invested. The value entered is stored in the field identified by the variable name A. The if statement on line 500 then checks if the value in A is less than the value in the field identified by the variable name A1. The value 100000.00 was placed in A1 at initialization time.

If the value in A is less than the value in A1, control is passed to the statement on line 560, and the loop is never entered. If, however, the value in A is not less than the value in A1, the loop is entered, and the statements on lines 510–540 are executed. The error messages are printed by the print statements on lines 510–520. The print statement on line 520 utilizes the value in A1 as part of the error message. Thus, the value in A1 is used for comparing on line 500 and in an error message on line 520. This is an example of the value in a variable field being used in more than one place in a program. If the value in A1 were to be changed, for example to $200,000.00, the programmer needs to change only the let statement which places the value in the field in the initialization portion of the program. The statements on lines 500 and 520 need not be changed.

Figure 6-29 The print statement on line 520 includes a variable field (A1). In addition, the statement ends with a semicolon. Therefore, the data entered in response to the input statement on line 530 is displayed on the same line as the prompt printed by the print statement on line 520.

Note also that the print statement on line 520 ends with a semicolon. Therefore, after the print statement is complete, the cursor will remain on the same line as the message. The input statement on line 530 then allows the user to enter the new value on the same line as the message (Figure 6–29).

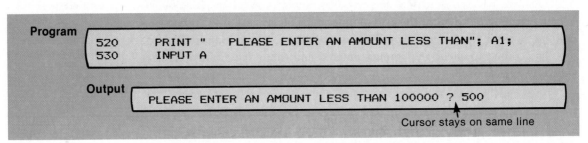

After the new amount has been entered, the goto statement on line 540 passes control to line 500, where the amount just entered is checked. This loop will continue until the amount entered is less than $100,000.00.

Similar processing is performed by the coding in Figure 6–28 to check the interest rate.

Clear screen instruction

After the amount and interest rate have been entered, the investment chart is printed. So that other information will not appear on the screen at the same time the investment chart is displayed, the clear screen instruction is used in this program. This instruction completely blanks the CRT screen and places the cursor in the upper left corner of the screen. The clear screen instruction on many computer systems consists of the statement CLS (Figure 6–30).

```
640     CLS
650     PRINT USING F2$; A, R
```

Figure 6-30 The CLS instruction is used to clear the CRT screen and place the cursor in the upper lefthand corner.

The CLS instruction on line 640 will clear the screen and place the cursor in the top lefthand corner. Therefore, the line printed by the print using statement on line 650 will be the first line on the screen.

All computer systems have an instruction which will clear the screen, but the instruction is not always CLS. On some systems, the instruction is HOME, while on others it could be still different. The programmer should check the system being used for the instruction which will clear the screen.

In the sample program, the value of the amount invested is to be calculated and printed for each of ten years. The formula for calculating the value of an investment at the end of any given year is:

For-next loop

$$V = A * (1 + (R / 100)) \uparrow Y$$

Where:

V = The value of the investment at the end of the year
A = The amount invested
R = The interest rate specified as a whole number
     (example: 25, not .25)
Y = Years amount has been invested

Figure 6-31 This figure shows the formula required to calculate the value of the investment for each year.

The formula in Figure 6-31 must be repeated for each year that is to be calculated. Therefore, in the sample program, it will be repeated ten times.

As noted previously, when presented with a logic design problem, the programmer must determine the proper logic structure. To calculate the investment value for each of the ten years, the formula must be repeated ten times. This, then, appears to be a perfect application for a loop logic structure, since the same processing must be repeated until a given condition occurs; that is, until all ten years have been calculated. The logic from the sample program to solve this problem is shown in Figure 6-32.

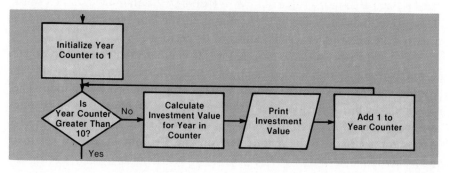

Figure 6-32 The loop to calculate the investment follows the exact format of the loop logic structure — initialize, test, execute loop instructions, modify, and exit.

The logic illustrated in Figure 6-32 to calculate and print the investment value follows the typical looping structure. The first step is to initialize the counter which indicates the year being processed. The control variable (year counter) is then tested to determine if the loop should be entered. Within the loop, the investment value is calculated and printed. The control variable is then modified when the year counter is incremented by 1.

Since this loop is to be executed based upon the value in a counter, and since the value in the counter is to be incremented by the same value each time through the loop, it can be easily implemented in BASIC using the for-next statements (Figure 6-33).

```
460 IF R$ = "NO" THEN 840
470    CLS
       .
690    FOR Y = 1 TO U STEP 1
700       LET V = A * (1 + (R / 100)) ↑ Y
710       PRINT USING F1$; Y, V
720    NEXT Y
730                                                          REM
740    PRINT " "
750    PRINT "DO YOU WANT TO PERFORM ANOTHER CALCULATION?"
760    INPUT "ENTER YES OR NO: "; R$
770                                                          REM
780    IF R$ = "YES" OR R$ = "NO" THEN 820
790       INPUT "    INVALID RESPONSE - PLEASE ENTER YES OR NO: "; R$
800    GOTO 780
810                                                          REM
820 GOTO 460
```

Figure 6-33 A for-next loop is used to calculate and print the investment values for each of the ten years. When the loop is completed, the statements on lines 740 - 800 obtain from the user a response (YES or NO) which will determine whether the main processing loop will be entered again. This response is checked on line 460.

When the for statement on line 690 is executed, the value 1 is placed in the field identified by the variable name Y. This value is then compared to the value in U. If the value in Y is less than or equal to the value in U, the statements on lines 700 and 710 are executed. The value 10 was placed in U when the variables were initialized.

Within the loop, the investment value (V) is calculated and the year (Y) and the investment value are printed. The next statement on line 720 passes control back to the for statement, where the value in Y is incremented by 1 and then is compared to the value in U. This looping will continue until the value in Y is greater than the value in U. At that time, the loop is terminated, and the user is asked if another calculation is to be performed.

The statements on lines 740–800 ask if another calculation is to be performed and verify that a valid response is made. These statements modify the control variable, R$, which is used to control the main processing loop. They obtain data which indicates whether the main processing loop is to be executed again (YES in R$) or terminated (NO in R$). The goto statement on line 820 passes control back to the if statement on line 460 which checks if the main loop should be entered.

The function performed by the statements on lines 740–800 is very similar to that performed by the read statement in previous programs. Therefore, these statements must be the last statements within the loop in the same manner that the read statement in previous programs was the last statement within the loop. It is a design error to pass control back to any statement located before the if statement on line 460.

The looping logic structure and its implementation in BASIC is very important. All material covered in this chapter should be thoroughly understood before continuing to subsequent chapters.

The following tips should be kept in mind when coding a program: **Coding tips**

1. The constant values which are used in a program should be placed in fields with variable names by the initialization portion of the program. When this is done, the maintenance task is much easier and less prone to error.

2. Whenever new, unrelated subject matter is to be displayed on a CRT screen, the screen should be cleared first. This allows the user to see only that information which is required for the response.

3. When editing data entered via the input statement, never assume that if one value was not entered, another value was entered. For example, when editing the response to the question, Do you want to perform an investment calculation, do not assume that if the value entered is not yes, it is no. Both possible values must be explicitly checked. If a valid response is not entered, an error message should be printed and a correct response asked for.

4. Loops, whether they are implemented using an if statement and a goto statement or for-next statements, should be preceded by and followed by a blank line. Writing loops this way enables a reader of a program to quickly and easily spot the beginning and ending of a loop.

5. The first statement in a loop (either an if statement or a for statement) and the last statement in a loop (either a goto statement or a next statement) should be vertically aligned. All statements within the loop should be indented two columns from the beginning and ending statements.

6. Loops should be implemented using the for-next statements when the execution of the loop is dependent upon the value in a counter and the value in the counter is incremented by the same amount each pass through the loop. Otherwise, loops should be implemented using the if and the goto statements.

7. It is quite important that the users of a program understand the messages written on the CRT screen in response to a value entered.

Therefore, the error messages written by a program should be self-explanatory and should indicate to the user why the input entered was in error. For example, if a user enters an interest rate greater than 24%, the message should explain that the interest rate must be less than 25%. If the message just said ''Error — reenter'', the user would have no guidance and may, therefore, never figure out why the entry was in error.

Sample program   The complete listing for the sample program is shown below and on the next page.

```
100 REM INVEST                DECEMBER 28              SHELLY/CASHMAN
110                                                                REM
120 REM THIS PROGRAM CALCULATES THE VALUE OF AN AMOUNT INVESTED
130 REM FOR EACH OF TEN YEARS. THE USER ENTERS AN AMOUNT LESS
140 REM THAN $100,000.00 AND AN INTEREST RATE LESS THAN 25%
150                                                                REM
160 REM VARIABLE NAMES:
170 REM    R$....RESPONSE TO IS THERE ANOTHER CALCULATION
180 REM    A.....AMOUNT TO BE INVESTED - ENTERED BY USER
190 REM    A1....AMOUNT ENTERED MUST BE LESS THAN THIS AMOUNT
200 REM    R.....RATE OF INTEREST - ENTERED BY USER
210 REM    R1....RATE ENTERED MUST BE LESS THAN THIS RATE
220 REM    V.....VALUE AT THE END OF EACH YEAR
230 REM    Y.....YEARS COUNTER
240 REM    U.....NUMBER OF YEARS FOR WHICH TO CALCULATE VALUE
250 REM    F1$...PRINT USING FORMAT FOR OUTPUT LINE
260 REM    F2$...PRINT USING FORMAT FOR HEADING LINE
270                                                                REM
280 REM ***** INITIALIZATION OF VARIABLES *****
290                                                                REM
300 LET A1 = 100000#
310 LET R1 = 25
320 LET U = 10
330 LET F1$ = "               ##             $$##,###.##"
340 LET F2$ = "INVESTMENT CHART FOR $$#,###.## AT ##.##% INTEREST"
350                                                                REM
360 REM ***** PROCESSING *****
370                                                                REM
380 CLS
390 PRINT "DO YOU WANT TO PERFORM AN INVESTMENT CALCULATION?"
400 INPUT "ENTER YES OR NO: "; R$
410                                                                REM
420 IF R$ = "YES" OR R$ = "NO" THEN 460
430    INPUT "   INVALID RESPONSE - PLEASE ENTER YES OR NO: "; R$
440 GOTO 420
450                                                                REM
460 IF R$ = "NO" THEN 840
470    CLS
480    INPUT "ENTER AMOUNT TO BE INVESTED: "; A
490                                                                REM
```

Figure 6-34 Sample program (Part 1 of 2)

```
500     IF A < A1 THEN 560
510        PRINT "    AMOUNT ENTERED IS TOO HIGH"
520        PRINT "    PLEASE ENTER AN AMOUNT LESS THAN"; A1;
530        INPUT A
540     GOTO 500
550                                                             REM
560     INPUT "ENTER INTEREST RATE: "; R
570                                                             REM
580     IF R < R1 THEN 640
590        PRINT "    INTEREST RATE IS TOO HIGH"
600        PRINT "    PLEASE ENTER A RATE LESS THAN"; R1; "%: ";
610        INPUT R
620     GOTO 580
630                                                             REM
640     CLS
650     PRINT USING F2$; A, R
660     PRINT " "
670     PRINT "              YEAR              AMOUNT"
680                                                             REM
690     FOR Y = 1 TO U STEP 1
700        LET V = A * (1 + (R / 100)) ^ Y
710        PRINT USING F1$; Y, V
720     NEXT Y
730                                                             REM
740     PRINT " "
750     PRINT "DO YOU WANT TO PERFORM ANOTHER CALCULATION?"
760     INPUT "ENTER YES OR NO: "; R$
770                                                             REM
780     IF R$ = "YES" OR R$ = "NO" THEN 820
790        INPUT "    INVALID RESPONSE - PLEASE ENTER YES OR NO: "; R$
800     GOTO 780
810                                                             REM
820 GOTO 460
830                                                             REM
840 PRINT " "
850 PRINT "END OF INVESTMENT PROGRAM"
860 END
```

Figure 6-35 Sample program (Part 2 of 2)

SUMMARY

The following points have been discussed and explained in this chapter.

1. Looping can be used in any problem which requires repetitive actions until a given condition occurs.

2. Interactive programming is when the user enters data from a keyboard or other input device and the program processes the data immediately.

3. A prompt is a message which prompts a person to enter data or otherwise interact with a program. Prompts are used in interactive programming. Prompts should clearly state the action to be taken by the person using the program.

4. The process of checking input data is called data editing.

5. The input statement causes the program to pause until the user has entered one or more values or characters through the computer or terminal keyboard.

6. Data entered via the keyboard as a result of the input statement is displayed on the CRT screen and stored in main computer storage.

7. The input statement contains a line number, the word INPUT, and one or more variable names of fields where data will be stored when it is entered on the keyboard.

8. When the input statement is executed, a question mark is displayed on the CRT screen and the program waits for data to be entered.

9. When the variable name specified in an input statement is a numeric variable name, the data entered must be numeric (numbers or a single decimal point).

10. String variables can be used with the input statement.

11. A prompt can be included within an input statement.

12. A prompt in an input statement is a string constant which must be contained within double quotation marks. When the input statement is executed, the prompt is printed prior to the program's halting for the data to be entered.

13. The print statement can be used instead of or together with the prompt in the input statement to prompt users.

14. When two lines of prompt messages are to be printed, the print statement must be used for at least the first message.

15. If variables are to be printed on the prompt line, the print statement must be used to print the prompt.

16. More than one numeric or string variable name may be specified in a single input statement. The names are separated by commas in the input statement. When the data is entered from the keyboard, the values for each variable must be separated by commas.

17. If the return or enter key is depressed before all values have been entered in response to an input statement with multiple variable names, some

computer systems will ask for more values while others will require all of the data to be reentered.

18. A loop consists of five elements: a) Initialize the control variable; b) Test the control variable; c) Execute the loop statements; d) Modify the control variable; e) Exit from the loop.

19. The read loops which have been used in previous programs contain all the elements of a loop.

20. The basic loop structure is always the same, regardless of the function of the loop and the processing which occurs within the loop.

21. A loop should be used whenever a series of instructions is to be repeated until a given condition occurs.

22. For those problems in which one set of instructions is to be executed if a condition is true and another set of instructions is to be executed if the condition is false, the if-then-else logic structure is appropriate. If a set of instructions is to be repeatedly executed until a condition is true, the loop logic structure is appropriate.

23. When a loop is to be executed based upon the uniform incrementing of a counter, the For and Next statements in BASIC provide a convenient and easy-to-use method for controlling the execution of the loop.

24. The for statement consists of a line number, the word FOR, the variable name of the counter-variable, an equal sign, the initial and final values of the counter-variable, and the optional step entry.

25. The next statement consists of a line number, the word NEXT, and the variable name of the counter-variable used in the corresponding for statement. The next statement marks the end of a for-next loop.

26. The for-next loop operates in one of two ways, depending on the BASIC interpreter being used. Some interpreters will cause the statements within the loop to be executed one time regardless of the initial value in the counter-variable. Other interpreters will check the initial value of the counter-variable. If the initial value is greater than the final value, the statements within the loop will not be executed.

27. A for-next loop will continue execution until the value in the counter-variable field is greater than the final value specified in the for statement.

28. The for-next loop has all the elements of the standard looping logic structure.

29. All properly designed loops have a single entry point and a single exit point. This includes loops implemented using the for and next statements.

30. Statements within a for-next loop should be executed only after the for statement has been executed. The only way a for-next loop should be terminated is that the for statement determines that the value in the control variable field is greater than the final value specified in the for statement.

31. The step increment in the for statement need not be the value one. It can be any positive or negative value required by the application.

32. When the step increment is negative in a for statement, the test for termination of the loop is whether the value in the control-variable field is less than the final value specified in the for statement.

33. If the step increment is omitted from a for statement, the default increment is a positive one.

34. Variable names may be used in the for statement as the initial value, the final value, and the incremental value. In many cases, the use of variable names is preferable to literal values for maintenance reasons.

35. For-next loops can be nested within other for-next loops.

36. An inner, or nested, for-next loop must be entirely contained within the outer for-next loop.

37. In a flowchart, the page connector is used to indicate that control is passed to another page of the flowchart.

38. Whenever a set of instructions is to be executed multiple times until a condition occurs, a loop is the proper logic structure to use.

39. In most interactive applications, it is desirable to perform a check on data entered by the user to ensure that the value is reasonable; that is, the value is not below or above values which have been designated as reasonable.

40. The clear screen instruction (CLS) is used to clear the CRT screen of any information and to place the cursor in the upper leftmost position of the screen. On some computer systems, the instruction HOME or other instructions may be used instead of the CLS instruction for this same function.

41. Generally, whenever new, unrelated subject matter is to be displayed on the CRT screen, the screen should be cleared first. This allows the user to see only that information which is required for the response.

42. Loops, regardless of whether they are coded with if and goto statements or with for-next statements, should always be preceded by and followed by a blank line.

43. The first statement in a loop and the last statement in a loop should be vertically aligned. All statements within the loop should be indented two columns from the beginning and ending statements.

44. Loops should be implemented using the for-next statements when execution of the loop is dependent upon the value in a counter and the value in the counter is incremented by the same amount each pass through the loop. Otherwise, loops should be implemented using the if and goto statements.

1. What are some of the characteristics of interactive programming?
2. When the input statement is executed: a) Data is moved from the data statement to the variable following the word INPUT; b) The program halts, waiting for the programmer to code the appropriate data statements; c) The program halts and will continue when the programmer types CONT; d) The program halts, waiting for the computer operator to enter data.
3. If a numeric variable is specified with the input statement and string data is entered, the BASIC interpreter will convert the data to a numeric format (T or F).
4. What is a prompt? Why is a prompt used?
5. When multiple variable names are used with an input statement, they must be of the same type — either both numeric or both string (T or F).
6. What are the five basic elements of a loop structure? Describe each one.
7. What will occur if the control variable in a loop is not modified?
8. Loops: a) Must always be executed at least one time; b) May be executed zero or more times; c) Will be executed the number of times equal to the value of the control variable; d) Must always begin with an if statement.
9. A loop should be used whenever one set of instructions is to be executed when a condition is true, and another set of instructions is to be executed when the condition is false (T or F).
10. The counter-variable in a for statement must always be numeric (T or F).
11. The single entry point in a loop is: a) The next statement in the for-next loop; b) The step which modifies the control-variable; c) The decision which determines if the loop is to be executed; d) The statement which initializes the control-variable field.
12. What is meant by a single exit point in a loop?
13. When a negative step increment is used in a for statement: a) The counter variable is initialized with the value and then the value is decremented by one each pass through the loop; b) The final value is decremented each time by the value in the step increment; c) The value in the counter-variable is decremented by the value in the step increment; d) The step increment is converted to a positive number prior to being used.
14. The value in the counter-variable field must be less than the final value when a negative step increment is used (T or F).
15. The sample program is to be modified by restricting the amount of money to be invested to $50,000.00 and the interest rate can be as high as 40%. Make the changes in the sample program to implement these modifications.
16. Management has now realized that investments can be made over varying lengths of time. They have asked, therefore, that the program be modified to allow the user to enter the number of years of the investment. The minimum number of years is 1, and the maximum number of years is 15. Make the changes to the program to implement this modification.

Chapter 6
DEBUGGING EXERCISES

The following lines of code contain one or more coding errors. Circle each of the errors and write the coding to correct the errors.

1.
```
640    CLS
650    PRINT USING F2$   A, R
660    PRINT " "
670    PRINT "              YEAR              AMOUNT"
680                                                    REM
690    FOR Y = 1 TO U STEP 1
700      LET V = A * (1 + (R / 100) ↑ Y
710      PRINT USING F1$; Y, V
720    NEXT U
730                                                    REM
740    PRINT " "
750    PRINT "DO YOU WANT TO PERFORM ANOTHER CALCULATION?"
760    INPUT "ENTER YES OR NO: ";R$
770                                                    REM
780    IF R$ = "YES" OR R$ = "NO" THEN 820
790      INPUT "   INVALID RESPONSE - PLEASE ENTER YES OR NO: ; R$
800    GOTO 780
```

2.
```
380 CLS
390 PRINT "DO YOU WANT TO PERFORM AN INVESTMENT CALCULATION?"
400 INPUT "ENTER YES OR NO: ";R$
410                                                    REM
420 IF R$ = YES OR R$ = NO THEN 460
430    INPUT "   INVALID RESPONSE - PLEASE ENTER YES OR NO: " R$
440 GOTO 420
450                                                    REM
460 IF R$ = "NO" THEN 840
470    CLS
480    INPUT "ENTER AMOUNT TO BE INVESTED: ": A
490                                                    REM
500    IF A < A1 THEN 560
510      PRINT "   AMOUNT ENTERED IS TOO HIGH"
520      PRINT "   PLEASE ENTER AN AMOUNT LESS THAN": A1:
530      INPUT A
540    GOTO 500
```

Chapter 6
PROGRAM DEBUGGING

The following program was designed and written to produce the investment chart using the input data as shown in Figure 6–1 (page 6.1). The results
actually obtained from the program are illustrated on page 6.38. Analyze the
results to determine if they are correct. If they are in error, circle the errors in
the program and write corrections.

```
100 REM INVEST                 DECEMBER 28              SHELLY/CASHMAN
110                                                                REM
120 REM THIS PROGRAM CALCULATES THE VALUE OF AN AMOUNT INVESTED
130 REM FOR EACH OF TEN YEARS. THE USER ENTERS AN AMOUNT LESS
140 REM THAN $100,000.00 AND AN INTEREST RATE LESS THAN 25%
150                                                                REM
160 REM VARIABLE NAMES:
170 REM    R$....RESPONSE TO IS THERE ANOTHER CALCULATION
180 REM    A.....AMOUNT TO BE INVESTED - ENTERED BY USER
190 REM    A1....AMOUNT ENTERED MUST BE LESS THAN THIS AMOUNT
200 REM    R.....RATE OF INTEREST - ENTERED BY USER
210 REM    R1....RATE ENTERED MUST BE LESS THAN THIS RATE
220 REM    V.....VALUE AT THE END OF EACH YEAR
230 REM    Y.....YEARS COUNTER
240 REM    U.....NUMBER OF YEARS FOR WHICH TO CALCULATE VALUE
250 REM    F1$...PRINT USING FORMAT FOR OUTPUT LINE
260 REM    F2$...PRINT USING FORMAT FOR HEADING LINE
270                                                                REM
280 REM ***** INITIALIZATION OF VARIABLES *****
290                                                                REM
300 LET A1 = 100000#
310 LET R1 = 25
320 LET U = 10
330 LET F1$ = "              ##              $$###,###.##"
340 LET F2$ = "INVESTMENT CHART FOR $$#,###.## AT ##.##% INTEREST"
350                                                                REM
360 REM ***** PROCESSING *****
370                                                                REM
380 CLS
390 PRINT "DO YOU WANT TO PERFORM AN INVESTMENT CALCULATION?"
400 INPUT "ENTER YES OR NO: ";R$
410                                                                REM
420 IF R$ = "YES" OR R$ = "NO" THEN 460
430    INPUT "    INVALID RESPONSE - PLEASE ENTER YES OR NO: "; R$
440 GOTO 420
450                                                                REM
460 IF R$ = "NO" THEN 840
470    CLS
480    INPUT "ENTER AMOUNT TO BE INVESTED: "; A
490                                                                REM
500    IF A < A1 THEN 560
510       PRINT "    AMOUNT ENTERED IS TOO HIGH"
520       PRINT "    PLEASE ENTER AN AMOUNT LESS THAN"; A1;
530       INPUT A
540    GOTO 500
```

```
550                                                                    REM
560     INPUT "ENTER INTEREST RATE: "; R
570                                                                    REM
580     IF R > R1 THEN 640
590       PRINT "    INTEREST RATE IS TOO HIGH"
600       PRINT "    PLEASE ENTER A RATE LESS THAN"; R1; "%: ";
610       INPUT R
620     GOTO 580
630                                                              •  REM
640     CLS
650     PRINT USING F2$; A, R
660     PRINT " "
670     PRINT "              YEAR              AMOUNT"
680                                                                    REM
690     FOR Y = 1 TO U STEP 1
700       LET V = A * (1 + (R / 100)) ↑ Y
710       PRINT USING F1$; Y, V
720     NEXT Y
730                                                                    REM
740     PRINT " "
750     PRINT "DO YOU WANT TO PERFORM ANOTHER CALCULATION?"
760     INPUT "ENTER YES OR NO: ";R$
770                                                                    REM
780     IF R$ = "YES" OR R$ = "NO" THEN 820
790       INPUT "    INVALID RESPONSE - PLEASE ENTER YES OR NO: "; R$
800     GOTO 780
810                                                                    REM
820 GOTO 460
830                                                                    REM
840 PRINT " "
850 PRINT "END OF INVESTMENT PROGRAM"
860 END
```

Program Results

```
DO YOU WANT TO PERFORM AN INVESTMENT CALCULATION?
ENTER YES OR NO: ? YES
```

```
ENTER AMOUNT TO BE INVESTED: ? 10000
ENTER INTEREST RATE: ? 20
    INTEREST RATE IS TOO HIGH
    PLEASE ENTER A RATE LESS THAN 25 %: ? 10
    INTEREST RATE IS TOO HIGH
    PLEASE ENTER A RATE LESS THAN 25 %: ? 15
    INTEREST RATE IS TOO HIGH
    PLEASE ENTER A RATE LESS THAN 25 %: ? 1
    INTEREST RATE IS TOO HIGH
    PLEASE ENTER A RATE LESS THAN 25 %: ? 24
    INTEREST RATE IS TOO HIGH
    PLEASE ENTER A RATE LESS THAN 25 %: ?
```

Chapter 6
PROGRAMMING ASSIGNMENT 1

Sales charts must be prepared by a fast food restaurant listing the cost of 1 to 10 items of the various products sold. Design and code the BASIC program to produce the sales charts.

Instructions

The user will enter the cost of one food item. The data entered should be edited to ensure that the amount is less than $10.00.

Input

The program should be designed using good interactive programming techniques. The program begins by asking the user if a sales chart is to be prepared. If the answer is no, the program should be terminated. If the answer is yes, the user should be asked to enter the cost of one item. A chart should then be printed listing the cost of 1 through 10 items. The format of the output is illustrated below. In the example, 1.25 was entered as the cost of one item.

Output

```
DO YOU WANT TO PRODUCE A SALES CHART?
ENTER YES OR NO: ? YES

ENTER COST OF ONE ITEM: ? 1.25
```

```
              SALES CHART
      ITEMS              AMOUNT

        1               $ 1.25
        2               $ 2.50
        3               $ 3.75
        4               $ 5.00
        5               $ 6.25
        6               $ 7.50
        7               $ 8.75
        8               $10.00
        9               $11.25
       10               $12.50

   DO YOU WANT ANOTHER SALES CHART?
   ENTER YES OR NO:  ?
```

Chapter 6
PROGRAMMING ASSIGNMENT 2

Instructions A report is to be prepared listing the cost of one to ten gallons of gasoline based upon the cost per liter. Design and code the BASIC program to produce the desired report.

Input The user will input the current cost of one liter of gasoline. The data entered should be edited to ensure that the amount does not exceed $.99 per liter.

Output The program should begin with a question to the user asking if a gasoline charges report is to be prepared. If the answer is no, the program should be terminated. If the answer is yes, the user should then be asked to enter the cost of one liter of gasoline. The output should contain the number of gallons (from one to ten), the corresponding number of liters, and the cost for the gallon of gas. Liters are obtained by multiplying the number of gallons by 3.785. The cost of each gallon is obtained by multiplying the liters in each gallon by the cost per liter entered by the user. In the example below, the cost per liter was entered as $.39 by the user. The format of the output is illustrated below.

```
DO YOU WANT TO PRODUCE A GASOLINE CHART?
ENTER YES OR NO: ? YES

ENTER THE COST OF ONE LITER: ? .39
```

```
                    GASOLINE CHARGES
        GALLONS         LITERS              COST

           1             3.785           $  1.48
           2             7.570           $  2.95
           3            11.355           $  4.43
           4            15.140           $  5.90
           5            18.925           $  7.38
           6            22.710           $  8.86
           7            26.495           $10.33
           8            30.280           $11.81
           9            34.065           $13.29
          10            37.850           $14.76

        DO YOU WANT TO PRODUCE ANOTHER CHART?
        ENTER YES OR NO: ?
```

Chapter 6
SUPPLEMENTARY PROGRAMMING ASSIGNMENTS

A payroll program should be prepared listing the hourly, weekly, monthly, **Program 3**
and yearly salaries for a series of hourly rates. The beginning and ending
hourly rates which are to appear on the report are to be entered by the user.
The weekly pay rate is calculated by multiplying the hourly rate by 40. The
monthly rate is calculated by multiplying the weekly rate by 52 and dividing by
12. The yearly rate is calculated by multiplying the weekly rate by 52. The
beginning pay rate should not be less than 3.50, and the ending pay rate should
not be more than 20.00. The user should also input an increment to the beginning hourly pay rates. This increment should not be less than .10 nor greater
than 5.00. The program should ask the user if a chart is to be prepared. The
screens obtaining the user information are illustrated below.

```
DO YOU WANT TO PRODUCE A PAY CHART?
ENTER YES OR NO: ? YES
```

```
ENTER BEGINNING HOURLY RATE: ? 5.00
ENTER ENDING HOURLY RATE: ? 10.00
ENTER HOURLY PAY RATE INCREMENT: ? 1.00
```

A program should be designed and written that will prepare a report reflecting **Program 4**
the inflation rate of any value from $100.00 to $99,999.99 over a period of
years. The user should enter the dollar amount, the percentage of inflation
(from 1% through 25%), the beginning year for the report, and the ending
year for the report. The report should contain the year and the value for that
year. The value for any given year is the value from the previous year plus the
increase calculated by multiplying the percentage entered by the user by the
previous year's value. An example of the input entered by the user in this
program is shown below.

```
DO YOU WANT TO PRODUCE THE CHART?
ENTER YES OR NO: ? YES
```

```
ENTER VALUE: ? 1000
ENTER RATE OF INFLATION: ? 10
ENTER BEGINNING YEAR: ? 1983
ENTER ENDING YEAR: ? 1986
```

ARRAYS

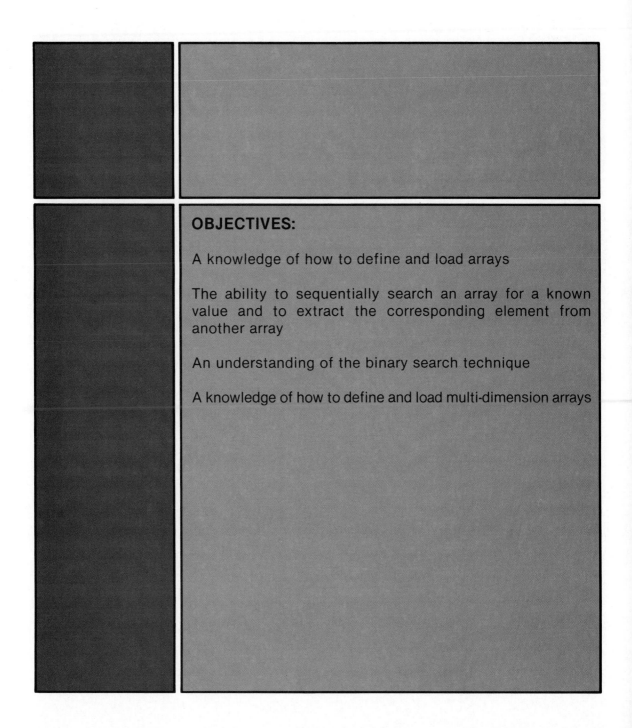

OBJECTIVES:

A knowledge of how to define and load arrays

The ability to sequentially search an array for a known value and to extract the corresponding element from another array

An understanding of the binary search technique

A knowledge of how to define and load multi-dimension arrays

CHAPTER SEVEN   ARRAYS

Tables are commonly used to look up information or to extract values for use in calculations. For example, one might use a table of distances between various cities when making a trip. Income tax tables, insurance tables, or sales tax tables may be used when extracting a value for use in a calculation. When a table is used, it must be searched in order to extract the proper information.

Tables also play an important part in computer programming. They are used to store data which can be extracted based upon given information. As an example, in the following illustration the user enters a flight number on the terminal keyboard. The program stored in main computer storage will search a table containing valid flight numbers. When the flight number which has been entered is found, the flight number and the departure time of the flight are displayed on the CRT screen.

Figure 7-1 When the user enters a flight number, the flight number table is searched until an equal flight number is found. The corresponding departure number is then displayed on the CRT screen.

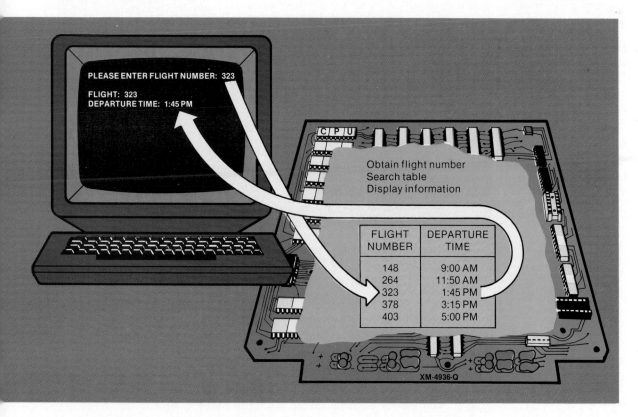

PLEASE ENTER FLIGHT NUMBER: 323

FLIGHT: 323
DEPARTURE TIME: 1:45 PM

C P U

Obtain flight number
Search table
Display information

FLIGHT NUMBER	DEPARTURE TIME
148	9:00 AM
264	11:50 AM
323	1:45 PM
378	3:15 PM
403	5:00 PM

XM-4936-Q

In the example above, the terminal operator entered the flight number — 323. The program stored in main computer storage used that value to search the table containing the flight numbers. The search could proceed by examining the first flight number (148). Since this flight number is not equal to the one entered on the terminal, the program would examine the second flight number. Again, the flight numbers are not equal, so the third flight number in the table is examined. In this case, the flight numbers are equal. Therefore, the corresponding departure time is extracted from the table and is displayed on the CRT screen.

Sample program   The sample program in this chapter illustrates an application in which flight information is made available to airline terminal operators. If the operators wish to make an inquiry, they are asked to enter the flight number. When the flight number is entered, the origination point, destination point, and departure time are displayed on the CRT screen (Figure 7–2).

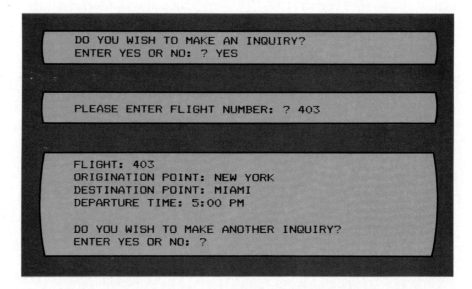

Figure 7-2 In the sample program, the user enters a flight number, and the origination point, destination point, and departure time of the flight are displayed on the CRT.

The first message sent to the terminal operator is "DO YOU WISH TO MAKE AN INQUIRY?". If the answer is no, the program is terminated. If the answer is yes, such as in the example above, the operator is asked to enter the flight number. In this case, flight number 403 was entered. The program will then search the flight number table. When flight number 403 is found in the table, the origination point, destination point, and departure time are extracted from corresponding tables and are printed on the screen.

In order to accomplish the processing shown in this example, three steps must be followed in the program. First, the tables must be created in the program. Second, data must be placed within the tables. And third, the tables must be searched and the correct data extracted from the tables.

These three steps are explained on the following pages.

When programming in BASIC, a table is normally referred to as an array. The first step in a program which will search an array is to reserve areas in main computer storage for the entries within the array. These entries are called elements of the array. This is accomplished through the use of the DIM (DIMension) statement. The general format of the DIM statement, an example of its use, and the results of its use are shown in Figure 7-3.

Creating an array

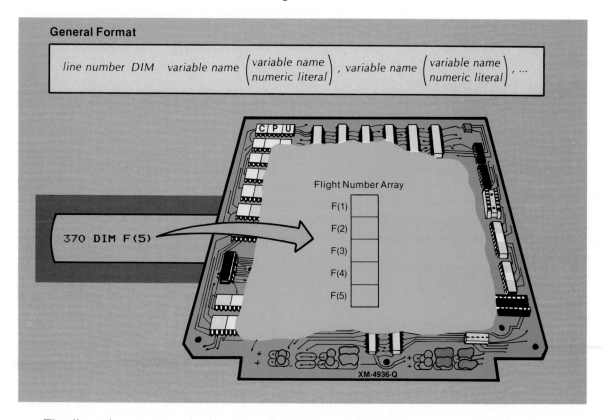

The dimension statement begins with a line number, followed by one or more spaces. The word DIM is specified next. One or more spaces follow the word DIM. The next entry is a variable name. This variable name is used to reference the array. Immediately following the variable name, with no intervening spaces, is a set of parentheses. Within the parentheses is a numeric literal, a numeric variable, or an arithmetic expression which indicates the number of elements in the array. In the example in Figure 7-3, the numeric literal 5 is specified. Therefore, the dimension statement reserves space in the F array for five elements in the array.

The F array is an array which will contain numeric values in each element because the variable name F is a numeric variable name. Each element in the array is referenced through the use of a subscript. A subscript is a numeric value, either a literal or a variable name representing a numeric value,

Figure 7-3 When the dimension statement is executed, storage is reserved for the number of elements in the array specified within the parentheses. In this example, the F array will have five elements. The dimension statement does not place data in the array — it merely reserves storage and informs the BASIC interpreter of the number of elements in the array.

specified in parentheses following the array name. It identifies the element within the array which is being referenced. For example, the entry F(2) specifies that the second element of the array is to be referenced. The entry F(4) specifies that the fourth element of the array is referenced.

It should be noted that some BASIC interpreters begin numbering elements within an array with the subscript 0. Therefore, a dimension statement DIM F(5), such as shown in Figure 7–3, would reserve space for six elements. The first element would be specified as F(0). In this text, the first element referenced in an array will always be identified with a subscript of 1; that is, F(1). In addition, some BASIC interpreters do not require a dimension statement if the array contains ten or fewer elements. It is suggested, however, that a dimension statement always be used to specify the exact number of elements in an array.

Loading the array   After an array has been defined using the dimension statement, the data must be placed in each element. Although a number of different techniques exist to perform this task, the most commonly found uses a for-next loop and the read statement. The coding to load the flight number array defined in Figure 7–3 is shown below.

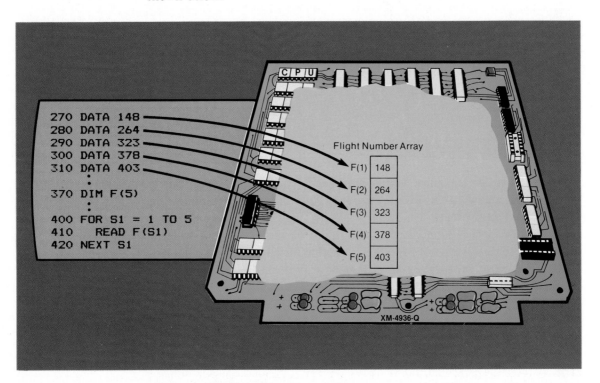

Figure 7-4 The for-next loop is used to load data into the flight number array.

The data statements on lines 270 – 310 each define the data which is to be placed in an element of the F array. The dimension statement on line 370 reserves computer storage for an array with the name F that will contain five elements. The for-next loop on lines 400 – 420 is used to transfer the data from the data statements to the array elements.

It will be recalled that the counter-variable in a for statement is initialized with the initial value specified in the statement. Therefore, in Figure 7–4, the counter-variable S1 will be initialized with the value 1. This value is then compared to the final value, 5. Since one is not greater than five, the loop is entered.

There, a read statement is executed. The read statement will transfer the data in the first data statement to the field identified by the variable following the word READ. In this example, the variable is F(S1), which is the array name F followed by a variable field which acts as the subscript. When the value in S1 is equal to 1, then the first element of F is referenced. When the value in S1 is equal to 2, the second element of F is referenced, and so on. On the first pass of the for-next loop, the value in S1 will be 1, so the read statement will transfer the value 148 from the data statement to the first element of the F array.

When the Next statement on line 420 is encountered, control is passed back to the for statement on line 400. The value in S1 is incremented by 1 and is compared to the final value, 5. Since the value in S1, 2, is less than the final value, the loop is once again entered. There, the read statement will transfer data from the second data statement to the F(S1) element of the F array. Since the value in S1 is 2, the data in the data statement on line 280 is transferred to the second element of the array.

This processing continues for the third, fourth, and fifth elements of the array. When the value in the counter-variable S1 reaches 6, the loop is terminated. From this example, it can be seen that the value in the counter-variable of the for-next loop is used as the subscript to reference the elements within the F array. This is the most commonly used means for loading an array in the BASIC language.

When array search is to occur in a program, more than one array is required in the program. The dimension statement is used to define these arrays, as shown in Figure 7–5.

Multiple arrays

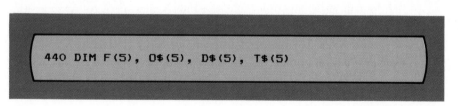

```
440 DIM F(5), O$(5), D$(5), T$(5)
```

Figure 7-5 Multiple arrays can be defined with a single dimension statement. If required by the application, each of the arrays defined by a single dimension statement could contain a different number of elements.

The dimension statement in Figure 7–5 defines four arrays. The F array has been seen in previous examples. The O$ array, which will contain string data because a string variable name is used, also contains five elements. Similarly, the D$ and T$ arrays contain five elements of string data. These arrays are used in the sample program to contain the flight numbers, the origination points (O$), the destination points (D$), and the departure times (T$).

These four arrays are loaded in the same fashion as the single F array in Figure 7–4. The following example illustrates loading these four arrays.

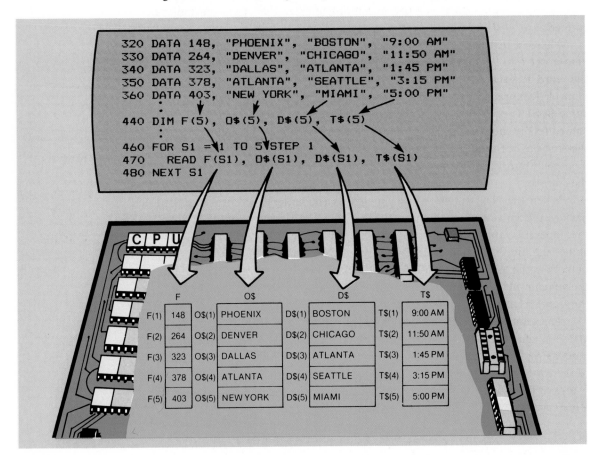

Figure 7-6 The single read statement in the for-next loop (line 470) is used to place data in four arrays. This single loop, which is executed five times, will work for all arrays which contain five elements. If an array contains a different number of elements, it will have to be loaded by a different for-next loop which is executed the same number of times as there are elements in the array.

In Figure 7–6, each data statement contains one element for each array. Thus, the data statement on line 320 contains an element for the flight number array (148), an element for the origination point array (PHOENIX), an element for the destination point array (BOSTON), and an element for the departure time array (9:00 AM). The next four data statements contain data for the other four elements of the arrays.

The for-next loop on lines 460 – 480 loads the arrays using the technique illustrated in Figure 7-4. The only difference here is that four elements are read with the single read statement. When the read statement on line 470 is executed the first time, the first entry in the data statement on line 320 is placed in the first element of the flight number array. The first element of the flight number array is used because the value in S1 on the first pass through the for-next loop is 1. After the first entry in the data statement is placed in the flight number array, the second entry in the data statement (PHOENIX) will be transferred to the first element of the O$ array. Then, the third entry in the data statement (BOSTON) is placed in the first element of the D$ array. Finally, the last entry in the data statement on line 320 (9:00 AM) is placed in the first element of the T$ array.

After the read statement has been completed, the Next statement on line 480 transfers control to the for statement on line 460 where the value in S1 is incremented by one. The same process is repeated for the data statement on line 330. This time the data is placed in the second element of each of the arrays. This processing will continue until all five elements of the arrays have been loaded with data.

Although the read statement within a for-next loop is the most commonly used means for placing data in an array, the exact method shown in Figure 7-6 need not always be used. Because of the manner in which the read and data statements work, different configurations of the data, read, and for-next statements can be used.

In order to understand these configurations, it is necessary to understand how the read and data statements work together. Regardless of the number of entries in the data statements, these statements merely define a list of data to be referenced by read statements. This is illustrated below.

The read and data statements

Coding

```
240 DATA 1, 2, 3, 4, 5
250 DATA 6, 7, 8, 9, 10
```

OR

```
240 DATA 1, 2, 3
250 DATA 4, 5, 6
260 DATA 7, 8, 9
270 DATA 10
```

OR

```
240 DATA 1, 2, 3, 4, 5, 6, 7, 8, 9, 10
```

All Yield: 1, 2, 3, 4, 5, 6, 7, 8, 9, 10

Figure 7-7 Regardless of the way in which data is specified in the data statement, the result is a single string of data. Each single entry in the string is read sequentially by the read statement(s) within the program. Thus, the first time a read statement is executed, the value 1 will be read. The next time a read statement is executed, the value 2 will be read.

Regardless of the format of the data statements in Figure 7–7, the results are identical — a list of the data entries specified in the data statements. When a read statement is executed, the next entry from the list is transferred to an area of storage referenced by the variable in the read statement. Therefore, from the data in Figure 7–7, the first read statement executed in the program would transfer the value 1 to a variable. The second read statement in the program, either the same read statement being executed a second time or another read statement being executed the first time, will transfer the value 2 from the data list to the variable field specified in the read statement. This is illustrated in Figure 7–8.

Figure 7–8 When a read statement is executed, it uses the next entries in the list generated by the data statements. If the read statement has a single variable name, the next entry in the data list is placed in the variable. If the read statement contains multiple variable names, the next entry in the data list is placed in the first variable field. The following entry in the data list is then placed in the second variable field. Thus, when the read statement on line 570 is executed, the first entry in the list is placed in the first variable field (A). The second entry in the data list is placed in the second variable field (B). This processing continues for all read statements in the program. If all of the entries in a data list have been used and a read statement is executed, the BASIC interpreter will write an "out of data" message, and the program will be terminated.

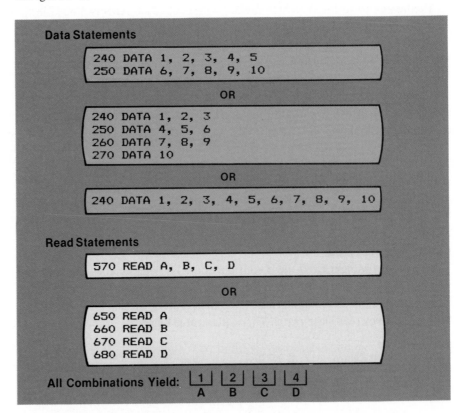

Data Statements

```
240 DATA 1, 2, 3, 4, 5
250 DATA 6, 7, 8, 9, 10
```

OR

```
240 DATA 1, 2, 3
250 DATA 4, 5, 6
260 DATA 7, 8, 9
270 DATA 10
```

OR

```
240 DATA 1, 2, 3, 4, 5, 6, 7, 8, 9, 10
```

Read Statements

```
570 READ A, B, C, D
```

OR

```
650 READ A
660 READ B
670 READ C
680 READ D
```

All Combinations Yield:

1	2	3	4
A	B	C	D

The entries in the data statements are always made available sequentially to the read statements. Each subsequent entry in the list generated by the data statements will be transferred to the field identified by a variable name in the read statements. Therefore, in the example in Figure 7–8, without regard to the manner in which the data statements are written, the read statement on line 570 will place the first data entry (1) into the field identified by the variable A, the second entry in the list (2) into the B field, the third entry (3) into the field identified by the variable name C, the fourth entry (4) into the D field.

The four read statements on lines 650 – 680 will cause exactly the same transfer of data to occur because the list of entries generated from the data statements is available to all read statements in the program. The next entry in the list is used for whichever read statement is executed next.

The number of entries in the list generated from data statements will normally be equal to the number of times read statements will be executed in the program. In some applications, however, a large number of read statements may be executed, but the actual amount of data to be read is small; that is, the same data is used over and over again. In some instances, it may not be known how many times this data is to be read. This condition can be solved through the use of the restore statement. After the restore statement is executed, the next read statement will obtain data from the first entry in the data list of the program, as shown in Figure 7-9.

Restore statement

```
250 DATA 1, 2
      •
630 READ A, B
640                              REM
650 FOR C = 1 TO 300
660    LET A = (A * C) / B
      •
740    RESTORE
750    READ A, B
760 NEXT C
```

Figure 7-9 After the restore instruction is executed, the next read statement will obtain its data from the first entry in the data list generated by the data statements in the program. Here, the read statement on line 750 will read the first entry from the data statement on line 250 because of the restore statement on line 740.

In the example above, the single data statement on line 250 contains two entries. The read statement on line 630 will transfer the first entry from the list generated by the data statement to the field identified by the variable name A and the second entry to the B field. Within the for-next loop, the calculation performed by the let statement on line 660 alters the value in A. To allow the read statement on line 750 to replace the calculated value in A by the first value in the data list, the restore statement on line 740 is executed. After its execution, the next read statement will obtain its data from the beginning of the data list. Therefore, when the read statement on line 750 is performed, the first value in the data list (1) will be placed in the A field. The value 2 will be placed in the B field. Although not widely used, the restore statement at times is a useful instruction.

Based upon the previous discussion, it is possible to arrange data statements and read statements in a number of configurations to load arrays. The example in Figure 7-6 illustrated the most commonly found means for loading four arrays with the same number of elements, but the examples on the following page illustrate several other means which could be used.

Loading arrays

Figure 7-10 Examples of
the data and read statements
to load arrays with an equal
number of elements.

Loading an array — Example 1

```
320 DATA 148, "PHOENIX", "BOSTON", "9:00 AM"
330 DATA 264, "DENVER", "CHICAGO", "11:50 AM"
340 DATA 323, "DALLAS", "ATLANTA", "1:45 PM"
350 DATA 378, "ATLANTA", "SEATTLE", "3:15 PM"
360 DATA 403, "NEW YORK", "MIAMI", "5:00 PM"
      .
440 DIM F(5), O$(5), D$(5), T$(5)
      .
460 FOR S1 = 1 TO 5 STEP 1
470    READ F(S1)
480    READ O$(S1)
490    READ D$(S1)
500    READ T$(S1)
510 NEXT S1
```

Loading an array — Example 2

```
320 DATA 148
330 DATA "PHOENIX"
340 DATA "BOSTON"
350 DATA "9:00 AM"
360 DATA 264
370 DATA "DENVER"
380 DATA "CHICAGO"
390 DATA "11:50 AM"
      .
740 DIM F(5), O$(5), D$(5), T$(5)
      .
760 FOR S1 = 1 TO 5 STEP 1
770    READ F(S1), O$(S1), D$(S1), T$(S1)
780 NEXT S1
```

Loading an array — Example 3

```
320 DATA 148
330 DATA "PHOENIX"
340 DATA "BOSTON"
350 DATA "9:00 AM"
360 DATA 264
370 DATA "DENVER"
380 DATA "CHICAGO"
390 DATA "11:50 AM"
      .
740 DIM F(5), O$(5), D$(5), T$(5)
      .
760 FOR S1 = 1 TO 5 STEP 1
770    READ F(S1)
780    READ O$(S1)
790    READ D$(S1)
800    READ T$(S1)
810 NEXT S1
```

As shown in Figure 7-10, a variety of methods can be used to load an array. The methods shown are not exhaustive — there are many more ways to load an array as well. These, however, illustrate the more commonly found methods.

After an array is loaded with data, it can be used for a variety of applications. In the sample program in this chapter, an array search is required. An array search consists of searching the array until a desired value is found. When the value is found, a corresponding element from another array is extracted and used.

The sample program requires the user to enter a flight number. Based upon the flight number, the origination point, the destination point, and the departure time are displayed (see Figure 7-2). The process of performing the array search consists of the following steps (Figure 7-11): 1) The flight number is obtained from the user; 2) The flight number is compared to each flight number in the array until an equal flight number is found; 3) The corresponding values for the other arrays are extracted and displayed on the CRT screen.

Searching

Figure 7-11 When the array search occurs, the flight number entered by the user is compared to the elements in the flight number array (F) until an equal flight number is found. When an equal number is found, the corresponding entries from the origination point array (O$), the destination point array (D$), and the departure time array (T$) are extracted and displayed on the screen.

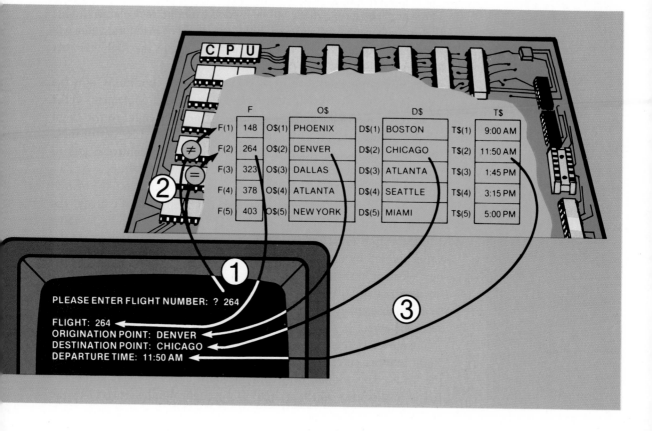

When the flight number is entered, it is compared to each successive flight number in the F array until an equal flight number is found. In the example in Figure 7-11, the second element in the flight array contains flight number 264, which is the number entered by the user. Since the second element in the flight number array contains the equal flight number, the second element in the other arrays will be extracted and displayed on the CRT screen. Thus, DENVER from the O$ array, CHICAGO from the D$ array, and 11:50 AM from the T$ array are extracted and displayed. Each of these elements is addressed by using the same subscript as the equal element in the F array.

When an array is searched, there is the possibility that the value being searched for does not exist. For example, if the computer user entered flight number 400, an equal condition would not occur because there is no flight 400 in the F array. Therefore, whenever an array search is performed in a program, there must always be provision for the case where an equal element in an array is not found.

Array search logic

The logic to perform the search illustrated in Figure 7-11 is shown by the flowchart in Figure 7-12. The numbered steps are explained below:

1. The flight number to be found in the array is entered on the keyboard.
2. The search subscript which will be used to examine each element in the flight number array is set to an initial value of 1. This initial value will allow the search to begin with the first element in the flight number array.
3. A decision is made to enter a loop based on two conditions — is the value in the search subscript greater than the number of elements in the array, or is the flight number entered by the user equal to the flight number in the element of the array being examined. If either of these conditions is true, the loop is not entered. Instead, control passes to the if-then-else structure at step 4.

   If, however, the flight numbers are not equal and the search subscript is not greater than the number of entries in the array, the loop is entered. The only statement within the loop is to add the value 1 to the search subscript. This processing means that the next time the value entered by the user is compared to an element in the array, the next element in the array is examined. Thus, if the first element of the array is not equal to the flight number entered by the user, after the search subscript is incremented the next comparison will be to the second element in the array.

   Control is then passed back to the start of the loop where the flight number entered by the user is compared to the next element in the array. This looping will continue until either a flight number is found in the array which is equal to the flight number entered by the

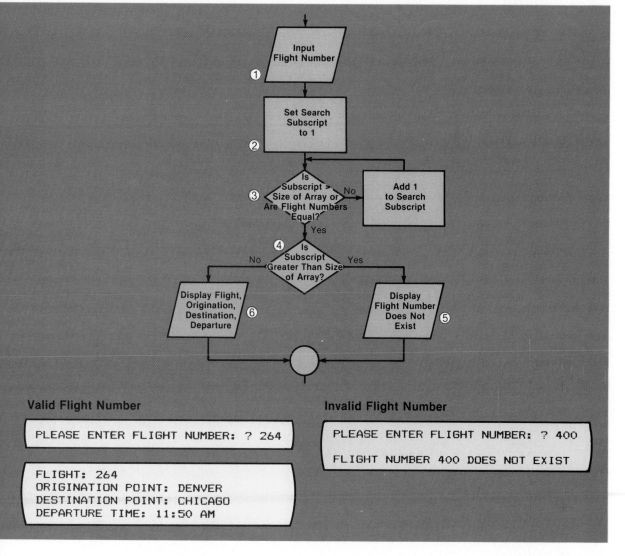

Valid Flight Number

```
PLEASE ENTER FLIGHT NUMBER: ? 264
```

```
FLIGHT: 264
ORIGINATION POINT: DENVER
DESTINATION POINT: CHICAGO
DEPARTURE TIME: 11:50 AM
```

Invalid Flight Number

```
PLEASE ENTER FLIGHT NUMBER: ? 400

FLIGHT NUMBER 400 DOES NOT EXIST
```

user or until the value in the search subscript is greater than the number of entries in the array.

4. When the exit from the loop occurs, the next task is to determine why the exit took place. There are two possible reasons — either a flight number was found in the array which was equal to the flight number entered by the user, or the value in the search subscript became greater than the number of elements in the array. If the value in the subscript is greater than the number of elements in the array, it indicates that the flight number does not exist in the array because all elements have been compared and none have been found to be equal.

5. When a flight number is not found in the flight number array, the message FLIGHT NUMBER 400 DOES NOT EXIST is printed. The flight number in the message is the invalid flight number entered by the user. Control is then passed to the next portion of the program.

Figure 7-12 The six steps required for the logic of an array search are shown by the flowchart. If an equal flight number is found in the flight number array, the flight number, origination point, destination point, and departure time are displayed. If an equal flight number is not found, an error message is displayed.

6. If the subscript is not greater than the size of the array, it means a flight number was found in the array that was equal to the flight number entered by the user. Therefore, the flight number, origination point, destination point, and departure time are displayed on the screen.

The steps in the flowchart for the first element in the flight number array are illustrated in the example in Figure 7–13.

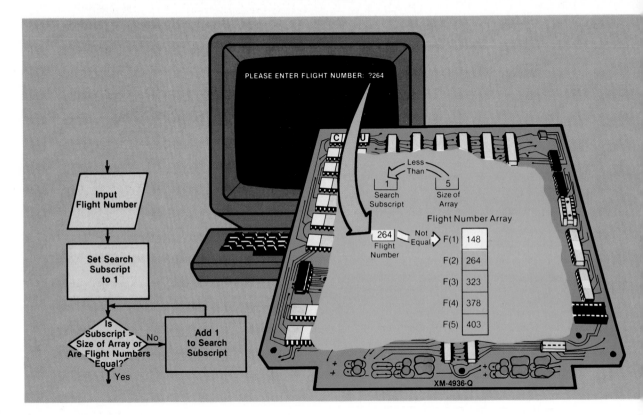

Figure 7-13 In this example, flight number 264 is entered by the user. This flight number is not equal to the first element in the flight number array. Therefore, the subscript must be incremented by one, and the next element in the array is compared.

In the example above, the user enters flight number 264. The search subscript is set to the value 1. It is then compared to the size of the array, where it is found the subscript is less than the size of the array. The flight number entered by the user is compared to the first element in the flight number array. They are not equal. Therefore, the loop must be entered to increment the subscript by one and continue the search (Figure 7–14).

After the search subscript is incremented by one, control passes back to the decision statement which again checks if the value in the subscript is greater than the size of the array. Since it is not, the flight number entered is compared to the second element of the flight number array. In this case, they are equal. Therefore, the loop is terminated, and control is passed to the if-then-else structure.

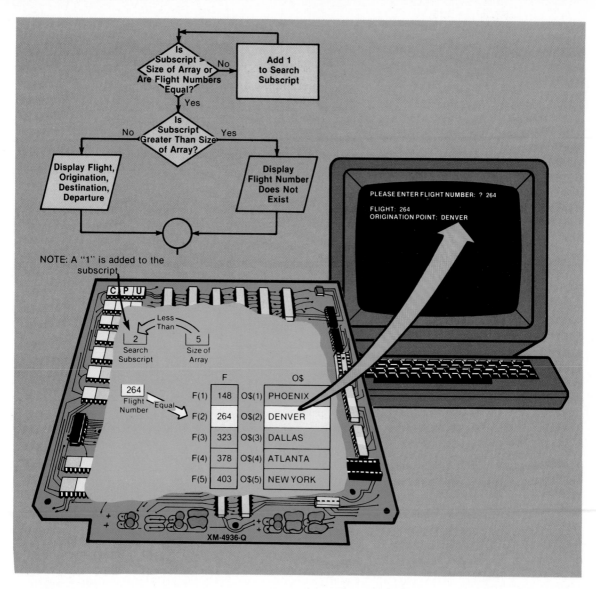

Figure 7-14 Flight number 264 is equal to the flight number in the second element of the flight number array. Therefore, the corresponding elements of the other arrays are accessed, and the data is displayed on the screen.

The decision at the entry point to the if-then-else structure tests if the subscript is greater than the size of the array. In this example, it is not (2 is not greater than 5). Therefore, an equal flight number had to be found. As a result, the flight number, origination point, destination point, and departure time are extracted from the arrays and displayed on the CRT screen. The subscript value used when the equal flight number was found (2) is used to reference the elements in the origination, destination, and departure time arrays.

To summarize the search logic, the value to be found in an array is compared to the first element of the array. If they are equal, the corresponding elements from the other arrays are extracted and printed, and the search process is complete. If the value to be found is not equal to the first element in the array, the subscript is incremented by one. The value is then compared to the second element in the array. This process will continue until the value to be found is equal to an element in the array, or all of the elements of the array have been examined and none is equal to the value. If none is equal, an error message is displayed. If an equal element is found, the corresponding elements from the other arrays are printed.

It is important that the programmer thoroughly understand this logic and processing prior to designing and coding a program which will search an array.

Coding the array search

After the logic for the array search has been designed, the coding to implement the logic must be written. The coding to implement the logic of the flowchart in Figure 7-12 is illustrated below.

```
450 INPUT "PLEASE ENTER FLIGHT NUMBER: "; F1
460 LET S = 1
470                                              REM
480 IF S > 5 THEN 530
490 IF F1 = F(S) THEN 530
500    LET S = S + 1
510 GOTO 480
520                                              REM
530 IF S > 5 THEN 600
540    PRINT "FLIGHT: "; F(S)
550    PRINT "ORIGINATION POINT: "; O$(S)
560    PRINT "DESTINATION POINT: "; D$(S)
570    PRINT "DEPARTURE TIME: "; T$(S)
580    GOTO 640
590                                              REM
600    PRINT " "
610    PRINT "FLIGHT NUMBER"; F1; "DOES NOT EXIST"
620    GOTO 640
630                                              REM
640      .
         .
         .
```

Figure 7-15 The coding for the array search consists of two major parts — the loop to search for an equal flight number and the if-then-else structure to determine the results of the search.

The input statement on line 450 obtains the flight number from the user which will be used to search the flight number array. This value is stored in the F1 field. The subscript field, S, is then set to the value 1.

The if statement on line 480 checks if the value in the subscript field, S, is greater than the size of the array, which is 5. If so, then the entire array has been searched, and a flight number equal to the one entered by the user has not been found. If the value in S is greater than 5, control is passed to line 530, where further checking is done.

If the value in S is not greater than 5, the if statement on line 490 tests if the value entered by the user is equal to the element in the array addressed by the entry F(S). This entry addresses the element in the F array corresponding to the value in the subscript field, S. If the value in S is one, the first element of the F array is compared. If the value in S is two, the second element of the F array is compared, and so on. If the value in F1 is equal to the element in the array being compared, an equal flight number was found. Control is passed to line 530 for further checking.

If neither of the if statement conditions is true, the statement on line 500 adds 1 to the subscript field (S) so that the next element of the flight number array can be compared. The goto statement on line 510 then passes control back to the if statement at line 480.

On line 530, the value in the subscript field is checked to determine if it is greater than 5. If so, no equal flight number was found in the array, and control is passed to line 600, where the error message is printed. If the value in S is not greater than 5, an equal flight number in the array was found. The value in S will point to the element which contains the equal flight number. This value is used to reference the elements in the other arrays to print the origination point (line 550), the destination point (line 560), and the departure time (line 570).

As will be noted from both the flowchart in Figure 7–12 and the coding in Figure 7–15, a loop is used to search the array. The if-then-else structure is then used to determine the results of the array search and take appropriate action.

The if statements on lines 480 and 490 both pass control to the same point if they are true. Therefore, it can be asked why the OR logical operator cannot be used to join these conditions. If either or both of the conditions are true, line 530 will receive control (Figure 7–16).

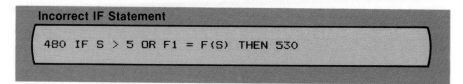

Incorrect IF Statement

```
480 IF S > 5 OR F1 = F(S) THEN 530
```

Figure 7–16 Whenever a subscript is to be used with an array name, the value in the subscript must not be greater than the number of elements in the array. If it is, the program will be terminated. Therefore, this if statement cannot be used in an array search because the value in S could be greater than 5, which is the number of elements in the F array.

The reason this statement will not work properly is that when the if statement is evaluated, both conditions are examined before it is determined whether the if statement is true. The value in the subscript S can be greater than 5; indeed, this is tested in the if statement. If the value in S is greater than 5, however, the entry F(S) is invalid because there are only five elements in the F array. The error message SUBSCRIPT OUT OF RANGE will be printed by the BASIC interpreter if the value in the subscript field is greater than the number of elements in the array. Therefore, not only must the conditions be tested separately, the test for the subscript value being greater than the number of elements in the array must be performed before the comparison to the element in the array. This is true for all array searches.

**Misuse of
for-next loop**

In some programs, it will be found that the programmer used for-next statements to perform the array search. The typical coding which is used is shown in Figure 7–17.

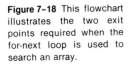

Figure 7-17 A for-next loop should never be used to search an array because it violates the single exit point rule of the loop logic structure.

Invalid array search using for-next loop

```
480 FOR S = 1 TO 5
490    IF F1 = F(S) THEN 550
500 NEXT S
510                                                      REM
520 PRINT "FLIGHT NUMBER"; F1; "DOES NOT EXIST"
530 GOTO 600
540                                                      REM
550 PRINT "FLIGHT: "; F(S)
560 PRINT "ORIGINATION POINT: "; O$(S)
570 PRINT "DESTINATION POINT: "; D$(S)
580 PRINT "DEPARTURE TIME: "; T$(S)
590
600
```

From the example above, it can be seen that the for-next loop is used to increment the subscript by one each pass through the loop. If the loop is completed by the value in S becoming greater than 5, then the element in the array is not equal to the value to be found and an error message is written. The if statement on line 490 compares the value entered (F1) to the element in the flight number array. If they are equal, control is passed to the statement at line 550 which will print the data from the arrays.

This coding violates the single exit rule of the loop logic structure, as shown by the flowchart in Figure 7–18. The if statement within the for-next loop exits from the loop at a second exit point. It passes control to a different statement from the normal exit of the loop. Because of these violations of the single exit rule, the for-next loop should never be used for array search. The

Figure 7-18 This flowchart illustrates the two exit points required when the for-next loop is used to search an array.

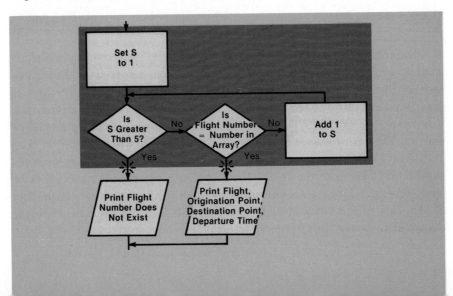

for-next loop is used only when the exit from the loop is controlled by the value in the counter-variable.

Binary array search

The previous examples have illustrated a sequential array search, where the first element of the array is examined, and then the second element, and then the third element, and so on in succession. This type of array search is useful when the number of elements in the array is relatively small, on the order of fewer than one hundred. When arrays with a larger number of elements must be searched, other searching techniques which produce a faster search can be used. When the elements of the array can be arranged in an ascending or descending sequence, one of the more widely used techniques is the binary search.

The binary search is used to eliminate portions of an array that do not contain the value for which a search is being conducted. To illustrate, the example in Figure 7-19 contains eleven flight numbers that are arranged in ascending sequence in the flight number array. This means that the flight number in the first element of the array is less than the flight number in the second element; the flight number in the second element is less than the flight number in the third element, and so on. The steps involved in a binary search of the array are:

1. The flight number to be found in the array (587) is entered from the keyboard.
2. The middle item in the array (the sixth flight number) is compared to

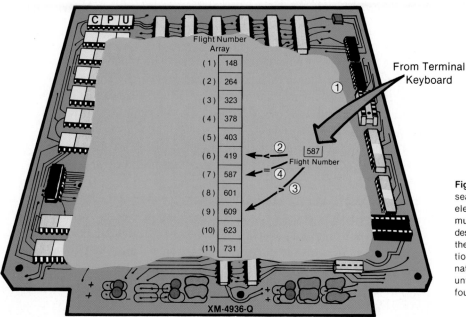

Figure 7-19 When a binary search is to be used, the elements within the array must be in an ascending or descending sequence. When the search takes place, portions of the array are eliminated from consideration until the equal element is found.

the flight number to be found. The flight number in the sixth element of the array (419) is less than the flight number entered by the user (587). Since the flight numbers in the array are in ascending sequence, the flight numbers in elements 1 – 5 are also less than the flight number entered by the user. Therefore, these elements of the array need not be compared. From this one comparison, then, more than half of the array has been removed from consideration when attempting to find an equal flight number.

3. This step compares the flight number entered by the user to the flight number in the middle element of those elements remaining in consideration (elements 7 – 11). The middle element between 7 and 11 is element 9. Thus, the second comparison compares flight number 587 to flight number 609, which is found in the ninth element of the array. Flight number 587 is less than flight number 609. Therefore, since 589 is greater than the value in the sixth element and less than the value in the ninth element, only element 7 or element 8 can contain the equal flight number.

4. Since there is no single middle element between element 6 and element 9, the lower of 7 and 8 is chosen for the comparison. When flight number 587 is compared to the flight number in the seventh element of the array, it is found that the flight numbers are equal. Therefore, the array search is terminated.

Note in this example that only three comparisons were required to find the equal flight number, while if a sequential array search were used, seven comparisons would have been required. In larger arrays, more savings in time can be realized. For example, in an array with 1,000 elements, the maximum number of comparisons using a binary search to find an equal element is ten.

Logic for a binary search

The logic to perform a binary search must calculate which element within the array is to be compared on each pass through the search. The search continues until either an equal element has been found or until all possible elements have been examined and found to be not equal. The flowchart of the logic used in a binary search is shown in Figure 7–20.

The steps to search the array illustrated in Figure 7–19 for flight number 587 using the logic shown in the flowchart are explained below:

1. The upper limit, which is a numeric value used in the calculation of the element to be compared, is set to the value 12 (the size of the array plus 1). The lower limit, another value used in the calculation, is set to zero.

2. The subscript used for the comparison is calculated by adding the upper limit and lower limit, and dividing the result by 2. In the example, the sum of the upper and lower limits is 12. Twelve divided

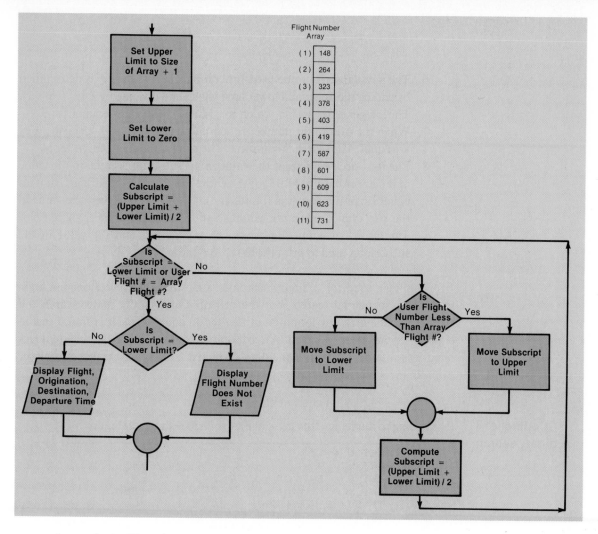

Flight Number
Array

(1)	148
(2)	264
(3)	323
(4)	378
(5)	403
(6)	419
(7)	587
(8)	601
(9)	609
(10)	623
(11)	731

by two is six. Therefore, the first element to be compared is 6.

3. The subscript (6) is not equal to the lower limit (0), nor is the user flight number (587) equal to the flight number in the sixth element (419). Therefore, a check is made to determine if the user flight number is less than the array flight number. Flight number 587 is not less than 419. Therefore, the subscript is moved to the lower limit field. The lower limit field now contains the value 6.

4. The subscript for the next element in the array to be compared is calculated by adding the value in the upper limit field (12) to the value in the lower limit field (6) and dividing the result (18) by 2. From this calculation, the subscript value 9 will be used for the next comparison.

5. The subscript is not equal to the lower limit, and the flight number (587) is not equal to the flight number in the ninth element of the array (609). Therefore, the search loop is entered, and it is found that the user flight number (587) is less than the array flight number (609). As a result, the value in the subscript (9) is placed in the upper limit field.

Figure 7-20 The principle used in a binary search is the same as that used in a sequential search — use a loop to perform the search and then use the if-then-else logic structure to determine the results of the search.

6. The new subscript to be used for comparing in the array is determined by adding the upper and lower limit values and dividing by 2 ((9 + 6) / 2). The integer of the result, which is 7, is used for the next comparison.

7. When the user flight number is compared to the seventh element, they are equal. The search is complete. The program exits from the loop.

8. The next decision tests if the value in the subscript is equal to the value in the lower limit field. If so, the entire table has been searched, and no equal flight number was found. In this example, however, the value in the subscript field is not equal to the value in the lower limit field. Therefore, an equal flight number was found, and the value in the subscript is used to print the data from the arrays.

The logic used for a binary search is somewhat different from the logic used for a sequential search, but the principle used is the same: search the elements in the array by looping until either an equal element is found or the entire array has been searched. After looping, determine whether an equal element was found. If so, print the data extracted from other arrays; otherwise, print an error message.

Coding for a binary search

The coding to implement the logic in Figure 7–20 is shown in Figure 7–21.

```
220     LET U = 12
230     LET L = 0
240     LET S = INT((U + L) / 2)
250                                     REM
260     IF S = L THEN 380
270     IF F1 = F(S) THEN 380
280       IF F1 < F(S) THEN 320
290         LET L = S
300         GOTO 350
310                                     REM
320         LET U = S
330         GOTO 350
340                                     REM
350       LET S = INT((U + L) / 2)
360     GOTO 260
370                                     REM
380     IF S = L THEN 460
390       CLS
400       PRINT "FLIGHT NUMBER: "; F1
410       PRINT "ORIGINATION POINT: "; O$(S)
420       PRINT "DESTINATION POINT: "; D$(S)
430       PRINT "DEPARTURE TIME: "; T$(S)
440       GOTO 490
450                                     REM
460       PRINT "FLIGHT NUMBER"; F1; "DOES NOT EXIST"
470       GOTO 490
480                                     REM
490
```

Figure 7-21 The coding for the binary search reflects exactly the logic of the flowchart in Figure 7-20. Note the use of the integer function (int) to ensure an integer for the subscript. Numbers used as subscripts to reference an array cannot contain digits to the right of the decimal point.

The coding is straight forward. Since subscripts must be whole numbers, not real numbers, the calculation of the subscript uses the integer (int) function. It will be recalled that the integer function returns the next lowest integer from the number within parentheses.

The binary search is quite a powerful tool when searching larger arrays. There are other search techniques which can be used as well, depending upon the nature of the data in the array. The programmer who understands the sequential search and the binary search, however, will usually be able to adequately design and write any array searching required in a program.

Multi-dimension arrays

The arrays which have been examined thus far in this chapter have been single dimension arrays; that is, a single subscript is required to determine where in the array an element is located. In some applications, multi-dimension arrays are required. A multi-dimension array is one which requires two subscript values, one for the rows of the array and one for the columns of the array, to identify an element within the array. The mileage chart below is an example of a two-dimension array.

		Column 1	Column 2	Column 3	Column 4	Column 5	Column 6
		ATLANTA	CHICAGO	DALLAS	MIAMI	NEW YORK	SEATTLE
Row 1	ATLANTA	—	712	791	663	854	2820
Row 2	CHICAGO	712	—	921	1423	809	2060
Row 3	DALLAS	791	921	—	1385	1614	2183
Row 4	MIAMI	663	1423	1385	—	1279	3486
Row 5	NEW YORK	854	809	1614	1279	—	2878

The mileage array in Figure 7-22 consists of rows and columns. To determine the distance from Dallas to Miami, the user of the array would search each row until Dallas is found. Then, within the Dallas row, each column is examined until the Miami column is found. At the intersection of the Dallas row and the Miami column is the mileage from Dallas to Miami.

To reference the location where the mileage from Dallas to Miami is found, the row and then the column can be specified. Thus, the location can be addressed as row 3, column 4. Two values are required to address the location — a row and a column. Therefore, this array is a two-dimensional array because two identifiers are required to address an element within the array.

A two-dimensional array is defined in BASIC using the dimension statement. The dimension statement which could be used to define the array in Figure 7-22 is shown in Figure 7-23 on page 7.24.

Figure 7-22 This mileage chart is an example of a two-dimension array because two subscript values are required to locate an element in the chart. The first subscript value specifies the row the desired element occupies, and the second subscript value specifies the column.

Figure 7-23 The dimension statement is used to define a two-dimension array. The first number in parentheses specifies the number of rows in the array; the second number in parentheses specifies the number of columns.

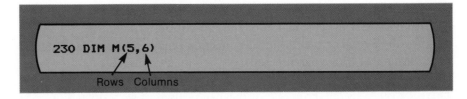

```
230 DIM M(5,6)
        ↑   ↑
    Rows  Columns
```

The format of the dimension statement used for multi-dimension arrays is the same as that used for one-dimension arrays. The only difference is that both the number of rows and the number of columns must be specified in the parentheses following the array name. Thus, in Figure 7–23, the M array will consist of five rows and six columns.

Loading a two-dimension array

As with a one-dimension array, the for-next loop provides the best technique for loading a two-dimension array. However, a nested for-next loop must be used to load a two-dimension array. The statements to load the array defined by the dimension statement in Figure 7–23 are illustrated below.

```
230 DIM M(5,6)
240                                              REM
250 DATA 0, 712, 791, 663, 854, 2820
260 DATA 712, 0, 921, 1423, 809, 2060
270 DATA 791, 921, 0, 1385, 1614, 2183
280 DATA 663, 1423, 1385, 0, 1279, 3486
290 DATA 854, 809, 1614, 1279, 0, 2878
300                                              REM
310 FOR R = 1 TO 5
320    FOR C = 1 TO 6
330       READ M(R, C)
340    NEXT C
350 NEXT R
360                                              REM
```

Figure 7-24 To load a two-dimension array, a nested for-next loop, such as shown in this example, is commonly used.

The dimension statement on line 230 defines the two-dimension array. The data statements on lines 250 – 290 contain the data which is to be placed in the array. Note that each data statement contains the data for one row in the array. As with one-dimension arrays, many different schemes can be used for loading the arrays. The technique shown here has proved to be easy to use and easy to understand.

The for statement on line 310 establishes a loop for each of the rows of the array. Within each row, six columns must be filled with data. The for statement on line 320 establishes a loop for each column within a row. The read statement on line 330 reads a number from a data statement and places it in the element of the M array corresponding to the subscripts R and C. The first time the read statement is executed, the value in R will be one and the value in C will be one. Thus, the first number read will be placed in row one, column one of the M array.

When the read statement is executed the second time, the value in C will be incremented by 1 by the for statement on line 320, but the value in R will still be one. Therefore, the second time the read statement is executed, the data will be placed in the row 1, column 2 element of the M array. The remainder of row 1 will be filled in this same manner by the for-next loop on lines 320 – 340. When this loop is completed, control will be passed to the next statement on line 350 and then to the for statement on line 310. The value in R will be increased by 1 to 2. The loop on lines 320 – 340 will again be executed in its entirety, this time for the second row of the array. This processing will continue for all five rows of the M array.

Once data has been stored in the multi-dimension array, it can be accessed in much the same manner as one-dimension arrays. To perform an array search process, the normal procedure is to define a one-dimension array representing the rows of the two-dimension array and a one-dimension array representing the columns of the two-dimension array. Each of these one-dimension arrays is searched to determine the two subscripts required to access the two-dimension array. This process is illustrated in Figure 7–25.

Multi-dimension array search

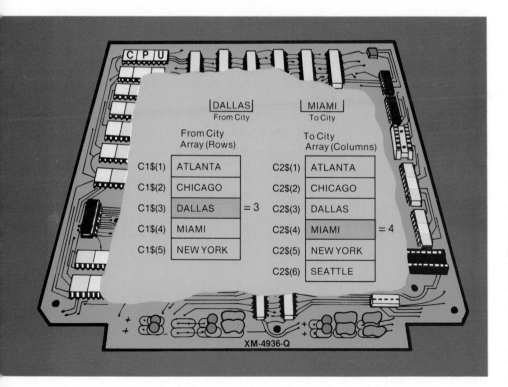

Figure 7-25 To search a two-dimension array, a common technique is to define two one-dimension arrays — one for the rows and one for the columns of the two-dimension arrays. By searching each of the one-dimension arrays, the subscripts required to reference elements in the two-dimension arrays can be determined. Here, Dallas is the third element in the C1$ array, and Miami is the fourth element in the C2$ array. These subscripts (3, 4) can be used to reference the two-dimension mileage array.

In the example in Figure 7–25, the row array contains all of the city names in the rows of the multi-dimension array. The column array contains all the cities in the columns of the multi-dimension array. The row array is searched until the from city is found. In the example, the city to be found is Dallas. Dallas is found in the third element of the row array. Therefore, when the two-dimension array is accessed, the row subscript will be three.

Similarly, the column array is searched to find the to city, which is Miami in the example. Miami is found in the fourth element of the column array. Thus, when the mileage array is referenced, the column subscript will be 4.

To extract the distance from Dallas to Miami, the row subscript and the column subscript determined in the searches are used. Therefore, the entry $M(3,4)$ could be used to reference the mileage array. Normally, the subscripts used to reference the array would be variable names such as in the entry $M(R,C)$, where R contains the value 3 and C contains the value 4.

Multi-dimension arrays can be quite useful in some applications. The programmer should be familiar with the techniques used to process them.

Sample program

The sample program in this chapter uses a flight number entered from a terminal or computer keyboard to search arrays and print the flight number, the origination point, the destination point, and the departure time of the flight. The output produced by the program is illustrated in Figure 7–2 on page 7.2. The input to the program is the flight number entered by the user. The arrays used by the program to store the flight information are shown in Figure 7–6 on page 7.6.

When the program is executed, the user enters a flight number. If the flight number is found in the flight number array, the corresponding information is displayed on the screen; if the flight number is not found, an error message is displayed on the screen. The user is then asked if another inquiry is to be made. If so, the process is repeated. If not, the program is terminated.

Program design

The tasks which must be accomplished by the program are specified below.

Program Tasks

1. Load arrays.
2. Obtain flight number and ensure valid user entries.
3. Perform array search.
4. Write flight information and error messages.

Program flowchart

The logic for this program is shown by the flowchart in Figures 7–26 and 7–27.

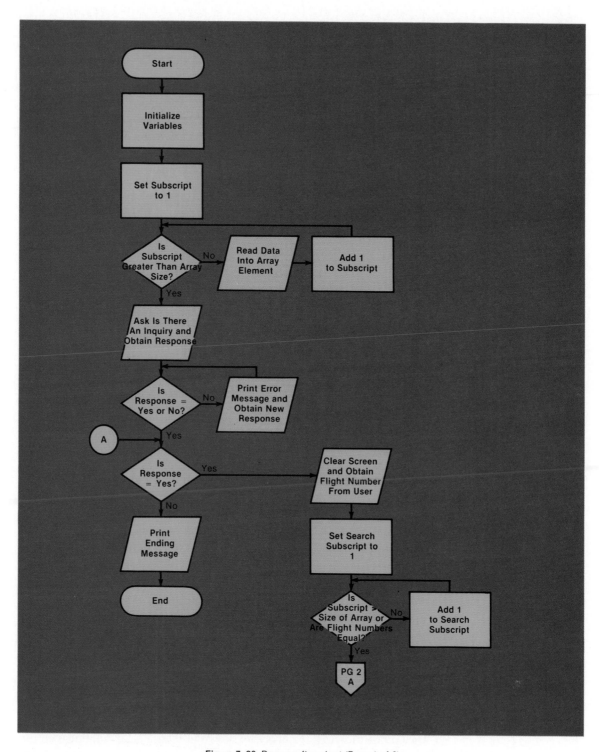

Figure 7-26 Program flowchart (Page 1 of 2)

Figure 7-27 Program flowchart (Page 2 of 2)

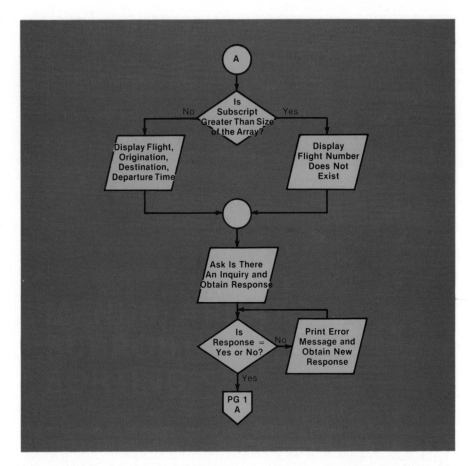

Program coding

The coding to load the arrays used in the sample program is illustrated in Figure 7-28. The technique shown is virtually the same as explained in the chapter. The only difference is that the size of the arrays (five elements each) is placed in the variable field N in the initialization portion of the program. The dimension statement on line 440 uses this value when defining the size of the arrays.

The for-next loop on lines 460 – 480 is used to load the arrays by reading data and placing it in each of the elements of the arrays. The variable N is also used in the for statement on line 460 to control the number of times the loop will be executed. Thus, if the number of elements in the arrays were to be changed, the only statement which would have to be modified in the program is the let statement on line 400. The dimension statement and the loop to load the arrays would not have to be modified. If more elements were added to the arrays, the data statements would also have to be changed to provide more data for the arrays.

The coding to search the arrays is shown in Figure 7-29. On line 650, the if statement tests whether the value in the search subscript, S2, is greater than

```
300 REM ***** DATA TO LOAD ARRAYS *****
310                                                         REM
320 DATA 148, "PHOENIX", "BOSTON", "9:00 AM"
330 DATA 264, "DENVER", "CHICAGO", "11:50 AM"
340 DATA 323, "DALLAS", "ATLANTA", "1:45 PM"
350 DATA 378, "ATLANTA", "SEATTLE", "3:15 PM"
360 DATA 403, "NEW YORK", "MIAMI", "5:00 PM"
370                                                         REM
380 REM ***** INITIALIZATION OF VARIABLES *****
390                                                         REM
400 LET N = 5
410                                                         REM
420 REM ***** DEFINE AND LOAD ARRAYS *****
430                                                         REM
440 DIM F(N), O$(N), D$(N), T$(N)
450                                                         REM
460 FOR S1 = 1 TO N STEP 1
470    READ F(S1), O$(S1), D$(S1), T$(S1)
480 NEXT S1
```

Figure 7-28 Definition and loading of program arrays for sample program

the number of elements in the array (the value in N). Once again, note that if the number of elements in the array was changed, this if statement would not have to be modified. If the value in S2 is not greater than the value in N, then the element in the array F(S2) is compared to the flight number entered by the user, F1. If they are equal, control is passed to line 700, where, since S2 is not greater than N, the flight number, origination point, destination point, and departure time are printed. This array search processing is the same as that previously explained in detail in this chapter.

Figure 7-29 Array search coding from sample program

```
630     LET S2 = 1
640                                                         REM
650     IF S2 > N THEN 700
660     IF F(S2) = F1 THEN 700
670       LET S2 = S2 + 1
680     GOTO 650
690                                                         REM
700     IF S2 > N THEN 780
710       CLS
720       PRINT "FLIGHT:"; F(S2)
730       PRINT "ORIGINATION POINT: "; O$(S2)
740       PRINT "DESTINATION POINT: "; D$(S2)
750       PRINT "DEPARTURE TIME: "; T$(S2)
760       GOTO 820
770                                                         REM
780       PRINT " "
790       PRINT "   FLIGHT NUMBER"; F1; "DOES NOT EXIST"
800       GOTO 820
810                                                         REM
820     PRINT " "
```

Sample program   The complete listing of the sample program is illustrated in Figure 7–30 and
Figure 7–31.

```
100 REM AIRLINE                 JANUARY 23              SHELLY/CASHMAN
110                                                              REM
120 REM THIS PROGRAM LOADS AIRLINE ARRAYS CONTAINING FLIGHT
130 REM NUMBERS, ORIGINATION POINTS, DESTINATION POINTS, AND
140 REM DEPARTURE TIMES. THE USER CAN ENTER THE FLIGHT NUMBER
150 REM TO OBTAIN THE OTHER INFORMATION.
160                                                              REM
170 REM VARIABLE NAMES:
180 REM    F()...FLIGHT NUMBER ARRAY
190 REM    O$()..ORIGINATION POINT ARRAY
200 REM    D$()..DESTINATION POINT ARRAY
210 REM    T$()..DEPARTURE TIME ARRAY
220 REM    F1....FLIGHT NUMBER FOR INQUIRY
230 REM    S1....SUBSCRIPT TO LOAD ARRAYS
240 REM    S2....SUBSCRIPT TO SEARCH ARRAY AND REFERENCE ALL
250 REM          ARRAYS WHEN SEARCH IS SUCCESSFUL
260 REM    N.....NUMBER OF ENTRIES IN ARRAYS
270 REM    R$....INPUT AREA FOR RESPONSE TO QUESTION
280 REM          "DO YOU WISH TO MAKE AN INQUIRY?"
290                                                              REM
300 REM ***** DATA TO LOAD ARRAYS *****
310                                                              REM
320 DATA 148, "PHOENIX", "BOSTON", "9:00 AM"
330 DATA 264, "DENVER", "CHICAGO", "11:50 AM"
340 DATA 323, "DALLAS", "ATLANTA", "1:45 PM"
350 DATA 378, "ATLANTA", "SEATTLE", "3:15 PM"
360 DATA 403, "NEW YORK", "MIAMI", "5:00 PM"
370                                                              REM
380 REM ***** INITIALIZATION OF VARIABLES *****
390                                                              REM
400 LET N = 5
410                                                              REM
420 REM ***** DEFINE AND LOAD ARRAYS *****
430                                                              REM
440 DIM F(N), O$(N), D$(N), T$(N)
450                                                              REM
460 FOR S1 = 1 TO N STEP 1
470    READ F(S1), O$(S1), D$(S1), T$(S1)
480 NEXT S1
490                                                              REM
500 REM ***** PROCESSING *****
510                                                              REM
520 CLS
530 PRINT "DO YOU WISH TO MAKE AN INQUIRY?"
540 INPUT "ENTER YES OR NO: "; R$
550                                                              REM
560 IF R$ = "YES" OR R$ = "NO" THEN 600
570    INPUT "   INVALID RESPONSE - PLEASE ENTER YES OR NO: "; R$
580 GOTO 560
590                                                              REM
```

Figure 7-30 Sample program (Part 1 of 2)

```
600 IF R$ = "NO" THEN 920
610   CLS
620   INPUT "PLEASE ENTER FLIGHT NUMBER: "; F1
630   LET S2 = 1
640                                                      REM
650   IF S2 > N THEN 700
660   IF F(S2) = F1 THEN 700
670     LET S2 = S2 + 1
680   GOTO 650
690                                                      REM
700   IF S2 > N THEN 780
710     CLS
720     PRINT "FLIGHT:"; F(S2)
730     PRINT "ORIGINATION POINT: "; O$(S2)
740     PRINT "DESTINATION POINT: "; D$(S2)
750     PRINT "DEPARTURE TIME: "; T$(S2)
760     GOTO 820
770                                                      REM
780     PRINT " "
790     PRINT "   FLIGHT NUMBER"; F1; "DOES NOT EXIST"
800     GOTO 820
810                                                      REM
820   PRINT " "
830   PRINT "DO YOU WISH TO MAKE ANOTHER INQUIRY?"
840   INPUT "ENTER YES OR NO: "; R$
850                                                      REM
860   IF R$ = "YES" OR R$ = "NO" THEN 900
870     INPUT "   INVALID RESPONSE - PLEASE ENTER YES OR NO: "; R$
880   GOTO 860
890                                                      REM
900 GOTO 600
910                                                      REM
920 PRINT " "
930 PRINT "END OF FLIGHT INFORMATION INQUIRY"
940 END
```

Figure 7-31 Sample program (Part 2 of 2)

SUMMARY   The following points have been discussed and explained in this chapter.

1. Tables, or arrays as they are called in BASIC programming, are commonly used to search for information or to extract values for use in calculations. They play an important role in computer programming.

2. To process data in an array, three steps must be accomplished: Create the array, load data into the array, and search the array.

3. To create an array, areas in main computer storage must be reserved for the array. This is accomplished with the dimension statement.

4. In the dimension statement, the array name and the number of elements within the array must be specified. An element is a single entry in an array.

5. Numeric and string arrays can be defined by the dimension statement.

6. An element within the array is addressed by specifying the name of the array and the number of the element within the array in a subscript. For example, the entry F(2) references the second element in the F array. The number 2 is called a subscript. A variable name representing a numeric field can be used as the subscript as well as a numeric literal or an arithmetic expression.

7. After the array has been defined using the dimension statement, the data must be placed in each element of the array. This is normally accomplished through the use of a for-next loop and the read and data statements.

8. When the read statement in a for-next loop is used to load data into an array, the variable specified in the read statement is the name of the array and a variable name which acts as the subscript. The variable name which acts as the subscript is normally the same name as the counter-variable in the for statement.

9. A dimension statement can be used to define more than one array. The names of each array to be defined are specified, separated by a comma. The arrays can be string or numeric arrays, and each array can have a different number of elements if required by the application.

10. A single read statement can be used to load multiple arrays, provided the data in the data statement is defined in the correct sequence. The read statement contains multiple array names when this is to occur.

11. Data statements merely define a list of data to be referenced by read statements. When a read statement is executed, the next entry from the list is transferred to the variable in the read statement. It does not matter whether one data statement or many data statements are used — the result is a single list of data whose members are referenced in sequence by each subsequent read statement that is executed.

12. The restore statement allows the next executed read statement to obtain data from the first entry in the list generated by the data statements in a program.

13. A variety of methods can be used to load an array.

14. After an array is loaded with data, it can be searched and corresponding data can be extracted from other arrays based on the search. This process consists of searching an array until a desired value is found. When the value is found, a corresponding element from another array is extracted and used.

15. When an array is searched, each element in the array is compared to a value to be found. This process continues until either an equal element in the array is found or until all elements of the array have been searched and no equal element is found.

16. When an array is searched, there is the possibility that the value being searched for does not exist. Therefore, whenever an array search is performed in a program, there must always be provision for the case where an equal element in an array is not found.

17. The array search logic is: a) Set the search subscript to 1; b) If the search subscript is greater than the number of elements in the array or the value being searched for is found, do not enter a loop. If neither of these conditions is true, enter a loop where the search subscript is incremented by one and the test for these conditions occurs again; c) When the exit from the loop occurs, test the value in the search subscript. If it is greater than the number of elements in the array, the loop terminated because an equal element was not found. In this case, an error message should be written. If the search subscript is not greater than the number of elements in the array, an equal element was found, and it can be used in whatever manner is required by the application.

18. To code an array search, the if statement and the goto statement are used to establish the search loop.

19. An if-then-else structure is used to determine why the search loop was terminated and to initiate the correct processing based on that reason.

20. The OR logical operator cannot be used when the size of the search subscript is tested at the start of the search loop because if the subscript is greater than the size of the array, the test for equality will cause a subscript error, and the program will be terminated.

21. The for-next loop is not used to search an array because its use violates the single exit rule for the loop logic structure.

22. When a sequential array search is conducted, the first element of the array is examined, followed by the second element, the third element, and so on.

23. A binary search eliminates portions of an array which cannot contain the value being searched for. It is used on larger arrays where the elements of the array can be arranged in an ascending or descending sequence, based upon the value being searched for.

24. The basic binary search logic is: a) Examine the middle element in the array; b) If the value being searched for is greater than the middle element, the desired element must be in the upper half of the array. If the value being searched for is less than the middle element, the desired element must be in the lower half of the array; c) Look at the middle element in either the upper or

lower half of the array, based upon the results in step b; c) Continue splitting the array in half until either the desired element is found, or all of the possible elements have been examined, and the desired element is not found.

25. In large arrays, a binary search technique can save a great deal of time. For example, the maximum number of comparisons to find an element in a 1,000 element array is 10 when the binary search technique is used.

26. The logic to implement the binary search is somewhat different from the sequential search, but the principle is the same: search the elements in the array by looping until either an equal element is found, or the entire array has been searched. After looping, determine whether an equal element was found. If so, print the data extracted from other arrays; otherwise, print an error message.

27. The binary search requires that the search subscript be calculated on each pass through the loop.

28. A two-dimension array is one which requires two subscript values, one for the rows of the array and one for the columns of the array, to identify an element within the array.

29. To define a two-dimension array, the dimension statement is used. It must contain the number of rows and the number of columns in the array.

30. A two-dimension array can be loaded using nested for-next loops and the read statement.

31. To perform an array search, the normal procedure is to define a one-dimension array representing the rows of the two-dimension array and a one-dimension array representing the columns of the two-dimension array. Each of these one-dimension arrays is searched to determine the two subscripts required to access the two-dimension array.

1. The steps to process data in an array are: a) Create the array, load data into the array, and search the array; b) Create the array, search the array, and calculate the subscript; c) Create the array, load data into the array, and divide the array in half; d) Load data into the array, search the array, and calculate the subscript.

2. The _____ statement is used to reserve storage for an array.

3. An element in an array is addressed by specifying the name of the array (T or F).

4. A for-next loop is not used to place data in an array because it violates the single exit rule for the loop logic structure (T or F).

5. Data statements: a) Load data into an array; b) Must be used in conjunction with a for-next loop; c) Define a list of data to be referenced by read statements; d) Must be subscripted when being used to define data for an array.

6. When an array is searched, it is possible that the value being searched for does not exist in the array. What steps must be taken in the program to account for this possibility?

7. Write the steps used in the sequential array search logic.

8. The _____ statement and the _____ statement are used to establish the search loop.

9. The OR logical operator cannot be used when the size of the search subscript is tested at the start of the search loop because: a) It causes a syntax error; b) It is too complex and violates good program design; c) It may cause a subscript error, and the program will be terminated; d) No such thing exists in the BASIC language.

10. A binary search is generally faster than a sequential search. The only requirement for a binary search is: a) The elements must be arranged in an ascending or descending sequence, based upon the value being searched for; b) The computer system being used must use binary coding rather than octal or hexadecimal; c) It can be used only for small arrays; its use for larger arrays requires too much main computer storage and is inefficient; d) It must be used for large arrays with 1,000 or more elements.

11. The airline using the sample program in this chapter has requested that the program be modified to show not only the departure time, but the arrival time as well. The arrival times for the cities used are: Boston — 3:30 pm; Chicago — 2:40 pm; Atlanta — 5:45 pm; Seattle — 5:30 pm; Miami — 8:10 pm. Make the required changes in the sample program to accomplish these modifications.

12. Four more cities are to be added to the flight schedule used in the sample program. The information is: Flight #419–Denver — Dallas 4:50 pm; Flight #587–Atlanta — Miami 2:10 pm; Flight #601–Boston — New York 11:10 am; Flight #609–Memphis — Washington 3:30 pm. Make the changes in the sample program to add these new flights.

Chapter 7
DEBUGGING EXERCISES

The following lines of code contain one or more coding errors. Circle each of the errors and write the coding to correct the errors.

1.
```
300 REM ***** DATA TO LOAD ARRAYS *****
310                                                    REM
320 DATA 148, "PHOENIX", "BOSTON", "9:00 AM"
330 DATA 264, "DENVER", "CHICAGO", "11:50 AM"
340 DATA 323, "DALLAS", "ATLANTA", "1:45 PM"
350 DATA 378, "ATLANTA", "SEATTLE", "3:15 PM"
360 DATA 403, "NEW YORK", "MIAMI", "5:00 PM"
370                                                    REM
380 REM ***** DEFINE AND LOAD ARRAYS *****
390                                                    REM
400 DIM F, O$, D$, T$
410                                                    REM
420 FOR S1 = 1 TO N STEP 1
430    READ F, O$, D$, T$
440 NEXT S1
```

2.
```
520 CLS
530 PRINT "DO YOU WISH TO MAKE AN INQUIRY?"
540 INPUT "ENTER YES OR NO: " R$
550                                                    REM
560 IF R$ = "YES" OR R$ = "NO" THEN 600
570    INPUT "   INVALID RESPONSE - PLEASE ENTER YES OR NO: "
590                                                    REM
600 IF R$ = "NO" THEN 920
610    CLS
620    INPUT "PLEASE ENTER FLIGHT NUMBER: "
```

3.
```
650    IF S2 > N THEN 700
660    IF F = F1(S1) THEN 700
670       LET S2 = S2 + 1
680    GOTO 660
690                                                    REM
700    IF S2 > N THEN 780
710       CLS
720       PRINT "FLIGHT:"; F(S2)
730       PRINT "ORIGINATION POINT: "; O$(S2)
740       PRINT "DESTINATION POINT: "; D$(S2)
750       PRINT "DEPARTURE TIME: "; T(S2)
760       GOTO 820
770                                                    REM
780       PRINT " "
790       PRINT "   FLIGHT NUMBER"; F1; "DOES NOT EXIST"
800       GOTO 820
810                                                    REM
820    PRINT " "
```

Chapter 7
PROGRAM DEBUGGING

The following program was designed and written to process airline information in the manner shown in Figure 7-2 on page 7.2. The results from running the program are shown on page 7.38. Analyze the results to determine if they are correct. If there is an error, circle the incorrect statement(s) in the program and write corrections.

```
100 REM AIRLINE               JANUARY 23              SHELLY/CASHMAN
110                                                              REM
120 REM THIS PROGRAM LOADS AIRLINE ARRAYS CONTAINING FLIGHT
130 REM NUMBERS, ORIGINATION POINTS, DESTINATION POINTS, AND
140 REM DEPARTURE TIMES. THE USER CAN ENTER THE FLIGHT NUMBER
150 REM TO OBTAIN THE OTHER INFORMATION.
160                                                              REM
170 REM VARIABLE NAMES:
180 REM    F()...FLIGHT NUMBER ARRAY
190 REM    O$()..ORIGINATION POINT ARRAY
200 REM    D$()..DESTINATION POINT ARRAY
210 REM    T$()..DEPARTURE TIME ARRAY
220 REM    F1....FLIGHT NUMBER FOR INQUIRY
230 REM    S1....SUBSCRIPT TO LOAD ARRAYS
240 REM    S2....SUBSCRIPT TO SEARCH ARRAY AND REFERENCE ALL
250 REM          ARRAYS WHEN SEARCH IS SUCCESSFUL
260 REM    N.....NUMBER OF ENTRIES IN ARRAYS
270 REM    R$....INPUT AREA FOR RESPONSE TO QUESTION
280 REM          "DO YOU WISH TO MAKE AN INQUIRY?"
290                                                              REM
300 REM ***** DATA TO LOAD ARRAYS *****
310                                                              REM
320 DATA 148, "PHOENIX", "BOSTON", "9:00 AM"
330 DATA 264, "DENVER", "CHICAGO", "11:50 AM"
340 DATA 323, "DALLAS", "ATLANTA", "1:45 PM"
350 DATA 378, "ATLANTA", "SEATTLE", "3:15 PM"
360 DATA 403, "NEW YORK", "MIAMI", "5:00 PM"
370                                                              REM
380 REM ***** INITIALIZATION OF VARIABLES *****
390                                                              REM
400 LET N = 5
410                                                              REM
420 REM ***** DEFINE AND LOAD ARRAYS *****
430              5                                               REM
440 DIM F(N), O$(N), D$(N), T$(N)
450                                                              REM
460 FOR S1 = 1 TO N STEP 1
470    READ F(S1), O$(S1), D$(S1), T$(S1)
480 NEXT S1
490                                                              REM
```

```
500 REM ***** PROCESSING *****
510                                                              REM
520 CLS
530 PRINT "DO YOU WISH TO MAKE AN INQUIRY?"
540 INPUT "ENTER YES OR NO: "; R$
550                                                              REM
560 IF R$ = "YES" OR R$ = "NO" THEN 600
570   INPUT "  INVALID RESPONSE - PLEASE ENTER YES OR NO: "; R$
580 GOTO 560
590                                                              REM
600 IF R$ = "NO" THEN 920
610   CLS
620   INPUT "PLEASE ENTER FLIGHT NUMBER: "; F1
630   LET S2 = 1
640                                                              REM
650   IF S2 > N THEN 700
660   IF F(S2) = F1 THEN 700
670     LET S2 = S2 + 1
680   GOTO 650
690                                                              REM
700   IF S2 < N THEN 780
710     CLS
720     PRINT "FLIGHT:"; F(S2)
730     PRINT "ORIGINATION POINT: "; O$(S2)
740     PRINT "DESTINATION POINT: "; D$(S2)
750     PRINT "DEPARTURE TIME: "; T$(S2)
760     GOTO 820
770                                                              REM
780     PRINT " "
790     PRINT "  FLIGHT NUMBER"; F1; "DOES NOT EXIST"
800     GOTO 820
810                                                              REM
820   PRINT " "
830   PRINT "DO YOU WISH TO MAKE ANOTHER INQUIRY?"
840   INPUT "ENTER YES OR NO: "; R$
850                                                              REM
860   IF R$ = "YES" OR R$ = "NO" THEN 900
870     INPUT "  INVALID RESPONSE - PLEASE ENTER YES OR NO: "; R$
880   GOTO 860
890                                                              REM
900 GOTO 600
910                                                              REM
920 PRINT " "
930 PRINT "END OF FLIGHT INFORMATION INQUIRY"
940 END
```

Program Results

①
```
DO YOU WISH TO MAKE AN INQUIRY?
ENTER YES OR NO: ? YES
```

③
```
PLEASE ENTER FLIGHT NUMBER: ? 321
```

②
```
PLEASE ENTER FLIGHT NUMBER: ? 264

  FLIGHT NUMBER 264 DOES NOT EXIST

DO YOU WISH TO MAKE ANOTHER INQUIRY?
ENTER YES OR NO: ? YES
```

④
```
FLIGHT:
Subscript out of range in 720
```

Chapter 7
PROGRAMMING ASSIGNMENT 1

A telephone number inquiry system is to be prepared. Design and code the BASIC program to implement the inquiry system.

Instructions

The input consists of telephone inquiries which specify the name of a business. The user will enter the name of a company for which the telephone number is desired.

Input

The data containing the company name, area code, and telephone number is stored in an array. The data to be used in this program is shown below.

Array data

NAME	AREA CODE	TELEPHONE NUMBER
COMPUTERLAND	714	527-0981
MICRO CITY	213	311-6699
SOFTECK	213	896-1032
DATATEC	714	370-1034
HITECC	213	455-6619

After the name of the company is entered by the user, the area code and telephone number should be displayed. The screens which should be used are shown below.

Output

```
DO YOU WANT TO MAKE A TELEPHONE INQUIRY?
ENTER YES OR NO: ? YES
```

```
ENTER THE NAME OF THE COMPANY: ? SOFTECK
```

```
COMPANY: SOFTECK
AREA CODE: 213
TELEPHONE NUMBER: 896-1032
```

```
DO YOU WISH TO MAKE ANOTHER INQUIRY?
PLEASE ENTER YES OR NO: ?
```

The data entered by the user should be checked as follows: The answer to the question asking if an inquiry is to be made must be yes or no. Any other entry should generate an error message asking for the correct input. If the company entered by the user is not in the array, an appropriate error message should be displayed, and then the user should be asked if there is another inquiry.

Chapter 7
PROGRAMMING ASSIGNMENT 2

Instructions   A price quotation system is to be prepared. Design and code the BASIC program to implement the quotation system.

Input   The input consists of inquiries for price quotations on software products. The user will enter the name of the company for which the quotation is made, the product which is to be quoted, and the quantity to be quoted on.

Array data   The data containing the software product and the price of the product is contained in an array. The data to be used in the program is shown below.

PRODUCT	PRICE
SPELL	15.00
GRAPHICS	26.00
PLOT	29.00
TUTOR	22.00
MATH	19.00

Output   After the inquiry data is entered by the user, a price quotation is to be printed. The screens to be used in the program are shown below.

```
DO YOU WISH A PRICE QUOTATION?
ENTER YES OR NO: ? YES
```

```
ENTER COMPANY NAME: COMPUTER CITY
ENTER PRODUCT NAME: SPELL
ENTER QUANTITY: 3
```

```
             COMPUTER CITY
             PRICE QUOTATION

PRODUCT   QUANTITY   PRICE     AMOUNT

SPELL         3       15.00   $ 45.00
```

```
DO YOU WISH ANOTHER PRICE QUOTATION?
ENTER YES OR NO: ?
```

The amount is calculated by multiplying the quantity times the price for the product. The following editing should take place. The answer to the question about whether a price quotation is to be prepared must be yes or no. An error message should be written for any other response. The value entered for the quantity must be 1 through 9. If the quantity is not 1 through 9, an appropriate error message should be written, and the user should reenter the quantity. If the product entered is not in the array, the message UNKNOWN PRODUCT should be displayed.

Chapter 7
SUPPLEMENTARY PROGRAMMING ASSIGNMENTS

The following programming assignments contain an explanation of the problem and list suggested array data. The student should design the output.

Instructions

An inquiry program should be written which will allow a user to enter the name of a state and receive back the approved post office abbreviation OR enter the abbreviation and receive back the name of the state. The array used should contain at least the following states.

Program 3

STATE	ABBREVIATION	STATE	ABBREVIATION
ALABAMA	AL	ARKANSAS	AR
ALASKA	AK	CALIFORNIA	CA
ARIZONA	AZ	COLORADO	CO

An inquiry program should be written which will allow a user to extract the maximum healthy weight for a young man from an array, compare it to the current weight of the person, and determine if the man is overweight and by how much. The array below contains the height of the man and maximum weight for that height. The user should enter the person's name, the person's height, and the person's weight. The output should list the person's name, height, current weight, and maximum weight. The program will find the maximum weight based upon the person's height. If the individual's current weight exceeds the maximum specified in the array, the message OVERWEIGHT BY XX POUNDS should be displayed. Appropriate editing and error messages should be designed by the programmer.

Program 4

HEIGHT (INCHES)	MAXIMUM WEIGHT	HEIGHT (INCHES)	MAXIMUM WEIGHT
66	156	70	174
67	160	71	178
68	166	72	184
69	168		

MENUS, ARRAYS, SUBROUTINES, AND SORTING

OBJECTIVES:

Familiarization with menus used in interactive programs

Ability to design and code programs using the case structure

Knowledge of the use of subroutines

Ability to use arrays in a variety of applications

Knowledge of sorting and ability to design and write an exchange sort

Ability to design a program by decomposing the program into a series of functional modules

MENUS, ARRAYS, SUBROUTINES, AND SORTING

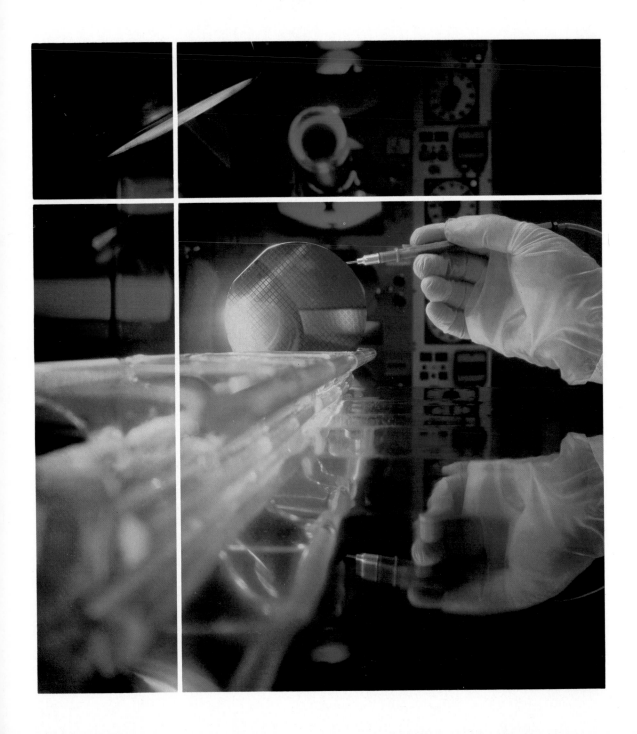

When computer terminals are used in an interactive mode, the user will often be able to make inquiries to obtain various types of information. Many times the type of inquiry available to the user will be displayed on a menu, which is a listing of those functions that can be performed by a program. The user chooses the desired function by entering a code from the terminal keyboard. The use of menus and the manner in which they are programmed will be explained in this chapter.

Introduction

The data which is displayed by an inquiry program or by other types of programs can be arranged in different sequences for presentation to the user. When the same data is to be made available in varying sequences, the data must be sorted prior to being displayed. Sorting is the process of placing data in an ascending or descending sequence based upon one or more values in the data. A method for programming a sort is shown in this chapter.

A program which performs multiple functions, such as sorting data and displaying it in various forms, may require the use of subroutines. A subroutine is a series of instructions which performs a particular function in a program. The design and use of subroutines is illustrated by the sample program in this chapter.

A menu lists the functions which can be performed by a program. To illustrate the use of a menu, the sample program in this chapter accepts and displays information concerning a baseball team. The menu for the program, which specifies the functions available, is shown in Figure 8-1.

Menus

```
B A S E B A L L    M E N U

CODE        FUNCTION

  1 - LOAD STARTING PLAYERS
  2 - DISPLAY STARTING PLAYERS IN BATTING ORDER
  3 - DISPLAY PLAYERS IN ALPHABETICAL SEQUENCE
  4 - END PROGRAM

ENTER A NUMBER 1 THROUGH 4:?
```

Figure 8-1 A menu lists the functions which can be performed by the program. The user enters a code to select the function desired.

The menu in Figure 8-1 consists of a group of codes and a group of functions. The four functions are those that the program can perform. Thus, the user can choose to load the starting players for a baseball team, display the starting players on the baseball team in batting order, display the players in alphabetical sequence, or end the program. The user selects which function will be performed by entering the appropriate code.

When the user wishes to enter the starting baseball players, which should normally be the first function performed, the value 1 is specified in response to the menu. The LOAD STARTING PLAYERS screen is then displayed (Figure 8-2).

Figure 8-2 When code 1 is selected in the sample program, the user enters the starting players in batting order.

```
LOAD STARTING PLAYERS

BATTER NUMBER 1

    ENTER PLAYER'S NAME:  ?
```

In response to the message ENTER PLAYER'S NAME, the user would enter the name of the player. In Figure 8-3, the user entered the name HANESLEY.

Figure 8-3 The user enters the player's name, position, number of at bats, and number of hits.

```
LOAD STARTING PLAYERS

BATTER NUMBER 1

    ENTER PLAYER'S NAME:  ? HANESLEY
    ENTER PLAYER'S POSITION:  ? SECOND BASE
    ENTER PLAYER'S AT BATS:  ? 100
    ENTER PLAYER'S HITS:  ? 28
```

After the name is entered, the user, in response to the prompts, will enter the player's position, the number of times the player has batted during the season, and the number of hits the player has had during the season. These latter two figures are used to calculate the batting average of the player (the number of hits divided by the number of times at bat).

In the sample program, this processing will continue until all nine players have been entered.

After the players have been entered, their names, positions, and batting averages can be displayed. The sequence in which they are displayed is determined by the entry made in response to the menu. If code 2 is entered, the display is in batting order sequence, which is the same sequence in which the players are entered. If code 3 is entered, the display is in alphabetical sequence based upon the player's name (Figure 8-4).

When the user enters code 4, the program will be terminated. Whenever a menu is used in a program, the user must always be given the option of terminating the processing whenever desired.

```
        STARTING PLAYERS              STARTING PLAYERS
        BATTING ORDER              ALPHABETICAL SEQUENCE

  NAME         POSITION     AVG      NAME        POSITION     AVG
HANESLEY    SECOND BASE   .280    ALLEN      THIRD BASE    .274
BLACKBURG   LEFT FIELD    .263    BLACKBURG  LEFT FIELD    .263
TRAMESMAN   FIRST BASE    .333    CRAIYERSON PITCHER       .115
WOODS       CATCHER       .341    GRANT      SHORTSTOP     .213
WAITENTON   CENTER FIELD  .245    HANESLEY   SECOND BASE   .280
SEREIN      RIGHT FIELD   .236    SEREIN     RIGHT FIELD   .236
ALLEN       THIRD BASE    .274    TRAMESMAN  FIRST BASE    .333
GRANT       SHORTSTOP     .213    WAITENTON  CENTER FIELD  .245
CRAIYERSON  PITCHER       .115    WOODS      CATCHER       .341
                                    TEAM BATTING AVERAGE .256
DEPRESS ENTER OR RETURN KEY      DEPRESS ENTER OR RETURN KEY
 TO RETURN TO THE MENU: ?         TO RETURN TO THE MENU: ?
```

Figure 8-4 The two reports from the program print the players in batting order and alphabetical sequence.

A menu is displayed by print statements. The statements which are to display the menu in the sample program, together with the input statement which is used to obtain the user response, are shown in Figure 8-5.

Processing a menu

Note that the first statement, on line 1050, is used to clear the screen. When a menu is to be written on a screen, it should normally be the only material on the screen. Therefore, the screen must be cleared prior to displaying the menu.

The print statements on lines 1060 through 1140 display the menu on the CRT screen. The input statement on line 1150 obtains the code selection from the user.

Figure 8-5 The menu is displayed through the use of print statements. The response by the user must be edited.

```
1000                                                              REM
1010 REM ***********************************************************
1020 REM * DISPLAY MENU AND GET SELECTION                         *
1030 REM ***********************************************************
1040                                                              REM
1050 CLS
1060 PRINT "B A S E B A L L    M E N U"
1070 PRINT " "
1080 PRINT "CODE       FUNCTION"
1090 PRINT " "
1100 PRINT " 1 - LOAD STARTING PLAYERS"
1110 PRINT " 2 - DISPLAY STARTING PLAYERS IN BATTING ORDER"
1120 PRINT " 3 - DISPLAY PLAYERS IN ALPHABETICAL SEQUENCE"
1130 PRINT " 4 - END PROGRAM"
1140 PRINT " "
1150 INPUT "ENTER A NUMBER 1 THROUGH 4:"; S
1160                                                              REM
1170 IF S >= 1 AND S <= 4 THEN 1230
1180    PRINT " "
1190    PRINT " "; S; "IS INVALID"
1200    INPUT "        PLEASE REENTER 1, 2, 3, OR 4: "; S
1210 GOTO 1170
1220                                                              REM
1230 RETURN
```

Whenever a code is obtained from a menu selection, it should be edited to ensure that it is valid. In the sample program, the user can enter the codes 1, 2, 3, or 4 to choose a function to be performed by the program. Therefore, the coding on lines 1170 – 1210 check to ensure that the code entered by the user is one of these values. The if statement on line 1170 ensures that the value entered by the user and stored in the S field is 1, 2, 3, or 4. Note the use of the logical operator AND in this example. The value in S must be both equal to or greater than 1 and equal to or less than 4. In comparisons such as this, there may be a tendency to use the OR logical operator; that is, the thinking by the programmer is the value must be greater than or equal to 1 OR less than or equal to 4. This thinking is invalid, however, because any value which is entered will satisfy the condition. Therefore, the AND logical operator is required.

If the value entered by the user is not 1, 2, 3, or 4, a loop is entered where an error message is printed and the user is requested to reenter the value. Note that the error message informs the user the value entered is in error. It also specifies what the valid values are. It is important when designing interactive programs that the communication between the program and the user be as clear and precise as possible. A message such as used in this program is much better than one which would say, INVALID CODE — REENTER. This message tells the user nothing that would help in entering a correct code.

Case structure

After the code is entered by the user in response to the menu, the program must determine which code was entered and then perform the requested function. A flowchart of the processing required is shown in Figure 8-6.

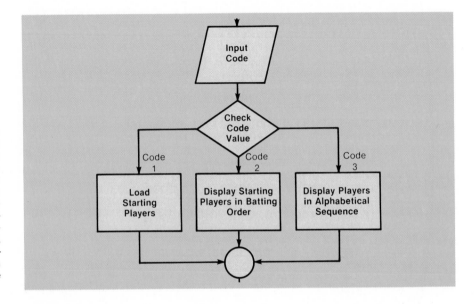

Figure 8-6 The case structure, a special application of the if-then-else logic structure, is used when multiple operations can occur based upon the value in a single field. Here, three different actions — Load Starting Players, Display Starting Players in Batting Order, and Display Players in Alphabetical Sequence — can occur based upon the value in the code field.

In the flowchart in Figure 8–6, the code is accepted by the program. Based upon the code entered, the appropriate processing occurs. This type of comparing where multiple operations can occur based upon the value in a single field is called the case structure. The case structure is a special version of the if-then-else logic structure.

One method for implementing the case structure is the use of nested if-then-else structures. The coding in Figure 8–7 illustrates the if statements which could be used for the case structure shown in Figure 8–6.

Implementing the case structure — if statements

```
290 INPUT S
300 IF S = 1 THEN 440
310    IF S = 2 THEN 600
320       IF S = 3 THEN 770
             .
             .
             .
440 CLS
450 PRINT "LOAD STARTING PLAYERS"
460    .
       .
580 GOTO 920
       .
600 CLS
610 PRINT "STARTING PLAYERS"
620 PRINT " BATTING ORDER"
630    .
       .
750 GOTO 920
       .
770 CLS
780 PRINT " STARTING PLAYERS"
790 PRINT "ALPHABETICAL ORDER"
800    .
       .
       .
       .
900 GOTO 920
910
920    .
       .                                    REM
```

Figure 8-7 To implement the case structure, the BASIC if statement can be used.

The if statements on lines 300, 310, and 320 test for the value in the field identified by the variable S, which is the field used with the input statement to obtain the menu code. If the code is equal to 1, the routine at line 440 is used. If the code is equal to 2, the routine beginning at line 600 is used while if the code is equal to 3, the routine beginning at line 770 is used. When the processing in each of these routines is completed, they pass control to line 920, which is the common exit point for the nested if-then-else structures. The use of nested if-then-else structures to implement the case structure will allow any number of cases to be implemented in the same manner, and the field on which the case structure depends can be a numeric or string field.

On goto statement

When the value which the case structure checks is numeric, a BASIC statement called the on goto statement can be used to implement the case structure. The general format of the on goto statement together with its use to implement the processing shown in Figure 8–7 is illustrated below.

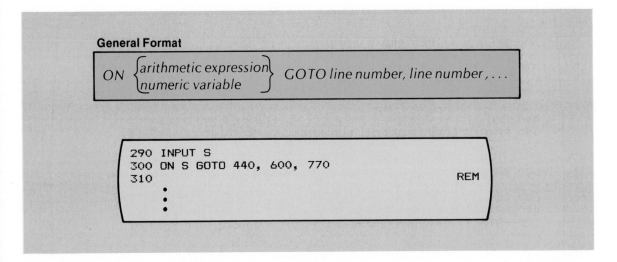

General Format

$$ON \begin{Bmatrix} \textit{arithmetic expression} \\ \textit{numeric variable} \end{Bmatrix} GOTO \textit{ line number, line number, . . .}$$

```
290  INPUT S
300  ON S GOTO 440, 600, 770
310                                                    REM
       .
       .
       .
```

Figure 8–8 The ON GOTO statement is used in this example to implement the case structure. If the value in S is equal to 1, the statement at line 440 will be given control. If the value in S is equal to 2, the statement at line 600 is given control. If the value in S is equal to 3, the statement at line 770 is given control. If the value in S is not equal to 1, 2, or, 3, the statement on line 310 will be executed next.

When the on goto statement is executed, the integer portion of the arithmetic expression or numeric variable specified is evaluated. If the value is equal to 1, control is transferred to the first line number following the word GOTO. Thus, in the example, if the value in S is equal to 1, control will be transferred to line 440. If the value in the variable or arithmetic expression is equal to 2, control is passed to the second line number following the word GOTO. In the example, if the value in S is equal to 2, the statement at line number 600 will be given control. This evaluation by the on goto statement will continue for the maximum number of line numbers which can be listed, which on most computer systems is 255 lines.

If the value in the numeric variable or arithmetic expression is equal to zero or is greater than the number of line numbers specified in the statement, then the statement immediately following the on goto statement is executed. In the example in Figure 8–8, if the value in S is zero or is greater than 3, then the statement on line 310 would be given control. If the value is negative, most systems will issue an error message, and the program will be terminated.

When a program becomes larger than several pages, it will many times become quite difficult to read and understand simply because of its size. In addition, as programs become larger, the logic may become much more difficult. Generally in computer programming, largeness leads to complexity.

One way in which programs are kept less complex is to subdivide a large program into two or more smaller parts called subroutines, or modules. Each subroutine performs a particular task in the program. The overall program is simpler because it consists of a number of simple, easy to understand subroutines rather than one large, complex piece of code. In the sample program, a number of different tasks must be accomplished. One task requires displaying the menu and obtaining the selection code from the user. This task can be placed in a subroutine to be executed when desired. The concept of a subroutine is illustrated in the drawing in Figure 8–9.

SUBROUTINES

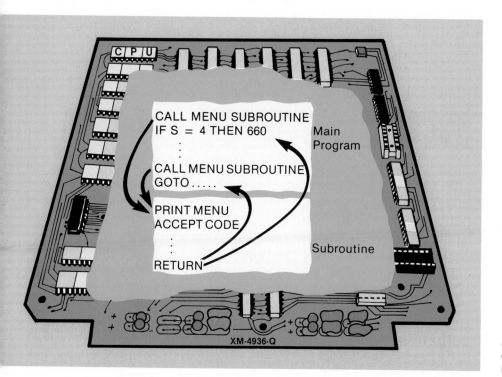

Figure 8-9 When a subroutine is called, control is passed to the first statement in the subroutine. When the subroutine has completed its processing, it passes control back to the statement in the main program immediately following the statement which called it. In this example, the subroutine is called from two different places in the main program. When its processing is complete, control is returned to two different points in the main program.

In the example above, the main program issues a "call" to the subroutine. A call means that control is transferred from the main program to the first statement in the subroutine. The statements within the subroutine are then executed. The last statement in the subroutine is an instruction which returns control to the statement in the main program immediately following the statement which called the subroutine.

The sequence for executing a subroutine, then, consists of the following steps: 1) The subroutine is called; 2) The instructions within the subroutine are executed; 3) The subroutine returns control to the statement immediately following the statement which called the subroutine.

Note in Figure 8-9 that the menu subroutine is called from two different points in the main program. In each case, the subroutine must return control to the statement immediately following the statement which called it. Therefore, the statement which calls the subroutine must establish linkage between the calling program and the called subroutine. In most languages, a special instruction is available to call a subroutine. In BASIC, the GOSUB statement is used to call a subroutine and establish the linkage between the calling program and the called subroutine.

GOSUB statement

The format of the gosub statement and an example of its use are shown in Figure 8-10.

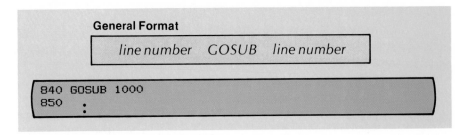

Figure 8-10 The GOSUB statement passes control to the subroutine which begins at the line number specified following the word GOSUB. It also establishes the linkage which allows the subroutine to return control to statement 850.

As with all BASIC statements, the gosub statement begins with a line number. The line number is followed by one or more spaces and then the word GOSUB. The line number following the word GOSUB specifies the first line number in the subroutine which is being called. When the gosub instruction is executed, control is passed to the line number following the word GOSUB.

The gosub instruction not only passes control to the specified line number, it also establishes the linkage which will allow the subroutine to return control to the statement following the gosub statement. To cause this to occur, the return statement is used in the subroutine. The format of the return statement is contained in Figure 8-11.

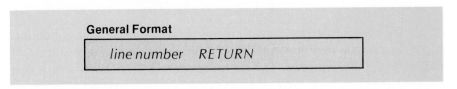

Figure 8-11 The RETURN statement, which is the last statement executed in a subroutine, returns control to the statement in the calling program which immediately follows the gosub statement that called the subroutine.

The word RETURN, preceded by a line number, is all that is required for the subroutine to return control to the statement following the gosub statement which called the subroutine. An example of the implementation of the gosub and return statements is illustrated in Figure 8-12.

```
590 GOSUB 1000
600                                                              REM
610 IF S = 4 THEN 660
    .
    .
    .
1000                                                             REM
1010 REM ***********************************************************
1020 REM * DISPLAY MENU AND GET SELECTION                        *
1030 REM ***********************************************************
1040                                                             REM
1050 CLS
1060 PRINT "B A S E B A L L    M E N U"
1070 PRINT " "
1080 PRINT "CODE        FUNCTION"
    .
    .
    .
1240 RETURN
```

In the example, the gosub statement on line 590 passes control to the subroutine beginning on line 1000. The subroutine displays the menu and obtains a selection from the user. After the subroutine has completed its task, the return statement on line 1240 will pass control back to the statement on line 600, which is the statement following the gosub that called the subroutine. Whenever a subroutine is used, control should always be passed back to the statement following the gosub statement that called it.

Figure 8-12 In this example, the gosub statement on line 590 passes control to the first line of the subroutine (line 1000). When the subroutine has completed processing, the last statement executed (the return statement on line 1240) returns control to line 600.

Subroutines which are used in a program may correspond to the tasks which must be performed in a case structure. When this occurs, the ON GOSUB statement can be used to call subroutines based upon each case. The general format of the on gosub statement together with an example of its use in the sample program is shown in Figure 8-13.

ON GOSUB statement

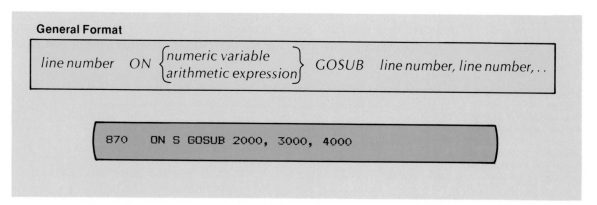

General Format

line number   ON $\left\{ \begin{array}{l} \textit{numeric variable} \\ \textit{arithmetic expression} \end{array} \right\}$ GOSUB   line number, line number, . .

870   ON S GOSUB 2000, 3000, 4000

Figure 8-13 The ON GOSUB statement calls the subroutines based upon the value in a numeric variable.

The format of the on gosub statement is quite similar to that of the on goto statement explained previously. The statement begins with a line number and then the word ON. A numeric variable or arithmetic expression is specified next. If the value in the numeric variable or arithmetic expression is one, the subroutine beginning at the first line number following the word GOSUB is given control. If the value is two, the subroutine at the second line number is given control, and so on. In the example, if the value in S is equal to 1, the subroutine at line 2000 is passed control; if the value in S is equal to 2, the subroutine at line 3000 is given control; and if the value in S is equal to 3, the subroutine at line 4000 will gain control. If the value in the numeric variable or arithmetic expression is equal to zero or is greater than the number of line numbers specified, the statement immediately following the on gosub statement is given control.

When the subroutine has finished processing and issues the return statement, control is passed to the statement immediately following the on gosub statement in the same manner as the gosub statement.

When the tasks to be performed in a case structure involve more than a few processing statements, it will many times be found that they should be performed by subroutines. When that is the case, the on gosub statement provides a convenient mechanism for implementing the subroutines in a case structure where the controlling field is numeric.

ARRAY PROCESSING

The sample program in Chapter 7 illustrated the use of arrays when array search was required for the application. Arrays can be used in a number of other ways in addition to array search. The following sections illustrate some additional applications of array processing.

Loading an array

As has been illustrated, an array can be loaded using the read and data statements in a for-next loop. An array can also be loaded from the data entered by a user from the keyboard through the use of the input statement. The following coding illustrates the use of the for-next statement and input statement to load an array.

Figure 8-14 This for-next loop will load the G$ array. The control-variable J in the loop determines which element of the G$ array receives data when the input statement is executed.

```
400 FOR J = 1 TO 5
410    INPUT G$(J)
420 NEXT J
```

In the example above, the for-next loop will be executed five times. On each pass through the loop, the input statement on line 410 will be executed.

On the first pass, the value in J will be 1; therefore, when the input statement is executed, the value entered by the user will be stored in the first element of the G$ array.

On the second pass of the for-next loop, the data entered by the user in response to the input statement will be stored in the second element of the G$ array. This processing will continue for the five passes through the loop. When the for-next loop is complete, the first five elements of the G$ array will contain data entered by the user.

In the sample program, the user enters the player position, the player name, the number of hits, and the number of times at bat for each of the nine players on the team. The loop which accomplishes this processing is illustrated in Figure 8–15.

```
2050 FOR S1 = 1 TO E
2060    CLS
2070    PRINT "LOAD STARTING PLAYERS"
2080    PRINT " "
2090    PRINT "BATTER NUMBER"; S1
2100    PRINT " "
2110    INPUT "    ENTER PLAYER'S NAME: "; N$(S1)
2120    PRINT " "
2130    INPUT "    ENTER PLAYER'S POSITION: "; P1$(S1)
2140    PRINT " "
2150    INPUT "    ENTER PLAYER'S AT BATS: "; B(S1)
2160    PRINT " "
2170    INPUT "    ENTER PLAYER'S HITS: "; H(S1)
2180 NEXT S1
```

Figure 8–15 In this example from the sample program, the S1 counter-variable in the for-next loop serves as the subscript to reference the elements within the arrays where data is to be loaded. Thus, when the value in S1 is equal to 1, the first element of the N$, P1$, B, and H arrays will receive the data entered by the user. When the value in S2 is equal to 2, the second elements of the arrays will receive data, and so on.

The processing begins with a for statement that establishes the loop. The value in the variable E has been initialized to 9. Therefore, the loop will occur nine times. The subscript to be used to reference the elements in the arrays is the counter-variable S1. The input statement on line 2110 will place the name entered by the user into the N$ array. The element in the N$ array to be used is identified by the value in S1. If the value in S1 is equal to 1, the first element in the N$ array is used; if the value in S1 is equal to 2, the second element is used. This continues for all nine passes through the loop.

The same processing occurs for the position array (P1$), the at bats array (B), and the hits array (H). When the processing within the for-next loop is completed, all nine elements of the N$, P1$, B, and H arrays have been loaded with data entered by the user in response to the input statement. From this example, it can be seen that arrays can be dynamically loaded with different data each time the program is executed rather than with data which is defined by data statements in the program as was illustrated in Chapter 7.

**Adding elements
of arrays**

In some applications, all the values stored in the elements of an array must be added together. Such is the case in the sample program, where the batting average for the entire baseball team is to be calculated and printed when the team members are printed in alphabetical sequence (see Figure 8-4). To calculate the team batting average, all of the at bats and all of the hits for the entire team must be added together. The total hits are then divided by the total at bats to obtain the team batting average. The coding to perform this operation is illustrated in Figure 8-16.

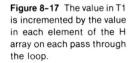
Figure 8-16 The numeric fields T1 and T2 are used to accumulate the values in the H and B arrays.

```
4210 LET T1 = 0
4220 LET T2 = 0
4230                                                     REM
4240 FOR X = 1 TO E
4250    LET T1 = T1 + H(X)
4260    LET T2 = T2 + B(X)
4270 NEXT X
4280                                                     REM
4290 PRINT USING F3$; T1 / T2
```

On lines 4210 and 4220, the accumulators T1 and T2 are initialized to the value zero. The for-next loop on lines 4240 through 4270 is used to accumulate the total hits and the total at bats. On line 4250, the value in T1 and the value in H(X) are added together. On the first pass through the loop, the value in T1 is zero. The value in the counter-variable X, which is also used as the subscript for the hits array, is one. Thus, on the first pass of the loop, the value in the first element of the H array is added to zero, and the result is stored in T1 (Figure 8-17).

Figure 8-17 The value in T1 is incremented by the value in each element of the H array on each pass through the loop.

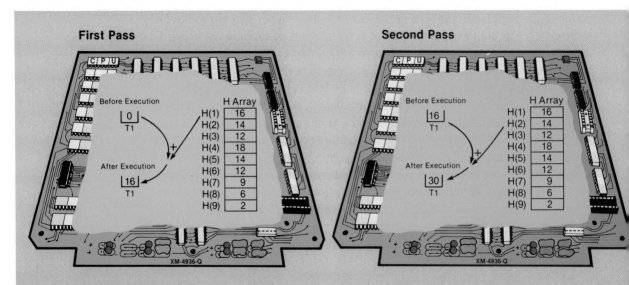

On the second pass through the loop, the value in T1 is 16. The second element of the H array will be added to this value because the counter-variable X contains the value 2. The same processing which happens for the H array will also happen for the B array, so that both the hits (H) and the at bats (B) are being accumulated by the for-next loop.

The looping will continue until the value in X is greater than the value in E. Control then exits from the loop, and the print statement on line 4290 is executed. This print statement displays the batting average (T1 / T2).

As can be seen from this example, numeric values in a numeric array can be accumulated through the use of a for-next loop.

Printing an array

In many applications, the elements within an array must be printed. This processing is easily accomplished using a for-next loop. The example in Figure 8-18 illustrates the for-next loop used in the sample program to print the baseball players in batting order sequence, which is the same sequence in which they are stored in the array.

```
3000                                                          REM
3010 REM ******************************************************
3020 REM * DISPLAY PLAYERS IN BATTING ORDER                  *
3030 REM ******************************************************
3040                                                          REM
3050 CLS
3060 PRINT "          STARTING PLAYERS"
3070 PRINT "          BATTING ORDER"
3080 PRINT " "
3090 PRINT "    NAME         POSITION       AVG"
3100                                                          REM
3110 FOR S3 = 1 TO E
3120    PRINT USING F1$; N$(S3), P1$(S3), H(S3) / B(S3)
3130 NEXT S3
```

Figure 8-18 The for-next loop on lines 3110 – 3130 prints the elements from the four arrays in the sample program. The control variable S3 acts as the subscript which references the elements of the arrays.

In the example above, the headings for the screen are printed on lines 3050 – 3090. A for-next loop is then entered to print the elements from the N$ and P1$ arrays, and to calculate the batting average for each player by dividing the number of hits (H array) by the number of at bats (B array). The numeric variable S3 is used as both the counter-variable in the for-next loop and the subscript which references the elements in the arrays.

On the first pass of the for-next loop, the value in S3 will be one. Therefore, the first elements of the N$ array and the P1$ array will be printed. The first elements of the H array and the B array are used in the calculation of the player's batting average, which is also printed. After the first line is printed, the next statement on line 3130 transfers control to the for statement on line 3110, where the value in S3 is incremented by one and the loop is executed again. On the second pass, the value in S3 is equal to 2, so the second element in each of the arrays is printed and used in the calculation.

This processing continues until the value in S3 exceeds the value in the field identified by the variable name E. The value was set to 9 in the initialization portion of the program. As a result of this loop, all the elements of the arrays specified are printed. The elements of any array can normally be printed through the use of a for-next loop.

After the arrays are printed, the user will normally wish to view the screen to read the information displayed. Therefore, program execution should be halted until the user has read the screen and is ready to continue. The method used in the subroutine which prints the players in batting order sequence makes use of the input statement (Figure 8-19).

Figure 8-19 A "dummy" input statement allows the user to view the screen until a return to the menu is desired. The Z$ field will contain no meaningful data. It is used because a variable field must be specified with the input statement.

```
                •
                •
3150 PRINT " "
3160 PRINT "DEPRESS ENTER OR RETURN KEY"
3170 INPUT " TO RETURN TO THE MENU: "; Z$
3180 RETURN
                •
                •
                •
```

The print statement and the input statement on lines 3160 – 3170 display a message to the user and then halt while the user reads the screen. When the user is ready to return to the menu, the enter or return key is depressed. The variable field used with the input statement is Z$. This field is used only because a field must be used with an input statement. The user will enter no meaningful data in the Z$ field. When the user depresses the enter or return key, the return statement on line 3180 will be executed and control will return to the main processing routine, which called this subroutine. The menu will then be displayed.

Summary of array processing

The previous examples have illustrated some of the ways in which arrays can be used within a program. Whenever more than one piece or set of data is to be processed in the same manner, consideration should be given to storing the data in an array. As has been seen, data that is stored in an array will normally be processed within a loop because each element of the array can be processed by merely changing the subscript to address the appropriate element. If an application is found that uses arrays, the programmer should immediately think in terms of loop when developing the logic for processing the arrays.

The combination of arrays and loops is one of the more powerful tools available to the programmer. The good programmer should be able to use them properly whenever the need arises.

One of the options in the sample program is to print the list of baseball players in alphabetical sequence by player name. In order to produce this report, the players' names must be sorted in alphabetical sequence.

Sorting is the process of placing data in a prescribed sequence based upon one or more values in the data being sorted. In the sample program, the data will be placed in alphabetical sequence based upon the names of the players (Figure 8-20).

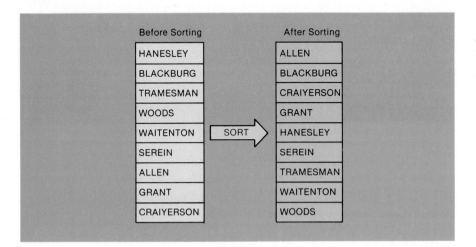

Figure 8-20 Before sorting, the names in this example are in the order entered by the user. After sorting, the names are in alphabetical sequence.

In the example above, prior to sorting, the players are stored in batting order sequence, which is the sequence in which they were entered by the user. After the sorting process takes place, the players' names are stored in alphabetical sequence. The following sections explain the processing required to sort the players' names in alphabetical sequence.

An algorithm is a series of steps which can be followed to produce a desired result. The algorithm used in the sample program to sort the players' names into alphabetical sequence is known as the exchange sort because the data being sorted is exchanged as the algorithm takes place.

The essential idea in an exchange sort is to examine the data to be sorted with the goal of placing the data with the highest key in the highest position. The key of the data being sorted is the field or fields on which the sort is taking place. In the sample program, the key to the data being sorted is the players' names.

When the sort takes place, the first name in the list of names to be sorted is compared to the second name in the list of names to be sorted. If the first name is greater than the second name, the two names are exchanged; that is, the first name is placed in the second position, and the second name is placed in the first position.

Sorting algorithm

If, on the other hand, the first name is not greater than the second name, the names are not exchanged. This processing is illustrated in Figure 8-21.

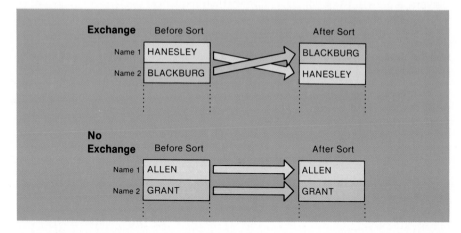

Figure 8-21 An exchange sort requires that elements in the array being sorted are exchanged if the value in a lower element is greater than the value in a higher element. Here, since HANESLEY is greater than BLACKBURG, the names are exchanged. ALLEN, however, is not greater than GRANT; therefore, the elements are not exchanged.

In the exchange example above, the first name, HANESLEY, is greater than the second name, BLACKBURG. Therefore, the names are exchanged, with BLACKBURG going to the first name position and HANESLEY going to the second name position. In the no exchange example, the first name, ALLEN, is not greater than the second name, GRANT. Therefore, no exchange occurs.

Through the use of exchanges, each pass through the sort loop will place the highest name in the highest available position of the array containing the names being sorted. The examples in Figure 8-22 illustrate the first two passes through the sort loop.

In step 1 of the first pass, the name in the first element of the array (HANESLEY) is compared to the name in the second element of the array (BLACKBURG). Since Hanesley is greater than Blackburg, an exchange occurs, placing Hanesley in the second element of the array. In step 2, the name in the second element of the array (HANESLEY) is then compared to the name in the third element of the array (TRAMESMAN). Since Tramesman is greater than Hanesley, no exchange occurs. Note at this point that the third element of the array contains the highest name that has been examined. It should be recalled that the purpose is to place the highest name in the highest available position on each pass through the loop.

In step 3, the name in the third element (TRAMESMAN) is compared to the name in the fourth element (WOODS). Since Woods is greater than Tramesman, no exchange takes place. In step 4, the name in the fourth element (WOODS) is compared to the name in the fifth element (WAITENTON). Since Woods is greater than Waitenton, an exchange takes place. Similarly, in step 5 Woods is greater than Serein, so an exchange occurs. In steps 6 through 8, Woods is also greater than the names found in the array, so exchanges

FIRST PASS OF LOOP

Step 1
Name 1	HANESLEY
Name 2	BLACKBURG
Name 3	TRAMESMAN
Name 4	WOODS
Name 5	WAITENTON
Name 6	SEREIN
Name 7	ALLEN
Name 8	GRANT
Name 9	CRAIYERSON

Step 2
Name 1	BLACKBURG
Name 2	HANESLEY
Name 3	TRAMESMAN
Name 4	WOODS
Name 5	WAITENTON
Name 6	SEREIN
Name 7	ALLEN
Name 8	GRANT
Name 9	CRAIYERSON

Step 3
Name 1	BLACKBURG
Name 2	HANESLEY
Name 3	TRAMESMAN
Name 4	WOODS
Name 5	WAITENTON
Name 6	SEREIN
Name 7	ALLEN
Name 8	GRANT
Name 9	CRAIYERSON

Step 4
Name 1	BLACKBURG
Name 2	HANESLEY
Name 3	TRAMESMAN
Name 4	WOODS
Name 5	WAITENTON
Name 6	SEREIN
Name 7	ALLEN
Name 8	GRANT
Name 9	CRAIYERSON

Step 5
Name 1	BLACKBURG
Name 2	HANESLEY
Name 3	TRAMESMAN
Name 4	WAITENTON
Name 5	WOODS
Name 6	SEREIN
Name 7	ALLEN
Name 8	GRANT
Name 9	CRAIYERSON

Step 6
Name 1	BLACKBURG
Name 2	HANESLEY
Name 3	TRAMESMAN
Name 4	WAITENTON
Name 5	SEREIN
Name 6	WOODS
Name 7	ALLEN
Name 8	GRANT
Name 9	CRAIYERSON

Step 7
Name 1	BLACKBURG
Name 2	HANESLEY
Name 3	TRAMESMAN
Name 4	WAITENTON
Name 5	SEREIN
Name 6	ALLEN
Name 7	WOODS
Name 8	GRANT
Name 9	CRAIYERSON

Step 8
Name 1	BLACKBURG
Name 2	HANESLEY
Name 3	TRAMESMAN
Name 4	WAITENTON
Name 5	SEREIN
Name 6	ALLEN
Name 7	GRANT
Name 8	WOODS
Name 9	CRAIYERSON

After First Pass of Loop
Name 1	BLACKBURG
Name 2	HANESLEY
Name 3	TRAMESMAN
Name 4	WAITENTON
Name 5	SEREIN
Name 6	ALLEN
Name 7	GRANT
Name 8	CRAIYERSON
Name 9	WOODS

SECOND PASS OF LOOP

Step 1
Name 1	BLACKBURG
Name 2	HANESLEY
Name 3	TRAMESMAN
Name 4	WAITENTON
Name 5	SEREIN
Name 6	ALLEN
Name 7	GRANT
Name 8	CRAIYERSON
Name 9	WOODS

Step 2
Name 1	BLACKBURG
Name 2	HANESLEY
Name 3	TRAMESMAN
Name 4	WAITENTON
Name 5	SEREIN
Name 6	ALLEN
Name 7	GRANT
Name 8	CRAIYERSON
Name 9	WOODS

Step 3
Name 1	BLACKBURG
Name 2	HANESLEY
Name 3	TRAMESMAN
Name 4	WAITENTON
Name 5	SEREIN
Name 6	ALLEN
Name 7	GRANT
Name 8	CRAIYERSON
Name 9	WOODS

Step 4
Name 1	BLACKBURG
Name 2	HANESLEY
Name 3	TRAMESMAN
Name 4	WAITENTON
Name 5	SEREIN
Name 6	ALLEN
Name 7	GRANT
Name 8	CRAIYERSON
Name 9	WOODS

Step 5
Name 1	BLACKBURG
Name 2	HANESLEY
Name 3	TRAMESMAN
Name 4	SEREIN
Name 5	WAITENTON
Name 6	ALLEN
Name 7	GRANT
Name 8	CRAIYERSON
Name 9	WOODS

Step 6
Name 1	BLACKBURG
Name 2	HANESLEY
Name 3	TRAMESMAN
Name 4	SEREIN
Name 5	ALLEN
Name 6	WAITENTON
Name 7	GRANT
Name 8	CRAIYERSON
Name 9	WOODS

Step 7
Name 1	BLACKBURG
Name 2	HANESLEY
Name 3	TRAMESMAN
Name 4	SEREIN
Name 5	ALLEN
Name 6	GRANT
Name 7	WAITENTON
Name 8	CRAIYERSON
Name 9	WOODS

After Second Pass of Loop
Name 1	BLACKBURG
Name 2	HANESLEY
Name 3	TRAMESMAN
Name 4	SEREIN
Name 5	ALLEN
Name 6	GRANT
Name 7	CRAIYERSON
Name 8	WAITENTON
Name 9	WOODS

Figure 8-22 This example illustrates the first two passes through the sort loop which places the names in alphabetical order.

occur. After the first pass through the loop, then, the name WOODS is placed in the highest position of the array containing the names to be sorted. This, of course, is the object of the exchange sort.

When the second pass of the sort loop begins, the name in the first element of the array (BLACKBURG) is again compared to the name in the second element of the array (HANESLEY). Since Hanesley is greater than Blackburg, the names are not exchanged. In step 2, HANESLEY, the name in the second element, is compared to TRAMESMAN, the name in the third element. Since Tramesman is greater than Hanesley, no exchange takes place. No exchange occurs until step 4, where WAITENTON is greater than SEREIN. Therefore, these two names are exchanged. In steps 5 through 7, it is found that Waitenton is greater than the names found in elements 6 through 8, so names are exchanged. After step 7, Waitenton is in element 8 of the name array. There is no need to compare Waitenton to the value in element 9 (WOODS) because the first pass through the loop placed the highest name in the array (WOODS) in the highest element (element 9).

On subsequent passes through the sort loop, the name with the highest value will be placed in the highest available element of the name array. Thus, on pass three, the highest name will be placed in element 7 of the array; on pass 4, the highest name will be placed in the sixth element, and so on, until the names are in alphabetical order. At that time, the sorting is complete.

The flowchart for the exchange sort algorithm is shown in Figure 8-24. Each of the steps accomplished using the logic in the flowchart will be explained in the following examples.

The first steps in the flowchart are to set the maximum number of comparisons to the number of values to be sorted less one, and to set the termination indicator to the value 0 (Figure 8-23). The maximum number of comparisons field (M) contains the number of comparisons which will have to be performed to place the highest value being sorted in the highest position of the array containing the data. For the sample program, the number of values to be sorted is nine. Therefore, the value in this field is set to eight. The termination indicator (T3) is used to identify when the sorting process can be terminated. As will be seen, when this field contains the value 1, the sorting is complete. This value is initially set to zero so that when it is checked the first time, the sorting loop will be entered.

Figure 8-23 The field M contains the maximum number of comparisons which will have to be made on any single pass through the sort loop. Prior to any processing through the loop, the field is initialized to the number of elements to be sorted less one. The termination indicator field (T3) indicates when the sorting is completed. It is initialized to zero so that the sort loop will be entered.

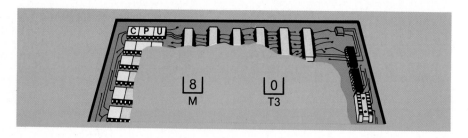

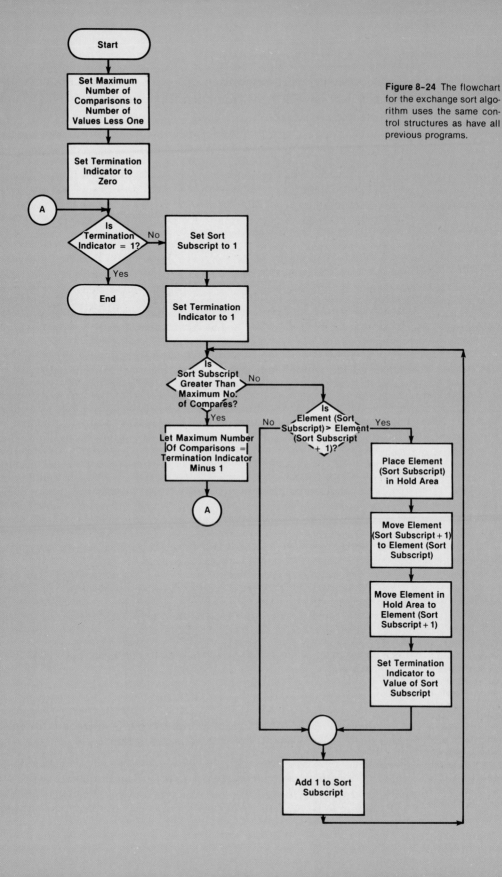

Figure 8-24 The flowchart for the exchange sort algorithm uses the same control structures as have all previous programs.

The next step in the exchange sort logic is to check the value in the termination indicator (T3) to determine if it is equal to 1. If it is, the sort processing is complete. The value in this field is not equal to one, however, because it was initialized to the value zero. Therefore, the sorting loop is entered (Figure 8–25).

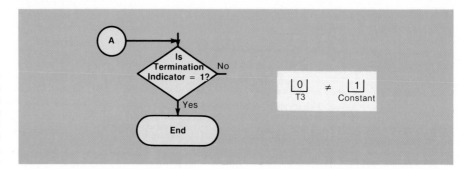

Figure 8-25 When the termination indicator contains the value 1, the sorting has been completed. Since the T3 field was initialized with the value zero, the sort is not complete. Therefore, the sorting loop is entered.

The first steps within the sorting loop are to set the sort subscript (S2) to 1 and set the termination indicator (T3) to 1 (Figure 8–26). The data to be sorted is stored in an array. In the sample program, this data consists of names of the baseball players. To reference the data being sorted, subscripts must be used. On each sorting pass, the first element in the array will be compared to the second element in the array. Therefore, the sort subscript is initially set to the value 1.

The termination indicator is reset to the value 1 once the loop is entered. If no exchanges take place in the sorting, the value in this field will not be changed, indicating that the sorting is completed.

Figure 8-26 The sort subscript (S2) is set to 1 so that the first element in the array being sorted will be compared. The termination indicator (T3) is set to 1. If an exchange takes place in the course of the loop processing, the value in the termination indicator will be changed to the value of the subscript which references the lower element that was exchanged. If the fifth and sixth elements are exchanged, for example, the termination indicator will be set to 5. If, however, no exchanges take place, or the only exchange which occurs is between the first and second elements, then the value in T3 at the end of the loop will be one, and the sort will be complete.

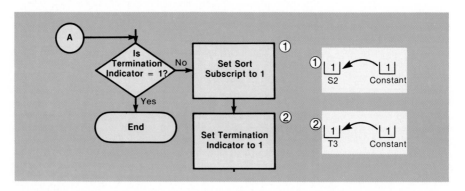

After setting the sort subscript to 1 and the termination indicator to 1, the loop which steps through each of the elements in the array and performs the exchanges is entered (Figure 8–27). The test to enter the loop is whether the value of the sort subscript is greater than the maximum number of comparisons to be performed. In the example shown, the value of the sort subscript (S2) is equal to 1, and the value in the maximum number of comparisons field (M) is equal to 8. Therefore, the loop is entered.

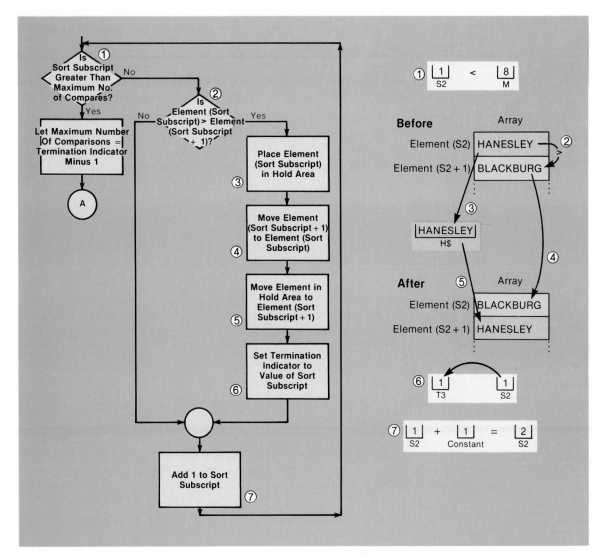

Within the loop, the test to determine if an exchange should take place is conducted. If the element referenced by the value in the sort subscript (S2) is greater than the element referenced by the value in the sort subscript plus 1 (S2 + 1), an exchange takes place. If not, no exchange occurs. In the example, the value in the sort subscript (S2) is 1. Therefore, the first element in the array is compared to the second element in the array. The first element contains the name HANESLEY, and the second element contains the name BLACKBURG. The name in the first element is greater than the name in the second element. Therefore, an exchange should occur.

To make the exchange, the value in element 1 (HANESLEY) is temporarily

Figure 8-27 On the first pass through the sort loop, the value in the first element (HANESLEY) is greater than the value in the second element (BLACKBURG). Therefore, the two names are exchanged. The termination indicator is set to the value in the subscript of the lower element in the exchange (1) because an exchange took place.

moved to another area (H$) in computer storage. The value in element 2 (BLACKBURG) is then moved to element 1. Finally, the value in H$ is moved to the second element in the array. As can be seen, the values in these two elements have been exchanged.

After the exchange takes place, the value of the sort subscript is moved to the termination indicator field. In the example, the value in S2 (which is 1) is moved to T3. The value in the subscript field is incremented by 1 so that the next elements in the array can be compared. Control is then sent back to the decision which determines if this pass through the sort loop is complete.

To determine if the sort loop pass is complete, the value in the sort subscript field (S2) is compared to the maximum number of comparisons to be made on this pass, which is stored in M (Figure 8–28).

Figure 8-28 When the second and third elements in the array being sorted are compared, the value in the second element (HANESLEY) is less than the value in the third element (TRAMESMAN). Therefore, no exchange takes place. The value in the termination indicator (T3) is not changed.

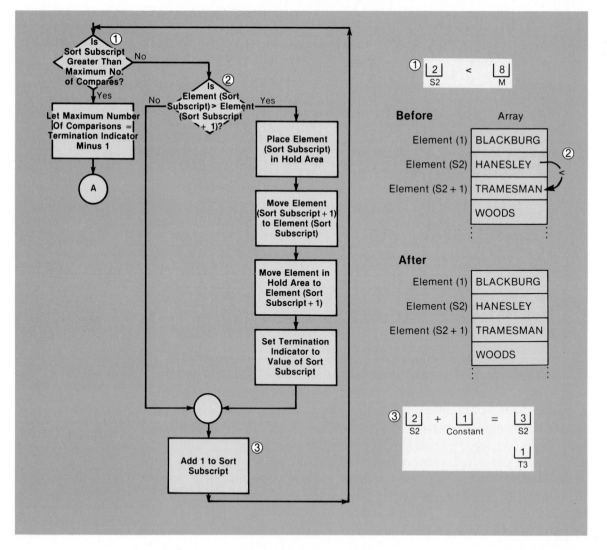

Since the value in S2 is 2 and the value in M is 8, the loop will again be entered. The first instruction in the loop tests if the value in the second element (referenced by S2) is greater than the value in the third element (referenced by S2 + 1). The value in the second element, HANESLEY, is not greater than the value in the third element, TRAMESMAN. Therefore, an exchange does not occur. Instead, as shown in Figure 8–28, the sort subscript (S2) is incremented by one, and control is returned to the entry point of the loop.

Several points should be noted from Figure 8–28. First, an exchange did not occur, meaning that the second and third elements are in the correct sequence. Secondly, the termination indicator (T3) has not been modified because no exchange took place. Third, the sort subscript (S2) is incremented to the value 3 so that the third and fourth elements in the array can be compared.

On the third pass of the loop, the sort subscript is compared to the maximum number of comparisons to be made to determine if the loop should be entered again. Since the subscript contains the value 3, the loop will again be entered. The third element in the array will be compared to the fourth element in the array. Since the name WOODS is greater than the name TRAMESMAN, no exchange will take place. The sort subscript is then incremented to 4. Control is passed to the decision to enter the loop.

This processing will continue until the value in the sort subscript (S2) is greater than the number of comparisons to be made on the sort pass. At that time, the maximum number of comparisons field is set to the value in the terminations indicator field less 1. Control is then passed back to determine if the sort process is complete (Figure 8–29).

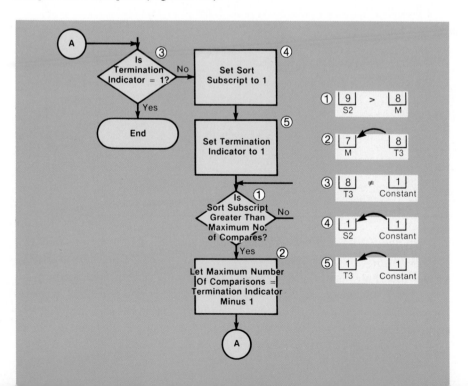

Figure 8-29 After all elements in the array being sorted have been compared one time, the value in the sort subscript is equal to 9. Since this value is greater than the value in the maximum number of compares field (M = 8), the first pass of the loop is completed. Note at the conclusion of the first pass that the value in the termination indicator (T3) is equal to 8. This is because the last elements to be exchanged were the eighth and ninth elements (see Figure 8–22, first pass of the loop), and the value in the termination indicator will always be equal to the subscript of the lower element in an exchange.

If the value in the termination indicator (T3) is equal to 1, the sorting process is complete. If the value is not equal to 1, it indicates that at least one more pass is required to place all of the data in the required sequence. When another pass is required, the sort subscript is set to 1, and the termination indicator is set to one. The loop which performs the exchanges is then entered.

The processing just described will continue until all of the elements in the array being sorted have been placed in the proper sequence. The sort is then complete. The sort processing is terminated, and the sorted data can be used as required in the program.

Sort coding   The coding to implement this logic is shown in Figure 8–30.

```
5000                                                                REM
5010 REM ***********************************************************
5020 REM * SORT DATA IN N$ ARRAY.                                  *
5030 REM ***********************************************************
5040                                                                REM
5050 LET M = E - 1
5060 LET T3 = 0
5070                                                                REM
5080 IF T3 = 1 THEN 5280
5090    LET S2 = 1
5100    LET T3 = 1
5110                                                                REM
5120    IF S2 > M THEN 5250
5130      IF N$(S2) > N$(S2 + 1) THEN 5160
5140        GOTO 5220
5150                                                                REM
5160        LET H$ = N$(S2)
5170        LET N$(S2) = N$(S2 + 1)
5180        LET N$(S2 + 1) = H$
5190        LET T3 = S2
5200        GOTO 5220
5210                                                                REM
5220      LET S2 = S2 + 1
5230    GOTO 5120
5240                                                                REM
5250    LET M = T3 - 1
5260 GOTO 5080
5270                                                                REM
5280 RETURN
```

Figure 8-30 The coding shown in this example implements the logic illustrated in the previous examples. The relationship between the coding and the sort logic should be carefully studied.

On line 5050, the value in the maximum number of comparisons field (M) is set to one less than the number of elements to be sorted (the value in E). The termination indicator (T3) is initialized to the value zero on line 5060.

The if statement on line 5080 tests if the termination field contains the value 1. If so, the sort processing is complete. If not, the sort subscript (S2) is initialized to the value 1 on line 5090, and the value 1 is placed in the T3 field on line 5100.

The exchange loop is entered on line 5120, where the value in the sort subscript is checked against the value in the maximum number of comparisons field (M). If the value in S2 is greater than the value in M, the pass through the loop to place the highest value being sorted in the highest element of the array is complete. Control is passed to line number 5250, where the value in M is replaced by the value in T3 less one.

If the value in S2 is not greater than the value in M, then the if statement on line 5130 determines if an exchange should occur. When the value in the element identified by the sort subscript, N$(S2), is greater than the element identified by the sort subscript plus 1, N$(S2 + 1), then an exchange must take place. The coding on lines 5160 – 5180 implements the exchange by moving the element at N$(S2) to H$, moving the element at N$(S2 + 1) to the element N$(S2), and then moving the data from H$ to N$(S2 + 1). The value in the sort subscript is then moved to the termination control indicator (T3).

Regardless of whether an exchange occurred, the statement on line 5220 increments the subscript by one so that the next element in the array can be examined. The loop from line 5120 through line 5230 will continue until the value in the subscript is greater than the value in M. At that time, the value in M is reset by the let statement on line 5250, and control is passed to line 5080, where the value in T3 is checked. This looping will continue until all data in the N$ array has been sorted.

Calling the sort module

The example in Figure 8–30 illustrates the code that could be used to sort the names contained in the N$ array. It will be recalled, however, that the N$ array is used to store the players' names when they are entered by the user (see Figure 8–15). In addition, the N$ array is used to print the players in batting order sequence (see Figure 8–18). If the sort processing illustrated in Figure 8–30 took place, the names in the N$ array would be permanently placed in alphabetical sequence, and the listing generated by the coding in Figure 8–18 would not be in batting order sequence.

Together with this is the fact that sorting is a task commonly required in programs. Tasks which are commonly used can many times be written as a subroutine and then be included in any program which requires them. For example, the sort processing shown in Figure 8–30 can be written as a subroutine. Then, if the same sort processing is required in another program, this subroutine can be copied into the other program without requiring that the subroutine be redesigned and rewritten.

To generalize the sort subroutine and to overcome the problem with the N$ array, it is necessary to place the data to be sorted in a different array prior to calling the subroutine. In this way, the data in the N$ array will not be rearranged, and the sort subroutine will sort whatever data is passed to it, regardless of what that data is.

To cause this to occur, a for-next loop is commonly used. The example in Figure 8–31 illustrates the coding used in the sample program to load the names in the N$ array into a sort work array called D$. The sort subroutine then sorts the data in the D$ array.

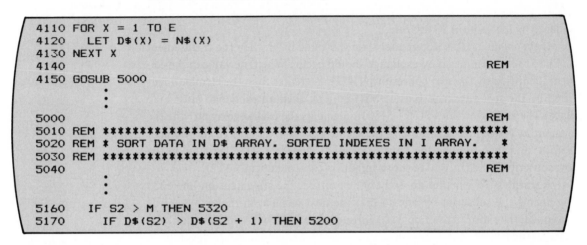

```
4110 FOR X = 1 TO E
4120    LET D$(X) = N$(X)
4130 NEXT X
4140                                                             REM
4150 GOSUB 5000
        •
        •
        •
5000                                                             REM
5010 REM *******************************************************
5020 REM * SORT DATA IN D$ ARRAY. SORTED INDEXES IN I ARRAY.   *
5030 REM *******************************************************
5040                                                             REM
        •
        •
        •
5160    IF S2 > M THEN 5320
5170        IF D$(S2) > D$(S2 + 1) THEN 5200
```

Figure 8-31 The for-next loop on lines 4110 – 4130 places the elements in the N$ array into the corresponding elements of the D$ array. When control is passed to the sort subroutine by the GOSUB statement on line 4150, the data in the D$ array will be sorted. The if statement on line 5170 compares the elements in the D$ array.

In the example above, the for-next loop on lines 4110 – 4130 places each element in the N$ array into a corresponding element of the D$ array. The gosub statement on line 4150 passes control to the sort subroutine at line 5000.

Within the sort subroutine, the data in the D$ array is sorted (see Figure 8–30 for the complete sort subroutine). When the sort is complete, the calling program can use the data in the D$ array as required by the application while still having access to the data in batting order sequence in the N$ array.

A generalized subroutine is one which can be used in more than one program to perform its task. In almost all cases, a generalized subroutine should be passed data in a work area of some sort, such as the D$ array. This accomplishes two things: First, the data which is required within the program, such as the data in N$, is not disturbed by the processing in the subroutine. Secondly, the subroutine can be used to perform its task regardless of the variable names in the program which calls it. That is, so long as the data to be sorted is placed in the D$ array, it does not matter what names or what types of data are used in the program which calls the sort module. This is very important when using a generalized subroutine.

A generalized subroutine which performs a commonly required task, such as sorting, is a very important tool for the programmer. It can save considerable time and effort because new code need not be designed, written, and tested.

Most generalized subroutines have certain rules which must be followed in order to use them. For example, when using the sort subroutine, the calling program will have to place the number of elements to be sorted in the field identified by the variable name E, and will have to place the data to be sorted in the D$ array. The programmer should know how to write a generalized subroutine and how to use subroutines which might be available.

In the sample program, the sorting takes place on the names of the players. There is other data stored in arrays in the sample program which is associated with the players' names. The positions of each player are stored in the P1$ array, the number of at bats of a player are stored in the B array, and the number of hits for the player are stored in the H array (see Figure 8-15). When the names are sorted, the elements in these other arrays should be placed in the sorted sequence so that they still correspond to the names. Otherwise, the correct positions, at bats, and hits will not be associated with the correct players.

Pointers to array elements

This problem can be handled in one of two ways. One way is to exchange the elements in these arrays in the same manner as the names are exchanged when the sort is taking place. Thus, when one name is exchanged with another, the positions, at bats, and hits corresponding to the names would also be exchanged. Since the data in these arrays is required in other parts of the program, the positions, at bats, and hits would have to be placed in work arrays in the same way that the elements of the N$ array are placed in the D$ array. As can be seen, this method requires additional arrays, additional procedures by the calling program to load the work arrays, and additional exchanging in the sort module to exchange all of the elements. Moreover, the addition of all these arrays requires the sort subroutine to specifically process these arrays. It loses its generality. In summary, then, this approach requires considerably more processing for both the calling program and the sort subroutine; and, the sort subroutine is no longer a generalized subroutine. Therefore, it is not recommended that this approach be used.

A second means to solve this problem is to use elements of an array as pointers to elements of other arrays. This concept is illustrated in Figure 8-32.

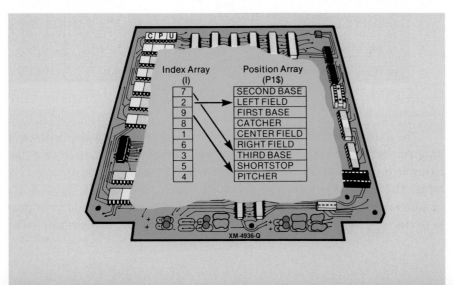

Figure 8-32 The elements in the index array I contain values which can be used as subscripts to reference the elements in the position array. For example, the first element in the I array contains the value 7. This value can be used as the subscript to reference the seventh element in the position array (THIRD BASE).

In Figure 8–32, the position array contains the player positions in the sequence in which they were entered by the user. The index array contains numeric values in each element that correspond to an element in the position array. Thus, the value in the first element of the index array, 7, is used to point to the seventh element in the position array. The value in the second element of the index array, 2, is used to point to the second element in the position array. The value in the third element of the index array, 9, is used to point to the ninth element in the position array. Elements in the index array can be used as subscripts to reference the elements in the position array.

This principle can be used in the sort subroutine by placing the original subscripts of the sorted data in a sorted sequence in the index array (Figure 8–33).

Figure 8-33 When an index array is used, only the actual data being sorted and the values in the index array must be exchanged. All other arrays which must be referenced in the sorted sequence can remain without change. Thus, after sorting, the elements in the D$ array have been placed in sorted sequence, and the elements in the index array (I) have been placed in a sequence corresponding to the sorted sequence. The other arrays, however, have have not been altered from their sequence prior to sorting.

Before sorting

D$	I	N$	P1$	B	H
HANESLEY	1	HANESLEY	SECOND BASE	100	28
BLACKBURG	2	BLACKBURG	LEFT FIELD	76	20
TRAMESMAN	3	TRAMESMAN	FIRST BASE	75	25
WOODS	4	WOODS	CATCHER	82	28
WAITENTON	5	WAITENTON	CENTER FIELD	98	24
SEREIN	6	SEREIN	RIGHT FIELD	110	26
ALLEN	7	ALLEN	THIRD BASE	62	17
GRANT	8	GRANT	SHORTSTOP	94	20
CRAIYERSON	9	CRAIYERSON	PITCHER	26	3

After sorting

D$	I	N$	P1$	B	H
ALLEN	7	HANESLEY	SECOND BASE	100	28
BLACKBURG	2	BLACKBURG	LEFT FIELD	76	20
CRAIYERSON	9	TRAMESMAN	FIRST BASE	75	25
GRANT	8	WOODS	CATCHER	82	28
HANESLEY	1	WAITENTON	CENTER FIELD	98	24
SEREIN	6	SEREIN	RIGHT FIELD	110	26
TRAMESMAN	3	ALLEN	THIRD BASE	62	17
WAITENTON	5	GRANT	SHORTSTOP	94	20
WOODS	4	CRAIYERSON	PITCHER	26	3

The illustration in Figure 8–33 shows the arrays involved in the baseball program before sorting and after sorting. Before sorting, note that the elements in the D$ array are in the same sequence as the elements in the N$ array. The D$ array is loaded by the coding shown previously in Figure 8–31. In addition, the elements in the P1$, B, and H arrays are in the same sequence as the players' names in the N$ array. Thus, Hanesley (the first element in the

N$ array), plays second base (the first element in the P1$ array), has 100 at bats (the first element in the B array), and has 28 hits (the first element in the H array).

Prior to the sort, each element in the index array (I) contains a value corresponding to the position of the element in the array. The first element contains the value 1, the second element contains the value 2, and so on.

After sorting, there has been no change to the N$, P1$, B, or H arrays. They are in the same sequence as before the sort. The elements in the D$ array, however, have been placed in alphabetical sequence because the D$ array is used in the exchange of elements in the sorting subroutine. The values in the elements of the I array have also been placed in the sorted sequence. The name Allen, which is the first name in the sorted data, was the seventh name in the unsorted data. Therefore, the value in the first element of the I array is seven. This value can be used as the subscript to reference the name Allen in the N$ array, the position third base in the P1$ array, the number of at bats Allen has (62) in the B array, and the number of hits Allen has (17) in the H array.

Similarly, the value in the second element of the I array, 2, can be used to reference the information for the second player in the sorted sequence. The player is Blackburg, who plays left field, has 76 at bats, and 20 hits. The value in the third element of the I array is 9. The player Craiyerson is the ninth player in the batting order but the third player in alphabetical order.

The value in each of the elements of the I array, then, can be used to reference the elements of the other arrays. To accomplish this, a double subscript is used in the statement which references the arrays (Figure 8–34).

Figure 8-34 To use the elements in an index array as subscripts, a double subscript is required. In this example, the value in S4 is used to identify which element in the I array is to be referenced. The element in the I array acts as the subscript for the N$ array.

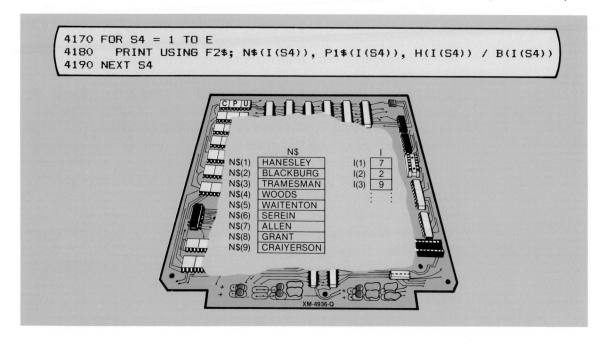

```
4170 FOR S4 = 1 TO E
4180    PRINT USING F2$; N$(I(S4)), P1$(I(S4)), H(I(S4)) / B(I(S4))
4190 NEXT S4
```

In the print using statement in Figure 8–34, the first data to be printed is specified as N$(I(S4)). The data is to be taken from the N$ array. The subscript used to reference the N$ array is specified as I(S4). This subscript is taken from the I array. The element in the I array to be used is identified by the value in S4, which acts as the subscript for the I array.

To obtain an element from the N$ array, then, the value in S4 is used to specify an element in the I array. The value in the I array element is used as the subscript for the N$ array. For example, if the value in S4 is 1, the value in the first element of the I array (7) is used as the subscript to reference the N$ array; if the value in S4 is 2, the value in the second element in the I array (2) is used; and so on. Therefore, in the print using statement in Figure 8–34, when the value in S4 is equal to 1, the value in the seventh element in the N$ array (ALLEN) will be printed.

This methodology is used to reference elements in the P1$, H, and B arrays as well. A major advantage is that the data in these arrays need not be disturbed when the sorting takes place.

The sort subroutine illustrated in Figure 8–30 and Figure 8–31 must be modified slightly to initialize the index array (I) and to exchange the elements in the I array when the sort is taking place. The actual sort subroutine used in the sample program is shown in Figure 8–35. The for-next loop on lines 5050 – 5070 initialize the I array. The counter-variable X is used to control the loop. On each pass through the loop, the let statement on line 5060 places the value of X in the Xth element of the array. For example, when the value in X is equal to 1, one is placed in the first element of the I array. When the value in X is equal to 2, the value 2 is placed in the second element of the I array, and so on. When the for-next loop is completed, the I array will contain the data shown in the before sorting portion of Figure 8–33.

When the index array is used, the elements in it must be exchanged in the same manner as the elements in the D$ array which are actually being sorted. In the sort subroutine in the sample program (Figure 8–35), the exchange takes place on lines 5200 – 5220. The data in the element in the I array identified by the value in the S2 subscript is temporarily moved to a hold area, H. The data in the element identified by the subscript S2 + 1 is then moved to the element identified by the subscript S2. The last step in the exchange is to move the data in the hold area H to the element identified by S2 + 1. This exchange follows the same logic as that used to exchange the elements in D$ which are actually being sorted. With the use of an index array, these are the only two exchanges which must be made regardless of the number of arrays which will be referenced by the values in the index array.

Generalized sort subroutine

The prime advantage in the use of an index array in the sort subroutine is that the subroutine becomes able to sort any string array and allows other arrays

```
5000                                                              REM
5010 REM ***********************************************************
5020 REM * SORT DATA IN D$ ARRAY.  SORTED INDEXES IN I ARRAY.    *
5030 REM ***********************************************************
5040                                                              REM
5050 FOR X = 1 TO E
5060    LET I(X) = X
5070 NEXT X
5080                                                              REM
5090 LET M = E - 1
5100 LET T3 = 0
5110                                                              REM
5120 IF T3 = 1 THEN 5350
5130    LET S2 = 1
5140    LET T3 = 1
5150                                                              REM
5160    IF S2 > M THEN 5320
5170      IF D$(S2) > D$(S2 + 1) THEN 5200
5180        GOTO 5290
5190                                                              REM
5200        LET H = I(S2)
5210        LET I(S2) = I(S2 + 1)
5220        LET I(S2 + 1) = H
5230        LET H$ = D$(S2)
5240        LET D$(S2) = D$(S2 + 1)
5250        LET D$(S2 + 1) = H$
5260        LET T3 = S2
5270        GOTO 5290
5280                                                              REM
5290      LET S2 = S2 + 1
5300      GOTO 5160
5310                                                              REM
5320    LET M = T3 - 1
5330 GOTO 5120
5340                                                              REM
5350 RETURN
```

Figure 8-35 The sort subroutine used in the sample program initializes the elements in the index array (I) and then exchanges the elements in the index array at the same time the elements in the array being sorted, D$, are exchanged.

to be referenced in the sorted sequence. For example, although it is not a part of the sample program in this chapter, assume that a report was to be generated in alphabetical sequence by position. That is, the first line on the report should be catcher, followed by center field, first base, and so on. The sort subroutine illustrated in Figure 8–35 can be used to sort the position array in this manner. The only requirement is that the position array be loaded into the D$ array, as shown in Figure 8–36. When control is passed to the sort subroutine, the data in D$ is sorted, and the subscripts for the sorted data are placed in the I array. The values in the I array can be used as subscripts to reference any other arrays in the program.

```
2730 FOR X = 1 TO E
2740    LET D$(X) = P1$(X)
2750 NEXT X
2760                                          REM
2770 GOSUB 5000
```

Figure 8-36 Since the sort subroutine shown in Figure 8-35 is a generalized subroutine, it can be used to sort any string data. Here, elements from the P1$ array are placed in the D$ array. Control is then passed to the sort subroutine at line 5000, where the data in the D$ array is sorted.

The sort subroutine illustrated in Figure 8–35 can also be used to sort data stored in numeric arrays provided the values in the arrays are all positive. The only requirement is that when the data is moved to the D$ array, a special instruction called STR$ is used to change the data from numeric to string. The use of this instruction is described in detail in Chapter 9.

It is important that consideration be given to making subroutines as generalized as possible. The sort subroutine in Figure 8–35 is an example of a subroutine that can be used in any program to sort data in a string array.

Sample program

The sample program in this chapter is used to load the starting line-up of a baseball team and then create reports in batting order sequence and alphabetical sequence by player name. The reports generated are shown in Figure 8–4 on page 8.3. The input data is entered by the user, as shown in Figure 8–15 on page 8.11. The user selects the processing to be done by responding to a menu (see Figure 8–1 on page 8.1).

Program design

As with previous programs, the program design begins by specifying the program tasks to be accomplished. The tasks for the sample program are listed below.

Program Tasks

*1. Display the menu and obtain a user selection.
 2. Determine the selection to be performed.
*3. Load the starting players.
*4. Display the players in batting order.
*5. Display the players in alphabetical sequence.

As programs become larger, they generally become more complex. As noted previously in this chapter, one way to keep the complexity of a program to a minimum is to subdivide the program into a series of smaller subroutines. The program then consists of a number of relatively simple subroutines rather than one large, complex piece of code. The preferred method for decomposing the program into a series of subroutines, or modules, is to analyze the program tasks. Any program task that performs a specific function and appears to require more than 10 – 15 BASIC statements can be placed in a subroutine.

In the sample program, five tasks are specified. The first task, display the menu and obtain a user selection, performs a specific task and seems to require more than 10 – 15 programming statements. Therefore, it will be a subroutine in the sample program. The asterisk specified beside the program task indicates that the task will be performed by a subroutine.

The second task, determine the selection to be performed, will probably require fewer than 10 statements, so it will not be a subroutine in the program. It should be noted here that the judgment about how many statements will be required does not have to be 100% accurate. It is only an estimate to aid in decomposing the program into a series of subroutines. The primary reason for breaking a program into a series of subroutines is to simplify the program. If a routine within the program consists of a large number of statements, it will probably be a difficult routine to understand. Therefore, in most cases, it should be subdivided into smaller subroutines.

The third task, load the starting players, is estimated to require more than 10 – 15 statements. Therefore, it will also be a separate subroutine. The same analysis holds for the fourth task and the fifth task. Thus, after the analysis of the tasks to be performed in the program, it is found that four tasks will be subroutines in the program.

When a program is to consist of a series of subroutines, the relationships of the subroutines in the program will normally be shown through the use of a hierarchy chart. The hierarchy chart derived from the analysis of the tasks in the sample program is shown in Figure 8–37.

Figure 8-37 The hierarchy chart is used to show the relationships of subroutines and tasks within the program. The tasks specified within the rectangles will be performed in subroutines. The task below the horizontal line will not be performed in a subroutine.

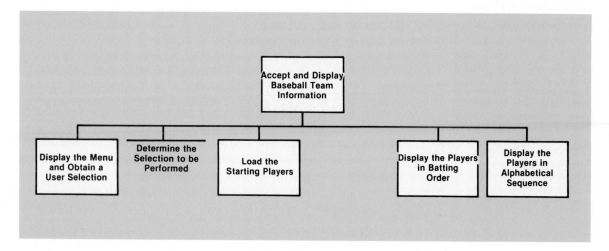

The rectangles each represent a separate module or subroutine in the program. The tasks to be performed by each module are specified within the rectangle. The top module's task is to accept and display baseball team information, which is the task of the entire program. The top module in a hierarchy chart will normally specify the role of the program itself.

The second level of the hierarchy chart contains those tasks which were identified on page 8.32. The tasks which are to be subroutines in the program are placed in rectangles. The task which is not to be done in a subroutine is placed under a horizontal line. Thus, from viewing the hierarchy chart, a programmer can see which tasks will be performed in subroutine and which will not be performed in a subroutine.

When a program will contain one or more subroutines, the subroutines themselves should be analyzed to determine if they should utilize subroutines. Therefore, the programming tasks in each of the subroutines must be defined. In Figure 8–38, the tasks for the subroutine which displays the menu and obtains a user selection are listed.

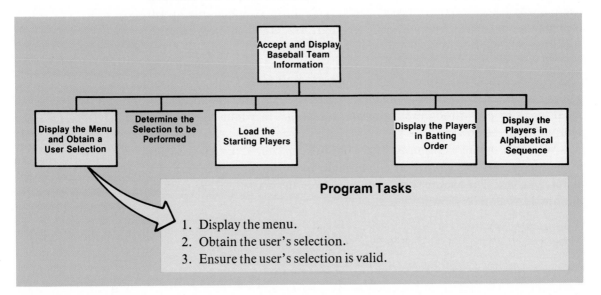

Figure 8-38 The subroutines used in a program must themselves be analyzed to determine the program tasks they must accomplish. Here, the program tasks for the module which displays the menu and obtains a user selection are specified. Each of these tasks must be examined to determine if it is lengthy or complex. If so, the task should be performed in a separate module. In this case, none of the tasks will be performed by a subroutine.

When the tasks are identified for a subroutine, the same analysis on these tasks takes place as on the tasks identified for the top-level module. Any task which performs a specific function and appears to require more than 10–15 BASIC statements can be placed in a subroutine. In the tasks specified above, none of the three seems to be either large or complex. Therefore, none of them will be a subroutine, or a separate module, in the program.

This same process must be performed for the module which loads the starting players (Figure 8–39). The five tasks — Display the screen headings, Obtain the players' names, Obtain the players' positions, Obtain the players' at bats, and Obtain the players' hits — seem to be neither large nor complex. Therefore, they will not be subroutines.

The tasks for the subroutine which displays the players in batting order are shown in Figure 8–40. None of the three tasks — Display the screen headings, Display the lines on the report, and Obtain a response to return to the menu — appears to be either large or complex. Therefore, none of them will be a subroutine.

Note from the hierarchy chart in Figure 8–40 that the structure of the program is apparent. Each task which is performed in the program and where it is performed can be easily seen. If, at some future time, the program must be modified in some manner, the hierarchy chart provides a map to where each

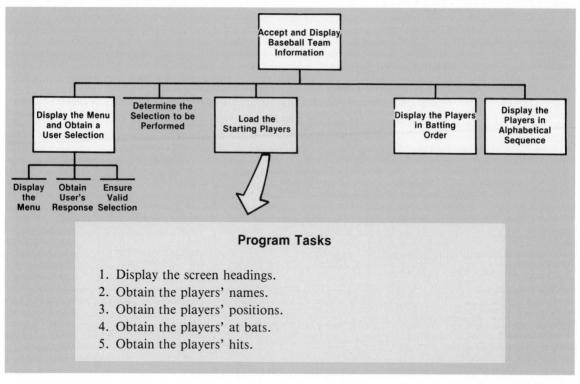

Figure 8-39 The analysis of the tasks to be performed by the module which loads the starting players reveals that none of the tasks should be accomplished in a separate subroutine because none of them appears to be large or complex.

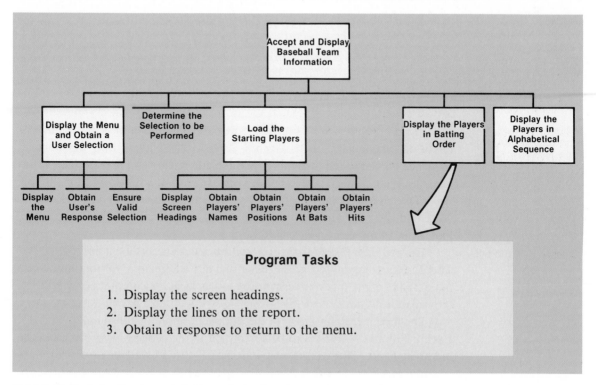

Figure 8-40 Displaying the players in batting order involves three program tasks. These tasks are performed within the module.

task is performed.

The last module on the second level to analyze is the module whose task is to display the players in alphabetical sequence. The program tasks for this module are shown in Figure 8–41.

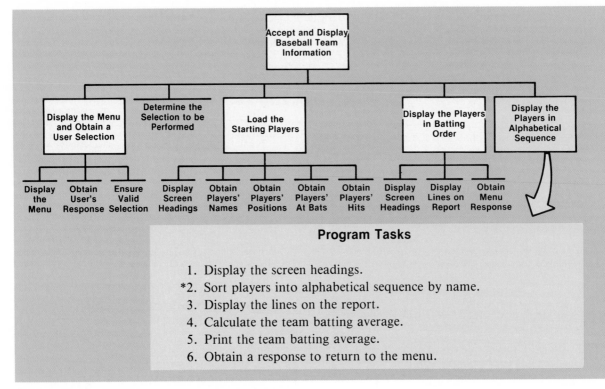

Program Tasks

1. Display the screen headings.
*2. Sort players into alphabetical sequence by name.
3. Display the lines on the report.
4. Calculate the team batting average.
5. Print the team batting average.
6. Obtain a response to return to the menu.

Figure 8-41 Six identifiable tasks must be accomplished by the module which displays the players in alphabetical sequence. The task of sorting the players into alphabetical sequence appears to be reasonably large and perhaps complex. Therefore, as indicated by the asterisk, this task will be performed in a subroutine.

The six program tasks for the module are analyzed in the same manner as discussed previously. Task number 2, sort the players into alphabetical sequence by name, requires more than ten statements and is reasonably complex (see Figure 8–35). Therefore, a separate module will be used for the sort task. The hierarchy chart resulting from this analysis is shown in Figure 8–42. Note that the task which will sort the players is specified within a rectangle, indicating a subroutine will be used.

The program tasks for the sort subroutine are also shown in Figure 8–42. These tasks are analyzed in the same manner as previous subroutines. Since none of the three tasks appears to be either large or complex, they will not require subroutines.

The final hierarchy chart for the sample program is shown in Figure 8–43. Each of the tasks which is to be performed in the program is specified in the hierarchy chart. Those tasks which are large (10 – 15 statements or more) are separate modules, or subroutines, in the program. They are indicated by rectangles. Those tasks which are not separate modules are described under the

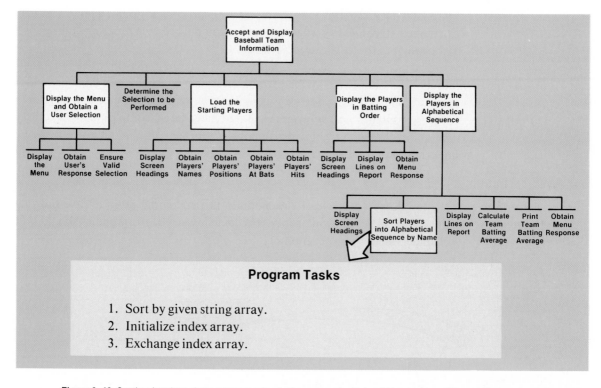

Program Tasks

1. Sort by given string array.
2. Initialize index array.
3. Exchange index array.

Figure 8-42 Sorting involves three programming tasks, none of which will be performed in a separate module.

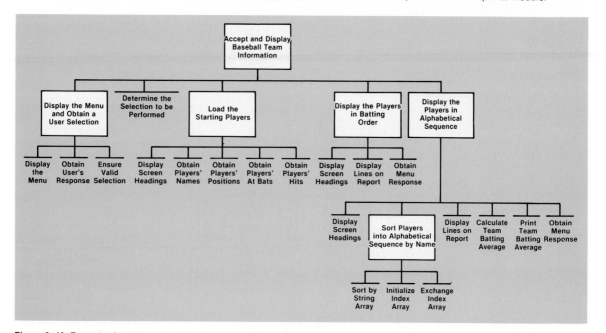

Figure 8-43 From the final hierarchy chart for the sample program in this chapter, it is clear what tasks are being performed by the program and where in the program these tasks are being performed. The hierarchy chart acts as a map to the program.

horizontal lines. By reviewing the hierarchy chart of a program, a programmer can immediately identify what tasks are accomplished by a program and where in the program the tasks are performed.

The methodology shown in this sample program to decompose a program into modules should always be used on programs which contain large or complex program tasks. In this way, complexity is reduced because the program consists of small simple subroutines rather than a large, complex piece of code. The ability to analyze and decompose a program into modules is a very important skill for the accomplished programmer.

Program flowcharts

The flowcharts for each of the modules in the sample program are shown below and on the following pages. The logic in each of the modules should be well understood by the programmer.

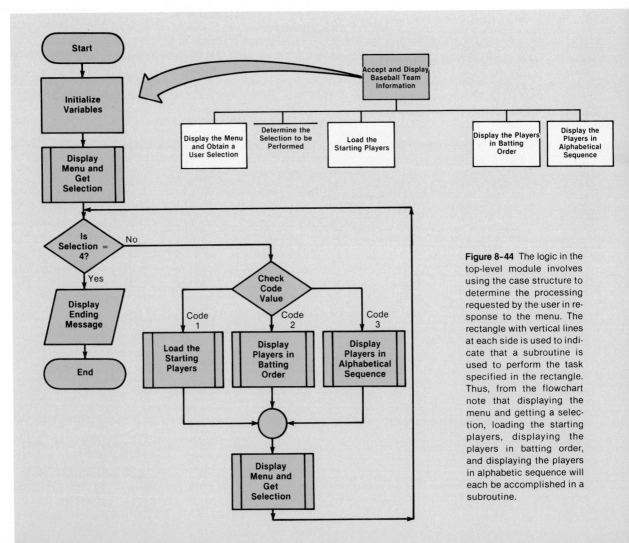

Figure 8-44 The logic in the top-level module involves using the case structure to determine the processing requested by the user in response to the menu. The rectangle with vertical lines at each side is used to indicate that a subroutine is used to perform the task specified in the rectangle. Thus, from the flowchart note that displaying the menu and getting a selection, loading the starting players, displaying the players in batting order, and displaying the players in alphabetic sequence will each be accomplished in a subroutine.

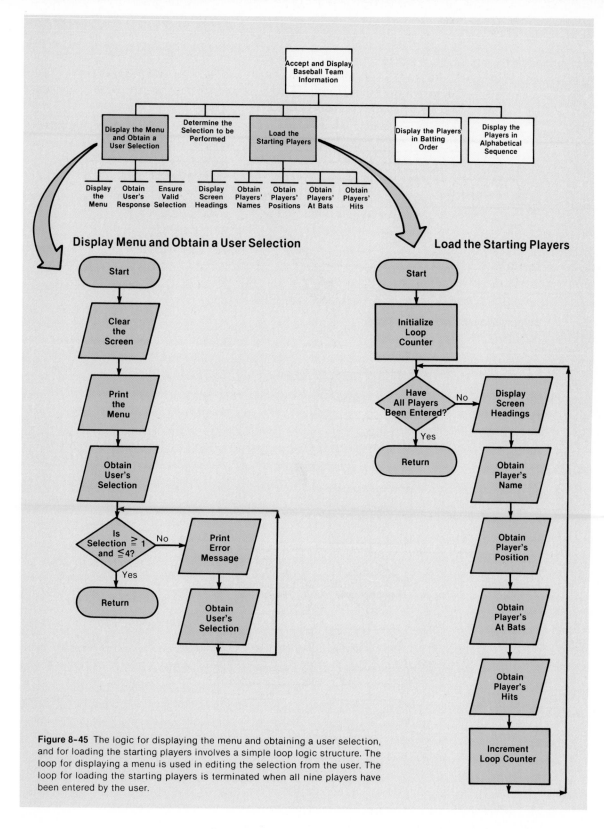

Figure 8–45 The logic for displaying the menu and obtaining a user selection, and for loading the starting players involves a simple loop logic structure. The loop for displaying a menu is used in editing the selection from the user. The loop for loading the starting players is terminated when all nine players have been entered by the user.

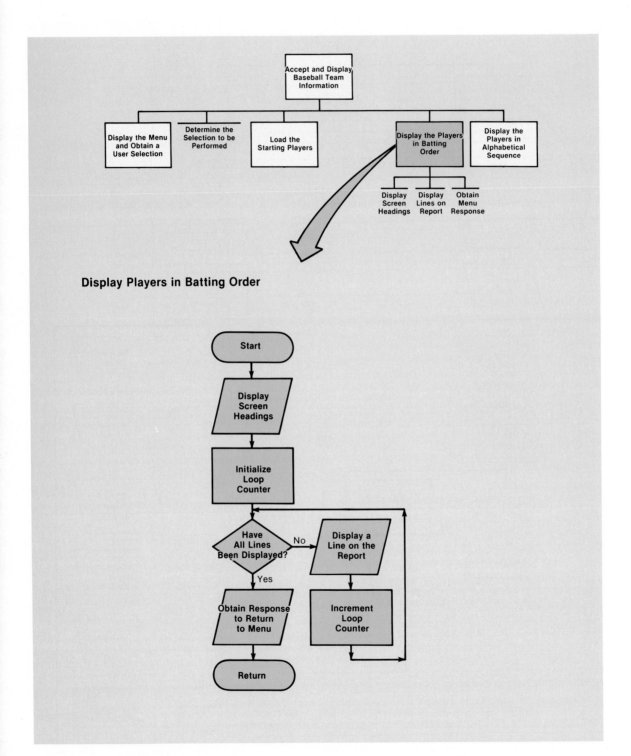

Figure 8-46 A simple loop is used to print the players in batting order sequence.

Display Players in Alphabetical Sequence

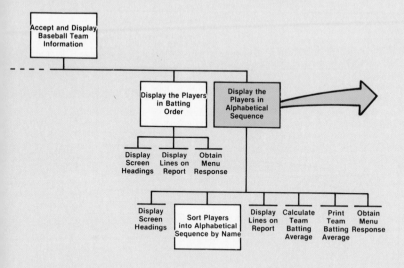

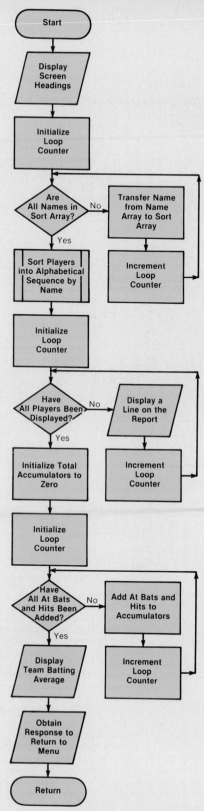

Figure 8-47 When the players are displayed in alphabetical sequence, they must be sorted first. Therefore, this module loads the sort array with the names to be sorted and then passes control to the sort subroutine. The sort subroutine is identified by the rectangle with vertical lines inside each side. After the names are sorted, a loop is used to print them. The total hits and at bats are then accumulated using a loop so that the team batting average can be printed.

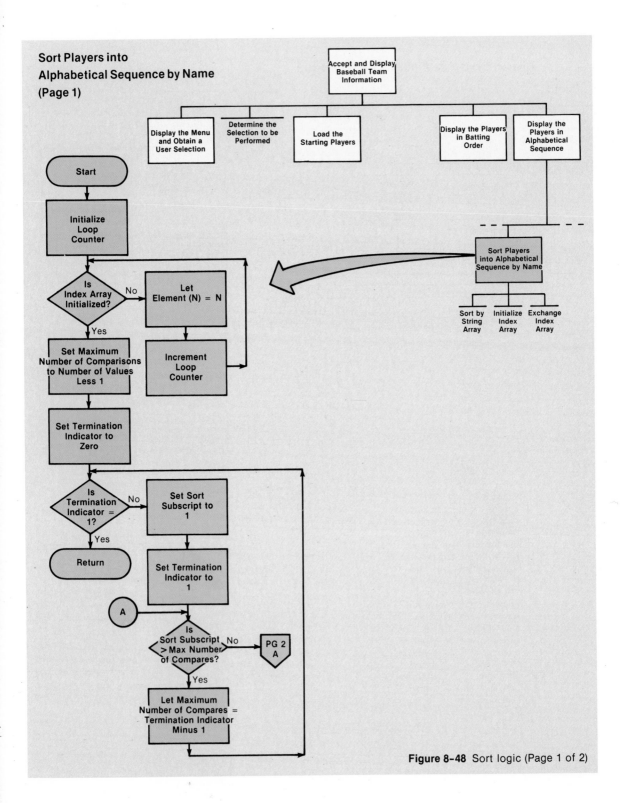

Figure 8-48 Sort logic (Page 1 of 2)

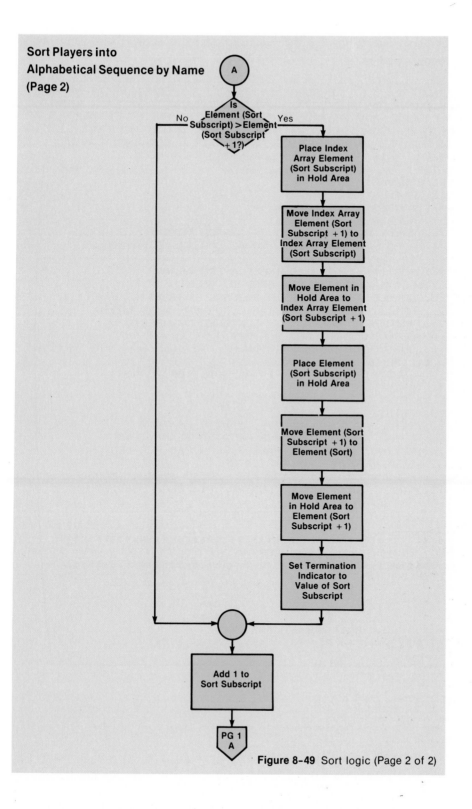

Figure 8-49 Sort logic (Page 2 of 2)

Sample program   The complete listing for the sample program is shown below and on the following pages.

```
100 REM BASEBALL              FEBRUARY 10              SHELLY/CASHMAN
110                                                              REM
120 REM THIS PROGRAM ALLOWS THE STARTING PLAYERS ON A BASEBALL
130 REM TEAM TO BE LOADED INTO AN ARRAY. THEN, A LISTING OF
140 REM THESE PLAYERS IN LINE-UP OR ALPHABETICAL SEQUENCE CAN BE
150 REM PRODUCED. THIS HAPPENS BY RESPONDING TO A MENU.
160                                                              REM
170 REM VARIABLE NAMES:
180 REM    N$()..PLAYER NAME ARRAY
190 REM    B()...NUMBER OF AT BATS ARRAY
200 REM    H()...NUMBER OF HITS ARRAY
210 REM    I()...ARRAY OF SUBSCRIPTS OF SORTED DATA
220 REM    D$()..ARRAY IN WHICH DATA TO BE SORTED IS PASSED
230 REM           TO THE SORT MODULE
240 REM    P1$().POSITIONS OF STARTING PLAYERS ARRAY
250 REM    P$....PLAYER POSITION ENTERED BY USER
260 REM    E.....NUMBER OF ENTRIES IN BASEBALL ARRAYS
270 REM    X.....UTILITY COUNTER VARIABLE FOR FOR-NEXT LOOPS
280 REM    S.....MAIN MENU SELECTION - ENTERED BY USER
290 REM    S1....SUBSCRIPT TO LOAD PLAYERS
300 REM    S2....SUBSCRIPT FOR SORT MODULE
310 REM    S3....LINE-UP DISPLAY SUBSCRIPT
320 REM    S4....SUBSCRIPT TO PRINT IN ALPHABETICAL ORDER
330 REM    F1$...PRINT USING FORMAT
340 REM    F2$...PRINT USING FORMAT
350 REM    F3$...PRINT USING FORMAT
360 REM    T1....TOTAL AREA FOR NUMBER OF HITS BY TEAM
370 REM    T2....TOTAL AREA FOR NUMBER OF AT BATS BY TEAM
380 REM    M.....MAXIMUM NUMBER OF PASSES REQUIRED FOR SORT
390 REM    T3....SORT TERMINATION INDICATOR
400 REM    H.....HOLD AREA FOR SUBSCRIPTS - USED BY SORT MODULE
410 REM    H$....HOLD AREA FOR SORT CONTROL FIELDS - USED BY
420 REM           THE SORT MODULE
430 REM    Z$....WORK AREA FOR ENTER OR RETURN KEY
440                                                              REM
450 REM ***********************************************************
460 REM * INITIALIZATION OF VARIABLES                            *
470 REM ***********************************************************
480                                                              REM
490 LET E = 9
500 LET F1$ = "\           \ \              \ .###"
510 LET F2$ = "\           \ \              \ .###"
520 LET F3$ = "   TEAM BATTING AVERAGE .###"
530 DIM N$(E), B(E), H(E), P1$(E), L(E), D$(E), I(E)
540                                                              REM
```

```
550 REM ***********************************************************
560 REM * MAIN PROCESSING MODULE                                  *
570 REM ***********************************************************
580                                                             REM
590 GOSUB 1000
600                                                             REM
610 IF S = 4 THEN 660
620    ON S GOSUB 2000, 3000, 4000
630    GOSUB 1000
640 GOTO 610
650                                                             REM
660 PRINT " "
670 PRINT "END OF BASEBALL PROGRAM"
680 END
1000                                                            REM
1010 REM ***********************************************************
1020 REM * DISPLAY MENU AND GET SELECTION                          *
1030 REM ***********************************************************
1040                                                            REM
1050 CLS
1060 PRINT "B A S E B A L L    M E N U"
1070 PRINT " "
1080 PRINT "CODE        FUNCTION"
1090 PRINT " "
1100 PRINT " 1 - LOAD STARTING PLAYERS"
1110 PRINT " 2 - DISPLAY STARTING PLAYERS IN BATTING ORDER"
1120 PRINT " 3 - DISPLAY PLAYERS IN ALPHABETICAL SEQUENCE"
1130 PRINT " 4 - END PROGRAM"
1140 PRINT " "
1150 INPUT "ENTER A NUMBER 1 THROUGH 4:"; S
1160                                                            REM
1170 IF S >= 1 AND S <= 4 THEN 1230
1180    PRINT " "
1190    PRINT "  "; S; "IS INVALID"
1200    INPUT "        PLEASE REENTER 1, 2, 3, OR 4: "; S
1210 GOTO 1170
1220                                                            REM
1230 RETURN
2000                                                            REM
2010 REM ***********************************************************
2020 REM * LOAD STARTING PLAYERS                                   *
2030 REM***********************************************************
2040                                                            REM
2050 FOR S1 = 1 TO E
2060    CLS
2070    PRINT "LOAD STARTING PLAYERS"
2080    PRINT " "
2090    PRINT "BATTER NUMBER"; S1
2100    PRINT " "
2110    INPUT "   ENTER PLAYER'S NAME: "; N$(S1)
2120    PRINT " "
2130    INPUT "   ENTER PLAYER'S POSITION: "; P1$(S1)
2140    PRINT " "
2150    INPUT "   ENTER PLAYER'S AT BATS: "; B(S1)
2160    PRINT " "
2170    INPUT "   ENTER PLAYER'S HITS: "; H(S1)
2180 NEXT S1
2190                                                            REM
2200 RETURN
```

```
3000                                                         REM
3010 REM ******************************************************
3020 REM * DISPLAY PLAYERS IN BATTING ORDER                  *
3030 REM ******************************************************
3040                                                         REM
3050 CLS
3060 PRINT "        STARTING PLAYERS"
3070 PRINT "         BATTING ORDER"
3080 PRINT " "
3090 PRINT "   NAME         POSITION      AVG"
3100                                                         REM
3110 FOR S3 = 1 TO E
3120    PRINT USING F1$; N$(S3), P1$(S3), H(S3) / B(S3)
3130 NEXT S3
3140                                                         REM
3150 PRINT " "
3160 PRINT "DEPRESS ENTER OR RETURN KEY"
3170 INPUT " TO RETURN TO THE MENU: "; Z$
3180 RETURN
4000                                                         REM
4010 REM ******************************************************
4020 REM * DISPLAY PLAYERS IN ALPHABETICAL SEQUENCE          *
4030 REM ******************************************************
4040                                                         REM
4050 CLS
4060 PRINT "        STARTING PLAYERS"
4070 PRINT "    ALPHABETICAL SEQUENCE"
4080 PRINT " "
4090 PRINT "   NAME         POSITION      AVG"
4100                                                         REM
4110 FOR X = 1 TO E
4120    LET D$(X) = N$(X)
4130 NEXT X
4140                                                         REM
4150 GOSUB 5000
4160                                                         REM
4170 FOR S4 = 1 TO E
4180    PRINT USING F2$; N$(I(S4)), P1$(I(S4)), H(I(S4)) / B(I(S4))
4190 NEXT S4
4200                                                         REM
4210 LET T1 = 0
4220 LET T2 = 0
4230                                                         REM
4240 FOR X = 1 TO E
4250    LET T1 = T1 + H(X)
4260    LET T2 = T2 + B(X)
4270 NEXT X
4280                                                         REM
4290 PRINT USING F3$; T1 / T2
4300 PRINT "DEPRESS ENTER OR RETURN KEY"
4310 INPUT " TO RETURN TO THE MENU: "; Z$
4320 RETURN
```

```
5000                                                          REM
5010 REM *******************************************************
5020 REM * SORT DATA IN D$ ARRAY.  SORTED INDEXES IN I ARRAY.  *
5030 REM *******************************************************
5040                                                          REM
5050 FOR X = 1 TO E
5060    LET I(X) = X
5070 NEXT X
5080                                                          REM
5090 LET M = E - 1
5100 LET T3 = 0
5110                                                          REM
5120 IF T3 = 1 THEN 5350
5130    LET S2 = 1
5140    LET T3 = 1
5150                                                          REM
5160    IF S2 > M THEN 5320
5170       IF D$(S2) > D$(S2 + 1) THEN 5200
5180          GOTO 5290
5190                                                          REM
5200          LET H = I(S2)
5210          LET I(S2) = I(S2 + 1)
5220          LET I(S2 + 1) = H
5230          LET H$ = D$(S2)
5240          LET D$(S2) = D$(S2 + 1)
5250          LET D$(S2 + 1) = H$
5260          LET T3 = S2
5270          GOTO 5290
5280                                                          REM
5290       LET S2 = S2 + 1
5300    GOTO 5160
5310                                                          REM
5320    LET M = T3 - 1
5330 GOTO 5120
5340                                                          REM
5350 RETURN
```

SUMMARY

The following points have been discussed and explained in this chapter.

1. A menu is a listing of those functions that can be performed by a program. The user chooses the function by entering a code from the keyboard.

2. Sorting is the process of placing data in an ascending or descending sequence based upon one or more values in the data.

3. A subroutine is a series of instructions which performs a particular function in a program.

4. Whenever a menu is used in a program, the user must always be given the option of terminating the processing whenever desired.

5. A menu is normally displayed by print statements.

6. When a menu is to be written on a screen, it should normally be the only material on the screen. Therefore, the screen must be cleared prior to displaying the menu.

7. Whenever a code is obtained from a menu selection, it should be edited to ensure that it is valid.

8. When if statements are written to edit input data, the differences between the AND logical operator and the OR logical operator should be carefully evaluated.

9. When designing interactive programs, the communication between the program and the user should be as clear and precise as possible.

10. The type of comparing where multiple operations can occur based upon the value in a single field is called a case structure.

11. The case structure can be implemented through the use of nested if-then-else structures.

12. The use of nested if-then-else structures to implement the case structure will allow any number of cases to be implemented in the same manner, and the field on which the case structure depends can be a numeric or string field.

13. When the value which the case structure checks is numeric, the on goto statement can be used to implement the case structure.

14. When the on goto statement is executed, the integer portion of the specified arithmetic expression or numeric variable is evaluated. If the value is equal to 1, control is transferred to the first line number following the word GOTO. If the value in the variable or arithmetic expression is equal to 2, control is passed to the second line number following the word GOTO, and so on.

15. If the value in the numeric variable or arithmetic expression evaluated by the on goto statement is equal to zero or is greater than the number of line numbers specified in the statement, then the statement immediately following the on goto statement is executed.

16. As programs become larger, the logic may become more complex. Generally in computer programming, largeness leads to complexity.

17. One way in which programs are kept less complex is to subdivide a

large program into two or more smaller parts called subroutines, or modules. Each subroutine performs a particular task in the program. The overall program is simpler because it consists of a number of simple, easy to understand subroutines rather than one large, complex piece of code.

18. A call to a subroutine means that control is transferred from the main program (i.e., the calling program) to the first statement in the subroutine.

19. The last statement in a subroutine returns control to the statement in the calling program immediately following the statement which called the subroutine.

20. The sequence for executing a subroutine consists of the following: a) The subroutine is called; b) The instructions within the subroutine are executed; c) The subroutine returns control to the statement immediately following the statement which called the subroutine.

21. The statement which calls the subroutine establishes a linkage between the calling program and the subroutine. In BASIC, the gosub statement is used to call a subroutine and establish the linkage between the calling program and the called subroutine.

22. The gosub statement consists of a line number, the word GOSUB, and the line number of the first statement in the subroutine which will receive control.

23. The return statement returns control from a subroutine to the statement following the gosub statement in the calling program. It consists of a line number and the word RETURN.

24. The on gosub statement can be used to call subroutines based upon the value in a numeric variable or arithmetic expression.

25. The format of the on gosub statement is the same as the on goto statement except that the line numbers specified after the words ON GOSUB are the beginning lines of a subroutine.

26. When a subroutine is called using the on gosub statement and the subroutine issues the return statement, control is passed from the subroutine to the statement following the on gosub statement.

27. An array can be loaded from data entered by a user from the keyboard through the use of the input statement. The variable specified for the input statement is the name of the array together with the subscript.

28. To add the values in array elements, a for-next loop can be used.

29. A for-next loop can be used to print the elements in an array.

30. When a report is displayed on the CRT screen, the input statement can be used to temporarily halt processing while the user views the report. When finished viewing, the user should depress the return or enter key to return to the menu.

31. Whenever more than one piece or set of data is to be processed in the same manner, consideration should be given to storing the data in an array. Data that is stored in an array will normally be processed in a loop because

each element of the array can be processed by merely changing the subscript to address the appropriate element.

32. If an application is found that uses arrays, the programmer should immediately think in terms of loops when developing the logic for processing the arrays.

33. An algorithm is a series of steps which can be followed to produce a desired result.

34. The essential idea in an exchange sort is to examine the data to be sorted with the goal of placing the data with the highest key in the highest position.

35. The key of the data being sorted is the field or fields on which the sort is taking place.

36. When an exchange sort takes place, the elements of the array being sorted are exchanged if an element in a lower position has a key greater than an element in a higher position.

37. Tasks which are commonly used can many times be written as a subroutine and then be included in any program which requires them. For example, a sort subroutine can be written and then be used by any program which requires sorting.

38. When a generalized subroutine which will be used by many programs is written, the data which it will process should be passed to it in areas different from those used in the program so that the program data is not disturbed. In addition, this allows the subroutine to always use the same variable names regardless of the variable names used in the program which calls it.

39. A generalized subroutine which performs a commonly required task, such as sorting, is a very important tool for the programmer. It can save considerable time and effort because new code need not be designed, written, and tested.

40. Most generalized subroutines have certain rules which must be followed in order to use them.

41. The programmer should know how to write a generalized subroutine and how to use subroutines which might be available.

42. When the elements within multiple arrays must be placed in the same sequence as the data being sorted, there are two methods which can be used. First, the data in the other arrays can be exchanged in the same manner as the data being sorted. This creates more work, more arrays, and can cause the sort subroutine to lose its generality. This approach is not recommended. A second means to solve this problem is to use elements of an array as pointers to elements of other arrays.

43. The elements of an index array contain values which are used as subscripts to reference elements in other arrays. A double subscript consisting of the following is required: a) A subscript to reference the element in the index array; b) The element in the index array which acts as the subscript to actually reference the other array.

44. A major advantage of using an index array is that the arrays being referenced by the index array need not be disturbed.

45. The prime advantage in the use of an index array in a sort subroutine is that the subroutine becomes able to sort any array and allows other arrays to be referenced in the sorted sequence.

46. As programs become larger, they generally become more complex. One way to keep the complexity of a program to a minimum is to subdivide the program into a series of smaller subroutines. The program then consists of a number of relatively simple subroutines rather than one large, complex piece of code.

47. The preferred method for decomposing the program into a series of subroutines, or modules, is to analyze the program tasks. Any program task that performs a specific function and appears to require more than 10 – 15 BASIC statements should be placed in a subroutine.

48. The judgment about how many statements will be required for a program task does not have to be 100% accurate. It is only an estimate to aid in decomposing the program into a series of subroutines.

49. The primary reason for breaking a program into a series of subroutines is to simplify the program.

50. When a program is to consist of a series of subroutines, the relationships of the subroutines in the program will normally be shown through the use of a hierarchy chart.

51. When a program will contain one or more subroutines, the subroutines themselves should be analyzed to determine if they should utilize subroutines.

52. The hierarchy chart of the program shows the structure of the program. Each task which is performed and where within the program it is performed can easily be seen. If, at some future time, the program must be modified in some manner, the hierarchy chart provides a map to where each task is performed.

53. The ability to analyze and decompose a program into modules is a very important skill for the accomplished programmer.

1. What is a menu? What is it used for?
2. The case structure can be implemented using which of the following BASIC statements: a) ON SUB statement; b) ON GO statement; c) IF statement; d) All of the above.
3. Generally in computer programming, largeness leads to simplicity (T or F).
4. A subroutine is a series of programming statements that performs a given task within a program (T or F).
5. The last statement in a subroutine: a) Terminates the program; b) Returns control to the start of the program; c) Returns control to the start of the subroutine; d) Returns control to the statement immediately following the statement which called the subroutine.
6. The sequence for executing a subroutine is: a) _____; b) _____; c) _____.
7. A _____ loop can be used to print the elements of an array.
8. Data that is stored in an array will normally be processed: a) By a subroutine; b) In a loop; c) Through the use of the ON GOTO and RETURN statements; d) Without the benefit of certain BASIC instructions because array elements cannot be used in all BASIC statements.
9. What is an algorithm? What is its value?
10. The key of the data being sorted is the field or fields on which the sort is taking place (T or F).
11. What is an exchange sort? Describe the processing that takes place in an exchange sort.
12. A generalized subroutine is one which: a) Performs many functions which can be chosen by the user when the program is written; b) Performs one function and can be used by any program which requires that function to be done; c) Must always begin with the same line number in every BASIC program in which it is used so that it can be called from anywhere in the program; d) Must normally be written in a language other than BASIC.
13. The primary reason for breaking a program into a series of subroutines: a) Is to make the program execute faster; b) Is to make the program require less main computer storage; c) Is to simplify the program; d) Is to develop a hierarchy chart to show the structure of the program.
14. The baseball manager who uses the sample program in this chapter has found that in many instances the player who is originally entered for a position does not start the game at that position because of last minute decisions. Therefore, the manager has requested that a change be made to the program. The request is that the manager can enter the position, name, at bats, and hits of a new player to replace the player currently in the line-up at the position entered. The batting order does not change. Make the appropriate changes to the sample program to accomplish this.

Chapter 8
DEBUGGING EXERCISES

The following lines of code contain one or more coding errors. Circle each of the errors and write the coding to correct the errors.

1.
```
610 IF S = 4 THEN 660
620    ON GOSUB 2000, 3000, 4000
630    GOSUB 1000
640 GOTO 610
```

2.
```
1150 INPUT "ENTER A NUMBER 1 THROUGH 4:"; S
1160                                                     REM
1170 IF S >= 1 AND S <= 4 THEN 1230
1180    PRINT " "
1190    PRINT " "; S; "IS INVALID"
1200    PRINT "        PLEASE REENTER 1, 2, 3, OR 4: "; S
1210 GOTO 1170
```

3.
```
4110 FOR X = 1 TO E
4120    LET D$(X) = N$(X)
4130 NEXT E
4140                                                     REM
4150 GOSUB 5000
4160                                                     REM
4170 FOR S4 = 1 TO E
4180    PRINT USING F2$; N$(I(S4), P1$(I(S4)), H((I(S4)) / B((S4)
4190 NEXT S4
4200                                                     REM
4210 LET T1 = 0
4220 LET T2 = 0
4230                                                     REM
4240 FOR X = 1 TO E
4250    LET T1 = T1 + H(E)
4260    LET T2 = T2 + B(E)
4270 NEXT X
```

Chapter 8
PROGRAM DEBUGGING

The following program was designed and written to process the baseball team information using the same players, positions, at bats, and hits as shown in Figure 8-4 on page 8.3. The results obtained from the program are illustrated on page 8.57. Analyze the results to determine if they are correct. If they are in error, circle the errors in the program and write corrections.

```
100 REM BASEBALL          FEBRUARY 10          SHELLY/CASHMAN
110                                                      REM
120 REM THIS PROGRAM ALLOWS THE STARTING PLAYERS ON A BASEBALL
130 REM TEAM TO BE LOADED INTO AN ARRAY. THEN, A LISTING OF
140 REM THESE PLAYERS IN LINE-UP OR ALPHABETICAL SEQUENCE CAN BE
150 REM PRODUCED. THIS HAPPENS BY RESPONDING TO A MENU.
160                                                      REM
170 REM VARIABLE NAMES:
180 REM    N$()..PLAYER NAME ARRAY
190 REM    B()...NUMBER OF AT BATS ARRAY
200 REM    H()...NUMBER OF HITS ARRAY
210 REM    I()...ARRAY OF SUBSCRIPTS OF SORTED DATA
220 REM    D$()..ARRAY IN WHICH DATA TO BE SORTED IS PASSED
230 REM          TO THE SORT MODULE
240 REM    P1$().POSITIONS OF STARTING PLAYERS ARRAY
250 REM    P$....PLAYER POSITION ENTERED BY USER
260 REM    E.....NUMBER OF ENTRIES IN BASEBALL ARRAYS
270 REM    X.....UTILITY COUNTER VARIABLE FOR FOR-NEXT LOOPS
280 REM    S.....MAIN MENU SELECTION - ENTERED BY USER
290 REM    S1....SUBSCRIPT TO LOAD PLAYERS
300 REM    S2....SUBSCRIPT FOR SORT MODULE
310 REM    S3....LINE-UP DISPLAY SUBSCRIPT
320 REM    S4....SUBSCRIPT TO PRINT IN ALPHABETICAL ORDER
330 REM    F1$...PRINT USING FORMAT
340 REM    F2$...PRINT USING FORMAT
350 REM    F3$...PRINT USING FORMAT
360 REM    T1....TOTAL AREA FOR NUMBER OF HITS BY TEAM
370 REM    T2....TOTAL AREA FOR NUMBER OF AT BATS BY TEAM
380 REM    M.....MAXIMUM NUMBER OF PASSES REQUIRED FOR SORT
390 REM    T3....SORT TERMINATION INDICATOR
400 REM    H.....HOLD AREA FOR SUBSCRIPTS - USED BY SORT MODULE
410 REM    H$....HOLD AREA FOR SORT CONTROL FIELDS - USED BY
420 REM          THE SORT MODULE
430 REM    Z$....WORK AREA FOR ENTER OR RETURN KEY
440                                                      REM
450 REM ************************************************************
460 REM * INITIALIZATION OF VARIABLES                            *
470 REM ************************************************************
480                                                      REM
490 LET E = 9
500 LET F1$ = "\            \  \              \  .###"
510 LET F2$ = "\            \  \              \  .###"
520 LET F3$ = "    TEAM BATTING AVERAGE .###"
530 DIM N$(E), B(E), H(E), P1$(E), L(E), D$(E), I(E)
540                                                      REM
```

```
550 REM ***********************************************************
560 REM * MAIN PROCESSING MODULE                                 *
570 REM ***********************************************************
580                                                            REM
590 GOSUB 1000
600                                                            REM
610 IF S = 4 THEN 660
620   ON S GOSUB 2000, 3000, 4000
630   GOSUB 1000
640 GOTO 610
650                                                            REM
660 PRINT " "
670 PRINT "END OF BASEBALL PROGRAM"
680 END
1000                                                           REM
1010 REM **********************************************************
1020 REM * DISPLAY MENU AND GET SELECTION                        *
1030 REM **********************************************************
1040                                                           REM
1050 CLS
1060 PRINT "B A S E B A L L    M E N U"
1070 PRINT " "
1080 PRINT "CODE       FUNCTION"
1090 PRINT " "
1100 PRINT " 1 - LOAD STARTING PLAYERS"
1110 PRINT " 2 - DISPLAY STARTING PLAYERS IN BATTING ORDER"
1120 PRINT " 3 - DISPLAY PLAYERS IN ALPHABETICAL SEQUENCE"
1130 PRINT " 4 - END PROGRAM"
1140 PRINT " "
1150 INPUT "ENTER A NUMBER 1 THROUGH 4:"; S
1160                                                           REM
1170 IF S >= 1 AND S <= 4 THEN 1230
1180   PRINT " "
1190   PRINT " "; S; "IS INVALID"
1200   INPUT "         PLEASE REENTER 1, 2, 3, OR 4: "; S
1210 GOTO 1170
1220                                                           REM
1230 RETURN
2000                                                           REM
2010 REM **********************************************************
2020 REM * LOAD STARTING PLAYERS                                 *
2030 REM**********************************************************
2040                                                           REM
2050 FOR S1 = 1 TO E
2060   CLS
2070   PRINT "LOAD STARTING PLAYERS"
2080   PRINT " "
2090   PRINT "BATTER NUMBER"; S1
2100   PRINT " "
2110   INPUT "    ENTER PLAYER'S NAME: "; N$(S1)
2120   PRINT " "
2130   INPUT "    ENTER PLAYER'S POSITION: "; P1$(S1)
2140   PRINT " "
2150   INPUT "    ENTER PLAYER'S AT BATS: "; B(S1)
2160   PRINT " "
2170   INPUT "    ENTER PLAYER'S HITS: "; H(S1)
2180 NEXT S1
2190                                                           REM
2200 RETURN
```

```
3000                                                              REM
3010 REM ***********************************************************
3020 REM * DISPLAY PLAYERS IN BATTING ORDER                       *
3030 REM ***********************************************************
3040                                                              REM
3050 CLS
3060 PRINT "        STARTING PLAYERS"
3070 PRINT "         BATTING ORDER"
3080 PRINT " "
3090 PRINT "   NAME        POSITION     AVG"
3100                                                              REM
3110 FOR S3 = 1 TO E
3120    PRINT USING F1$; N$(S3), P1$(S3), H(S3) / B(S3)
3130 NEXT S3
3140                                                              REM
3150 PRINT " "
3160 PRINT "DEPRESS ENTER OR RETURN KEY"
3170 INPUT " TO RETURN TO THE MENU: "; Z$
3180 RETURN
4000                                                              REM
4010 REM ***********************************************************
4020 REM * DISPLAY PLAYERS IN ALPHABETICAL SEQUENCE               *
4030 REM ***********************************************************
4040                                                              REM
4050 CLS
4060 PRINT "        STARTING PLAYERS"
4070 PRINT "     ALPHABETICAL SEQUENCE"
4080 PRINT " "
4090 PRINT "   NAME        POSITION     AVG"
4100                                                              REM
4110 FOR X = 1 TO E
4120    LET D$(X) = N$(X)
4130 NEXT X
4140                                                              REM
4150 GOSUB 5000
4160                                                              REM
4170 FOR S4 = 1 TO E
4180    PRINT USING F2$; N$(I(S4)), P1$(I(S4)), H(I(S4)) / B(I(S4))
4190 NEXT S4
4200                                                              REM
4210 LET T1 = 0
4220 LET T2 = 0
4230                                                              REM
4240 FOR X = 1 TO E
4250    LET T1 = T1 + H(X)
4260    LET T2 = T2 + B(X)
4270 NEXT X
4280                                                              REM
4290 PRINT USING F3$; T1 / T2
4300 PRINT "DEPRESS ENTER OR RETURN KEY"
4310 INPUT " TO RETURN TO THE MENU: "; Z$
4320 RETURN
```

```
5000                                                                  REM
5010 REM **********************************************************
5020 REM * SORT DATA IN D$ ARRAY. SORTED INDEXES IN I ARRAY.    *
5030 REM **********************************************************
5040                                                                  REM
5050 FOR X = 1 TO E
5060    LET I(X) = X
5070 NEXT X
5080                                                                  REM
5090 LET M = E - 1
5100 LET T3 = 0
5110                                                                  REM
5120 IF T3 = 1 THEN 5350
5130    LET S2 = 1
5140    LET T3 = 1
5150                                                                  REM
5160    IF S2 > M THEN 5320
5170      IF D$(S2) > D$(S2 + 1) THEN 5200
5180        GOTO 5290
5190                                                                  REM
5200        LET H = I(S2)
5210        LET I(S2) = I(S2 + 1)
5220        LET I(S2 + 1) = I(S2)
5230        LET H$ = D$(S2)
5240        LET D$(S2) = D$(S2 + 1)
5250        LET D$(S2 + 1) = H$
5260        LET T3 = S2
5270        GOTO 5290
5280                                                                  REM
5290      LET S2 = S2 + 1
5300    GOTO 5160
5310                                                                  REM
5320    LET M = T3 - 1
5330 GOTO 5120
5340                                                                  REM
5350 RETURN
```

Output

```
B A S E B A L L    M E N U

CODE       FUNCTION

 1 - LOAD STARTING PLAYERS
 2 - DISPLAY STARTING PLAYERS IN BATTING ORDER
 3 - DISPLAY PLAYERS IN ALPHABETICAL SEQUENCE
 4 - END PROGRAM

ENTER A NUMBER 1 THROUGH 4:? 3
```

```
              STARTING PLAYERS
             ALPHABETICAL SEQUENCE

    NAME          POSITION       AVG
ALLEN           THIRD BASE       .274
ALLEN           THIRD BASE       .274
CRAIYERSON      PITCHER          .115
CRAIYERSON      PITCHER          .115
CRAIYERSON      PITCHER          .115
CRAIYERSON      PITCHER          .115
CRAIYERSON      PITCHER          .115
CRAIYERSON      PITCHER          .115
CRAIYERSON      PITCHER          .115
CRAIYERSON      PITCHER          .115
      TEAM BATTING AVERAGE .251
DEPRESS ENTER OR RETURN KEY
TO RETURN TO THE MENU: ?
```

Chapter 8
PROGRAMMING ASSIGNMENT 1

Instructions Bookstore listings of books are to be prepared. A program should be designed and coded in BASIC to produce the listings.

When the program in this programming assignment is tested, it may become tedious to enter the information required each time the program is executed. For testing purposes only, therefore, it is allowable to define the input data by data statements and use the read statement to load the arrays necessary for sorting and creating the reports. It must be noted, however, that the portion of the program which accepts the input data from the keyboard and edits that data must be tested and be part of the program when the program is completed.

Menu The program utilizes a menu which is illustrated below.

```
BOOKSTORE     MENU

CODE      FUNCTION

  1 - ENTER BOOK INFORMATION
  2 - LIST BOOKS BY TITLE
  3 - LIST BOOKS BY AUTHOR
  4 - END PROGRAM

ENTER CODE 1, 2, 3, OR 4:
```

The four functions which can be performed by the program allow the user to enter book information, list the books entered in alphabetical sequence by title, list the books entered in alphabetical sequence by author, and end the program.

Enter book information The following screen should be developed when book information is entered. For this program, six books should be entered by the user. The book information is shown on the reports on page 8.59.

```
ENTER BOOK INFORMATION

BOOK NUMBER 1

   BOOK TITLE:
   BOOK AUTHOR:
   QUANTITY:
   BOOK PRICE:
```

The following report should be prepared when the user selects menu code 2.

```
        BOOK REPORT BY TITLE

     TITLE          AUTHOR      QTY   PRICE

  FAST WATER      NUMOVICH      12   12.95
  SEA AND STONE   ALLERGEN       8   12.95
  SHOCK LIGHT     BRANNIGAN     21   14.95
  THE MARCHERS    IOTAY          8   10.95
  TORCH GAS       CRITENER      14   15.95
  WINDS OF TIME   POLLUTEY       4   12.95

  TOTAL QUANTITY:  67
  TOTAL VALUE: $   935.65

  DEPRESS ENTER OR RETURN KEY
   TO RETURN TO THE MENU:
```

Note that the report is in alphabetical sequence by book title. The total quantity of books is obtained by adding the quantity for each of the books. The total value of the books is obtained by multiplying the quantity of each book by the price for each book and adding the results.

The following report should be prepared when the user selects menu code 3.

```
        BOOK REPORT BY AUTHOR

     AUTHOR         TITLE       QTY   PRICE

  ALLERGEN     SEA AND STONE     8   12.95
  BRANNIGAN    SHOCK LIGHT      21   14.95
  CRITENER     TORCH GAS        14   15.95
  IOTAY        THE MARCHERS      8   10.95
  NUMOVICH     FAST WATER       12   12.95
  POLLUTEY     WINDS OF TIME     4   12.95

  DEPRESS ENTER OR RETURN KEY
   TO RETURN TO THE MENU:
```

The book report by author is in alphabetical sequence by author.

Appropriate editing and error messages should be designed by the programmer. It is store policy that the maximum quantity of any title is fifty books. No book should be priced under $1.00 or more than $49.95.

Chapter 8
PROGRAMMING ASSIGNMENT 2

Instructions

Class listings for a school are to be prepared. A program should be designed and coded in BASIC to produce the listings.

For testing purposes only, it is allowable to define the input data by data statements and use the read statement to load the arrays necessary for sorting and creating the reports. It must be noted, however, that the portion of the program which accepts the input data from the keyboard and edits that data must be tested and be part of the program when the program is completed.

Menu

The program utilizes a menu (page 8.61). The five functions which can be performed by the program allow the user to enter class information, display the classes in alphabetical sequence by class name, display the classes in alphabetical sequence by teacher name, and perform an inquiry to obtain the teacher name and class enrollment based upon the name of the class.

Enter class information

The screen on page 8.61 should be developed when class information is entered (menu code 1). For this program, six classes and the corresponding data should be entered. The class information is shown on the reports.

Class listing in class name sequence

The report on page 8.61 should be prepared when the user selects menu code 2. It is in alphabetical sequence by class name. The total enrollment for all classes is calculated by adding the enrollments for each of the classes.

Class listing in teacher name sequence

The class listing in alphabetical sequence by teacher name (page 8.61) should be prepared when the user selects menu code 3.

Teacher name and enrollment inquiry

When the user chooses code 4 from the menu, an inquiry should be performed to obtain the teacher name and class enrollment from the class name entered by the user (see page 8.61). The user should enter the class name. In response, the program should print the teacher name and the class enrollment.

Input editing

Appropriate editing and error messages should be designed by the programmer. No class is allowed to contain more than 600 or fewer than 10 students.

```
C L A S S    M E N U                                          Menu

CODE      FUNCTION

1 - ENTER CLASS INFORMATION
2 - DISPLAY IN CLASS NAME SEQUENCE
3 - DISPLAY IN TEACHER NAME SEQUENCE
4 - OBTAIN TEACHER NAME AND ENROLLMENT
5 - END PROGRAM

ENTER 1, 2, 3, 4, OR 5 TO MAKE SELECTION:
```

Menu

```
ENTER CLASS INFORMATION

    CLASS NUMBER 1

        ENTER CLASS NAME:
        ENTER TEACHER NAME:
        ENTER ENROLLMENT:
```

Code 1 - Enter Class Information

```
              CLASS LISTING
              CLASS SEQUENCE

    CLASS       TEACHER   ENROLL.

    BUS 231   HARRELSON      128
    BUS 429   ABBOTT          32
    CHE 112   CHEMONTE       359
    CHE 213   ZUNDERREY       21
    PHY 101   NOMMERREI      573
    SOC 219   BERRET          45


    TOTAL ENROLLMENT   1,158

DEPRESS ENTER OR RETURN KEY
  TO RETURN TO THE MENU:
```

Code 2 - Class Listing in Class Name Sequence

```
              CLASS LISTING
              TEACHER SEQUENCE

                    CLASS
    TEACHER         NAME   ENROLL.

    ABBOTT        BUS 429     32
    BERRET        SOC 219     45
    CHEMONTE      CHE 112    359
    HARRELSON     BUS 231    128
    NOMMERREI     PHY 101    573
    ZUNDERREY     CHE 213     21

DEPRESS ENTER OR RETURN KEY
  TO RETURN TO THE MENU:
```

Code 3 - Class Listing in Teacher Name Sequence

```
OBTAIN TEACHER NAME AND ENROLLMENT

    ENTER CLASS NAME:

    TEACHER:
    ENROLLMENT:


DEPRESS ENTER OR RETURN KEY
  TO RETURN TO THE MENU:
```

Code 4 - Obtain Teacher Name and Enrollment

STRING PROCESSING

OBJECTIVES:

An understanding of the process used to create a personalized letter using the string functions

The ability to edit input data using the string functions

The ability to use the string functions available with most BASIC interpreters

The ability to search strings for delimiters and substrings

An understanding of the design process for a program requiring numerous modules

STRING
PROCESSING

Many applications require the manipulation of string data. In word processing applications, for example, it is often necessary to place names and addresses at various points within letters or other correspondence. Information retrieval applications may require the text to be searched for the occurence of certain words, characters, or phrases. In addition, when interactive or transaction-oriented processing is taking place, the alphabetic or alphanumeric data entered by the user may have to be edited to ensure that valid data is entered in the prescribed format.

For applications of this type, BASIC provides a specific set of string functions which allows string data to be easily manipulated. This chapter illustrates the use of many of the string functions available with most BASIC interpreters.

The sample program in this chapter produces a personalized sales letter to be sent to selected individuals. The user enters the title (Mr. or Ms.), the first and last name of the individual to receive the letter, their address, their city and state, and their zip code. The program then generates a letter with their name and address printed in various places within the letter. The program also prints mailing labels for the people receiving the letters.

The program is menu-driven. The menu used in the program is shown in Figure 9–1.

```
S A L E S   L E T T E R   M E N U

   CODE          FUNCTION

    1 - DISPLAY INSTRUCTIONS
    2 - CREATE SALES LETTER
    3 - CREATE MAILING LABELS
    4 - END PROGRAM

  ENTER A NUMBER 1 THROUGH 4:  ?
```

Figure 9-1 The sales letter menu allows instructions for using the program to be displayed, the sales letter to be created, the mailing labels to be created, and the program to be terminated.

When the user selects code 1, detailed instructions specifying how to use the program are printed. In many applications, the user will never have used the program or will not have used the program for a long period of time. In addition, since the data entered by the user is edited, the user may want some help when entering data. Therefore, it is common for a selection on the menu to provide for printing instructions on how to use the program.

Instructions to the user

The instructions which are printed when code 1 is selected from the menu are illustrated in Figure 9-2.

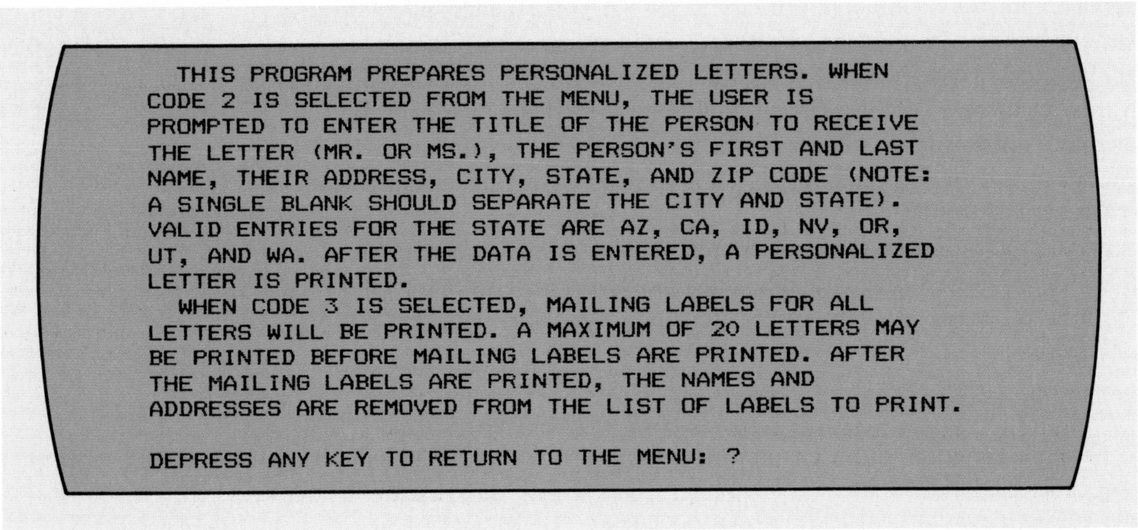

```
     THIS PROGRAM PREPARES PERSONALIZED LETTERS. WHEN
CODE 2 IS SELECTED FROM THE MENU, THE USER IS
PROMPTED TO ENTER THE TITLE OF THE PERSON TO RECEIVE
THE LETTER (MR. OR MS.), THE PERSON'S FIRST AND LAST
NAME, THEIR ADDRESS, CITY, STATE, AND ZIP CODE (NOTE:
A SINGLE BLANK SHOULD SEPARATE THE CITY AND STATE).
VALID ENTRIES FOR THE STATE ARE AZ, CA, ID, NV, OR,
UT, AND WA. AFTER THE DATA IS ENTERED, A PERSONALIZED
LETTER IS PRINTED.
   WHEN CODE 3 IS SELECTED, MAILING LABELS FOR ALL
LETTERS WILL BE PRINTED. A MAXIMUM OF 20 LETTERS MAY
BE PRINTED BEFORE MAILING LABELS ARE PRINTED. AFTER
THE MAILING LABELS ARE PRINTED, THE NAMES AND
ADDRESSES ARE REMOVED FROM THE LIST OF LABELS TO PRINT.

DEPRESS ANY KEY TO RETURN TO THE MENU:  ?
```

Figure 9-2 When code 1 is selected from the menu, instructions for using the program are displayed.

The instructions state what the program does and how the user can implement its functions. If, when using the program, there are any questions, the user can refer to these instructions for guidance.

Creating the personalized letter

When code 2 is selected, the sales letter is created. The data is entered by the user, and the letter is printed. The user is first directed to enter the title and first and last name of the person to receive the letter. Next, prompts direct that their address, city and state, and zip code be entered. The screen used for this purpose is shown in Figure 9-3.

The prompts request each of the entries. The user must enter the data according to the format requirements of the program (see page 9.4 for a detailed explanation).

After the user has entered the data, the personalized letter is produced. The letter contains standard wording with the information entered by the user inserted at certain locations. The letter generated from the information entered in Figure 9-3 is shown in Figure 9-4.

The letter begins with the name, address, city and state, and zip code entered by the user. The salutation then uses the title and the last name entered (that is, Dear Mr. Whitley). The last name is inserted in the first sentence of

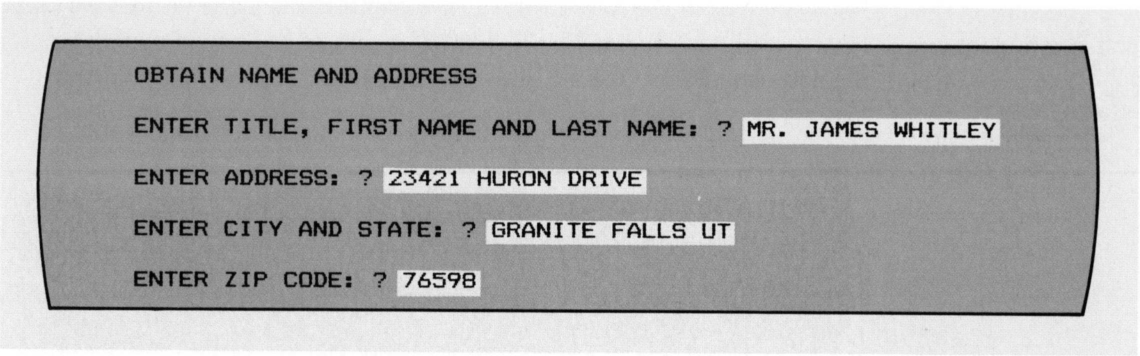

```
OBTAIN NAME AND ADDRESS

ENTER TITLE, FIRST NAME AND LAST NAME: ? MR. JAMES WHITLEY

ENTER ADDRESS: ? 23421 HURON DRIVE

ENTER CITY AND STATE: ? GRANITE FALLS UT

ENTER ZIP CODE: ? 76598
```

the letter (The Whitley family). The city entered is used in the third sentence (from your home in Granite Falls to Hawaii). Finally, the title and last name are used in the fourth sentence.

The data which is entered by the user is inserted in the letter through the use of special string functions available with most BASIC interpreters and compilers. Note that several different types of activities are performed. First, the title and name entered by the user must be searched to find and isolate the last name. Similarly, the title must be separated from the name. The city name must also be separated from the city and state which is entered. Finally, all this data must be inserted into the text of the letter at the appropriate places.

It is the purpose of this chapter to illustrate how this and other processing can be accomplished using string data.

Figure 9-3 When code 2 is selected, the user is first asked to enter name and address information for the person to receive the letter. When the information is entered, an exact format must be followed.

```
MR. JAMES WHITLEY
23421 HURON DRIVE
GRANITE FALLS, UT 76598

DEAR MR. WHITLEY:

     THE WHITLEY FAMILY HAS BECOME
ELIGIBLE TO RECEIVE AN EXPENSE-PAID TRIP
FROM YOUR HOME IN GRANITE FALLS TO HAWAII.
     MR. WHITLEY, PLEASE RETURN THE
ENCLOSED CARD TO DETERMINE IF YOU HAVE
WON YOUR FREE TRIP TO HAWAII.

          REAL ESTATE TIMESHARING

DEPRESS ANY KEY TO RETURN TO THE MENU: ?
```

Figure 9-4 After the information is entered, a letter is written using the information entered by the user. The name and city are inserted into the text of the letter.

**Creating the
mailing labels**

Selection 3 from the menu will cause mailing labels to be printed for those letters which have already been created. A sample of these mailing labels for the data entered in Figure 9-3 as well as another individual is illustrated in Figure 9-5.

```
MR. JAMES WHITLEY
23421 HURON DRIVE
GRANITE FALLS, UT 76598


MS. NANCY HALSTROM
3321 ROCKVALE LANE
SPRINGVILLE, OR 96439


DEPRESS ANY KEY TO RETURN TO THE MENU:  ?
```

Figure 9-5 When the user selects code 3 from the menu, the mailing labels for those people who have received a letter are printed.

As can be seen, the mailing labels consist of the information entered by the user. Up to twenty letters can be printed before the mailing labels are printed.

Editing input data

In previous sample programs, some of the data entered by the user has been edited to ensure that it is valid. For example, in response to a question, the user was required to answer yes or no. No other answer was accepted.

In most interactive programs, a great deal more editing is required. The editing attempts to ensure that valid data is being entered. In the sample program, the data must conform to the following formats and values:

1. The code entered by the user in response to the menu must be 1, 2, 3, or 4. No other value is valid.
2. The name title must be MR. or MS., including the periods. No other title is valid.
3. A single space must separate the title from the first name. More than one space or no space is not valid.
4. A single space must separate the first name from the last name. More than one space or no space is not valid.
5. The minimum number of characters for the title and name entry is seven (MS. F L).
6. The address is an optional entry. If no street address is required, the user should merely hit the enter or return key. If no address is entered by the user, the city and state should be printed on the line directly below the name. A blank line should not be printed on the letter or on the mailing labels.

7. The city and state entries must be separated by a single space. A comma is not to be specified in the city-state entry.
8. The state entry must be one of the following two-character codes: AZ, CA, ID, NV, OR, UT, or WA. Any other entry for the state is invalid.
9. The minimum number of characters for the city-state entry is four (C WA).
10. The zip code must consist of five digits or nine digits. Any other number of digits is invalid.

Each time the user enters data, the data will be edited against the criteria specified above. If any of the data entered violates these rules, an appropriate message will be displayed, and the user will be asked to enter correct data. The letter will be displayed only after valid data has been entered.

It should be noted that it is not possible for a program to determine that all entries made by a user are correct. For example, if a person's last name is spelled SMITH and the user enters SMYTH, the program has no way of determining that the name entered is invalid. The user, therefore, must examine the data that is entered to ensure that it is correct. The fact that the program will edit input data does not relieve the user of the responsibility for checking entries made on the keyboard.

STRING FUNCTIONS

To obtain user responses and edit the data, string functions are used. The following sections explain string functions that are commonly available with most BASIC interpreters.

INKEY$ function

In previous programs, the input statement has been used to obtain data from keyboard entries by the user. When a single character is to be entered from the keyboard, such as when the user chooses a selection from the menu, the INKEY$ function can be used. An example of the INKEY$ function is illustrated in Figure 9–6.

Figure 9-6 The INKEY$ function allows a single character to be entered by the user.

General Format

line number   LET   string variable = INKEY$

```
1150 PRINT "ENTER A NUMBER 1 THROUGH 4: ?";
1160 LET R$ = INKEY$
1170                                                     REM
1180 IF R$ <> "" THEN 1220
1190    LET R$ = INKEY$
1200 GOTO 1180
1210                                                     REM
1220 PRINT R$
```

In Figure 9-6, the prompt printed on line 1150 is followed by the let statement on line 1160 that contains the INKEY$ function. The INKEY$ function checks the keyboard to determine if a key has been struck. If a key has been depressed on the keyboard, the character entered is returned by the INKEY$ function. The let statement then places this character in the field identified by the string variable to the left of the equal sign. On line 1160, if a key on the keyboard has been depressed, the value entered will be stored in the R$ variable field by the let statement.

The INKEY$ function, unlike the input statement, does not cause the program to halt until the user enters a value and then depresses the enter or return key. Instead, if a key has not been depressed, a null character is returned, and control passes to the statement immediately following the let statement which contains the INKEY$ function. A null character signifies that no entry has been made from the keyboard. It is tested for through the use of double quotation marks with no space between the quotation marks. The if statement on line 1180 in Figure 9-6 tests if a null character has been returned.

Since the INKEY$ function does not halt to wait for a user response, the normal method for using this function is to place the program in a loop to await the response. The loop on lines 1180-1200 performs this task. The if statement on line 1180 tests for a null character. If the field identified by the variable name R$ does not contain a null character, then a character has been entered, and control is passed to line 1220. If the value in R$ is a null character, then a character has not yet been entered from the keyboard and the loop is entered. The only statement within the loop is a let statement containing the INKEY$ function. If a key on the keyboard has been depressed, the value entered will be placed in R$. Otherwise a null character is returned. The goto statement on line 1200 passes control back to the if statement on line 1180. This loop will continue until a key is depressed on the keyboard. When a key is depressed, the value which has been entered and stored in R$ can be displayed, compared, or used in any way required by the program.

A major reason the INKEY$ function finds use is that the return or enter key need not be depressed to enter data into main computer storage from the keyboard. Therefore, when only a single character must be entered, it is much faster to depress a single key and cause the desired processing to occur instead of depressing two keys (the key desired and the return or enter key).

An additional benefit of the INKEY$ function is that the operation of the program need not be interrupted while awaiting a response from the keyboard. This feature finds application in games which are played on a computer system where the user must depress a key to affect the playing of the game. To illustrate this feature of the INKEY$ function, the coding in Figure 9-7 will print the character entered from the keyboard across the screen. When a character is entered from the keyboard, that character is immediately printed across the screen. The character just entered will be printed until another

```
100 LET P$ = INKEY$
110                                                    REM
120 IF P$ <> "" THEN 160
130    LET P$ = INKEY$
140 GOTO 120
150                                                    REM
160 LET C$ = P$
170                                                    REM
180 IF C$ = "E" THEN 270
190    PRINT C$;
200    LET P$ = INKEY$
210    IF P$ = "" THEN 250
220       LET C$ = P$
230       GOTO 250
240                                                    REM
250 GOTO 180
260                                                    REM
270 PRINT " "
280 PRINT "END OF PROGRAM"
290 END
```

character is entered, at which time the new character will be printed. This will continue until the value E is entered, at which time the program is terminated.

The loop on lines 120 – 140 waits until a key is depressed for the first time before any printing takes place. Once a key is depressed, the value returned by the INKEY$ function that was stored in P$ by the let statement on line 130 is placed in the C$ field by the let statement on line 160. If the value entered is E, the processing is terminated. Otherwise, the value is printed, and the INKEY$ function is performed again (line 200). If a key has been depressed, the new value is placed in the C$ field (line 220). Otherwise, no change is made to the C$ field, and it is printed on the next pass of the loop.

The INKEY$ function is also used in the sample program to halt the processing while the user views the CRT screen. The coding to accomplish this is shown in Figure 9–8.

Figure 9-7 In this example, the loop on lines 180 – 250 will continually print a character across the screen. Although this particular application would not normally be used, the ability to dynamically enter data that alters the processing without requiring the program to halt can be mandatory in some applications.

```
2210 PRINT "DEPRESS ANY KEY TO RETURN TO THE MENU: ?";
2220 LET X$ = INKEY$
2230                                                   REM
2240 IF X$ <> "" THEN 2280
2250    LET X$ = INKEY$
2260 GOTO 2240
2270                                                   REM
2280 RETURN
```

Figure 9-8 The INKEY$ function is used here to allow the user to depress any key and continue with program execution. On some computer systems, the INKEY$ function is not available. Instead, the GET command may be used; or the computer system may not have the capability of the INKEY$ function.

The user is given the prompt to depress any key to continue by the print statement on line 2210. The let statement on line 2220 and the loop on lines 2240 to 2260 will wait until the user depresses a key. The value of the key is not checked. When any key is depressed, control exits from the loop, and the return statement on line 2280 is executed.

VAL function   Data which is stored in a string field cannot be used in calculations or other instructions where numeric fields are required. For example, the on gosub statement requires that the field specified be a numeric field. A string field cannot be used with the on gosub statement.

It often occurs, however, that a string field can contain numeric data which will have to be used in a statement which requires a numeric field. In the sample program, the INKEY$ function is used to obtain the menu selection from the user (see Figure 9–6). The value entered is stored in a string variable, as required by the INKEY$ function. To use this value in an on gosub statement, it must be allowed to be used as a numeric value. This can be accomplished by the VAL function, as illustrated in Figure 9–9.

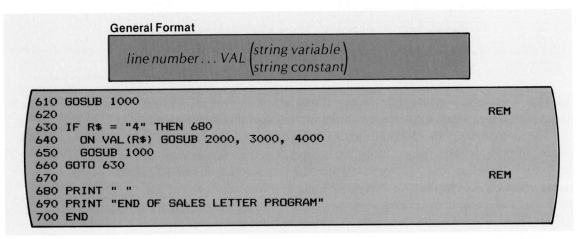

General Format

$$line\ number\ldots VAL \begin{pmatrix} string\ variable \\ string\ constant \end{pmatrix}$$

```
610 GOSUB 1000
620                                                              REM
630 IF R$ = "4" THEN 680
640    ON VAL(R$) GOSUB 2000, 3000, 4000
650    GOSUB 1000
660 GOTO 630
670                                                              REM
680 PRINT " "
690 PRINT "END OF SALES LETTER PROGRAM"
700 END
```

Figure 9-9 The VAL function is used to allow the value in a string field to be used in a statement that requires a numeric field. In this example, the VAL function allows the numeric value in R$ to be used with the on gosub statement.

The VAL function allows the data contained in the string variable field or string constant contained in the parentheses following the word VAL to be used in BASIC statements which require numeric fields or constants. In Figure 9–9, the value in R$ is between 1 and 4, as ensured by the editing of the menu selection entered by the user. If it is equal to 4, control is passed from the loop, and the program is terminated. If, however, the value in R$ is not equal to 4, the on gosub statement on line 640 is executed to send control to the appropriate subroutine. The VAL function with the R$ variable name in parentheses allows the value in R$ to be treated as a numeric value. Therefore, it can be used in the on gosub statement.

When a string contains one or more numeric values followed by alphanumeric characters, the leading number is referenced when using the VAL function and the alphanumeric data remaining in the field is ignored. This is illustrated in Figure 9–10.

Note that the string constant contains a number followed by alphabetic data. The VAL function utilizes the numeric data at the beginning of the constant and ignores the remaining data.

Program

```
5320 PRINT VAL("21 YEARS OF AGE")
```

Output

```
21
```

Figure 9-10 The leading numeric value is extracted from the constant and is printed. Note that the value returned by the VAL function is numeric and is printed according to the rules for numeric values; that is, when the numeric value is positive, the first position is printed as a blank.

If the string constant or variable field contains no numeric data when the VAL function is executed, the VAL function will return the value zero.

LEN function

The LEN function is used to determine the number of characters in a string constant or variable. The general format of the function, together with an example of its use, is shown in Figure 9-11.

Program

```
5320 PRINT LEN("MR. WILLIAM LOOMIS")
```

OR

```
5310 LET L = LEN("MR. WILLIAM LOOMIS")
5320 PRINT L
```

Output

```
18
```

Figure 9-11 The LEN function returns a numeric value that is the number of characters in a string constant or variable. Here, the string constant contains 18 characters. The value returned by the LEN function is numeric, so it is printed according to the rules for numeric values.

To utilize the function, the word LEN is followed by a string variable or constant enclosed within parentheses. Upon execution of the function, the length of the string is returned. Thus, when the print statement on line 5320 is executed, the number of characters in the constant contained within the parentheses is printed. The LEN function can be specified in any BASIC statement where a numeric value is allowed, as in the let statement on line 5310.

In the sample program in this chapter, the editing criteria specifies that the zip code must be five or nine digits in length. The coding from the sample program to input the zip code and check its length is illustrated in Figure 9-12.

Figure 9-12 The LEN function is used to edit the number of characters entered for the zip code. An element of a string array is used with the LEN function. Any string field or constant can be used. Note that the values 5 and 9 in the comparison are specified as numeric rather than string constants because the value returned by the LEN function is numeric.

```
3140 INPUT "ENTER ZIP CODE: "; Z$(I)
3150                                                        REM
3160 IF LEN(Z$(I)) = 5 OR LEN(Z$(I)) = 9 THEN 3220
3170    PRINT "   ERROR - ZIP CODE MUST BE 5 OR 9 DIGITS"
3180    PRINT " "
3190    INPUT " PLEASE REENTER ZIP CODE: "; Z$(I)
3200 GOTO 3160
```

The input statement on line 3140 will place the zip code entered by the user in the Ith element of the Z$ array. The if statement on line 3160 then tests if the length of the value entered is equal to 5 or 9. If so, control is passed to the statement at line 3220. If the number of digits entered is not equal to 5 or 9, then an error message is written, and the user is requested to reenter the zip code. This editing checks the number of digits entered but does not check that the correct zip code was entered. Therefore, this editing is to ensure that the correct format is used when entering the input data.

The variable name specified for the LEN function must be a string variable name. A numeric variable name or constant cannot be used for the LEN function.

STR$ function

In some applications, it may be necessary to determine the length of a numeric field. Since the LEN function requires a string variable, the numeric variable must be referenced as a string variable. This is accomplished through the use of the STR$ function (Figure 9–13).

Figure 9–13 The STR$ function allows a numeric field or constant to be referenced as a string field or constant. When the STR$ function is executed, if the number is positive, a blank precedes the first digit in the string field returned. If the number is negative, a negative sign is placed in the first position of the string field. In this example, since the quantity is positive, the string field will contain a blank in the first position. Therefore, if the number entered by the user is greater than three digits, the input statement on line 4350 will be executed.

General Format

$$STR\$ \begin{Bmatrix} numeric\ variable \\ numeric\ constant \end{Bmatrix}$$

```
4330 INPUT "ENTER INVENTORY QUANTITY: "; Q
4340 IF LEN(STR$(Q)) < 5 THEN 4390
4350   INPUT "QUANTITY IS TOO LARGE - PLEASE REENTER: "; Q
4360   :
```

The STR$ function allows the numeric constant or variable field specified within the parentheses to be treated as a string field. The entry STR$ (numeric variable name) can be used in any BASIC statement which requires or allows a string variable. On line 4330 of the example above, an inventory quantity is entered and stored in the field identified by the numeric variable name Q. The number of digits entered is checked by the if statement on line 4340. The LEN function requires a string variable. Therefore, the STR$ function is used to allow the numeric variable Q to be used with the LEN function.

LEFT$ function

The LEFT$ function is used to make available a specified number of characters from a string starting with the leftmost position. The general format and an example of the LEFT$ function is shown in Figure 9–14. The word LEFT$ must be specified as shown. The first entry within the parentheses is the string constant or string variable from which the characters are to be extracted. This entry must be followed by a comma.

The second entry specifies the number of digits beginning with the leftmost position that are to be extracted. In the example, the entry contains the

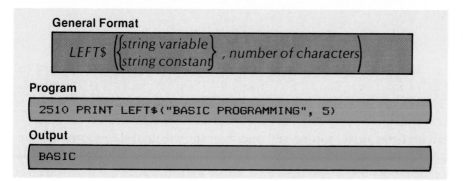

General Format

$$LEFT\$ \left\{ {string\ variable \atop string\ constant} \right\} ,\ number\ of\ characters$$

Program

```
2510 PRINT LEFT$("BASIC PROGRAMMING", 5)
```

Output

```
BASIC
```

Figure 9-14 The LEFT$ function in this example extracts the leftmost five characters of the string constant.

value five. Therefore, the five leftmost characters in the string constant (BASIC) are printed. The LEFT$ function can be used in any statement that requires or allows a string variable.

In the sample program, one editing requirement is that the title entered be either MR. or MS. The LEFT$ function is used when the title and name field is edited, as illustrated in Figure 9-15.

```
5470    IF LEFT$(N$, 3) = "MR." OR LEFT$(N$, 3) = "MS." THEN 5520
5480      PRINT "   ERROR - TITLE MUST BE MR. OR MS."
5490      LET E1$ = "ERROR IN NAME"
5500      GOTO 5520
5510        .                                                          REM
            .
5520        .
            .
```

The title, first name, and last name are stored in the string field identified by the variable name N$. The LEFT$ function in the if statement on line 5470 specifies that the leftmost three characters in the N$ field are to be compared to the constant MR. and the constant MS. If either of the comparisons is true, the data is valid, and control is passed to the statement on line 5520. If the leftmost three characters in the N$ field are not equal to MR. or MS., then an error message is written, and an indicator (E1$) is set to indicate that there is an error in the name entered by the user.

Figure 9-15 The LEFT$ function extracts the three leftmost characters in the N$ field for comparison to the constants MR. and MS.

String functions can be combined in a single statement. The print statement in Figure 9-16 illustrates the LEN and LEFT$ functions in the same statement.

Program

```
4120    PRINT LEFT$(C$(X), LEN(C$(X)) - 3); ", ";
```

Output

```
HARDROCK,
```

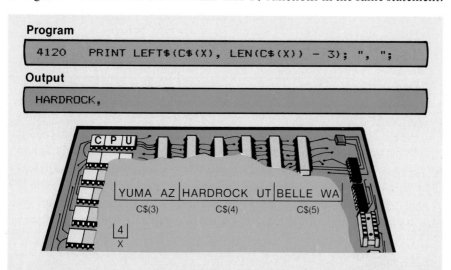

Figure 9-16 Any string field, including an element from a string array, can be used with the LEFT$ function. Here, elements from the C$ array are used.

The print statement in Figure 9–16 makes use of both the LEN and the LEFT$ functions. The LEFT$ function is used to specify that the leftmost characters in the C$(X) element will be printed. The LEN function is used to help determine how many characters will be printed. When the statement is executed, the LEN function will determine the length of the element containing the data to be printed. In the example, since the value in X is equal to 4, the element containing HARDROCK UT is to be used in the print statement. The length of the value in this element is 11 characters. Therefore, the value 11 will be returned by the entry LEN(C$(X)). Three is subtracted from this value to determine how many characters are to be printed. After the subtraction, it is found that the eight leftmost characters are to be printed. In the output, these eight characters are printed, followed by a comma. The comma follows immediately because it is separated from the LEFT$ entry by a semicolon.

Particular attention should be paid in this example to the sets of parentheses which are used. The entire entry used with the LEFT$ function is contained within parentheses. The subscript, X, which is used to reference a particular element in the C$ array, is contained within parentheses. Finally, the array element specified with the LEN function is contained within parentheses. The programmer must be extremely careful and thorough when using multiple string functions in a single statement, particularly when array elements are used as well, to ensure that no syntax errors are made in the use of parentheses.

RIGHT$ function

The RIGHT$ function performs the same task for the rightmost characters in a string variable or constant field as the LEFT$ function does for the leftmost characters. In Figure 9–16, the city and a comma were printed for the city-state portion of the letter address in the sample program. The print statement in Figure 9–17 uses the RIGHT$ function to print the state code and the zip code.

Figure 9-17 In this example, the two rightmost characters in an element of the C$ array are extracted and printed.

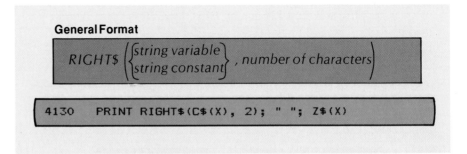

General Format

$$RIGHT\$ \left(\begin{Bmatrix} string\ variable \\ string\ constant \end{Bmatrix}, number\ of\ characters \right)$$

```
4130    PRINT RIGHT$(C$(X), 2); " "; Z$(X)
```

In the general format, the word RIGHT$ is followed immediately by a left parenthesis and then the string variable field or constant from which the rightmost characters will be taken. In the print statement on line 4130, the Xth element of the C$ array will be the field used. The field entry is followed by a comma. A numeric value, in the form of a numeric constant, a numeric variable, or an arithmetic expression that specifies the number of characters to be extracted, follows the comma. In the example, the numeric constant 2 is specified. Therefore, the two rightmost characters in the C$(X) element will be printed. The zip code is printed following a blank character.

The MID$ function can extract for use characters at any location within a string variable field or string constant. The programmer must specify the string field or constant from which the data is to be extracted, the beginning location of the data to be extracted, and the number of characters to be extracted. The example below illustrates the general format of the MID$ function, together with the coding required to extract the telephone area code from a string constant containing an entire telephone number.

MID$ function

General Format

$$MID\$ \left(\begin{Bmatrix} string\ constant \\ string\ variable \end{Bmatrix}, starting\ character,\ number\ of\ characters \right)$$

Program

```
6540 LET T$ = "TELEPHONE NUMBER: (714) 527-5131"
6550 PRINT "AREA CODE - "; MID$(T$, 20, 3)
```

Output

```
AREA CODE - 714
```

Figure 9-18 The MID$ function is used to extract three characters from the string field T$. The first character to be extracted is the 20th character in the field (7). The second character to be extracted is the twenty-first character in the field (1), and the third character extracted is the 22nd character (4).

The let statement on line 6540 places the constant in the T$ field. The print statement on line 6550 prints the constant AREA CODE and the area code from the value in T$. The first entry in the MID$ function is the string variable or string constant containing the data from which the characters (sometimes called the substring) are to be extracted. The second entry specifies the beginning point, relative to one, where the substring begins. This entry must be numeric and can be expressed as a constant, a numeric variable, or an arithmetic expression. The third entry specifies how many characters are to be extracted. It too must be a numeric value. When the MID$ function is executed, the substring identified by the beginning point and the number of characters specified is returned. The MID$ function can be included in any BASIC statement that allows or requires a string variable or constant.

As with the LEFT$ and the RIGHT$ functions, the MID$ function can be used to edit data entered by the user. It will be recalled that the city and state are entered by the user in the sample program. The format that is supposed to be

Editing with the MID$ function

followed is the city name, a single space, and then the two-character state code. The MID$ function is used to ensure that this format is followed. The coding in Figure 9-19 illustrates the method used in the sample program.

```
6550 LET C$ = C$(I)
6560 LET L2 = LEN(C$)
6570 IF L2 < 4 THEN 6830
6580    IF MID$(C$, L2-2, 1) = " " AND MID$(C$, L2-3, 1) <> " " THEN 6630
6590       PRINT "   ERROR - ENTRY MUST BE: CITY STATECODE"
6600       LET E2$ = "ERROR IN STATE CODE"
6610       GOTO 6870
```

Figure 9-19 The MID$ function is used to edit string data when it is entered by the user. Here, the MID$ function is used to identify where a space should be in the city-state data entered by the user.

The element from the C$ array which contains the entry to be edited is placed in the C$ field. This is done only to simplify the entries in the subsequent string functions and is not required. An element in an array can be used in the same manner as any string variable is used with the string functions.

The length of the entry in C$ is placed in the numeric variable L2 by the let statement on line 6560. Again, this is done merely to simplify the entries in the subsequent string functions. The entry LEN(C$) can be used as well.

The if statement on line 6570 checks if the length of the entry by the user is less than four characters. If so, the entry is in error because it must be at least four characters in length (i.e., a one-character city name, a blank, and a two-character state code). When the entry by the user is at least four characters, the if statement on line 6580 determines if the proper format was used. The last two characters in the city-state entry should be the state code. A single space should precede the state code.

To verify this condition, the first MID$ function identifies the position which should contain a space. The data and the manner of calculating which positions in the field are being referenced are illustrated in Figure 9-20.

Figure 9-20 The calculation of where the space should be is based upon the length of the data entered by the user. This length (16) is stored in the L2 numeric field. Since the state code is two characters in length, the calculation L2 - 2 identifies the position where a space should appear. The position L2 - 3 should not contain a space.

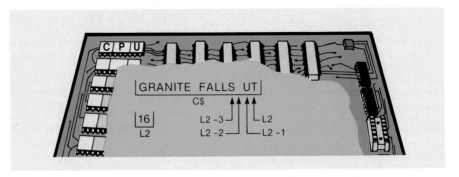

The value in the L2 numeric field is 16, which is the length of the data in C$. To reference the space preceding the state code (UT), the arithmetic expression L2 −2 can be used. This expression is specified in the second entry of the MID$ function to identify where the substring begins in C$. The third entry in the first MID$ function contains the value 1, which indicates that one character will be used. Therefore, the effect of the first portion of the if statement on line 6580 is to compare one character in the C$ field to the character blank.

The second MID$ function references the character in the field identified by the variable name C$ found at the L2 −3 location. From the drawing in Figure 9-20, note that the location referenced by L2 −3 should contain a non-blank character. If this location contains a blank, then the format specified has not been followed. The second portion of the if statement on line 6580, then, checks that this location does not contain a space. If both the conditions tested are true, the city and state have been entered in the proper format, and control is passed to the statement at line 6630 for further editing. If the city and state have not been entered in the proper format, an error message is printed, an error indicator is set to indicate that an error has occurred, and control is passed to the statement at line 6870.

Through the use of the string functions, text material can be searched for a delimiter. A delimiter is a value in a string of data that indicates the beginning or end of words, sentences, phrases, or paragraphs. Once the delimiter is found, portions of the text material can be extracted, moved, or otherwise processed as required by the application.

Searching using the MID$ function

To illustrate this processing, the sample program requires that the last name be extracted from the title and name entered by the user so that it can be used in the salutation and elsewhere in the letter (see Figure 9-4). The method used to extract the last name is to search the title and name entry, beginning at the rightmost position, until a blank is found. When the blank is found, the characters to the right constitute the last name (Figure 9-21).

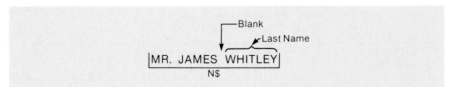

Figure 9-21 The last name of the individual can be found in the N$ field by beginning with the rightmost character and searching to the left for a blank. When the blank is found, all characters to the right constitute the last name.

The blank space preceding the last name is the delimiter which is searched for. When it is found, the characters to the right are the last name. If a blank space is not found, an error message must be written because the name has been entered in the wrong format. Whenever a string is searched, provision must be made for not finding the delimiter.

The essential process to search a string is to do the following: a) Establish the beginning point of the search; b) Determine the criteria which will end the search (usually finding the delimiter or searching the string without finding the delimiter); c) Establish the loop which will search the string text until the criteria in b is satisfied.

The flowchart and coding used in the sample program to search the title and name field for a space are shown in Figure 9-22. The beginning point of the search is the last character entered by the user. The search continues until a space is found, or, if a space is not found, to the point where the title MR. or

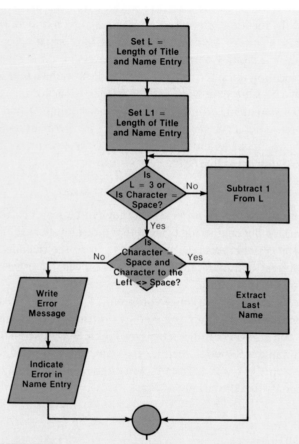

Figure 9-22 This logic and coding will search the data in the N$ field for the first blank to the left of the right-most character. When it is found, the last name is extracted by the let statement on line 5710. If a blank is not found prior to the right-most position of the title (L = 3), then the entry is in error, and the appropriate error message is printed.

```
5580     LET L = LEN(N$)
5590     LET L1 = LEN(N$)
5600                                                    REM
5610     IF L = 3 OR MID$(N$, L, 1) = " " THEN 5650
5620       LET L = L - 1
5630     GOTO 5610
5640                                                    REM
5650     IF MID$(N$, L, 1) = " " AND MID$(N$, L-1, 1) <> " "THEN 5710
5660       PRINT "    ERROR - ENTRY MUST BE: MR. FIRSTNAME LASTNAME"
5670       PRINT "         OR MS. FIRSTNAME LASTNAME"
5680       LET E1$ = "ERROR IN NAME"
5690       GOTO 5930
5700                                                    REM
5710       LET L$ = MID$(N$, L + 1, L1 - L)
```

MS. should end (the third position beginning with the leftmost character). If a space is not found, the data has not been entered in the proper format.

The first two statements place the length of the title and name entry into the L and L1 fields. The value in the L field is used as the pointer to examine each character in the text, while the value in the L1 field is used in the calculation to determine the length of the last name. The search for a space begins in the coding on line 5610, where the value in L is compared to 3, and the character identified by the entry MID$(N$, L, 1) is compared to a space. If the value in L is equal to 3, the search should be terminated because the value in L points to the rightmost position of the title.

If the value in L is not equal to 3, then it is used to point to the character in the N$ field which will be examined for a space. It will be recalled that the length of N$ is loaded into L prior to beginning this search. Therefore, the first time this comparison occurs, the rightmost character in the N$ field will be examined (Figure 9–23).

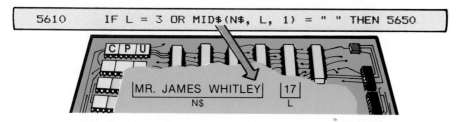

```
5610      IF L = 3 OR MID$(N$, L, 1) = " " THEN 5650
```

Figure 9-23 The entry MID$(N$, L, 1) identifies the character to be examined in the N$ field. When the value in L is equal to 17, the rightmost character is compared to a blank.

The value in L, 17, is the number of characters in the title and name entered by the user. When used in the MID$ function, it specifies the last character in the data entered by the user. From both the flowchart and the coding, it can be seen that if the value in L is not equal to 3 and the character compared is not equal to a space, the value in L is decreased by 1 (line 5620), and control is passed back to the if statement. On the second pass through the loop, the character in the 16th position of the N$ field will be compared to a space. If, as in the example in Figure 9–23, the character is not equal to a space, the value in L will again be decreased by one, and control is passed back to the if statement on line 5610.

When either a space is found or the value in L equals 3, an exit from the loop occurs, and control is passed to the if statement on line 5650. This statement first checks if the reason for exiting the loop was because a space was found. It also checks if the position to the left of the space (identified by L –1) contains a non-blank character. If both conditions are not true, then an error message is displayed by the print statements on lines 5660 and 5670, an error indicator is set by the let statement on line 5680, and control is passed to the statement at line number 5930.

If, however, the name was entered in the proper format, control is passed to the statement at line number 5710. The let statement extracts the last name from the string that was searched and places it in the field identified by the variable name L$ (Figure 9–24).

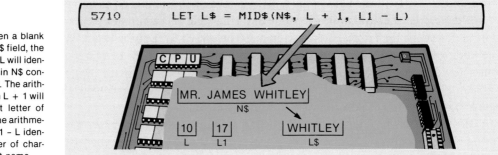

Figure 9-24 When a blank is found in the N$ field, the numeric value in L will identify the position in N$ containing the blank. The arithmetic expression L + 1 will identify the first letter of the last name. The arithmetic expression L1 – L identifies the number of characters in the last name.

The value in L indicates the position of the blank character preceding the last name in the N$ field. Therefore, the arithmetic expression L + 1 points to the first character of the last name. The arithmetic expression L1 – L equals the number of characters in the last name that should be extracted by the MID$ function. This is calculated as follows: The value in L1 is the number of characters in the N$ field. The value in L is the position in the field that contains the blank preceding the last name. The difference between these two values is the number of characters in the last name. In the example in Figure 9–24, the value in L1 is 17, and the value in L is 10. The difference between these two numbers, 7, is the number of characters in the last name (WHITLEY).

From this example, it can be seen how a string field can be searched for a delimiter. The delimiter can be any character or set of characters defined in the application. When the delimiter is found, the program can extract the appropriate data.

Searching for a substring

There are many applications in which it is required to search a string, such as a sentence or a paragraph, to find a substring within the string. For example, in an information retrieval application in a library, it might be desirable for a user to enter one or more words on a computer terminal to determine if the word or words are contained in a paragraph. The example in Figure 9–25 illustrates this concept.

Figure 9-25 The value entered by the user is used to search a paragraph. In this example, the user entered the value BASIC. When the value is found in the paragraph, a message to that effect is printed and then the paragraph is printed.

```
ENTER ONE OR MORE WORDS TO BEGIN THE SEARCH: ? BASIC

-BASIC- IS CONTAINED WITHIN THE PARAGRAPH.

THE PARAGRAPH FOLLOWS:

    IN 1965, BASIC WAS DEVELOPED AT DARTMOUTH COLLEGE.
```

In the example, the word BASIC is entered by the user. The program searches the paragraph to determine if this substring is contained within the paragraph. In this example, the message from the program indicates that the word BASIC was found in the paragraph. The paragraph is then displayed.

If a word is entered that is not contained within the paragraph, a message is printed indicating that the word or phrase entered was not found in the paragraph (Figure 9–26).

```
ENTER ONE OR MORE WORDS TO BEGIN THE SEARCH: ? FORTRAN

-FORTRAN- IS NOT CONTAINED WITHIN THE PARAGRAPH.
```

Figure 9-26 If the value entered by the user is not found in the paragraph being searched, a message notifying the user of this fact is displayed.

When the user entered the word FORTRAN, the paragraph was searched for this combination of letters. When they were not found, the program indicated this with the message.

The process of searching a string for a substring involves comparing the word or words entered by the user to an equal number of characters at the start of the paragraph (Figure 9–27). If an equal condition is found, then the word or words entered by the user are in the paragraph.

If an unequal condition is found, then the characters entered by the user are not the first word or words in the paragraph (A in Figure 9–27). Therefore, the data entered is compared to an equal number of characters in the paragraph, beginning with the second character in the paragraph (B in Figure 9–27). If an equal condition is not found, the data entered is compared to an equal number of characters in the paragraph beginning with the third character in the paragraph. This process continues until an equal condition occurs or until the entire paragraph has been searched (C in Figure 9–27).

Figure 9-27 The search for the substring is conducted one character at a time. The number of characters compared is equal to the number of characters entered by the user. The search terminates when an equal condition is found (such as in this example) or when the entire paragraph has been searched and an equal substring has not been found.

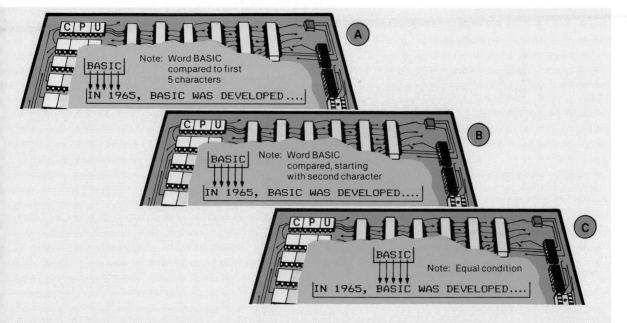

In Figure 9–27, the user entered the word BASIC as the value to be found in the paragraph. In example A, BASIC is compared to the first five characters of the paragraph (IN 19). Since these are not equal, and since the entire paragraph has not yet been examined, the word entered by the user will be compared to the paragraph beginning with the second character. Thus, the characters examined in the second comparison are N 196. Since these are not equal, the next comparison would compare the word entered to five characters in the paragraph beginning with the third character. This comparison continues until, as in the example, an equal condition is found; or until the entire paragraph has been compared and no equal condition is found.

The logic for conducting this search for a substring is shown in the flowchart in Figure 9–28.

Figure 9–28 The logic to perform a string search is virtually identical to that used when an array is searched. A loop is used to perform the actual search and then the if-then-else structure is used to determine the results of the search.

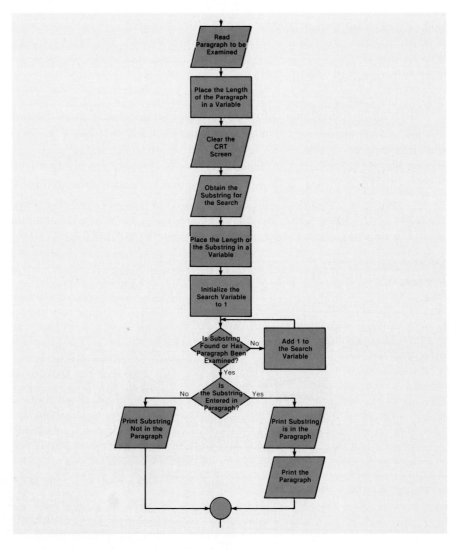

The paragraph to be searched must be placed in a string field. The length of the paragraph is then placed in a numeric variable. This value will be used to aid in determining if the entire paragraph has been searched without finding the desired substring. The CRT screen is then cleared, and the substring is obtained from the user. The length of the substring is placed in a numeric field.

The loop which performs the actual search is then implemented. The search variable is initialized to the value 1. This variable is used to identify the position in the paragraph that is the beginning point for the comparison. The loop then checks if the substring entered is in the paragraph or if the entire paragraph has been examined. If not, the search variable is incremented by 1, and the comparison takes place again. If so, control is passed to the next decision which asks if the substring was found in the paragraph. If so, a message to that effect is printed and then the paragraph is printed. If not, a message is printed stating the substring was not found. It should be noted that the logic used for this string search is virtually identical to that used for array searches in Chapter 7.

The coding to implement this logic is shown in Figure 9-29. As noted, the structure of the logic and, therefore, the structure of the code, is similar to that used for array lookups. Several statements, however, should be explained

Figure 9-29 The coding which implements the string search utilizes the string functions to perform the actual search and also to determine the values used to calculate when the search has been completed without finding the substring entered by the user.

```
2060 READ P$
2070 LET P1 = LEN(P$)
2080 CLS
2090 INPUT "ENTER ONE OR MORE WORDS TO BEGIN THE SEARCH: "; W$
2100 LET W1 = LEN(W$)
2110 LET C = 1
2120                                                          REM
2130 IF C = P1 - (W1 - 2) THEN 2180
2140 IF W$ = MID$(P$, C, W1) THEN 2180
2150    LET C = C + 1
2160 GOTO 2130
2170                                                          REM
2180 IF W$ = MID$(P$, C, W1) THEN 2230
2190    PRINT " "
2200    PRINT "-"; W$; "-"; " IS NOT CONTAINED WITHIN THE PARAGRAPH."
2210    GOTO 2310
2220                                                          REM
2230    PRINT " "
2240    PRINT "-"; W$; "-"; " IS CONTAINED WITHIN THE PARAGRAPH."
2250    PRINT " "
2260    PRINT "THE PARAGRAPH FOLLOWS:"
2270    PRINT " "
2280    PRINT "         "; P$
2290    GOTO 2310
2300         :                                               REM
2310         :
3220 DATA "IN 1965, BASIC WAS DEVELOPED AT DARTMOUTH COLLEGE."
```

because they are unique. The if statement on line 2130 is used to determine that the entire paragraph has been examined for the substring, and the substring does not exist in the paragraph.

The field C contains the search variable. The field P1 contains the length of the paragraph, and the field W1 contains the length of the substring entered by the user. The calculation P1 – (W1 – 2) used in the if statement identifies the point in the paragraph at which the substring cannot be found. For example, the paragraph contains 50 characters. If the substring is 5 characters in length, the calculation will yield the value 47 (50 – (5 – 2)). If the 47th character is to be the first character in the comparison to the paragraph, the substring cannot be in the paragraph because only four characters remain in the paragraph for comparison (characters 47, 48, 49, and 50). Therefore, when the value in C is equal to 47, the loop should be terminated because the substring does not exist in the paragraph. The if statement on line 2130 will transfer control to statement 2180 when this condition occurs.

The if statement on line 2140 compares the substring stored in W$ to the paragraph. The MID$ function is used to identify those characters in the paragraph which are to be used in the comparison on each pass through the loop. The first entry for the MID$ function is P$, which is the field where the entire paragraph is stored. The second entry, C, identifies the first character to be used in the comparison. As noted previously, the value in C will be initialized to 1 and then will be incremented by 1 each time through the loop until either an equal string is found or until the substring is not found in the paragraph.

The value in W1, which is the length of the substring entered by the user, determines how many characters will be compared. For example, if the length of the substring is equal to 5, then each time the if statement is executed, five characters from the P$ field will be compared. If the substring is not equal to the characters from the P$ field, then the value in C is incremented by one (line 2150), and control is passed back to the if statement on line 2130. If the substring is equal to the characters in the paragraph, control is passed to line 2180.

In a manner similar to that used for array lookup, the if statement on line 2180 determines if a substring was found. If so, control is passed to the statement on line 2230, where a message is printed and then the paragraph is displayed. If a substring was not found, a message indicating that is printed by the statements on lines 2190 and 2200.

The ability to search a string of data for a substring is important in some applications. The technique illustrated can be used whenever this ability is required.

The data which is entered by the user and is edited using the techniques illustrated previously is used in the creation of the letter printed by the program. The letter which is created is shown in Figure 9–4 on page 9.3. The coding to create the letter is shown below.

Printing the letter with string functions

```
7050 CLS
7060 PRINT N$(I)
7070 IF LEN(A$(I)) = 0 THEN 7110
7080    PRINT A$(I)
7090    GOTO 7110
7100                                              REM
7110 PRINT LEFT$(C$(I), LEN(C$(I)) - 3); ", ";
7120 PRINT RIGHT$(C$(I), 2); " "; Z$(I)
7130 PRINT " "
7140 PRINT "DEAR "; LEFT$(N$(I), 3); " "; L$; ":"
7150 PRINT " "
7160 PRINT "      THE "; L$; " FAMILY HAS BECOME"
7170 PRINT "ELIGIBLE TO RECEIVE AN EXPENSE-PAID TRIP"
7180 PRINT "FROM YOUR HOME IN "; LEFT$(C$(I), LEN(C$(I)) - 3);
7190 PRINT " TO HAWAII."
7200 PRINT "      "; LEFT$(N$(I), 3); " "; L$; ", PLEASE RETURN THE"
7210 PRINT "ENCLOSED CARD TO DETERMINE IF YOU HAVE"
7220 PRINT "WON YOUR FREE TRIP TO HAWAII."
7230 PRINT " "
7240 PRINT "          REAL ESTATE TIMESHARING"
```

The print statement on line 7060 displays the entire title and name entered by the user. The if statement on line 7070 checks the length of the address entry. If no street address was entered, that is, the length of A$(I) is equal to zero, then control is passed to statement 7110, and no address is printed in the salutation of the letter. If the length is not zero, the address is printed by the print statement on line 7080.

Figure 9-30 The string functions are used to insert data within the text of the letter. The technique shown here can be used to personalize letters and other correspondence.

The print statements on lines 7110 and 7120 print the city, a comma, the state code, and the zip code. The LEFT$ function in statement 7110 will print all except the rightmost three characters of the field identified as C$(I). This element contains the city and state entered by the user. The rightmost three characters are not printed because they are a blank followed by the state code. In the print statement, the LEFT$ function is followed by a semicolon and then a string literal consisting of a comma and space. Therefore, the line will print as CITY,. The literal is followed by a semicolon, meaning that the data printed by the print statement on line 7120 will appear on the same line as the city name.

The RIGHT$ function in the print statement on line 7120 is used to extract the state code from the C$(I) element. The code is followed by a space and then the zip code — Z$(I).

The print statement on line 7140 prints the word DEAR, the title (identified by the LEFT$ function), the last name, and a colon. The remainder of the letter is then printed, with various pieces of data entered by the user inserted in portions of the letter. As can be seen from this example, the string functions can be used to insert data into text as well as extract data from text as shown in previous examples.

Concatenation of data

Concatenation is the process of joining together one or more pieces of data. String data may be concatenated using the addition arithmetic operator (+). The following example illustrates an application in which an employee number is generated from data which consists of the department number to which the employee is assigned and the employee's date of birth.

Figure 9-31 The addition arithmetic operator (+) is used to cause concatenation to occur. Here, the value in the D$ field is concatenated with the value in the B$ field. Concatenation can take place only on string constants or variables. Numeric constants or variables cannot be used.

```
Program
3170 LET D$ = "10"
3180 LET B$ = "122243"
3190 PRINT "EMPLOYEE NUMBER: "; D$ + B$
```

```
Output
EMPLOYEE NUMBER: 10122243
```

In Figure 9-31, the department number (10) is stored in the field identified by the string variable D$, and the birthdate of the employee (122243) is stored in the field identified by the string variable name B$. Concatenation can take place only on string fields. Therefore, D$ and B$ must be string fields.

When the print statement on line 3190 is executed, the data in D$ is concatenated with the data in B$ to form the employee number. Note that when two string fields are concatenated, they are joined with no intervening spaces and become a single field.

Any string fields, including string constants, can be concatenated. The example in Figure 9-32 illustrates concatenating the month, day, and year in the B$ field from Figure 9-31 so that the birthdate prints month/day/year.

Figure 9-32 The string functions can be used to identify substrings which will be concatenated, such as in this example where the slashes are inserted between the month and the day and between the day and the year.

```
Program
4230 LET B$ = "122243"
4240 PRINT "BIRTHDATE: "; LEFT$(B$, 2) + "/" + MID$(B$, 3, 2) +
"/" + RIGHT$(B$, 2)
```

```
Output
BIRTHDATE: 12/22/43
```

The let statement on line 4230 in Figure 9–32 places the birthdate into the field identified by the string variable name B$. The print statement on line 4240 uses the LEFT$, the MID$, and the RIGHT$ functions to extract the month, day, and year from the B$ field. The month, day, and year which are extracted from B$ are concatenated with the character slash (/) to form the birthdate in month/day/year format (12/22/43). Concatenation is a powerful tool when the application requires joining pieces of string data.

Mixing numeric and string data

All of the string functions discussed thus far require string variable names or string literals. Numerous applications arise where string and numeric data must be interchanged so that the requirements of the particular instructions being used are satisfied. To illustrate this, the following steps illustrate the processing which must occur to take a list of numeric digits, insert a decimal point, and edit the result as dollars and cents using the print using statement.

Step 1: Numeric digits are entered and stored in a numeric field.

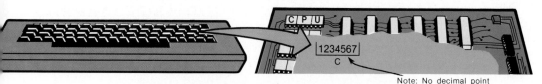

Note: No decimal point is entered in the list of numbers

Step 2: The digits are separated into dollars and cents.

Step 3: A decimal point is inserted between the dollars and cents fields.

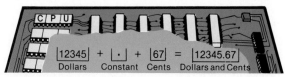

Step 4: The dollars and cents are edited and printed.

In step 1, the data is entered by the user and is stored in the field identified by the numeric variable C. Note that the data is a single list of numeric digits without a decimal point. Therefore, it is treated as a whole number.

In step 2, the two rightmost digits are separated from the remaining digits. A period is then inserted between the dollars and cents in step 3, and the numeric field with the decimal point in the proper position is printed in a dollars and cents format.

As noted, the data is first stored in a numeric field in step 1. In order for the processing of step 2 to occur, however, the data must be referenced as string data, since the string functions which separate these digits can only operate on string data. The third step involves concatenating the dollars and the cents with a period. This step again requires that the data be referenced as string data. Finally, in step 4, the data must be referenced as numeric data so that it can be edited in a dollars and cents format.

In summary, the data is entered as numeric data, must be referenced as string data to be placed in a dollars and cents format with a decimal point, and then referenced as numeric data to be edited by the print using statement.

The changes from numeric data to string data and back to numeric data are accomplished through the use of the STR$ and VAL functions. These functions, together with the MID$, LEN, and RIGHT$ functions, are combined in a print using statement to convert this string of numbers into an edited dollars and cents field on the CRT screen. The coding to accomplish this is shown in Figure 9-33, together with the screen produced from the coding.

Program

```
100 INPUT "ENTER CHECK AMOUNT: "; C
110 PRINT USING "CHECK AMOUNT IS: $$#,###.##"; VAL(MID$(STR$(C),
    2, LEN(STR$(C)) - 3) + "." + RIGHT$(STR$(C), 2))
```

Output

```
ENTER CHECK AMOUNT: ? 1234567
CHECK AMOUNT IS: $12,345.67
```

The print using statement should be examined in detail to understand the use of the STR$ function and the VAL function in the statement. The MID$ function extracts the dollars and the RIGHT$ function extracts the cents. The MID$ function begins with the second character of the field STR$(C) because the STR$ function always returns a blank in the first position of the string field when the numeric value is positive. For the same reason, the number of characters extracted by the MID$ function is the length of STR$(C) minus 3, rather than STR$(C) –2 as might be expected.

It should be noted from this example that the data stored in the field identified by the numeric variable C is used as string data, and then the resultant string data is converted back to numeric by the VAL function so that it can be edited as a dollars and cents field. Whenever multiple string functions are used in a single statement, such as in Figure 9–33, precision must be used to ensure that parentheses are in the proper positions, and that the data has been specified in the proper form for the function.

The STRING$ function makes available a string of characters of any length from 1 to 255. The general format of the STRING$ function and an example of its use are illustrated below.

STRING$ function

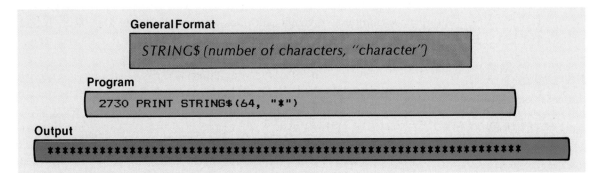

General Format

STRING$ (number of characters, "character")

Program

```
2730 PRINT STRING$(64, "*")
```

Output

```
****************************************************************
```

The STRING$ function returns a string of the character specified. The string contains the number of characters specified. In the example, therefore, sixty-four asterisks are returned by the STRING$ function. They are printed by the print statement.

Figure 9-34 In this example, the STRING$ function returns sixty-four asterisks. These are printed by the print statement.

On many computer systems each number, letter of the alphabet, or special character entered into main computer storage is recorded as a series of seven electronic impulses called bits. A bit (BInary Digit) may be considered either "on" or "off." A combination of seven bits being on or off determines what character is stored in a position of memory.

The ASCII (American Standard Code for Information Interchange) code is widely used to represent data in main computer storage. It specifies what combination of seven bits represents any given character. For example, when the digit 1 is entered from the keyboard and is stored in main computer storage, it will be stored using a unique combination of bits on and bits off (Figure 9-35).

The ASCII code

Figure 9-35 When the ASCII code is used, numbers, letters of the alphabet, and special characters are stored through a combination of seven bits being on and off. Here, the number one is represented by the combination of the first bit off, the next two bits on, the next three bits off, and the last bit on.

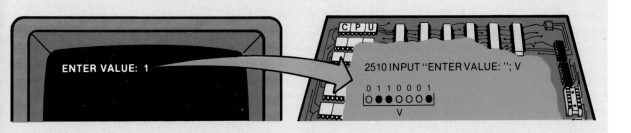

In the example in Figure 9–35, the O represents the bits that are off, and the ● represents the bits that are on. The 1's above the ● also represent bits that are on, while the zeros above the O represent bits that are off. Therefore, when using the ASCII code, the number 1 can symbolically be represented as 0110001.

Expressing decimal values using two symbols (the zero and one) is called the binary numbering system. Each position in the binary numbering system is assigned a place value based upon a power of 2. The place values of a binary number, beginning at the right and moving to the left, are 1, 2, 4, 8, 16, 32, and 64 (Figure 9–36).

Figure 9-36 Each bit position in a storage location is given a place position based upon the binary numbering system. When a bit is on, the place value of that bit is added to a total which represents the decimal value of the character. In this example, the place values of 32 + 16 + 1 are added to determine a decimal value 49 which represents the number 1 in the ASCII code.

$$32+16 \qquad +1 \; = \; \text{Decimal 49}$$

$$0 \; 1 \; 1 \; 0 \; 0 \; 0 \; 1$$

O	●	●	O	O	O	●
64	32	16	8	4	2	1

As can be seen from the example above, the ASCII bit combination which represents the number 1 in main computer storage has a binary numbering system value of decimal 49 (32 + 16 + 1). When characters are stored in main computer storage using the ASCII representation, each will have a unique decimal value code based upon the bits which are on and the bits which are off. The chart in Figure 9–37 illustrates characters which can be stored in main computer storage and the related decimal value codes.

Figure 9-37 This chart shows all the commonly found letters, numbers, and special characters and their respective ASCII codes.

Code	Character	Code	Character	Code	Character	Code	Character	Code	Character
32	Space	52	4	72	H	92	↓ or]	112	p
33	!	53	5	73	I	93	←	113	q
34	"	54	6	74	J	94	→	114	r
35	#	55	7	75	K	95	—	115	s
36	$	56	8	76	L	96	@	116	t
37	%	57	9	77	M	97	a	117	u
38	&	58	:	78	N	98	b	118	v
39	'	59	;	79	O	99	c	119	w
40	(	60	<	80	P	100	d	120	x
41	)	61	=	81	Q	101	e	121	y
42	*	62	>	82	R	102	f	122	z
43	+	63	?	83	S	103	g	123	
44	,	64	@	84	T	104	h	124	
45	-	65	A	85	U	105	i	125	
46	.	66	B	86	V	106	j	126	
47	/	67	C	87	W	107	k		
48	0	68	D	88	X	108	l	127	
49	1	69	E	89	Y	109	m		
50	2	70	F	90	Z	110	n		
51	3	71	G	91	↑ or [	111	o		

From the chart, it can be seen that each character that can be stored in main computer storage is represented by a unique decimal value code.

The CHR$ function allows the programmer to reference these decimal codes (called ASCII codes) in a BASIC statement. The following example illustrates the general format of the CHR$ function and an example of its use.

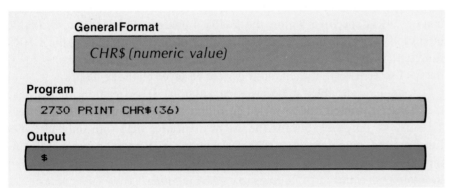

General Format

CHR$ (numeric value)

Program

    2730 PRINT CHR$(36)

Output

    $

The value within the parentheses following the word CHR$ is the ASCII code of the character to be processed. In the example, ASCII code 36 is specified. As a result, the print statement will print a dollar sign because a dollar sign is represented by ASCII code 36 (see Figure 9-37).

The value of this capability is that some computer systems do not have certain characters on the keyboard. Therefore, the only way to print these characters is through the use of the ASCII code for the character in conjunction with the CHR$ function. The CHR$ function can be specified in any statement or function that requires or allows a single string character.

The CHR$ function can be used to perform tasks that are not possible using standard BASIC statements. For example, to include quotation marks within a string constant requires the use of the CHR$ function because quotation marks are used as delimiters for string constants. The following example illustrates the use of the CHR$ function to allow quotation marks to be included within a string constant.

Program

    2190 PRINT "SHE SAID, "; CHR$(34); "HELLO."; CHR$(34)

Output

    SHE SAID, "HELLO."

In the example in Figure 9–39, quotation marks must appear around the word HELLO. Since, however, quotation marks are used as the delimiter identifying the beginning and ending of a string constant, the BASIC interpreter cannot distinguish when the quotes are used as delimiters and when the quotes are supposed to appear in the constant. Therefore, most BASIC interpreters use the double quotation marks strictly as a delimiter and, if quotes are to be included in the constant, the CHR$ function must be used.

In the print statement on line 2190, the ASCII code for double quotation marks, 34, is specified within the CHR$ function. This will cause double quotation marks to be printed (see output). Through the use of the CHR$ function, any character available on the computer system can be displayed on the CRT screen even if the character cannot be keyed on the keyboard.

A numeric variable can be specified with the CHR$ function. In this way, the character printed can be varied each time the print statement is executed. To illustrate this, and to show the use of a variable field with the STRING$ function, the example in Figure 9–40 will print the character corresponding to the numeric value entered by the user. In addition, the character will be printed the number of times corresponding to its ASCII code.

Figure 9-40 A variable value in the STRING$ function can allow a variable number of characters to be printed each time the function is executed. When the user enters a numeric value via the input statement on line 4240, that value is used to determine the number of characters which will be returned by the STRING$ function. The actual character that will be printed is the character whose ASCII code is entered by the user.

Program

```
4240 INPUT I
4250 PRINT STRING$(I, CHR$(I))
```

Output

```
? 49
1111111111111111111111111111111111111111111111111
```

The input statement on line 4240 obtains a numeric value from the user at the keyboard. The print statement on line 4250 prints a string of characters. The number of characters to be printed is equal to the value entered by the user. The character printed is the one whose ASCII code is equal to the number entered by the user. In the sample output, the value 49 was entered by the user. Therefore, the character corresponding to the ASCII code 49 (the number 1) is printed 49 times. Although this particular coding would not be widely used, it should be noted that variables can be used for both the STRING$ function and the CHR$ function. This may have particular application in graphing, where the number of characters to be printed and the character to be printed could depend upon a calculation made in the program.

ASC function   The ASC function returns the ASCII code for the first or only character in a string (Figure 9–41).

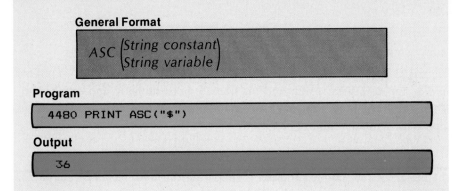

General Format

$$ASC \begin{pmatrix} String\ constant \\ String\ variable \end{pmatrix}$$

Program

```
4480 PRINT ASC("$")
```

Output

```
36
```

Figure 9-41 The ASC function will return the ASCII code of the number, letter, or special character enclosed within parentheses. Here, the ASCII code of a dollar sign is returned by the ASC function.

In the example above, the word ASC is followed in parentheses by the character whose code is to be returned. Thus, when the dollar sign is specified, the number value 36 is returned by the ASC function. This value is then printed. The ASC function can be used whenever a single numeric character is allowed or required in a BASIC statement.

Since the value returned by the ASC function is numeric, it can be used in a calculation. The example in Figure 9–42 illustrates its use to print the lower case representation of a letter for which the upper case ASCII code is known.

Program

```
5480 INPUT "PLEASE ENTER THE UPPERCASE LETTER: "; C$
5490   LET C = ASC(C$) + 32
5500   PRINT "THE LOWERCASE LETTER IS: "; CHR$(C)
5510   PRINT " "
5520 GOTO 5480
```

Output

```
PLEASE ENTER THE UPPERCASE LETTER: ? G
THE LOWERCASE LETTER IS: g

PLEASE ENTER THE UPPERCASE LETTER: ? Q
THE LOWERCASE LETTER IS: q

PLEASE ENTER THE UPPERCASE LETTER: ? R
THE LOWERCASE LETTER IS: r

PLEASE ENTER THE UPPERCASE LETTER: ?
```

Figure 9-42 The ASCII code for a lower case letter is always 32 greater than the representation of the upper case letter. When the user enters a letter in response to the input statement on line 5480, the ASC function is used to return the numeric code for the upper case letter. The let statement on line 5490 then adds that value to the constant 32, giving the numeric code for the lower case letter. The CHR$ function in the print statement on line 5500 then returns the lower case letter for the value contained in the numeric field C.

When the input statement on line 5480 is executed, the user will enter an upper case letter, which is stored in the field identified by the string variable C$. The let statement on line 5490 obtains the ASCII code for the letter entered, adds 32 to the code, and stores the result in the numeric field identified by the variable name C. This calculated value is the ASCII code for the lower case letter which was entered because the ASCII code for a lower case letter is always 32 greater than the ASCII code for the upper case letter (see Figure 9–37).

The print statement on line 5500 prints the character corresponding to the value in C by using the CHR$ function. Note on the output that the lower case letter is printed by this print statement.

**Summary of
string functions**
The string functions available with most BASIC interpreters and compilers provide the ability to search and manipulate both numeric and string data. When they are used properly, any data manipulation requirement in an application should be able to be solved.

PROGRAM
DESIGN
The design of the sample program is shown on this and the following pages.

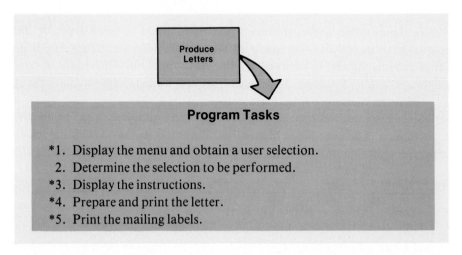

Program Tasks

*1. Display the menu and obtain a user selection.
 2. Determine the selection to be performed.
*3. Display the instructions.
*4. Prepare and print the letter.
*5. Print the mailing labels.

Figure 9–43 Four of the five tasks in the top-level module are done in separate modules.

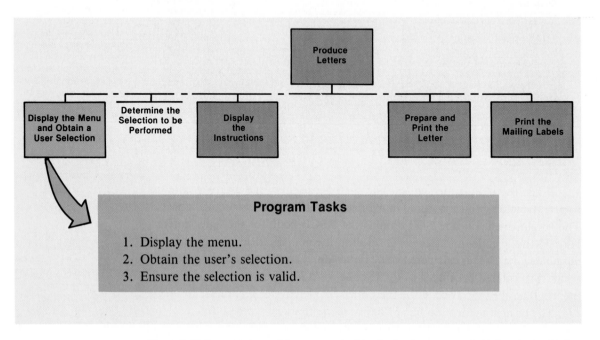

Program Tasks

1. Display the menu.
2. Obtain the user's selection.
3. Ensure the selection is valid.

Figure 9–44 No separate modules are required to display the menu and obtain a user selection.

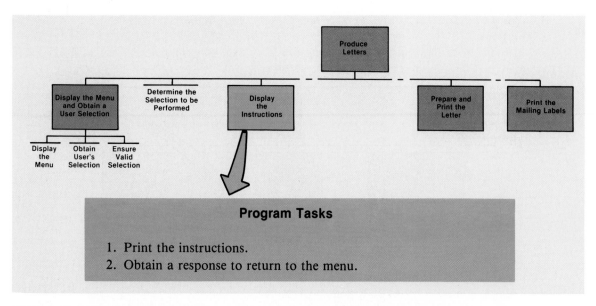

Figure 9-45 Two tasks are required to display the instructions, neither of which is large or complex.

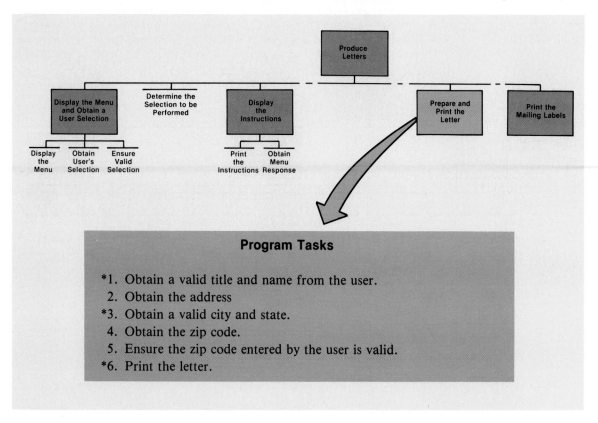

Figure 9-46 Of the six tasks required to prepare and print the letter, three require separate modules.

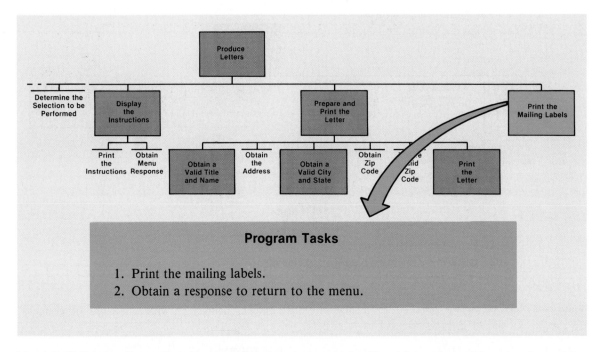

Figure 9-47 Printing the mailing labels requires two tasks which will not be performed in separate modules.

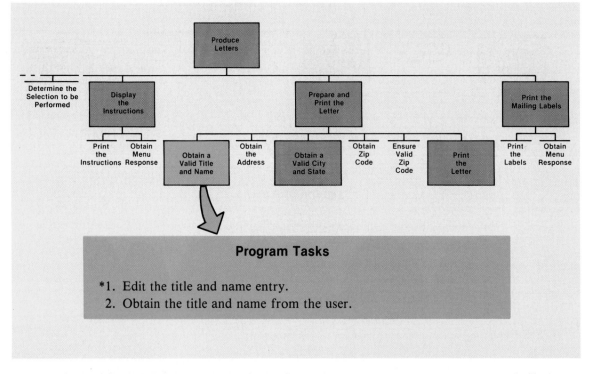

Figure 9-48 To obtain a valid title and name, the title and name must be obtained, and it must be edited.

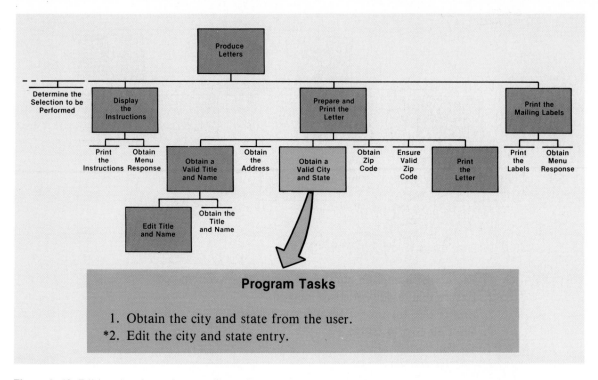

Figure 9-49 Editing the city and state will require a separate module while obtaining the data from the user will not.

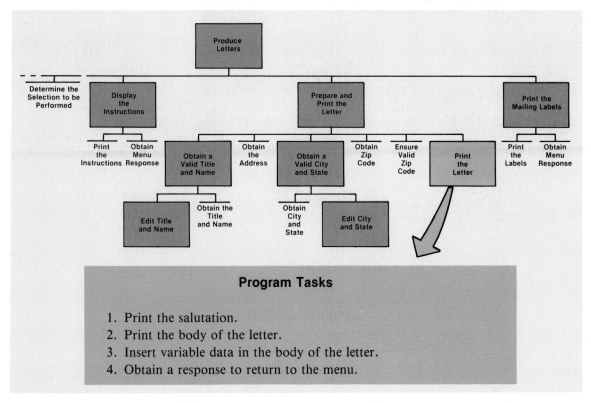

Figure 9-50 The four tasks required to print the letter will all be performed in the same module.

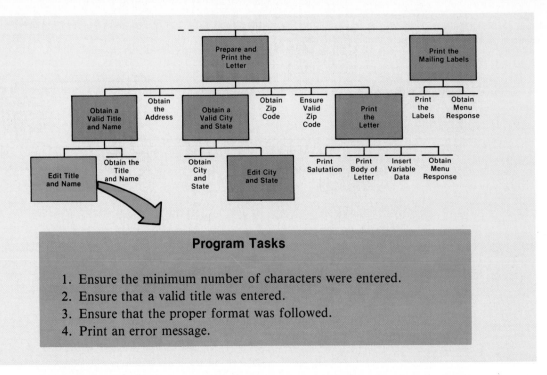

Program Tasks

1. Ensure the minimum number of characters were entered.
2. Ensure that a valid title was entered.
3. Ensure that the proper format was followed.
4. Print an error message.

Figure 9-51 Four tasks, none of which is large or complex, are required in order to edit the title and name.

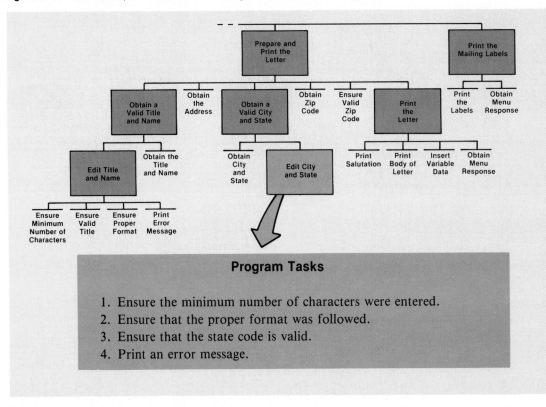

Program Tasks

1. Ensure the minimum number of characters were entered.
2. Ensure that the proper format was followed.
3. Ensure that the state code is valid.
4. Print an error message.

Figure 9-52 Editing the city and state requires four tasks, but none of them will be performed in a separate module.

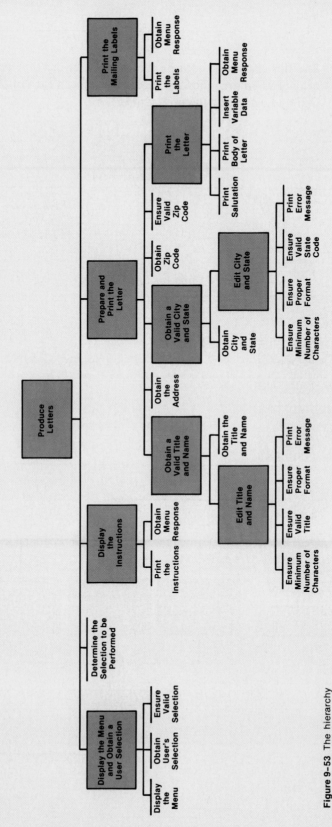

Figure 9-53 The hierarchy chart for the entire program illustrates where within the program all tasks are performed. The hierarchy chart is developed as the design of the program takes place and then serves as a map to anyone who must examine the program at some later time.

Program flowcharts The flowcharts for each of the modules in the sample program are shown below and on the following pages. The logic in each of the modules should be well understood by the programmer.

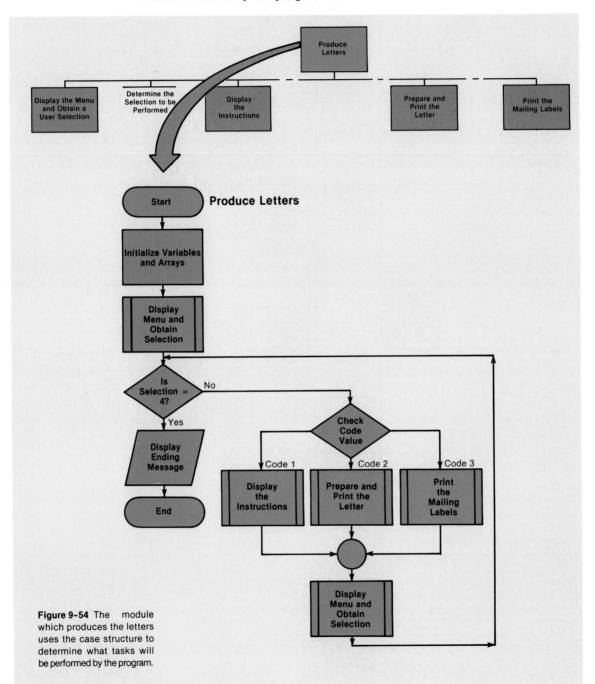

Figure 9-54 The module which produces the letters uses the case structure to determine what tasks will be performed by the program.

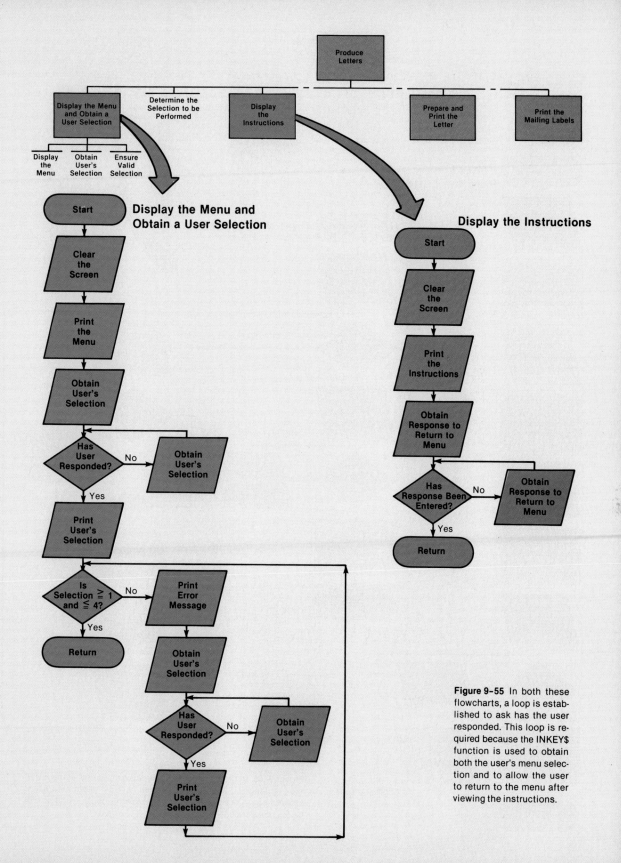

Produce Letters

Display the Menu and Obtain a User Selection — Determine the Selection to be Performed — Display the Instructions — Prepare and Print the Letter — Print the Mailing Labels

Display the Menu — Obtain User's Selection — Ensure Valid Selection

Display the Menu and Obtain a User Selection

Start

Clear the Screen

Print the Menu

Obtain User's Selection

Has User Responded? — No → Obtain User's Selection

Yes

Print User's Selection

Is Selection ≥ 1 and ≤ 4? — No → Print Error Message

Yes

Return

Obtain User's Selection

Has User Responded? — No → Obtain User's Selection

Yes

Print User's Selection

Display the Instructions

Start

Clear the Screen

Print the Instructions

Obtain Response to Return to Menu

Has Response Been Entered? — No → Obtain Response to Return to Menu

Yes

Return

Figure 9–55 In both these flowcharts, a loop is established to ask has the user responded. This loop is required because the INKEY$ function is used to obtain both the user's menu selection and to allow the user to return to the menu after viewing the instructions.

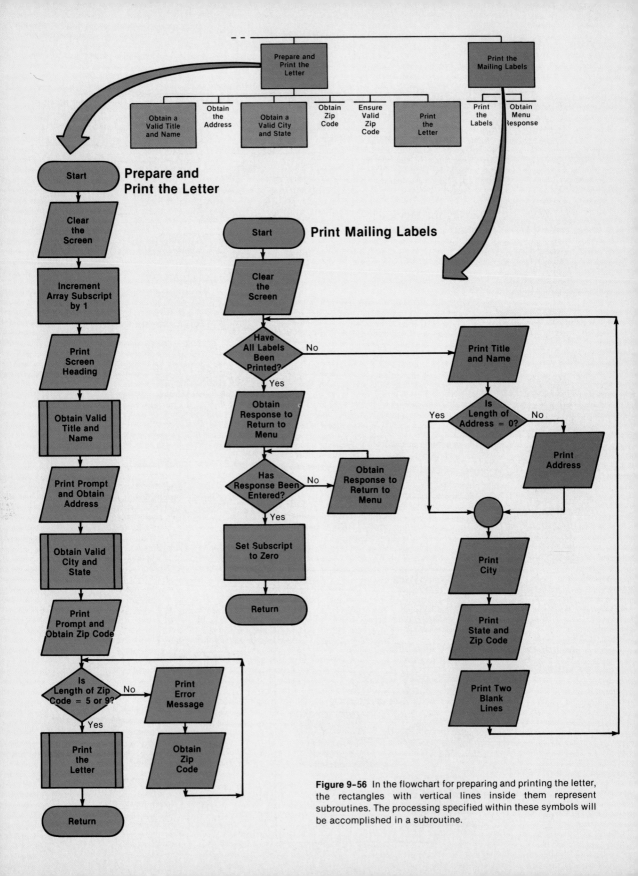

Figure 9-56 In the flowchart for preparing and printing the letter, the rectangles with vertical lines inside them represent subroutines. The processing specified within these symbols will be accomplished in a subroutine.

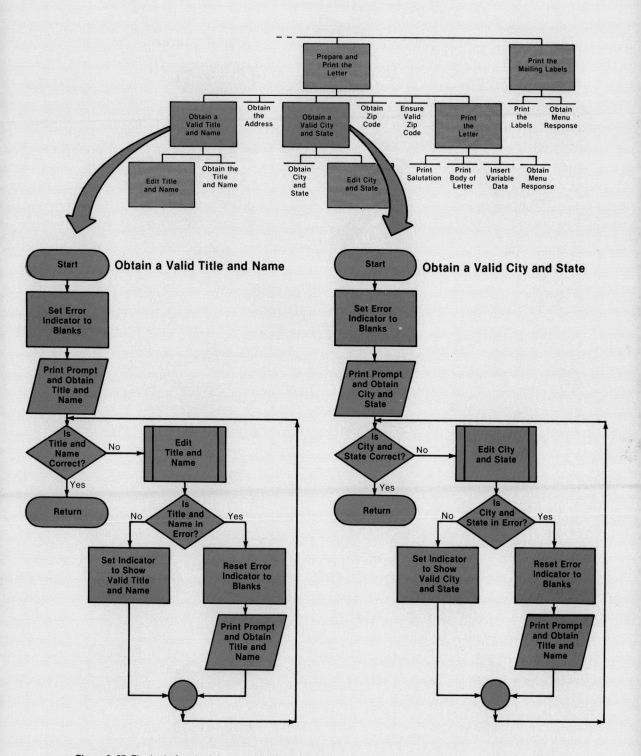

Figure 9-57 The logic for obtaining a valid title and name and for obtaining a valid city and state is virtually identical.

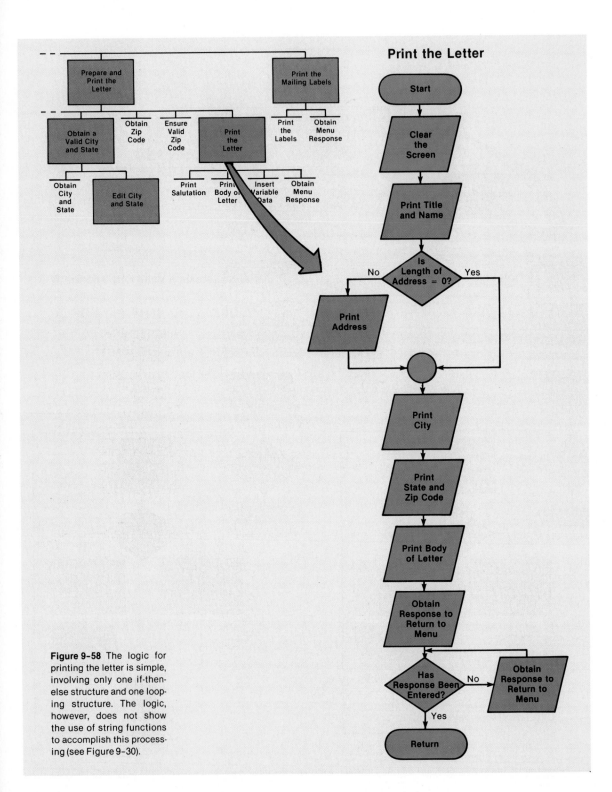

Print the Letter

Figure 9-58 The logic for printing the letter is simple, involving only one if-then-else structure and one looping structure. The logic, however, does not show the use of string functions to accomplish this processing (see Figure 9-30).

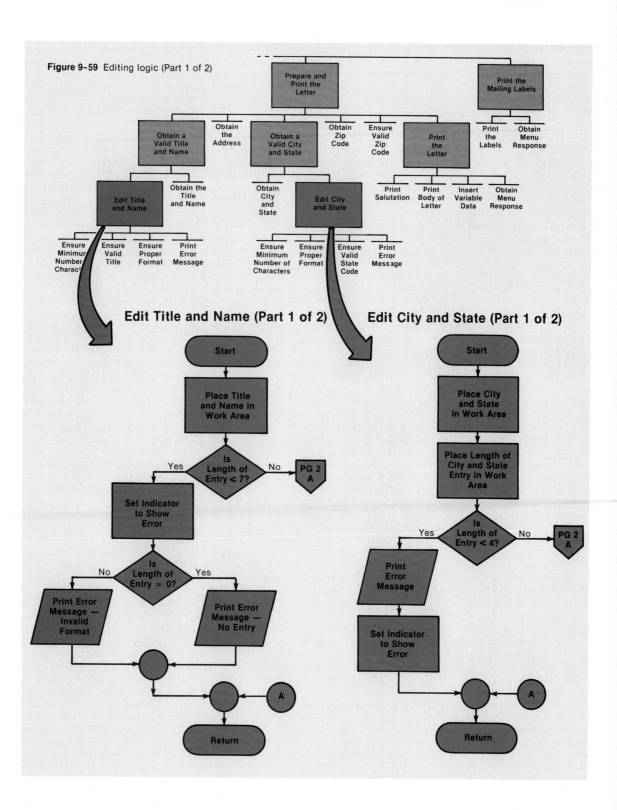

Figure 9-59 Editing logic (Part 1 of 2)

Edit Title and Name (Part 2 of 2)

Edit City and State (Part 2 of 2)

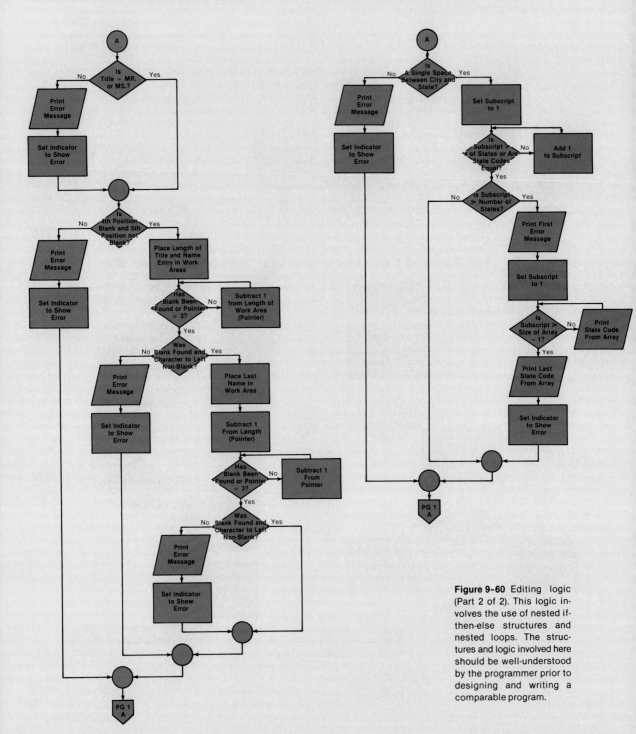

Figure 9-60 Editing logic (Part 2 of 2). This logic involves the use of nested if-then-else structures and nested loops. The structures and logic involved here should be well-understood by the programmer prior to designing and writing a comparable program.

The complete listing for the sample program is shown below and on the following pages.

Sample program

```
100 REM LETTER              MARCH 16          SHELLY/CASHMAN
110                                                     REM
120 REM THIS PROGRAM PREPARES SALES LETTERS FOR INDIVIDUALS.
130 REM MAILING LABELS CAN ALSO BE PREPARED.
140                                                     REM
150 REM VARIABLE NAMES:
160 REM    N$()..NAME ARRAY
170 REM    N$....NAME WORK AREA FOR EDITING
180 REM    A$()..ADDRESS ARRAY
190 REM    C$()..CITY-STATE ARRAY
200 REM    S$....CITY-STATE WORK AREA FOR EDITING
210 REM    Z$()..ZIP CODE ARRAY
220 REM    S$()..VALID STATE CODE ARRAY
230 REM    I.....COUNTER FOR NUMBER OF LETTERS WRITTEN -
240 REM          USED TO REFERENCE ARRAYS WHEN ENTERING DATA
250 REM    M.....MAXIMUM NUMBER OF ELEMENTS IN ARRAYS
260 REM    N.....NUMBER OF STATES IN VALID STATE ARRAY
270 REM    R$....RESPONSE FOR MENU SELECTION - ENTERED BY USER
280 REM    X.....UTILITY COUNTER-VARIABLE FOR FOR-NEXT LOOPS
290 REM    X$....UTILITY INPUT AREA FOR INKEY$ FUNCTION
300 REM    L$....LAST NAME OF PERSON RECEIVING LETTER
310 REM    E1$...ERROR INDICATOR FOR TITLE AND NAME
320 REM    E2$...ERROR INDICATOR FOR CITY-STATE
330 REM    L.....WORK AREA FOR LENGTH OF TITLE AND NAME ENTRY
340 REM    L1....WORK AREA FOR LENGTH OF TITLE AND NAME ENTRY
350 REM    L2....WORK AREA FOR LENGTH OF CITY AND STATE
360 REM    J.....COUNTER AND SUBSCRIPT TO EDIT STATE CODE
370                                                     REM
380 REM ***********************************************************
390 REM * DATA TO LOAD ARRAY                                    *
400 REM ***********************************************************
410                                                     REM
420 DATA "AZ", "CA", "ID", "NV", "OR", "UT", "WA"
430                                                     REM
440 REM ***********************************************************
450 REM * INITIALIZATION OF VARIABLES AND ARRAYS               *
460 REM ***********************************************************
470                                                     REM
480 LET I = 0
490 LET M = 20
500 LET N = 7
510 DIM N$(M), A$(M), C$(M), Z$(M), S$(N)
520                                                     REM
530 FOR X = 1 TO N
540    READ S$(X)
550 NEXT X
560                                                     REM
```

Figure 9-61 Sample program (Part 1 or 7)

```
570 REM ***********************************************************
580 REM * MAIN PROCESSING MODULE                                 *
590 REM ***********************************************************
600                                                            REM
610 GOSUB 1000
620                                                            REM
630 IF R$ = "4" THEN 680
640    ON VAL(R$) GOSUB 2000, 3000, 4000
650    GOSUB 1000
660 GOTO 630
670                                                            REM
680 PRINT " "
690 PRINT "END OF SALES LETTER PROGRAM"
700 END
1000                                                           REM
1010 REM **********************************************************
1020 REM * DISPLAY MENU AND GET SELECTION                        *
1030 REM **********************************************************
1040                                                           REM
1050 CLS
1060 PRINT "S A L E S   L E T T E R   M E N U"
1070 PRINT " "
1080 PRINT " CODE        FUNCTION"
1090 PRINT " "
1100 PRINT "  1 - DISPLAY INSTRUCTIONS"
1110 PRINT "  2 - CREATE SALES LETTER"
1120 PRINT "  3 - CREATE MAILING LABELS"
1130 PRINT "  4 - END PROGRAM"
1140 PRINT " "
1150 PRINT "ENTER A NUMBER 1 THROUGH 4: ?";
1160 LET R$ = INKEY$
1170                                                           REM
1180 IF R$ <> "" THEN 1220
1190    LET R$ = INKEY$
1200 GOTO 1180
1210                                                           REM
1220 PRINT R$
1230                                                           REM
1240 IF R$ >= "1" AND R$ <= "4" THEN 1370
1250    PRINT "  ERROR - "; R$; " IS AN INVALID ENTRY"
1260    PRINT " "
1270    PRINT " PLEASE REENTER 1, 2, 3, OR 4: ?";
1280    LET R$ = INKEY$
1290                                                           REM
1300    IF R$ <> "" THEN 1340
1310      LET R$ = INKEY$
1320    GOTO 1300
1330                                                           REM
1340    PRINT R$
1350 GOTO 1240
1360                                                           REM
1370 RETURN
```

Figure 9-62 Sample program (Part 2 or 7)

```
2000                                                            REM
2010 REM ****************************************************************
2020 REM * DISPLAY INSTRUCTIONS                                       *
2030 REM ****************************************************************
2040                                                            REM
2050 CLS
2060 PRINT "  THIS PROGRAM PREPARES PERSONALIZED LETTERS. WHEN"
2070 PRINT "CODE 2 IS SELECTED FROM THE MENU, THE USER IS"
2080 PRINT "PROMPTED TO ENTER THE TITLE OF THE PERSON TO RECEIVE"
2090 PRINT "THE LETTER (MR. OR MS.), THE PERSON'S FIRST AND LAST"
2100 PRINT "NAME, THEIR ADDRESS, CITY, STATE, AND ZIP CODE (NOTE:"
2110 PRINT "A SINGLE BLANK SHOULD SEPARATE THE CITY AND STATE)."
2120 PRINT "VALID ENTRIES FOR THE STATE ARE AZ, CA, ID, NV, OR,"
2130 PRINT "UT, AND WA. AFTER THE DATA IS ENTERED, A PERSONALIZED"
2140 PRINT "LETTER IS PRINTED."
2150 PRINT "  WHEN CODE 3 IS SELECTED, MAILING LABELS FOR ALL"
2160 PRINT "LETTERS WILL BE PRINTED. A MAXIMUM OF 20 LETTERS MAY"
2170 PRINT "BE PRINTED BEFORE MAILING LABELS ARE PRINTED. AFTER"
2180 PRINT "THE MAILING LABELS ARE PRINTED, THE NAMES AND"
2190 PRINT "ADDRESSES ARE REMOVED FROM THE LIST OF LABELS TO PRINT."
2200 PRINT " "
2210 PRINT "DEPRESS ANY KEY TO RETURN TO THE MENU: ?";
2220 LET X$ = INKEY$
2230                                                            REM
2240 IF X$ <> "" THEN 2280
2250   LET X$ = INKEY$
2260 GOTO 2240
2270                                                            REM
2280 RETURN
3000                                                            REM
3010 REM *****************************************************************
3020 REM * PREPARE AND PRINT LETTER                                    *
3030 REM *****************************************************************
3040                                                            REM
3050 CLS
3060 LET I = I + 1
3070 PRINT "OBTAIN NAME AND ADDRESS"
3080 PRINT " "
3090 GOSUB 5000
3100 PRINT " "
3110 INPUT "ENTER ADDRESS: "; A$(I)
3120 GOSUB 6000
3130 PRINT " "
3140 INPUT "ENTER ZIP CODE: "; Z$(I)
3150                                                            REM
3160 IF LEN(Z$(I)) = 5 OR LEN(Z$(I)) = 9 THEN 3220
3170   PRINT "  ERROR - ZIP CODE MUST BE 5 OR 9 DIGITS"
3180   PRINT " "
3190   INPUT " PLEASE REENTER ZIP CODE: "; Z$(I)
3200 GOTO 3160
3210                                                            REM
3220 GOSUB 7000
3230 RETURN
```

Figure 9-63 Sample program (Part 3 or 7)

```
4000                                                          REM
4010 REM ***********************************************************
4020 REM * PRINT MAILING LABELS                                   *
4030 REM ***********************************************************
4040                                                          REM
4050 CLS
4060 FOR X = 1 TO I STEP 1
4070   PRINT N$(X)
4080   IF LEN(A$(X)) = 0 THEN 4120
4090     PRINT A$(X)
4100     GOTO 4120
4110                                                          REM
4120   PRINT LEFT$(C$(X), LEN(C$(X)) - 3); ", ";
4130   PRINT RIGHT$(C$(X), 2); " "; Z$(X)
4140   PRINT " "
4150   PRINT " "
4160 NEXT X
4170                                                          REM
4180 PRINT "DEPRESS ANY KEY TO RETURN TO THE MENU: ?";
4190 LET X$ = INKEY$
4200                                                          REM
4210 IF X$ <> "" THEN 4250
4220   LET X$ = INKEY$
4230 GOTO 4210
4240                                                          REM
4250 LET I = 0
4260 RETURN
5000                                                          REM
5010 REM ***********************************************************
5020 REM * OBTAIN VALID TITLE AND NAME                            *
5030 REM ***********************************************************
5040                                                          REM
5050 LET E1$ = " "
5060 INPUT "ENTER TITLE, FIRST NAME AND LAST NAME: "; N$(I)
5070                                                          REM
5080 IF E1$ = "NAME IS VALID" THEN 5210
5090   GOSUB 5400
5100   IF E1$ = "ERROR IN NAME" THEN 5140
5110     LET E1$ = "NAME IS VALID"
5120     GOTO 5190
5130                                                          REM
5140     LET E1$ = " "
5150     PRINT " "
5160     INPUT " PLEASE REENTER TITLE, FIRST NAME AND LAST NAME: "; N$(I)
5170     GOTO 5190
5180                                                          REM
5190 GOTO 5080
5200                                                          REM
5210 RETURN
5400                                                          REM
5410 REM ***********************************************************
5420 REM * EDIT TITLE AND NAME ENTRY                              *
5430 REM ***********************************************************
5440                                                          REM
5450 LET N$ = N$(I)
5460 IF LEN(N$) < 7 THEN 5840
5470   IF LEFT$(N$, 3) = "MR." OR LEFT$(N$, 3) = "MS." THEN 5520
5480     PRINT "   ERROR - TITLE MUST BE MR. OR MS."
5490     LET E1$ = "ERROR IN NAME"
5500     GOTO 5520
5510                                                          REM
```

Figure 9-64 Sample program (Part 4 or 7)

```
5520     IF MID$(N$, 4, 1) = " " AND MID$(N$, 5, 1) <> " " THEN 5580
5530        PRINT "    ERROR - ENTRY MUST BE: MR. FIRSTNAME LASTNAME"
5540        PRINT "        OR MS. FIRSTNAME LASTNAME"
5550        LET E1$ = "ERROR IN NAME"
5560        GOTO 5930
5570                                                          REM
5580        LET L = LEN(N$)
5590        LET L1 = LEN(N$)
5600                                                          REM
5610        IF L = 3 OR MID$(N$, L, 1) = " " THEN 5650
5620          LET L = L - 1
5630        GOTO 5610
5640                                                          REM
5650        IF MID$(N$, L, 1) = " " AND MID$(N$, L-1, 1) <> " "THEN 5710
5660          PRINT "    ERROR - ENTRY MUST BE: MR. FIRSTNAME LASTNAME"
5670          PRINT "        OR MS. FIRSTNAME LASTNAME"
5680          LET E1$ = "ERROR IN NAME"
5690          GOTO 5930
5700                                                          REM
5710          LET L$ = MID$(N$, L + 1, L1 - L)
5720          LET L = L - 1
5730                                                          REM
5740          IF L = 3 OR MID$(N$, L, 1) = " " THEN 5780
5750            LET L = L - 1
5760          GOTO 5740
5770                                                          REM
5780          IF MID$(N$, L, 1) = " " AND MID$(N$, L-1, 1) <> " " THEN 5930
5790            PRINT "    ERROR - ENTRY MUST BE: MR. FIRSTNAME LASTNAME"
5800            PRINT "        OR MS. FIRSTNAME LASTNAME"
5810            LET E1$ = "ERROR IN NAME"
5820            GOTO 5930
5830                                                          REM
5840      LET E1$ = "ERROR IN NAME"
5850      IF LEN(N$) = 0 THEN 5900
5860        PRINT "    ERROR - ENTRY MUST BE: MR. FIRSTNAME LASTNAME"
5870        PRINT "        OR MS. FIRSTNAME LASTNAME"
5880        GOTO 5930
5890                                                          REM
5900        PRINT "    ERROR - NO TITLE AND NAME ENTERED"
5910        GOTO 5930
5920                                                          REM
5930 RETURN
6000                                                          REM
6010 REM ***********************************************************
6020 REM * OBTAIN VALID CITY AND STATE                            *
6030 REM ***********************************************************
6040                                                          REM
6050 LET E2$ = " "
6060 PRINT " "
6070 INPUT "ENTER CITY AND STATE: "; C$(I)
6080                                                          REM
6090 IF E2$ = "STATE IS VALID" THEN 6220
6100    GOSUB 6500
6110    IF E2$ = "ERROR IN STATE CODE" THEN 6150
6120      LET E2$ = "STATE IS VALID"
6130      GOTO 6200
6140                                                          REM
```

Figure 9-65 Sample program (Part 5 or 7)

```
6150      LET E2$ = " "
6160      PRINT " "
6170      INPUT " PLEASE REENTER CITY AND STATE: "; C$(I)
6180      GOTO 6200
6190                                                          REM
6200 GOTO 6090
6210                                                          REM
6220 RETURN
6500                                                          REM
6510 REM ***********************************************************
6520 REM * EDIT CITY AND STATE                                    *
6530 REM ***********************************************************
6540                                                          REM
6550 LET C$ = C$(I)
6560 LET L2 = LEN(C$)
6570 IF L2 < 4 THEN 6830
6580    IF MID$(C$, L2-2, 1) = " " AND MID$(C$, L2-3, 1) <> " " THEN 6630
6590      PRINT "   ERROR - ENTRY MUST BE: CITY STATECODE"
6600      LET E2$ = "ERROR IN STATE CODE"
6610      GOTO 6870
6620                                                          REM
6630      LET J = 1
6640                                                          REM
6650      IF J > N THEN 6700
6660      IF RIGHT$(C$, 2) = S$(J) THEN 6700
6670        LET J = J + 1
6680      GOTO 6650
6690                                                          REM
6700      IF J > N THEN 6730
6710        GOTO 6870
6720                                                          REM
6730      PRINT "   ERROR - STATE MUST BE: ";
6740                                                          REM
6750      FOR X = 1 TO N - 1
6760        PRINT S$(X); ", ";
6770      NEXT X
6780                                                          REM
6790        PRINT "OR "; S$(X)
6800        LET E2$ = "ERROR IN STATE CODE"
6810        GOTO 6870
6820                                                          REM
6830    PRINT "   ERROR - ENTRY MUST BE: CITY STATECODE"
6840    LET E2$ = "ERROR IN STATE CODE"
6850    GOTO 6870
6860                                                          REM
6870 RETURN
7000                                                          REM
7010 REM ***********************************************************
7020 REM * PRINT LETTER                                           *
7030 REM ***********************************************************
7040                                                          REM
7050 CLS
7060 PRINT N$(I)
7070 IF LEN(A$(I)) = 0 THEN 7110
7080    PRINT A$(I)
7090    GOTO 7110
7100                                                          REM
```

Figure 9-66 Sample program (Part 6 or 7)

```
7110 PRINT LEFT$(C$(I), LEN(C$(I)) - 3); ", ";
7120 PRINT RIGHT$(C$(I), 2); " "; Z$(I)
7130 PRINT " "
7140 PRINT "DEAR "; LEFT$(N$(I), 3); " "; L$; ":"
7150 PRINT " "
7160 PRINT "     THE "; L$; " FAMILY HAS BECOME"
7170 PRINT "ELIGIBLE TO RECEIVE AN EXPENSE-PAID TRIP"
7180 PRINT "FROM YOUR HOME IN "; LEFT$(C$(I), LEN(C$(I)) - 3);
7190 PRINT " TO HAWAII."
7200 PRINT "     "; LEFT$(N$(I), 3); " "; L$; ", PLEASE RETURN THE"
7210 PRINT "ENCLOSED CARD TO DETERMINE IF YOU HAVE"
7220 PRINT "WON YOUR FREE TRIP TO HAWAII."
7230 PRINT " "
7240 PRINT "         REAL ESTATE TIMESHARING"
7250 PRINT " "
7260 PRINT "DEPRESS ANY KEY TO RETURN TO THE MENU: ?";
7270 LET X$ = INKEY$
7280                                                    REM
7290 IF X$ <> "" THEN 7330
7300    LET X$ = INKEY$
7310 GOTO 7290
7320                                                    REM
7330 RETURN
```

Figure 9-67 Sample program (Part 7 or 7)

SUMMARY   The following points have been discussed and explained in this chapter.

1. BASIC provides a specific set of string functions which allow string data to be easily manipulated.

2. It is common for one selection on a menu to provide for printing instructions on how to use a program.

3. In most interactive programs, the data entered by the user will be edited against a criteria to attempt to ensure that the data entered is accurate. If the data entered is in error, the user will normally be asked to reenter the data.

4. It is not possible for a program to determine that all data entered is valid. Therefore, the user must examine the data entered to ensure it is correct. The fact that the program will edit input data does not relieve the user of the responsibility for checking entries made on the keyboard.

5. The INKEY$ function allows the user to enter a single character from the keyboard without requiring that the enter or return key be depressed.

6. The INKEY$ function checks the keyboard to determine if a key has been depressed. If so, the character is returned by the function. If not, a null character is returned by the function.

7. A null character is tested for through the use of the if statement and double quotation marks with no space between the quotation marks.

8. Since the INKEY$ function does not halt for a user response, the normal method for using this function is to place the program in a loop to await the response. If the variable field to the left of the equal sign in the let statement which contains the INKEY$ function contains a character, then a character has been entered. If the field contains a null character, a key has not been depressed on the keyboard.

9. The use of the INKEY$ function can allow single characters to be entered faster because only one key need be depressed. In addition, it can dynamically allow input to a program without requiring that the program halt while the user enters data.

10. Data which is stored in a string field cannot be used in calculations or other instructions where numeric fields are required. It often occurs, however, that a string field can contain numeric data which will have to be used in a statement which requires a numeric field. Allowing a string field to be used where a numeric field is required can be accomplished through the use of the VAL function.

11. When a string contains one or more numeric values followed by alphanumeric characters, the leading number is referenced when using the VAL function. If there is no leading numeric value in a field, the value zero is returned by the VAL function.

12. The LEN function is used to determine the number of characters in a string constant or field identified by a string variable. To utilize the function,

the word LEN is followed by a string variable or string constant enclosed within parentheses. The LEN function can be specified in any BASIC statement where a numeric value is required or allowed.

13. The variable name specified for the LEN function must be a string variable name. A numeric variable name or constant cannot be used for the LEN function.

14. The STR$ function allows a numeric constant or numeric variable field to be used in statements requiring a string constant or variable field. The entry STR$ (numeric variable name) can be used in any BASIC statement that requires or allows a string variable.

15. The STR$ function returns a string value. If the number in the numeric variable or constant is positive, a space is returned in the first position. If the value is negative, a minus sign is returned in the first position.

16. The LEFT$ function is used to make available a specified number of characters from a string starting with the leftmost position. The word LEFT$ is followed in parentheses by the string constant or the name of the string variable field from which the characters are to be made available and the number of characters to be made available. The LEFT$ function can be used in any statement that requires or allows a string variable.

17. String functions can be combined in a single statement. An important aspect is to identify which functions require string variables and which functions require numeric variables.

18. Particular attention must be paid to the sets of parentheses which are required when multiple functions are used in a single BASIC statement.

19. The RIGHT$ function makes available a specified number of characters from a string starting with the rightmost character and moving to the left. The word RIGHT$ is followed in parentheses by the string constant or the name of the string variable field from which the characters are to be made available and the number of characters to be made available. The RIGHT$ function can be used in any statement that requires or allows a string variable.

20. The MID$ function can extract any number of characters from any position within a string constant or variable string field. The programmer must specify the string constant or the variable name of the string field from which the data is to be taken, the beginning location of the data to be extracted, and the number of characters to be extracted.

21. The MID$, LEFT$, and RIGHT$ functions can be used to extract for editing data entered by a user.

22. The characters extracted from a string of data through the use of the MID$, RIGHT$, and LEFT$ functions are sometimes called a substring.

23. A delimiter is a value in a string of data that indicates the beginning or end of words, sentences, phrases, or paragraphs. String data can be searched for delimiters using string functions. Once the delimiter is found, portions of text material can be extracted, moved, or otherwise processed.

24. The essential process to search a string is to do the following: a) Establish the beginning point of the search; b) Determine the criteria which will end the search; c) Establish the loop which will search the string text until the criteria is satisfied.

25. A string search can be used to find a substring consisting of a word or words from a sentence or paragraph.

26. The process of searching a string for a substring involves comparing the word or words entered by the user to an equal number of characters at the start of the paragraph. If an equal condition is found, then the word or words entered by the user are in the paragraph. If an unequal condition is found, the data entered by the user is compared to the paragraph beginning with the next character. This process continues until an equal condition occurs or until the entire paragraph has been searched.

27. Concatenation is the process of joining together two or more pieces of data. String data may be concatenated using the addition arithmetic operator (+).

28. Concatenation can take place only on string fields. Any string fields, including constants, can be concatenated.

29. The STRING$ function makes available a string of characters of any length from 1 to 255. The number of repetitions of the character desired and the specific character are specified in parentheses following the word STRING$.

30. On many computer systems, each number, letter of the alphabet, or special character is stored in main computer storage as a series of seven electronic impulses called bits. The combination of seven bits being on or off determines the character stored.

31. The American Standard Code for Information Interchange (ASCII) code is widely used to represent data in main computer storage. It specifies what combination of seven bits represents any given character.

32. Expressing decimal values using two symbols (the zero and one) is called the binary numbering system. Each position in a binary numbering system is assigned a place value based upon a power of 2. The place values of a binary number, beginning at the right and moving to the left, are 1, 2, 4, 8, 16, 32, and 64.

33. The CHR$ function allows the programmer to specify ASCII codes to identify characters. The value within the parentheses following the word CHR$ represents the ASCII code of a particular character. This feature allows some characters which are not represented on a keyboard or which cannot legally be specified in a BASIC statement to be used with that statement.

34. The ASC function returns the ASCII code for the first or only character in a string. Since the value returned by the ASCII function is numeric, it can be used in calculations.

1. The _____ function allows the user to enter _____ character(s) from the keyboard without depressing the _____ or _____ key.

2. A null character is tested for using the if statement and double quotation marks with no space between the quotation marks (T or F).

3. Data which is stored in a string field: a) Can be used in a calculation; b) Cannot be used in a calculation; c) Cannot contain numbers; d) Can be used in a calculation only if the variable name of the field is used with the STR$ function.

4. The _____ function is used to determine the number of characters in a string constant or field identified by a string variable.

5. Which function allows a numeric constant or numeric variable field to be used in statements requiring a string constant or variable: a) STRING$; b) VAL; c) STR$; d) CHR$.

6. The LEFT$ function is used to make available a specified number of characters from a string starting from the leftmost position (T or F).

7. The RIGHT$ function can be used in any statement that requires or allows a numeric variable (T or F).

8. The three values which must be specified with the MID$ function are: a) The position of the first character, the position of the last character, and the number of characters to be extracted; b) The name of the field or the string constant from which the data is to be extracted, the position of the first character to be extracted, and the number of characters to be extracted; c) The number of characters to be extracted, the name of the field or the constant from which the data is to be extracted, and the position of the last character to be extracted; d) The name of the field or constant and the number of characters to be extracted.

9. A _____ is a value in a string of data that indicates the beginning or end of words, sentences, phrases, or paragraphs.

10. The logic for searching a string is virtually the same as the logic for the exchange sort (T or F).

11. Concatenation is the process of joining together: a) Two numeric fields; b) Two string fields or constants; c) Two numeric constants; d) Two or more BASIC statements.

12. ASCII stands for: a) Association for Standardization of Computer Information and Intelligence; b) American System Computer Information Institute; c) Association for Standard Computer Information Interchange; d) American Standard Code for Information Interchange.

13. The real estate company using the letter in the sample program in this chapter has determined that the letter is more effective if the first name is used in the salutation (DEAR JAMES:) rather than the title and last name. Make the changes in the sample program to cause this to happen.

Chapter 9
DEBUGGING EXERCISES

The following lines of code contain one or more coding errors. Circle each of the errors and write the coding to correct the errors.

1.

```
4050 CLS
4060 FOR X = 1 TO I STEP 1
4070    PRINT N$(X)
4080    IF LEN(A(X)) = "0" THEN 4120
4090       PRINT A(X)
4100       GOTO 4120
4110                                                                REM
4120    PRINT LEFT$(C$(X), LEN(C$(X) - 3); ", ";
4130    PRINT RIGHT$(C$(X), 2) " " Z$(X)
4140    PRINT " "
4150    PRINT " "
4160 NEXT I
4170                                                                REM
4180 PRINT "DEPRESS ANY KEY TO RETURN TO THE MENU: ?";
4190 LET X = INKEY
4200                                                                REM
4210 IF X <> "" THEN 4250
4220    LET X = INKEY
4230 GOTO 4210
4240                                                                REM
4250 LET I = 0
```

2.

```
7050 CLS
7060 PRINT N$(I)
7070 IF LEN(A$(I)) = "0" THEN 7110
7080    PRINT A$(I)
7090    GOTO 7110
7100                                                                REM
7110 PRINT LEFT(C$(I), LEN(C$(I) - 3); ", ";
7120 PRINT RIGHT(C$(I), 2); " "; Z$(I)
7130 PRINT " "
7140 PRINT "DEAR "; LEFT$(N(I), 3); " ": L$; ":"
7150 PRINT " "
7160 PRINT "       THE "; L$; " FAMILY HAS BECOME"
7170 PRINT "ELIGIBLE TO RECEIVE AN EXPENSE-PAID TRIP"
7180 PRINT "FROM YOUR HOME IN "; LEFT$(C$(I), LEN(C$(I) - 3;
7190 PRINT " TO HAWAII."
7200 PRINT "     "; LEFT$(N(I$), 3); " "; L$; ", PLEASE RETURN THE"
7210 PRINT "ENCLOSED CARD TO DETERMINE IF YOU HAVE"
7220 PRINT "WON YOUR FREE TRIP TO HAWAII."
7230 PRINT " "
7240 PRINT "         REAL ESTATE TIMESHARING"
7250 PRINT " "
7260 PRINT "DEPRESS ANY KEY TO RETURN TO THE MENU: ?";
```

Chapter 9
PROGRAMMING ASSIGNMENT 1

A credit collection letter that is sent to customers at least ten days late in   **Instructions**
paying their bills is to be prepared. In addition, a listing of customers who are
late is to be prepared, and mailing labels are to be prepared for those
customers receiving the letter. Design and code the BASIC program to
produce this material.

The program utilizes a menu which is illustrated below.   **Menu**

```
CREDIT COLLECTION LETTERS
        MENU

1 - CREATE COLLECTION LETTER
2 - PRINT LISTING OF CUSTOMERS
3 - PRINT MAILING LABELS
4 - END PROGRAM
```

    The four functions which can be performed by the program allow the user
to create the collection letter, print a listing of those customers receiving a
collection letter, print mailing labels, and terminate the program.

When code 1 is selected from the menu, the screen to create the collection   **Create collection**
letter should be displayed, as shown below.   **letter**

```
OBTAIN CUSTOMER INFORMATION

ENTER TITLE, FIRST NAME, AND LAST NAME:
ENTER STREET ADDRESS:
ENTER CITY AND STATE:
ENTER ZIP CODE:
ENTER NUMBER OF DAYS PAST DUE:
ENTER AMOUNT PAST DUE:
```

    The user should enter the title, first, and last name; the street address; the
city and state; the zip code; the number of days past due; and the amount past
due. The title and name entry must follow the same format as the sample program in this chapter. The street address can be omitted if there is none. The
city and state entry must follow the same format and contain the same states as
the sample program in this chapter. The number of days past due must be a
minimum of 10 and a maximum of 120. The amount past due must be a
minimum of 10.00 and a maximum of 5,000.00.

After the data has been entered, the letter should be printed, as shown below.

```
MR. NORMAN GREGORY
231 LOCUST AVENUE
BELL, CA 90811

DEAR MR. GREGORY:

    THE GREGORY ACCOUNT IS NOW 15 DAYS PAST DUE.
THIS IS UNDOUBTEDLY AN OVERSIGHT.
    I AM SURE YOU RECOGNIZE THE IMPORTANCE OF A GOOD
CREDIT RATING, MR. GREGORY. PLEASE REMIT $10.00 TO
BRING YOUR ACCOUNT UP TO DATE.

                    CREDIT MANAGER
```

Print listing of customers

When code two is selected from the menu, a listing of those people who have been entered should be printed, as illustrated below.

```
              CREDIT LETTERS

                                        AMOUNT
        NAME              CITY          PAST DUE

MR. NORMAN GREGORY      BELL           $10.00
MS. SUSAN BURNS         WESTSHIRE      $28.96

                        TOTAL PAST DUE  $38.96
```

Mailing labels

When code 3 is selected, mailing labels containing the title, first name and last name, address, city and state, and zip code should be printed. The format of mailing labels is the same as those in the sample program in this chapter.

Data editing

Data entered by the user should be edited by the program. For those fields not identified specifically in this assignment, the programmer should develop appropriate editing criteria and incorporate it into the program.

Chapter 9
PROGRAMMING ASSIGNMENT 2

A record store maintains a list of current best-selling records. This list is accessible from a computer. Design and write a BASIC program to access the list using a menu.

Instructions

The format of the menu is shown below.

Menu

```
       RECORD ACCESS
           MENU

1 - PRINT ALL SONGS
2 - SONG TITLE SEARCH INQUIRY
3 - END PROGRAM
```

The user can choose to print all the best selling songs, perform an inquiry, or terminate the program.

When selection one is chosen from the menu, the songs should be listed in the following format.

Printing the songs

```
    BEST-SELLING SONGS

I LOVE A COWBOY
LOVELY YOU
BETTER LATE THAN NEVER
COWBOY IN LOVE
I WANT TO BE IN LOVE IN TEXAS
LATER THAN EVER

DEPRESS ANY KEY TO RETURN TO THE MENU:
```

To make an inquiry, the user selects menu code 2. When the screen on page 9.60 appears, the user should enter one or more words or phrases which might be found in the title of the song. The program should then search each song title and, if the word or phrase entered by the user is found in the song title, the entire song title should be printed.

Inquiries

```
SONG TITLE SEARCH INQUIRY

ENTER ONE OR MORE LETTERS OR WORDS FROM
   A SONG TITLE: ?COWBOY

CURRENT SONGS WITH THE WORD COWBOY:

         I LOVE A COWBOY
         COWBOY IN LOVE

DEPRESS ANY KEY TO RETURN TO THE MENU:
```

If the word or phrase entered by the user does not appear in any of the current best-selling song titles, the message "—word entered by user— DOES NOT APPEAR IN ANY SONG TITLE" should be displayed.

For testing purposes, the song titles shown in the listing above should be used. The following words and phrases should be entered by the user: 1) I LOVE; 2) COWBOY; 3) EVER; 4) OKLAHOMA; 5) TEXAS; 6) LOVE.

CHAPTER
TEN

FILES, REPORT GENERATION, AND FUNCTIONS

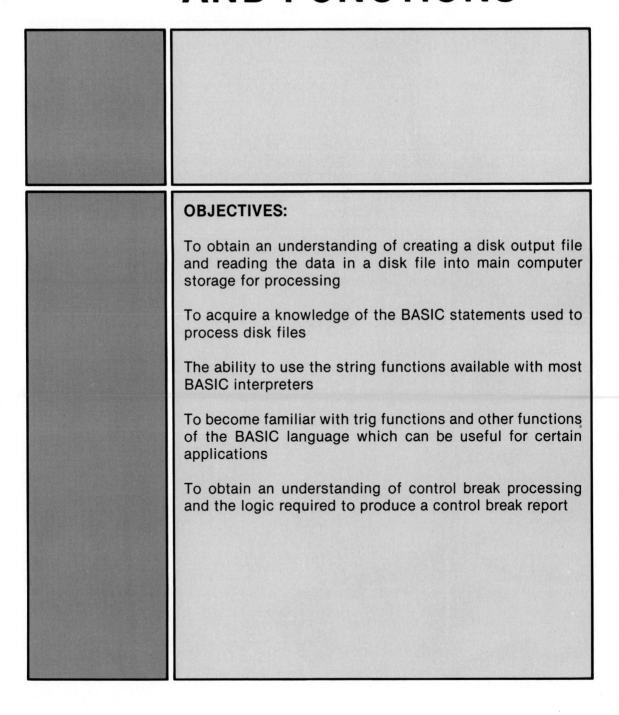

OBJECTIVES:

To obtain an understanding of creating a disk output file and reading the data in a disk file into main computer storage for processing

To acquire a knowledge of the BASIC statements used to process disk files

The ability to use the string functions available with most BASIC interpreters

To become familiar with trig functions and other functions of the BASIC language which can be useful for certain applications

To obtain an understanding of control break processing and the logic required to produce a control break report

CHAPTER
TEN
FILES, REPORT GENERATION, AND FUNCTIONS

In previous chapters, the data to be processed has been included in data statements or has been entered directly by the user in an interactive mode. In many applications, it is advantageous to permanently store data on an auxiliary storage device such as a floppy disk. When this is done, the data can be read from the floppy disk into main computer storage and be processed as required. Storing data on a floppy disk allows many programs to reference the same set of data. The statements to record data on a disk and the statements to read the data stored on a disk are explained in this chapter. In addition, a variety of other statements common to most BASIC interpreters are also discussed.

The diagram in Figure 10–1 illustrates the concept of storing data on a disk.

Introduction

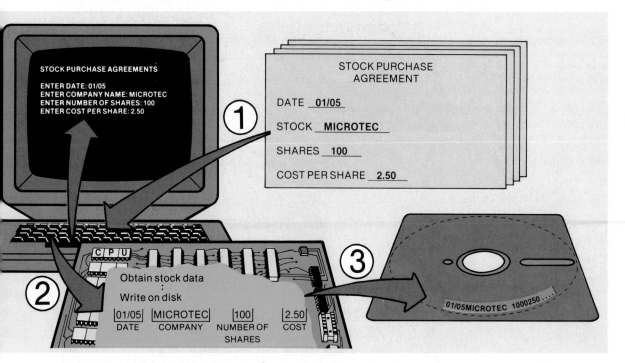

In the example, data from a stock purchase agreement is entered into main computer storage from a computer terminal. After the data has been entered into storage, the data is then written on a floppy disk.

After the data from the first stock purchase agreement is entered into storage and recorded on disk, the data from the next stock purchase agreement would be entered into storage via the computer terminal. This data would then be recorded on the disk immediately after the previous set of data.

Figure 10-1 The steps in storing data from a source document include: 1) Keying the data from the source document; 2) Storing the data in main computer storage as it is keyed; 3) Storing the data on a disk after it has been keyed.

Sequential files Each stock purchase agreement is considered a record. The collection of records, that is, all of the stock purchase agreements considered as a unit, is called a file. When records are stored on a disk one after the other, the collection of records on the disk is called a sequential file. Although records can be stored on the disk in any sequence, they are normally arranged in some sequence based upon a field in each record called a key. In the example on the previous page, the stock purchase agreements are recorded on the disk in date sequence. The date field, therefore, is the key or control field for the stock purchase file.

Records which are organized sequentially are usually retrieved sequentially. This means that when the records are read from the disk into main computer storage, they will be read one after the other in the same sequence as they are stored on the disk.

The diagram below illustrates reading data from a disk into main computer storage and preparing a report from the data in main computer storage.

Figure 10-2 When data is read from a disk file, it is read one record at a time into main computer storage When the record in this example is read, the date, company name, number of shares, and cost per share are placed in fields. The data in these fields can then be used for whatever processing is required, such as creating the report shown.

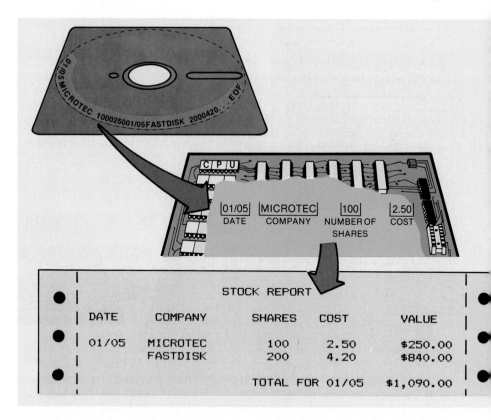

When data is read from a disk, the data is read a record at a time into main computer storage. To indicate the end of the file, an end of file indicator is recorded on the disk when the data is originally recorded. In the example above, the letters EOF are recorded in the date field to indicate end of file.

When data is stored on disk under the control of a BASIC program, the data to be written is moved from the individual fields to a reserved area of main computer storage called a buffer. The record formed in the buffer area is then written on the disk (Figure 10–3).

Storing data on disk

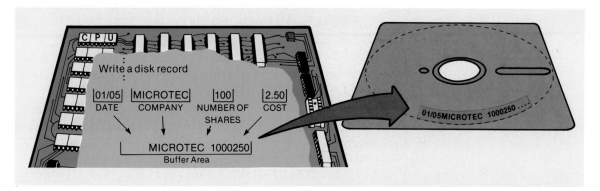

In the example above, the data from the individual fields is moved to the buffer area. The record is then written on the disk from the buffer area. Each file to be read or written in a program must have a buffer assigned to it. If there is one file in the program, then one buffer is required. If there are two files, then two buffers are required, and so on. These buffers are numbered by the BASIC interpreter. Most computer systems allow up to fifteen buffer areas. The instructions which cause a record to be written or read must refer to the proper buffer number.

Figure 10-3 A buffer area is used for both input and output disk files. The disk record is formed in the buffer area from the individual fields in the program and then is written when the file is an output file. When an input file is processed, the entire record is placed in the buffer area when it is read and then it is separated into each field.

When processing a sequential file using disk, the program must specify whether data is being recorded on the disk (an output file) or data is being read into main computer storage from a file already on the disk (an input file). In addition, the buffer to be used must be identified and a name must be assigned to the file. These tasks are accomplished by the OPEN statement.

The format of the open statement and an example of its use are illustrated below.

The OPEN statement

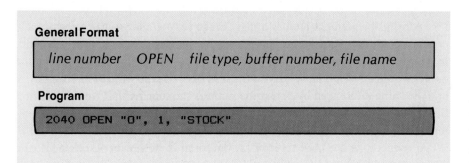

General Format

    line number   OPEN   file type, buffer number, file name

Program

    2040 OPEN "O", 1, "STOCK"

Figure 10-4 The open statement must be executed before any input/output operations occur with a disk file. The same filename used when the file is created as an output file must be used in the open statement that opens the file as an input file.

An open statement is required before a file on the disk can be referenced or accessed. The first entry following the word OPEN is the file type. For a sequential file, the entry may be the letter of the alphabet O, or the letter of the alphabet I. The entry must be included in quotation marks. The letter O signifies that an output file is to be recorded on the disk. The letter I indicates that an input file will be read from the disk. In the example in Figure 10-4, the open statement contains the letter O, signifying an output file.

Following the file type entry is a comma and then a buffer number. Buffer numbers normally begin with 1. In the example, buffer number 1 is specified. Each file defined by an open statement must have a unique buffer.

The last entry is a file name. The file name must be enclosed in quotation marks, and, for most systems, can consist of from 1 – 8 characters, the first of which must be alphabetic. In the example, the file name selected is STOCK.

The print # statement

The print # statement is used to sequentially write data in a file on a disk. The format of the print # statement and an example of its use for storing numeric data on disk is illustrated below.

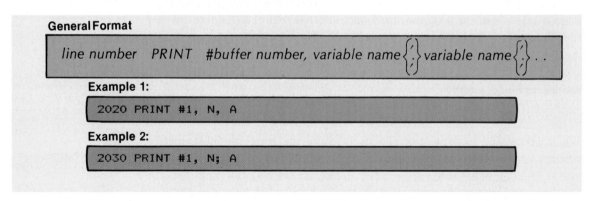

General Format

    line number   PRINT   #buffer number, variable name {,;} variable name {,;} . . .

Example 1:

    2020 PRINT #1, N, A

Example 2:

    2030 PRINT #1, N; A

Figure 10-5 The print # statement is used to write data in a disk file. The print # statement cannot be executed until an open statement for the same buffer number has been executed.

The print # statement writes data sequentially on a disk. The first entry following the print # entry is a buffer number. In the example above, buffer number 1 is specified. The buffer number is followed by a comma and then the variable names of the fields to be recorded.

A print # statement creates a disk image very similar to the screen image created by a print statement. Therefore, the punctuation in the print # statement is very important. In example 1 in Figure 10-5, the comma separating the names would cause blank spaces on the disk between the value referenced by N and the value referenced by A just the same as the spacing that would occur on the CRT. This is wasteful of disk storage. Therefore, semicolons should normally be placed between numeric variable names as illustrated in example 2. When semicolons are used to separate data names in a print # statement, the values are stored on disk with one blank space after the first number and one blank space before the next number. The effect is to separate each field so that the numeric fields may be referenced individually.

To store two or more adjacent string fields on a disk, the print # statement is used, followed by the buffer number, a comma, and the variable names referencing the fields to be stored on disk. It is important to note that each string field must be separated by a comma contained within quotation marks.

Storing string data on disk

```
2080 PRINT #1, D$; ","; N$
```

Figure 10-6 When writing string data in a disk file, the string fields should physically be separated by a comma. Generally, as in this example, a string constant containing a comma will be used.

This technique results in a comma being recorded on the disk to separate the string fields so that they may be accessed.

The following example illustrates portions of a program to accept data from the user and record the data onto disk.

```
2050 OPEN "O", 1, "STOCK"
     ⋮
2080 INPUT "ENTER DATE: "; D$
2090 INPUT "ENTER COMPANY NAME: "; C$
2100 INPUT "ENTER NUMBER OF SHARES: "; N
2110 INPUT "ENTER COST PER SHARE: "; P
     ⋮
3050 PRINT #1, D$; ","; C$; ","; N; ","; P
     ⋮
4230 CLOSE 1
```

Figure 10-7 The general sequence for storing data in a file on disk is to open the file as an output file, obtain the data which will be written on the file, and write the data on the file. The file is opened only one time. Usually, however, the processing to obtain data and write it on the file will be placed in a loop until all data has been written. At that time, the close statement for the file is executed.

In the example in Figure 10-7, after the open statement is specified, input statements are used to obtain stock data. The print # statement, when executed, stores the specified fields on the disk.

In the example in Figure 10-7, the last statement is the close statement, followed by a buffer number. The close statement terminates access to a file through the specified buffer. After a file has been opened and data has been processed, the file should always be closed prior to removing the disk from the system. Closing the file will ensure that all data is written on the disk.

The close statement

The input # statement is used to read data from the disk into main computer storage. The data is read one record at a time in the same sequence in which it is stored. The format of the input # statement and an example of its use are illustrated in Figure 10-8.

Reading data from disk

Figure 10-8 The INPUT #
statement is used to read
data from a disk file. The
buffer number specified
must be the same buffer
number specified in the
open statement for the file
to be read.

General Format

line number   INPUT   # buffer number, variable, variable,....

Program

```
2140 INPUT #1, D$, C$, N, P
```

When the input # statement in Figure 10-8 is executed, four fields from
the file using buffer #1 are read into the storage locations identified by the
variable names D$, C$, N, and P. This data may be processed in any manner
required by the program.

The following segment of code illustrates the entries to read data from the
disk and display the data on a CRT screen.

Figure 10-9 The sequence
for accessing data from a
file is first open the file and
then read data from the file
by using the input # statement. After all records have
been read and processed,
the file should be closed
with the close statement
(line 3250).

```
3130 OPEN "I", 1, "STOCK"
       ⋮
3150 INPUT #1, D$, C$, N, P
       ⋮
3190 PRINT D$, C$, N, P
       ⋮
3250 CLOSE 1
```

The open statement on line 3130 allows access to the sequential disk file
named STOCK using buffer number 1. The entry I enclosed in quotation
marks signifies that the file being accessed is an input file. The input # statement on line 3150 reads data from the disk and stores the data in main
computer storage in the areas referenced by D$, C$, N, and P.

The print statement on line 3190 displays the data on the CRT screen.

Additional BASIC functions and statements

There are a number of additional functions and statements that are available
with most BASIC interpreters. Some of these are explained on the following
pages.

RND function

The RND function generates random numbers. These numbers can be used for
simulations, games, or any application in which an unknown random number
must be used. The format of the RND function and the manner in which it
operates varies considerably from computer system to computer system. The
two most commonly found formats of the RND function are illustrated in
Figure 10-10 to generate a series of random numbers between 0 and 1.

In format 1, the value zero is specified within the parentheses following
the word RND. In format 2, any positive integer can be specified. Some com-

Program — Format 1

```
100 FOR I = 1 TO 12
110    PRINT RND(0),
120 NEXT I
```

OR

Program — Format 2

```
100 FOR I = 1 TO 12
110    PRINT RND(1),
120 NEXT I
```

Output

.7655695	.3558607	.3742327	.1388798
.8231488	.5232107	.1019188	.5166124
.2575781	.7670416	.9790686	.3092352

Figure 10-10 The random function (RND) is shown here in two formats that will return a random value between zero and one. The exact format and exact rules for the RND function should be checked in the BASIC programming manual for the computer system being used.

puter systems use format 1 and some computer systems use format 2. The user should check the programming manual for the particular computer system to determine which format is applicable.

In many applications where the random function will be used, there is a need to generate a range of integer values. For example, to simulate the roll of a pair of dice, the numbers 1 through 6 are desired. The routines in Figure 10-11 could be used to obtain these values.

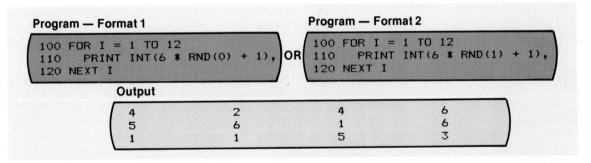

Program — Format 1

```
100 FOR I = 1 TO 12
110    PRINT INT(6 * RND(0) + 1),
120 NEXT I
```

OR

Program — Format 2

```
100 FOR I = 1 TO 12
110    PRINT INT(6 * RND(1) + 1),
120 NEXT I
```

Output

4	2	4	6
5	6	1	6
1	1	5	3

For both format 1 and format 2, the value between zero and one returned by the RND function is multiplied by six, and the value 1 is added to the result. The integer of that answer is then printed. This technique ensures that the value printed is a number 1 through 6. It will never be less than 1 because even if the value zero is returned by the random function, the one added to the value returned will cause a 1 to be printed. The value printed will never be greater than 6 because even if the maximum value (.9999999) returned is multiplied by six (.9999999 × 6 = 5.999999) and then a one is added (5.999999 + 1 = 6.999999), the integer function will return the next lowest integer (6). This technique can be used to generate random numbers within any given range by changing the six to the highest number greater than the lowest number in the range and replacing the one with the lowest number in the range of numbers.

The RND function will normally return the same sequence of random numbers each time a program is executed unless it is "seeded" with a new value each time. Some computer systems use a RANDOM function, while others use a RANDOMIZE function, and still others use different means to

Figure 10-11 In these examples, a value between zero and one will be returned by the RND function. The calculation, together with the integer function, then produces an integer between the values 1 through 6. This technique can be used for any application which requires random values between given boundaries.

seed the RND function. If it is important to ensure an unpredictable sequence of random numbers, the programmer should consult the programming guide for the particular computer system being used to determine the method for seeding the RND function with a new sequence each time the program is executed.

SQR function

Figure 10-12 The SQR function returns the square root of the value placed in parentheses. In the print statement on line 1010, the function is used to return the square root of an altitude entered by the user in response to the input statement on line 1000. The square root is multiplied by 1.22 to determine the number of miles that can be seen.

The square of a number is the value that results when a number is multiplied by itself. The square root of a number is a number which when multiplied by itself gives the original number. A square root is used in mathematical formulas for many applications.

The SQR function computes the square root of a number. To calculate the square root, the entry SQR, followed by a positive number, numeric variable, or expression enclosed in parentheses, is included in a BASIC statement. The following example illustrates the use of the SQR function to print the number of miles that can be seen from an airplane on a clear day. To perform this calculation, the square root of the altitude in feet is multiplied by 1.22.

General Format

$$SQR \begin{pmatrix} number \\ numeric\ variable \\ arithmetic\ expression \end{pmatrix}$$

Program

```
1000 INPUT "ENTER THE ALTITUDE: "; A
1010 PRINT "YOU CAN SEE"; SQR(A) * 1.22; "MILES FROM"; A; "FEET"
```

Output

```
ENTER THE ALTITUDE: ? 5000
YOU CAN SEE 86.26702 MILES FROM 5000 FEET
```

The SQR(A) entry returns the square root of the value in the numeric field A. The value in A must be positive. The SQR function can be used wherever a numeric value is required or allowed in a BASIC statement.

SGN function

The SGN function may be used to indicate the sign of a numeric value. To use the function, the entry SGN is included in a statement followed by a number, numeric variable, or expression in parentheses whose sign is to be determined. When included in a statement, the SGN function returns a –1 if the value is negative, a zero if the value is zero, and a + 1 if the value is positive. The following example illustrates the use of the SGN function in an on gosub statement.

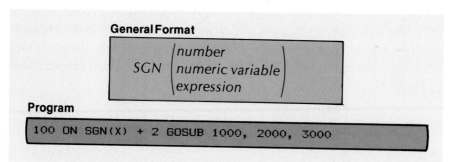

In the example in Figure 10–13, if the sign of the value in the field identified by the variable name X is negative, the entry SGN(X) will return the value –1. If the value in X is equal to zero, a zero is returned by SGN(X), while if the value in X is positive, the value + 1 is returned. Therefore, the arithmetic expression SGN(X) + 2 will compute a value of 1, 2, or 3, depending on whether the value is negative, zero, or positive. As a result, if the value in X is negative, the subroutine at line 1000 will be given control by the on gosub statement. If the value in X is zero, the subroutine on line 2000 will receive control; and if the value in X is positive, the subroutine beginning at line 3000 will be executed.

The BASIC language is frequently used for engineering, mathematical, and scientific applications. When certain values are required, these functions can be used to calculate the values. The table in Figure 10–14 lists the most frequently used functions.

Math and trigonometry functions

Figure 10-14 The math and trig functions shown here are to be used in math, scientific, and engineering applications. For several of the functions (COS, SIN, and TAN), the angle must be expressed in radians, not degrees. To calculate radians from degrees, the number of degrees is multiplied by the value PI/180 where PI is equal to 3.141593.

FUNCTION	EXPLANATION	EXAMPLE
ATN(X)	– Returns the arctangent of X in radians – X is a numeric value representing a tangent	210 LET Y = ATN(X)
COS(X)	– Returns the cosine of the angle X where X is expressed as radians *	440 LET X = COS(45 • 3.141593/180)
EXP(X)	– Returns the mathematical number e raised to the X power	270 LET M = EXP(30)
FIX(X)	– Truncates X to an integer – Fix does not return the next lower number when X is negative. H only truncates	320 LET M = FIX(25.63)
LOG(X)	– Returns the natural logarithm of X	390 PRINT LOG(A/B)
SIN(X)	– Returns the trigonometric sine of angle X where X is expressed as radians *	920 LET Q = SIN(45 •3.141593/180)
TAN(X)	– Returns the trigonometric tangent of angle X where X is expressed as radians *	340 LET T = TAN(L)

* To determine radians, multiply degrees by PI/180, where PI = 3.141593.

The DEF FN function

BASIC programmers can define their own one line functions using the DEF FN function. Through the use of this function, the repetition of coding complex statements can be avoided. An example of the use of the DEF FN function to code a general rounding function for use in a program is shown in Figure 10-15.

Figure 10-15 The DEF FN function allows a programmer to define a one-line function that can be called by using the name FNvariablename, where the variable name is a numeric or string variable name. In this example, the variable name chosen is R, so the function is called using the name FNR. The value(s) placed in the parentheses following the name of the function are used in the processing performed by the function. When the function is called, the variables or constants specified by the programmer are substituted for the variable names in the definition of the function. Here, on line 230, M is substituted for V; and on line 250, P is substituted for V.

Program

```
200 DEF FNR(V) = INT((V + .005) * 100) / 100
220 LET M = 250.255
230 PRINT FNR(M)
240 LET P = 456.984
250 PRINT FNR(P)
```

Output

```
250.26
456.98
```

The DEF FN function consists of a line number, the entry DEF, the entry FN, a numeric or variable name which serves to name the function, a variable name or names in parentheses, and the expression which constitutes the processing to take place. In the sample coding (line 200), the name of the function is FNR. R is a numeric variable name chosen by the programmer. If this variable name were a string variable name, then the function would process string data. The variable name in parentheses (V) represents the variable which will actually be used with the function. On the right side of the equal sign, the formula for rounding numeric values to dollars and cents is specified (see Figure 3-21 for an explanation of this formula).

The function is defined on line 200 and is used on lines 230 and 250. On line 220, the numeric value 250.255 is placed in the field identified by the numeric variable name M. On line 230, this value is rounded by the FNR function and is printed by the print statement. In this statement, the value in the field M is substituted for every occurrence of the field V as defined in the function (line 200). Similarly, on line 250, the value in P will be used in the formula at every occurrence of V.

Multiple variable names can be specified in the parentheses following the DEF FN entry. These variable names would then be substituted for by the values and variable names placed in parentheses when the function is used.

The DEF FN function can be useful when complex processing that is required at more than one point in the program is specified in a single statement.

Peek statement

The PEEK statement returns the ASCII code value of the character stored in computer storage at the address specified. The address must be in decimal form. For example, the following statement prints the contents of storage location 1.

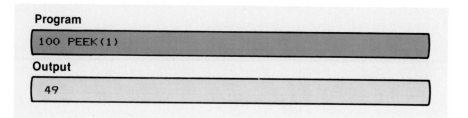

Program

    100 PEEK(1)

Output

    49

Figure 10-16 The PEEK
statement returns the ASCII
code value found at the address specified in the statement. Here, the ASCII code
49 is found at storage location 1.

To use the Peek, the address must be enclosed in parentheses following the entry Peek. In the example, storage location 1 contained the ASCII code value 49.

The POKE statement places a value into a specified address in computer storage. It requires two entries — an address in decimal form and a value.

Poke statement

The use of the Peek and Poke are very machine dependent. Their use will vary from computer system to computer system because the uses of various memory locations in each computer are different. With the Radio Shack TRS-80 computer, memory location (address) 15360 is the first position in storage used to store data that is displayed on the screen. This position represents the upper left corner of the screen. To cause a rectangular box to appear on the screen in the upper left hand corner, the following entries could be used. The ASCII code 191 represents the rectangular box.

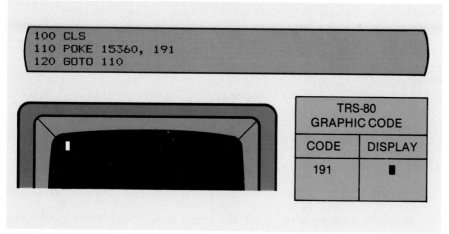

    100 CLS
    110 POKE 15360, 191
    120 GOTO 110

TRS-80 GRAPHIC CODE	
CODE	DISPLAY
191	■

Figure 10-17 The POKE
statement places a value at
the location specified in
the statement. In this example, the character corresponding to ASCII code 191
is placed at main computer
storage location 15360.

In the example in Figure 10–17, the graphic code 191 is "poked" into address 15360. The statement on line 120 causes the poke entry to be repeated. Therefore, the box appears permanently on the screen.

The program below illustrates a special graphic effect that may be obtained using the poke and the RND function to cause the box to appear on the screen at random, filling the screen with rectangular boxes.

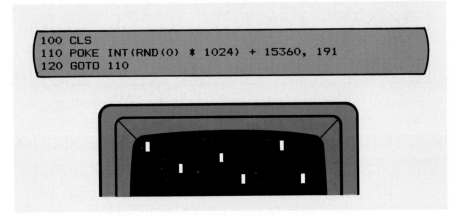

```
100 CLS
110 POKE INT(RND(0) * 1024) + 15360, 191
120 GOTO 110
```

For additional details concerning the use of graphics, the peek and the poke, refer to the reference manual for the computer system being used.

Control break logic

When sequential files are read from disk, the application may require a report of the data on the file. A common format for a report involves control breaks. A control break occurs when the data in a given field in an input record changes from the value found in the same field in the previous record. For example, in the report shown in Figure 10-19, all of the stock transactions for a given day are grouped together. When the day changes, a control break has occurred, and a total of the stock purchased for that day is printed.

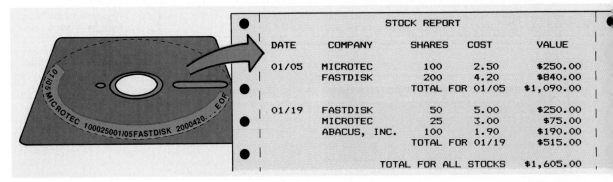

	STOCK REPORT			
DATE	COMPANY	SHARES	COST	VALUE
01/05	MICROTEC	100	2.50	$250.00
	FASTDISK	200	4.20	$840.00
	TOTAL FOR 01/05			$1,090.00
01/19	FASTDISK	50	5.00	$250.00
	MICROTEC	25	3.00	$75.00
	ABACUS, INC.	100	1.90	$190.00
	TOTAL FOR 01/19			$515.00
	TOTAL FOR ALL STOCKS			$1,605.00

Figure 10-19 On the stock report, when the value in the date field changes from one record to the next, a control break has occurred, and a total for the day is printed.

The logic to create a control break report is shown in Figure 10-20. The key to this logic is saving the control field (in this application, the date) in a compare area so that it can be compared to subsequent records that are read (see inset, Figure 10-20). When a subsequent record is read and the date in the new record is equal to the date in the compare area, no control break has

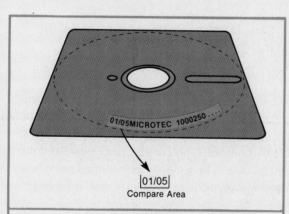

01/05
Compare Area

The date from the first record read must be moved to the date compare area. The date stored in the compare area will be compared to the date in each subsequent record which is read. When the date in the record is different from the date in the compare area, a control break has occurred. As part of the processing of the control break, the new date will be moved to the compare area.

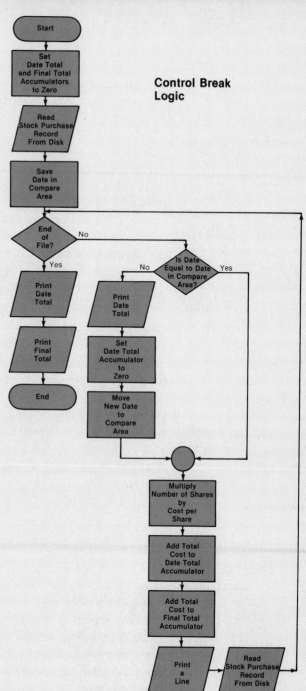

Control Break Logic

Figure 10-20 The logic for the control break report uses a loop which checks for end of file. The if-then-else structure tests for a control break. If the date read is equal to the date in the compare area, then a control break has not occurred. If the date read is not equal to the date in the compare area, a control break has occurred. When a control break occurs, the date total is printed, the date total accumulator is set to zero so that it can accumulate starting from zero the total for the next date, and the date from the record just read is placed in the compare area for comparisons to subsequent records.

occurred, so the calculations for the record are performed, and the data is written on the report.

When the date in the record is different from the date in the compare area, a control break has occurred. The total for the previous date is printed, and the new date is moved to the compare area. This processing occurs until all records have been read and processed. A final total is then printed.

Chapter 10
PROGRAMMING ASSIGNMENT 1

Instructions A program should be designed and coded in BASIC which provides for the entering of data concerning the stock purchases of an individual. The data should be stored on disk. After all stock purchase data has been entered, it should be possible to generate two types of reports. The first report should prepare a list of stocks purchased by date. The second report should provide a stock summary. Entering the data and preparing the reports should be under the control of a menu.

Menu The menu which should be utilized is illustrated below.

```
              STOCK MENU

    CODE              FUNCTION

    1 - LOAD STOCK INFORMATION
    2 - LIST STOCKS BY DATE OF PURCHASE
    3 - DISPLAY STOCK SUMMARY
    4 - END PROGRAM

    ENTER A NUMBER 1 THROUGH 4:
```

The menu selection should be edited to assure that an entry of 1, 2, 3, or 4 is made.

Entering stock purchases The screen for entering the stock purchase data is shown at the top of page 10.15. After all data has been entered and verified by the operator, it should be written on a disk file. The date of purchase should be a four-digit number consisting of a 2-digit month number and a 2-digit day number. For example, the date January 5 should be entered as 0105. The month number must be a valid number (01-12). The day entered should not be less than one nor more than the number of days in the month. For example, if the month entered is April, the maximum value of the day field is 30.

The number of shares purchased cannot be less than ten nor more than 1,000. The cost per share should not be less than $1.00 nor more than $500.00. After all entries have been entered, provision should be made for the operator to visually inspect all of the entries for accuracy. If the operator makes a NO response to the question HAS ALL DATA BEEN ENTERED CORRECTLY, the data should not be recorded on disk. Instead, the data entry should begin again with the date of purchase.

```
STOCK  PURCHASE  AGREEMENTS

ENTER  DATE:
ENTER  COMPANY  NAME:
ENTER  NUMBER  OF  SHARES:
ENTER  COST  PER  SHARE:

  HAS  ALL  DATA  BEEN  ENTERED  CORRECTLY?
      ENTER  YES  OR  NO:
```

When menu code 2 is selected by the user, a listing of the stocks by date of purchase is to be created. Note that the date is printed with a slash between the month and the day. When the date changes (i.e., a control break occurs), a total is to be printed of the total stock purchases for that day. After all records have been printed, the final total of all purchases should be printed.

List of stocks by date of purchase

```
                    STOCK  REPORT

DATE      COMPANY        SHARES    COST         VALUE

01/05   MICROTEC          100     2.50       $250.00
        FASTDISK          200     4.20       $840.00
                        TOTAL  FOR  01/05   $1,090.00

01/19   FASTDISK           50     5.00       $250.00
        MICROTEC           25     3.00        $75.00
        ABACUS,  INC.     100     1.90       $190.00
                        TOTAL  FOR  01/19     $515.00

                  TOTAL  FOR  ALL  STOCKS   $1,605.00
```

The stock summary report, illustrated below, should be prepared when the user selects menu code 3.

Stock summary report

```
              STOCK  SUMMARY

  COMPANY           TOTAL           TOTAL
   NAME             SHARES           COST

ABACUS,  INC.        100           190.00
FASTDISK             250         1,090.00
MICROTEC             125           325.00

        TOTAL  COST  OF  STOCK   $1,605.00
```

This report is in alphabetical sequence by company name. Therefore, the records on the disk will have to be read into main computer storage and be sorted by company name. This report is also a control break report; that is, when there is a change in company name, the total number of shares of stock owned and the total cost of those shares should be printed. After all company totals have been printed, the total value of all stocks should be printed.

Test data The following data should be entered to test the program.

DATE	STOCK	SHARES	COST PER SHARE
0105	MICROTEC	100	2.50
0105	FASTDISK	200	4.20
0119	FASTDISK	50	5.00
0119	MICROTEC	25	3.00
0119	ABACUS, INC.	100	1.90

Chapter 10
PROGRAMMING ASSIGNMENT 2

A program which registers people at a one-day computer conference should be designed and coded in BASIC. As registration data is entered, it should be stored on a disk file. Two classes are offered at the conference. A class in BASIC costs $150.00 to attend. A class in COBOL costs $100.00 to attend. After all people are registered, the user can select the processing from a menu.

Instructions

The menu used in the program is shown on the following page. The selections entered by the user should be edited to ensure they are valid.

Menu

The screen for code 1 from the menu is shown on page 10.18. The name should be entered in a first name-last name format. The course entered must be either BASIC or COBOL. Any other entry is invalid.

Conference registration

When the user selects code 2, a list of the individuals registered should be created (next page). The report is in alphabetical sequence by name, with the last name first and the first name last. After all records have been printed, the total enrollment and total registration fees are printed.

List of individuals registered

When the user selects code 3, a report in alphabetical sequence by class is produced (see following page). This report lists each person enrolled in the classes. When the class changes, the total enrollment in the class is printed.

Report by class

When the user requests code 4, an inquiry by last name should be performed to determine if the person is registered. The last name is entered. All persons with that last name should be listed (see next page).

Registrant inquiry

The following test data should be used for this program.

Test data

NAME	CLASS	NAME	CLASS
VIRGINIA CLANCY	COBOL	JACK DAYTON	BASIC
JULIE ABBOTT	BASIC	HENRY CLANCY	BASIC
ROBERT BUDD	COBOL		

Menu

```
REGISTRATION MENU

CODE          FUNCTION

  1 - ENTER NAMES OF REGISTRANTS
  2 - LIST INDIVIDUALS REGISTERED
  3 - REPORT BY CLASS
  4 - REGISTRANT INQUIRY
  5 - END PROGRAM

ENTER A NUMBER 1 THROUGH 5:
```

**Code 1 —
Conference
Registration**

```
CONFERENCE REGISTRATION

ENTER FIRST NAME AND LAST NAME:
ENTER COURSE:
```

**Code 2 —
Individuals
Registered**

```
             COMPUTER CONFERENCE
                REGISTRATION
      NAME                COURSE            FEE

ABBOTT, JULIE           BASIC            150.00
BUDD, ROBERT            COBOL            100.00
CLANCY, HENRY           BASIC            150.00
CLANCY, VIRGINIA        COBOL            100.00
DAYTON, JACK            BASIC            150.00

TOTAL ENROLLMENT   5
TOTAL FEES    $650.00
DEPRESS ANY KEY TO RETURN TO THE MENU:
```

**Code 3 —
Report by Class**

```
             CLASS REGISTRATION
COURSE          NAME                 FEE

BASIC       JULIE ABBOTT          150.00
            HENRY CLANCY          150.00
            JACK DAYTON           150.00
   TOTAL ENROLLMENT - 3   TOTAL FEES  $450.00

COBOL       ROBERT BUDD           100.00
            VIRGINIA CLANCY       100.00
   TOTAL ENROLLMENT - 2   TOTAL FEES  $200.00

TOTAL ENROLLMENT -   5   TOTAL FEES  $650.00
DEPRESS ANY KEY TO RETURN TO THE MENU:
```

**Code 4 —
Registrant Inquiry**

```
REGISTRANT INQUIRY

PLEASE ENTER REGISTRANT'S LAST NAME: CLANCY

THE FOLLOWING PEOPLE WITH CLANCY AS A LAST
   NAME ARE REGISTERED AT THE CONFERENCE:

        HENRY CLANCY              BASIC
        VIRGINIA CLANCY          COBOL

DEPRESS ANY KEY TO RETURN TO MENU:
```

INDEX